Genghis Khan

Genghis Khan

His Life and Legacy

Paul Ratchnevsky

Translated and Edited
by
Thomas Nivison Haining

BLACKWELL
Oxford UK & Cambridge USA

This English translation copyright © Basil Blackwell Ltd 1991

First published 1991
First published in USA 1992
Reprinted 1992

First published in Germany as *Činggis-Khan: Sein Leben und Wirken* by
Franz Steiner Verlag GMBH
Original German text copyright © 1983 Franz Steiner Verlag

Blackwell Publishers
108 Cowley Road, Oxford, OX4 1JF, UK

Three Cambridge Center
Cambridge, Massachusetts 02142, USA

British Library Cataloguing in Publication Data
A CIP catalogue record for this book is available from the British Library.

Library of Congress Cataloging in Publication Data
Ratchnevsky, Paul.
[Činggis-khan, sein Leben und Wirken. English]
Genghis Khan, his life and legacy/by Paul Ratchnevsky;
translated and edited by Thomas Nivison Haining.
p. cm.
Translation of: Činggis-Khan, sein Leben und Wirken.
Includes bibliographical references and index.
ISBN 0–631–16785–4:
1. Genghis Khan, 1162–1227.   2. Mongols—Kings and rulers
—Biography   I. Haining, Thomas Nivison.   II. Title.
DS22.RS3713   1992
950′.2′092—dc20
[B]   91–2295   CIP

Typeset in 11 on 12½ pt Garamond
by Times Graphic, Singapore
Printed in Great Britain by Hartnolls Limited, Bodmin, Cornwall

Contents

Contents

Illustrations

Editorial Foreword

The avowed aim of Ratchnevsky's *Činggis-Khan: sein Leben und Wirken* is 'to attempt to approach historical truth by undertaking a critical comparison of the original sources'. It is thus not surprising that the original is a work of great complexity, containing not only several hundred source references scattered throughout the text, but also more than 650 footnotes, many of great length and containing much substantive material. (The opening 450 words of the text of chapter 3, for example, attracted almost 1,100 words of notes!)

An early decision was taken by the publishers that, while striving to maintain the academic integrity of the original work, every effort should be made to present the English language version, *Genghis Khan: His Life and Legacy*, in a form which would make the book accessible to general as well as specialist readers. The text has, therefore, been purged of all references, which have been incorporated in the endnotes, and some 35 per cent of the substantive material in the original footnotes has been rewritten into the text. New appendices (Dynastic charts, Personalities, Chronology and Glossary of Foreign Terms) have also been added; these, it is hoped, will steer the reader through this exhaustive study of the early Mongol conquests.

A text based upon such a wide linguistic range of sources (Mongol, Turkic, Persian, Chinese and Russian are the major ones) presents any translator/editor with a veritable minefield. There is no universally accepted system of transliteration from Mongolian into English: ninety-one English language summaries of learned papers delivered at the August 1990 conference on the

Secret History which I attended in Ulan Bator provided evidence of some ten conflicting systems – not surprising, perhaps, given the different periods of the Mongol language and the idiosyncratic nature of the spelling in the *Secret History*. In addition, many Mongol words have commonly accepted English forms which differ considerably from the original Mongol spelling and, indeed, from scholarly transliterations; such accepted variants have been favoured in this translation. Add to these factors the differing German and English systems of transliteration, and one cannot hope to cross no man's land unscathed. One can only seek to be as consistent as possible and hope that the frequently strange names may be in forms which readers will find familiar or at least acceptable.

As regards detailed transcription, I have striven to do no violence to Mongol rules of vowel harmony. I have retained the Mongol diagraph *kh*, and, while I have transcribed the Mongol vowels y and ү (normally transcribed as *u* and *ü*) with a common *u*, I have felt it essential to retain *ö* as the transcription for the distinctive Mongol vowel ө. I have had the benefit of expert guidance in Arabic–Persian transcription and trust that I have not deviated too far from that guidance. In the case of Chinese names and places I have, with relief, usually felt able to adhere to Ratchnevsky's use of Pinyin. I have favoured *k* rather than *q* in transliteration and have been sparing in the use of diacritical marks in the text. I have, however, retained diacritical marks in the Notes and Bibliography in the hope that this will be welcomed by and useful to specialist readers.

Ratchnevsky points out that several women exerted considerable influence on Genghis Khan at different times in his career. Similar influences – quite apart from that of my commissioning editor, Alison Dickens and my desk editor, Pamela Thomas – lie behind the translation and editing of this English language edition of Ratchnevsky's biography of the World Conqueror. Mme Ochir Ina of Ulan Bator, sister-in-law of the great Mongolian writer Academician Rintchen, guided my first faltering steps in Mongolian history some twelve years ago; the late Lady Bettina Crowe (the author Peter Lum) encouraged me in my further studies and, because she always insisted that English-speaking readers deserved a new and authoritative biography of Genghis Khan, perhaps unwittingly guided me towards this present task;

my wife, Patricia, has not only shown much patience and understanding but has used her expertise in English language and literature to improve many shortcomings in my original manuscript.

I also owe a deep debt of gratitude to Dr David Morgan of the School of Oriental and African Studies, London. Not only did he advocate the production of an English language version of Ratchnevsky (as, indeed, did Professor Charles Bawden), he persuaded me to undertake the task of translation and editing – and my publishers to accept me. He also read my translation in manuscript, offering many valuable comments and corrections. He was, indeed, a ready source of advice at every stage.

The reader must now pass judgement whether the final offering, mine alone, justifies the encouragement and expert advice which has been so generously put at my disposal.

Thomas Nivison Haining

Preface

At the begining of the thirteenth century a small nation of hunters and herdsmen brought the Turkic-Mongolian peoples of Central Asia under its sway and in subsequent campaigns of conquest subjugated the most powerful and civilized states of Asia. The man who led this nation to victory was Temuchin, 'the smith', better known to history by the title which he adopted in 1206, Genghis Khan, 'The World Conqueror'.

The sources available to us originate from contemporaries or from witnesses of the aftermath of Genghis Khan's campaigns of conquest. These sources contain contradictory statements, their individual biases springing from the subjective attitude of the authors towards the World Conqueror, the aim of the work and the dependent relationship of each author on those for whom the work was written.

The present work will attempt to approach historical truth by undertaking a critical comparison of the original sources.

The written record of Genghis Khan's life and of the struggles for supremacy on the steppe, derives from two Mongolian works: *Mangqolun niuca tobchan* (*The Secret History of the Mongols*), which survived in Chinese phonetic script[1] and in excerpts in Uighur script cited in the *Altan tobchi* (*Golden Summary*);[2] also from the *Altan debter* (*Golden Book*), which has been lost, but which was known in the thirteenth century to the Persian chronicler, Rashid ad-Din, and which served as the source for the Chinese language chronicle, *Shenwu qinzheng lu* (*The Campaigns of Genghis Khan*), and for the *Yuanshi* (*The History of the Yuan Dynasty*).[3]

The *Secret History* was written immediately after Genghis Khan's death and it has been traditionally assumed that the Year of the Rat cited in the colophon refers to the year 1240. Established anachronisms in the text of the *Secret History* have, however, led to the postulation of a later dating,[4] but fresh and quite independent arguments have more recently been advanced to support the thesis that the original text dates from 1228.[5] The veterans of the military campaigns, gathered at the Great Khuriltai held by the Kerulen River would, during the long evenings, have recounted their deeds of valour; these stories provided the material for a work in which the anecdotes are only loosely connected. The author, possibly Shigi-Khutukhu, the adopted son of Genghis Khan, who was reared in the Conqueror's household, accompanied Genghis on campaigns and was one of the first Mongols to learn the Uighur script,[6] was obviously not concerned to offer a coherent picture of the course of history; his interest focused on the deeds of his heroes.

Judgements differ regarding the value of this work as a historical source. In form the *Secret History* closely resembles an epic poem in which imaginary dialogue, romantic embellishments and folkloric motifs serve to dramatize the events described. The work was dedicated to the Mongol ruling house and designed to keep alive the memory of the triumphs achieved by their followers. Glorification of the valiant deeds of those followers and of the Mongol army is the main aim of the author, who, as a supporter of the old order, openly disapproves of Genghis Khan's reforms.

Thanks to this critical attitude we have knowledge of some episodes in the life of Genghis Khan which are suppressed by the court historians as being detrimental to the reputation of the World Conqueror. Thus the *Secret History* is the only source which reports the murder of his half-brother Bekhter or the judgement on his brother Kasar, which mentions the abduction of Hö'elun by Yisugei, or suggests the illegitimate birth of Jochi. (Rashid ad-Din does report the abduction of Börte by the Merkits, but he presents a version of the incident designed to prove Jochi legitimate.) It also portrays as defeats for Temuchin such battles as Dalan Balzhut, although these are presented as victories in the official historiography. The author of the *Secret History* is also critical in his presentation of the World Conqueror's character: Temuchin is portrayed as a timorous person who fears dogs; he is dissuaded from reprehensible actions by his followers;[7] significant decisions such as the break with Jamuka, strained relations with the shaman Teb-tengri, even the nomination of Genghis' successor, are attributed to the influence of women around him rather than to his own decisiveness.

If one ignores the poetic elements and the unreliable chronology, then the *Secret History* must be regarded as our most valuable source concerning the youth of Temuchin and the struggle for mastery of the steppe. When the work was compiled, the events portrayed were well known to the veterans of the great Mongol campaigns of conquest and, of course, also to members of the ruling house, to which the work was dedicated.

Copious material about the life of Genghis Khan is provided by Rashid ad-Din, Jewish doctor and vizier of the Mongol Il-khans of Persia, in his monumental work *Jami' al-tawrikh* (*Collected Chronicles*). Rashid ad-Din wrote his work at the behest of the Il-khan, Ghazan. He was thus able to use not only the *Altan debter*, but also other documents which were preserved in the court archives. Additionally, he had the opportunity to acquaint himself with the oral Mongol tradition from an authoritative source – Khubilai Kha'an's ambassador at the court of the Il-khans, Pulad [Bolad] Chingsang, who was regarded as the greatest authority on the history of the Mongols and whose discourses, according to the historian Shams ad-Din Qashani, Rashid carefully recorded.[8]

Rashid ad-Din also learned much concerning the history of the Mongols from the il-khan himself: 'Ghazan knows the smallest details of the history of the Mongols, the names of their ancestors and of past and present emirs, the genealogy of most of the Mongol tribes. Apart from Pulad, no one knows these facts as well as he does. He alone knows Mongol secrets, but these are not included in this history,'[9] Rashid's confession is informative. He knew the 'secrets' of the life of Genghis Khan – and he makes other indirect allusions to this in his writings, especially in the *History of the Tribes*. As a court historian he was, however, bound by taboos; he conceals certain incidents which are detrimental to the reputation of Genghis Khan – or offers scarcely credible versions of them; and against his better judgement he presents Temuchin's defeats as victories. Rashid's work is of secondary importance for Genghis Khan's campaigns of conquest. His description of the western campaign follows the account of Juvaini, whose *Tarikh-i-jahan gushai* (*History of the World Conqueror*) is the most reliable source for that period.

The Chinese record of the life and deeds of Genghis Khan derives from the *Altan debter*. The *Shenwu qinzheng lu* deviates only in detail from Rashid ad-Din's account; tabooed incidents are omitted, defeats are transformed into victories. There is, however, one conspicuous difference; the history of Genghis Khan's ancestors, treated in detail by Rashid ad-Din, is missing from the modern version of this Chinese chronicle.

The *Yuanshi* repeats the same tradition, although it does contain the section about Genghis Khan's ancestors which is missing from the *Shenwu*. The text, edited by Khubilai, presents an official version, and the editing has the dry, laconic style typical of Chinese annals. In the biographical section of the *Yuanshi* there are also stories which can be traced back to the family tradition and these offer much valuable material regarding Genghis Khan's character.

There are thus two widely differing records available to us. On the one hand the *Secret History* offers an independent, uncensored record of events which were still fresh in the memories of the followers who represented the steppe tradition; on the other hand the official historiography presented by court historians offers only a censored version. The history of Genghis Khan's life thus contains many unresolved questions and the interpretations which follow are not the only possible ones; they do appear, however, to be the most plausible.

History has condemned Genghis Khan as a heartless conqueror. His conquests, it is true, brought death and disaster to countless human beings and destroyed irreplaceable cultural treasures, yet it would be unjust to judge him from the point of view of our own century. Genghis Khan was the product of his people and of his time. His actions were determined by the brutal law of the steppe, which knew no compassion towards enemies. His activities were not limited to the military field, his successes owed less to his military skills than to his astute policies and organizational abilities. The empire which he founded outlived him by more than a century and his demolition of barriers facilitated a brisk exchange of material and cultural wealth between the subject peoples, thus extending their horizons.

Genghis Khan's role in history is controversial and from time to time the debate about this role has become polemical as, for example, between Chinese and Soviet historians in the 1960s.[10] The extraordinary destiny of this exceptional man will, however, long command the interest of posterity.

The manuscript of this book was completed in 1978 and it has not been possible to take account of works which have appeared since that date. I owe a particular debt of gratitude to Professor Herbert Franke, who supported the publication of this work and who kindly edited the manuscript.

Paul Ratchnevsky

1

The Origins and Boyhood Years of Genghis Khan (Temuchin)

Homeland and ancestry

The vast steppes of the Mongolian plateau have, from time immemorial, been the setting for bitter struggles between the Turkic and the Mongol-Tungusic pastoral tribes. The bands of horsemen who swept across Asia and Europe came from this area. The Hsiung-nu, Hsien-pi, Tavghach, Juan-juan, Tu-chueh, Uighurs, Kirghiz and Khitans ruled the area and founded mighty empires; but these empires did not endure, usually collapsing in the third generation as the result of dissension among the tribal princes, or were the victims of incursions by fresh bands of nomads. Mastery of the steppe changed, but some of the conquered races remained in their old homelands, forming the substratum in the confederations of the conquerors and adopting the name of the victorious races; ethnic and linguistic dividing lines became increasingly blurred.

In the twelfth century mastery of Western Mongolia passed to the Naimans – the Mongol name for a group of the Turkic tribe *Säkiz Oghuz*, 'The Eight Oghuz', whose existence is recorded as early as an eighth century inscription. [1] When the Kirghiz defeated the Uighurs in 840 the Naimans, who remained in their homelands in the Altai Mountains, attached themselves to the victors; then, as their strength gradually increased, they pushed the Kirghiz to the River Yenesei. They also drove the Keraits from their hereditary lands on the Irtysch and in the Altai towards the east and in the face of these attacks the Khitans moved to northern China, where they founded the Liao dynasty. The area of which the Naimans now found themselves masters, stretched from the Black Irtysch to the Orkhon River, from the Altai to the Khangai Mountains.

Although the Naiman federation included foreign ethnic elements,[2] the Naiman ruling family and upper classes were of Turkic origin;[3] they maintained relations with their southern neighbours, the Uighurs, whose script and other elements of Inner Asiatic culture they adopted, and they possessed an organized administrative and financial infrastructure.[4] Diplomatic relations also existed with the Kara-Khitai empire, founded in the Tarim Basin when, after the collapse of the Liao dynasty, some of the Khitans, under the leadership of Yeliu-taishi, migrated to the west.[5] Such contacts contributed to the spread of the Mongol language among the Naimans and to their Mongolization.[6] 'Their customs and habits resemble those of the Mongols', comments Rashid ad-Din.[7]

The Naimans adopted Buddhism from the Uighurs, but Nestorian Christianity also made some inroads. Plano Carpini stated in 1245 that the Naimans were heathens (i.e. Buddhists); William of Rubruck, who travelled through the same area eight years later writes, however, that they were Nestorians.[8] Certainly, Kuchlug, son of the Naiman Tayang-khan, was originally a Nestorian, being converted to Buddhism only after he fled to Kara-Khitai. Profession of faith did not, however, exclude shamanist practices. The Naiman rulers had a reputation as great magicians, of associating with and having influence over demons. Buiruk-khan of the Naimans, for example, attempted to use his powers as a weather sorcerer on the battlefield of Köyitän.[9]

East of the Naimans, from the Orkhon in the west to the Onon and Kerulen rivers, was the extensive empire of the Keraits, whose rulers resided in the woodland areas of the Tula River. The origin of this people which, after the collapse of the Meng-ku empire in the middle of the twelfth century, exercised suzerainty over the largest part of eastern Mongolia and its tribes, is unclear. Tao Zongyi regards the Keraits as Mongols, Rashid ad-Din is less categorical. In his *History of the Tribes* he does comment that they belong to the Mongol nation, but he places them in a subgroup with the Naimans, Uighurs, Kirghiz, Kipchaks and other Turkic peoples; and in the 'Life of Genghis Khan' he speaks only of resemblances between the Keraits and the Mongols, whose customs, habits, dialects and vocabulary were related.[10] Tu Ji, in *Mengwuer shiji* (*History of the Mongols*), assumes a Turkic origin of the Keraits. He traces their origin to the Turkic Kangli and Ghuzz, 'whose height they shared', and comments that their language was that of the Tu-chueh, i.e. Turkic.[11]

Tu Ji's arguments may be open to refutation, but he is probably correct in attributing a Turkic origin to the Keraits. The names and titles of the Kerait rulers are Turkic. *To'oril* is the Mongolized form of the Turkic Toghrul;[12] Toghrul's father and grandfather bore the Turkic title *buiruk* ('commander'); the title of the Kerait princess, Dokuz-khatun, is Turkic, as is the title 'Yellow Khan' under which one Kerait leader is known.[13] The Turkic hypothesis is also supported by Rashid ad-Din's indication that the Kerait homelands were on the Irtysch and in the Altai,[14] an area inhabited by the Kirghiz before they were driven out by the Naimans. An important Kirghiz tribe bears the name *Kirai*, the Turkic element of Kerait,[15] and the possibility cannot be excluded that a branch of the Kirghiz moved eastwards from the Naiman attacks, although the main body of the tribe was thrown back on

1   *Fourth-century* BC *(possibly proto-Hun) stone-slab cist graves in Orkhon River Valley.*

the Yenesei. Such a hypothesis would explain the condescension shown by the Keraits towards the Mongols, which would then, as Grousset suspected, be based on racial prejudice.[16]

In these new surroundings and in contact with the Mongol tribes the Keraits quickly became assimilated, the Kerait tribal league losing its homogeneous character. When the Naimans drove back the Khitans, not all the Khitans followed the eastward exodus; some would have remained on the familiar pastures, attaching themselves to the Keraits.

The Keraits accepted the Nestorian faith by the end of the eleventh century at latest – although a letter cited by Abu'l Faraj, commonly known as Bar Hebraeus, reports the conversion of the Keraits as early as 1009, Kerait may be an interpolation[17] – and Toghrul's grandfather and father bore the Christian names Markus (Marghus) Kyriakus (Qurjaquz).[18] The Keraits, like the Naimans, were of a higher cultural level than the Mongols. They had a royal family and an organized military structure, from which Temuchin adopted the institution of a personal bodyguard. The Keraits also maintained friendly relations with the Khitans and it was in Kara-Khitai that Toghrul took refuge when expelled from his kingdom. There was enmity, however, with the Naimans, who had driven the Keraits from their traditional areas, also with the Tartars, who had handed over the Kerait king, Markus, to the leader of the Jurchid.[19] This enmity was exacerbated by political rivalry. After the fall of the Meng-ku empire[20] the Keraits, whose homelands lay on the Onon and Kerulen rivers – thus encompassing the lands of the Mongols[21] who, according to the Persian historian Juzjani, were subject to the Keraits and one other Turkic leader[22] – sought to achieve hegemony in eastern Mongolia, a hegemony to which the Tartars also aspired.

In olden times the Tartars were the most powerful tribe in eastern Mongolia.[23] Their name was recorded as early as the Kul-tegin inscription of 731/2 and was used, in Asia as well as in Europe, as the collective name for all the tribes and races of Central Asia. The Tartar nation consisted of some 70,000 households (perhaps some 350,000 individuals), according to Rashid ad-Din.[24] Their pastures lay by the Kulun and Buir lakes, between the Kerulen River and the central Khingan Mountains, an area rich in silver, from which they fashioned tools and utensils.

The *Secret History* tells not only of the silver cradle with a pearl-encrusted quilt which Temuchin carried off after his raid on the Tartars but also relates that Shigi-Khutukhu, abandoned in the plundered area, wore a golden nose-ring and a sable-lined damask jerkin.[25] The Tartars were the richest of all the nomads and had exercised power over the majority of the Mongol tribes. But quarrels and enmity were rife among the princes of this rapacious and bloodthirsty people; had they been united, no race, not even the Chinese, could have withstood them, comments Rashid.[26] In the twelfth century the Tartars served and paid tribute to the Chin emperors, but were often in rebellion against them.

The pastoral tribes of eastern Mongolia were constantly exposed to plundering by the savage and warlike Merkits,[27] who lived south of Lake Baikal on the lower Selenga. They lived by fishing and by hunting sable and wild animals, had a large army and rode tamed reindeer as if on horseback.[28] Tao Zongyi regards them as Mongols and Rashid ad-Din describes them as part of the Mongol nation. Writing more recently, Rockhill, who points to their Turkic origins, correctly challenges the assertion by Rubruck that the Merkits were Nestorian.[29] The Merkits had rebelled against the Liao emperors and been defeated in 1096.[30] Some of them thereafter attached themselves to the Khitan prince Yeliu-taishi when he moved westwards in 1115 after the fall of the Liao dynasty.[31]

Close to Lake Baikal lived the Oirats and other forest tribes, whose main occupation was hunting and fishing. The forest peoples clung to the old customs. The shamanist faith survived longest amongst them, their shamans enjoying the highest repu-tation among the nomads as soothsayers and healers. These shamans were most numerous in Bargu, east of Lake Baikal,[32] where the rulers usually bore the title *beki*, as in Tokto'a-beki of the Merkits and Kuduka-beki of the Oirats, the title indicating that they were arch-priests.[33]

The collective spirit of the herdsmen, who depended on a politico-military organization of the community to protect their herds from enemy attacks during the annual migrations, con-trasted with the free life of the forest hunters, who relied on the personal skill of the individual. The forest peoples considered their way of life to be the best in the world; herding sheep was regarded

2   *Orkhon Turk burial circles (fifth/sixth century) in Orkhon River Valley.*

by them as a disgrace, life in large encampments a punishment. Some of Genghis Khan's forebears belonged to the forest peoples, having been given the demeaning soubriquet *hoi-yin irgen* ('forest people') when the descendants of Nekun-taishi, a grandson of Kabul-khan and the brother of Genghis Khan's father, Yisugei, migrated to the Tayichi'ut.[34]

The Russian historian Vladimirtsov believes that the dividing line between pastoral and forest peoples was not firmly demarcated, and Rashid ad-Din comments that every tribe living near a forest was regarded as belonging to the forest peoples.[35] In the event of a successful series of plundering raids the hunters would acquire herds, as when Bodunchar and his brothers took control of a leaderless tribe 'and the five brothers acquired herds and supplies, servants and home'.[36] In contrast, plundered tribes were forced to adopt the life of a forest tribe – as Yisugei's family did after his death, living like the forest people and feeding themselves on wild berries, birds they had shot and by fishing.

Thus, the main factor in the struggle for supremacy on the steppe was not simply socio-political. It was not born merely of the contrast and conflict between the established, aristocratic order and those new, ambitious elements, which advocated recognition of the ability, skill and achievements of the individual, rather than of privileges which derived from mere birth and position in the tribal hierarchy. Economic factors, such as were evident in the antagonism between hunters and animal-breeders, or between shepherds and horse-breeders, were equally decisive.

The end of the eleventh century saw the emergence in eastern Mongolia of a nation which was to become known by the name *Mangqol* or *Mongqol* = *Mongol*[37] – *Menggu* in Chinese source.[38] At the time of Genghis Khan the Mongols, it should be noted, still described themselves as Tartars. The occurrence of the terms *Mangqol ulus* or *Mangqol irgen* in the *Secret History* does not, however, contradict this, since the work was not written until after Genghis Khan's death, when the term was applied, retrospectively, to the early days of the Mongol empire.

The origin of the Mongol nation is usually traced back to the Meng-ku (*Mengwu*) tribe which formed part of the Shiwei confederation during the Tang dynasty.[39] Vladimirtsov would have been thinking of the Meng-ku when he wrote: 'Kabul-khan gave the name *Mangqol* to his confederation in memory of an old and powerful nation or tribe.'[40] Li Xinchuan reports: 'The Menggu live to the northwest of the Jurchid; during the Tang dynasty they formed the tribe of the Mengwu. The people are strong and warlike, they can see in the night. They make armour from fish scales in order to protect themselves from stray arrows.' He also adds: 'They do not cook their food.' Although this last remark is quoted, word for word, by Yuwen Mouzhao in *Da-jin guozhi* (*Chronicle of the Great Chin*) the latter comments that the practice of cooking was gradually adopted by the children born of women who had been abducted by the Mongols in raids against such peoples as the Khitan and Han. Yuwen Mouzhao offers the following additional description of the *Menggu*:[41] 'They are eight feet tall, hunt and eat the flesh of wild deer. They can identify the smallest object at a distance of dozens of *li* because they do not smoke.'[42]

Li Xinchuan includes the Meng-ku among the 'Savage Tatars', a classification with which Ke Shaomin takes issue in *Xin Yuanshi kaozheng* (*Textual Research on the New History of the Yuan*), noting that Yuwen Mouzhao classifies the *Mengwu-Shiwei* as a branch of the Khitans.[43] The ethnogenesis of the Mongols raises problems which cannot be gone into here but, although Rubruck comments that the Mongols did not wish to be called Tartars, Ta-ta was a generally accepted collective terminology for the nomads of Mongolia. Zhao Hong reports in Meng-Da beilu (A Full Account of the Mongol-Tartars) that Mukali, the Mongol dignitary and military commander, spoke of himself as 'we Ta-Ta' and that 'They did not know that they were Meng[gu?], nor what kind of name that was.'[44]

In his note 'The Savage Tatars', Li Xinchuan reports additionally that the Tartars were warlike and subsisted only by hunting, that their land had no iron and that they therefore fashioned arrowheads from bone. The Liao were the first to institute barter markets with them – although the Tangut empire also carried on barter with the Tartars and the Meng-ku[45] – but firmly forbade the provision of iron to them, a prohibition rescinded only under the Chin dynasty in 1071.[46] After the relaxation of this ban on trading iron, the Tartars began to produce military equipment in large quantities and their strength quickly increased.[47]

The Qidan guozhi (Khitan Annals) indicates that the Meng-ku also practised animal husbandry. 'The Menguli people have no ruler and no chiefs. . .' (Juvaini and Rashid ad-Din also record that, in olden days, the Mongols never had a leader who ruled the whole nation, each tribe having its own princeling.) '. . . they have no agriculture, hunting is their primary occupation; they have no fixed abode but migrate, following the seasonal supplies of water and pasture; their food consists of meat and mares' milk; they do not fight with the Khitans but exchange with them cattle, sheep, camels, horses, also leather and wool products.'[48]

The transition to animal husbandry brought the Meng-ku a degree of prosperity. Monolun (Nomolun of the Secret History), wife of Dutum Menen, a grandson of Bodunchar the ancestor of the Borijigid, was a wealthy lady who had her innumerable herds brought before her every other day and herself checked whether any of them were missing.[49]

Monolun, however, was defeated by the Jalair tribe – Rashid ad-Din described them as resembling the Mongols in features and language, belonging to the Turkic tribes in olden days although now calling themselves Mongols.[50] Driven from their ancestral lands by the Jurchid, the Jalair invaded Monolun's pastures and

3 Khar Balghass. Eighth-century Uighur capital.

she and eight sons were killed. Kaidu, the only one surviving the catastrophe, was saved by his uncle, Nachin.[51] With his uncle's further assistance Kaidu was able to gather a following and eventually defeat the Jalair, thus laying the foundation for the growth of his tribe. The *Yuanshi* reports: 'Gradually his power grew; the clans and tribes who submitted to him became more numerous.'[52]

Under Kaidu's grandson, Kabul-khan, the Meng-ku became considerably stronger and, according to the *Secret History*, Kabul-khan ruled over all the Mongols.[53] The Jurchid had overthrown the Khitan Liao dynasty and founded the Chin (Golden) dynasty. The Chin emperor, Xi-zong, anxious to maintain peace in the North, therefore invited Kabul-khan to court, probably on the occasion of the emperor's coronation in 1125.[54] At the banquet the drunken Kabul-khan dared to tweak the emperor's beard. The emperor, who did not take this amiss, sent Kabul-khan home laden with gifts; but the obsequious courtiers were outraged by such *lèse majesté*, Horsemen were despatched to apprehend Kabul-khan, but he succeeded in escaping, an incident which led to extended hostilities between the Meng-ku and the Jurchid.[55] A

Chin army under command of Hushahu was forced to retreat in 1139 because of supply difficulties and, pursued by the Meng-ku, suffered a serious defeat at Hailing near the northern capital, Huining fu.[56]

In 1143 the Meng-ku again rebelled and the son of the king of Lu-kuo, seeking to avenge his executed father, joined them with his militia. The combined forces captured more than twenty Chin fortified localities and, according to the *Shenwu*, the Chin therefore equipped an army of 80,000 men in 1146 and dispatched it against the Meng-ku. This campaign was also unsuccessful[57] and the Chin emperor found himself compelled to enter into peace negotiations. In the eighth month of the sixth year *huantong* (September 1146) messengers were sent to the Meng-ku with peace proposals. The Jurchid were prepard to surrender twenty-seven fortified localities constructed under Taizong, the founder of the Chin dynasty, and to undertake heavy annual deliveries of cattle, sheep, rice and beans.[58] The Meng-ku princeling was offered the title 'King of the Meng-ku Empire', but he rejected the Chin proposals and peace was only concluded in the following year, 1147.

Jurchid sources suggest that the new peace agreement doubled the delivery of 250,000 head of cattle and sheep, and stipulated additional deliveries of 300,000 bales of fine silk (*quan*) and coarse silk (*mian*). As Wang Guowei notes,[59] these figures must be exaggerated. In the *Xinzheng lu* (*The Account of Later Campaigns*) the annual delivery is given as 50,000 head of cattle and of sheep, 50,000 *dou* of rice and beans, 300,000 bales of fine silk and the same amount of coarse silk. Li Xinchaun[60] regards even this assessment as exaggerated and has therefore replaced detailed figures with the phrase 'very generous deliveries'. The Meng-ku ruler (*olun beile*)[61] accepted the Chinese title *zuyuan huangdi*.[62]

The defeat of the Chin was serious, the peace humiliating. Unable to achieve military success, the Chin resorted to the proven Chinese tactic of exploiting the rivalry and enmity between individual tribes. After the death of Kabul-khan, Ambakai, great-grandson of Kaidu, was elected khan[63] – Rashid ad-Din corrects the erroneous attribution as grandson, found in the *Secret History*.[64] The Chin now took advantage of the enmity between the Tartars and the Meng-ku which, according to Rashid,[65] resulted from the murder of a Tartar shaman whose magic incantations had failed to save Sayan-tegin, the sick brother-in-law of Kabul-khan. With the help of the Tartars the Chin took Ambakai prisoner, apparently when he was either conducting his daughter to, or collecting a bride from, a Tartar tribe.[66]

Before his shameful death, nailed to a wooden donkey (Rashid reports that the eldest son of Kabul-khan, Ökin-barkak, was also captured by the Tartars, handed over to the Chin and suffered the same death), Ambakai called on his people to avenge him.[67] Kutula, a son of Kabul-khan, was now elected khan, and became a heroic figure in the Mongol saga. 'The warrior's voice was like thunder, his hands like the paws of a bear; and with these hands he could break the spine of the strongest man. If, when sleeping by the camp fire at night, glowing embers fell upon his body, he paid no attention – if this wakened him he thought that lice had bitten him, scratched himself and fell asleep again. He ate a three-year-old sheep and drank a huge bowl of *kumis* [mares' milk] at every meal and still could not satisfy his appetite.'[68]

Under Kutula's leadership the Mongol campaign of vengeance prospered; the Mongols inflicted a heavy defeat on the Chin and

4   *Khar-bukh balghassun. Tenth-century Khitan city.*

returned home laden with booty.[69] Their campaign of vengeance against the Tartars was less successful. 'They fought Koton-barak and Jali-buka on thirteen occasions, but were never able to take revenge for Ambakai-khan nor extract reparations.'[70] The Meng-ku empire finally collapsed at the beginning of the 1160s,[71] when the Tartars yielded to the demands of the Chin emperor and attacked the Meng-ku, inflicting a crushing defeat on them near Lake Buir. The collapse of their empire led to the political, social and economic decay of the Mongols.

Disunity and conflict were rife among the Mongol tribes; 'They had neither ruler nor leader. The tribes lived apart, singly or in twos; they were not united and were either at war or in a state of suspended enmity with each other; they were compelled to pay tribute to the Chin emperor and lived in abject poverty; they wore the skins of dogs and mice, ate the flesh of these and of other dead animals. Iron spurs were regarded as the mark of a great emir.' Thus does the Persian historian Juvaini describe the living conditions of the Mongols before the rise of Genghis Khan.[72]

Thirteenth-century travellers confirm that the Mongols were not fastidious in their eating habits. Plano Carpini comments: 'They consume everything which can be eaten – dogs, wolves, foxes, horses and, in an emergency, human flesh . . . They also eat the afterbirth of mares; we even saw them eating lice; and with our own eyes we saw them consume mice.'[73]

The shaman, Teb-tengri, reminded the sons of Genghis Khan of these olden days with the words: 'Before you were born the stars turned in the heavens. Everyone was feuding. Rather than sleep they robbed each other of their possessions. The earth and its crust had moved. The whole nation was in rebellion. Rather than rest they fought each other. In such a world one did not live as one wished, but rather in constant conflict. There was no respite, only battle. There was no affection, only mutual slaughter.'[74]

The kinship group lost its homogeneous character as a result of the constant plundering and retaliatory campaigns; defeated tribes and clans were incorporated into the victorious confederation or distributed individually among the dependants of the victors. The descendants of conquered tribes and clans became serfs (*ötögus bo'ol*) of the victorious leaders, serving these masters in peace and in war. Unlike a leader's followers (*nökhöd*), the serfs, although owning their personal possessions, could not leave their masters, being compelled to nomadize with them. Several factors, however, such as the period they lived together, the services and economic support rendered to their masters, tended to blur the social distinction between the *ötögus bo'ol* and the *nökhöd*. Such factors could even lead to family relationships between the *ötögus bo'ol* and their masters[75] and the status of *ötögus bo'ol* was certainly superior to that of a bonded serf (*bo'ol*). Many who belonged to the *ötögus bo'ol* distinguished themselves in the Mongol expansionist campaigns and achieved high honours.[76] Many, however, were exploited by masters such as the Tayichi'ut, who robbed the Jeuret of carts, horses and even food.[77] Such serfs felt bereft of all rights and strove to achieve independence.

The continuing state of war had serious consequences for the Mongol economy. Herds were stolen or slaughtered, horses were ridden to death − 'they collapsed from exhaustion and expired on the steppe', remarks Rashid ad-Din.[78] Such economic uncertainty and poverty motivated young, adventurous men to leave their clan and become followers (*nökhöd*) in the service of any leader who could provide for them, whose military or diplomatic skill offered them an opportunity to share rich booty and the possibility of rapid preferment. The *nökhöd* were freemen; they entered the service of a leader voluntarily and could leave him and attach themselves to another. They lived in their leader's household and were maintained by him. The *nökhöd* were constantly with their leader; in war they protected him from the enemy and guarded him while he slept; in peace they undertook household tasks, served him with soup and tended the herds. Such peacetime duties differed little from those of the *bo'ol*, the less fortunate who were given or sold into servitude by their fathers,[79] as Mukali was presented by his father to Temuchin as a threshold servant[80] and Malik of the Baya'ut exchanged his son for a haunch of venison.[81]

The destruction of the clan order, the basis of the old Mongol society, also affected the norms which regulated the social life of the Mongols. One maxim (*bilik*) preserved by Rashid ad-Din states: 'When in a tribe the sons do not heed the teachings of their fathers and the younger sons do not listen to the words of the elder sons, the husband has no trust in his wife and the wife does not obey the orders of her husband, the father-in-law does not approve of his daughters-in-law and these show no respect for their father-in-law, the great do not protect the common people and the latter do not obey the instructions of their superiors, . . . in such a tribe the robbers, the liars, the evil-doers, the good-for-nothings [will become so numerous that they] will overshadow the sun itself.' The moral decline went so far, comments Juvaini, that robbery and acts of violence, immorality and sexual offences were regarded by many as evidence of masculinity and superiority.[82]

The Mongol people longed for unity and for a state of order in which human life and property would be secure.

In this period of poverty, misery and decline, Genghis Khan was born. His father, Yisugei,[83] was a Kiyat-Borjigid,[84] a race which traced its family tree back to Bodunchar, the illegitimate son of Alan-ko'a. The legend of Bodunchar's birth relates how, after Dobun-mergen's death, Alan-ko'a bore Bodunchar, having been visited every night by a strange 'golden glittering' man.[85] Rashid ad-Din reports in greater detail: 'A red-haired, blue-(green-) eyed man approached her very slowly each night in her dream; he then slipped stealthily away.' The legend alludes to a possible foreign origin of the father, whom Dobun-mergen's sons suspected was the Baya'ut, Malik.[86] If so, he was not from the Mongol Baya'ut tribe, which belonged to the Borjigid, but rather from a Turkic tribe of that name, since Malik must have come from afar when he encountered Dobun-mergen, and been so exhausted that he sold his son for a haunch of venison.[87] The features attributed to the Borjigid suggest a Kirghiz origin – a hypothesis already put forward by Berezin – since the Kirghiz were tall, had red hair and blue (green) eyes; those with black hair and brown eyes were, according to the *Tangshu (History of the Tang)*, considered to be descendants of a Chinese general, Li Ling.[88]

The Kiyat were related to the Tayichi'ut,[89] a forest tribe whose main occupation was hunting and fishing and which, divided into numerous sub-clans, lived dispersed along the lower reaches of the Selenga, south-west of Lake Baikal.[90] Rashid ad-Din relates that, after the collapse of the Meng-ku empire, the Tayichi'ut assembled to elect a successor to Ambakai, but could not agree on any of the claimants. Some Tayichi'ut attached themselves to Yisugei but he never, as some sources claim, united all the clans, nor did he rule all the Mongol tribes. No less tendentious is the assertion by Zhao Hong that Yisugei's father was a mere troop commander.[91]

Yisugei was an aristocrat of the steppe and is correctly described by both the *Secret History* and Rashid ad-Din as a *ba'atur*. Although Genghis described his father posthumously as Khan,[92] this was never a title which Yisugei held during his lifetime; but he was a brave warrior who took part in the retaliatory campaign against the Jurchid.[93] Yisugei eventually acquired a certain power because when the Kerait ruler Toghrul was driven from his kingdom Yisugei helped him to regain the overlordship of the Kerait tribe.[94] In gratitude for this assistance, Toghrul swore blood-brothership (*anda*) with Yisugei.

Temuchin's birth

Rashid ad-Din maintains that Yisugei had many wives, but there is evidence of only two.

The aristocratic Mongol families were exogamous and traditional marriage arrangements existed between certain tribes. However, because of the dangers inherent in long trips, the nomads would sometimes avail themselves of chance encounters on the steppe to abduct women. Yisugei acquired his senior wife, Hö'elun, in this manner when, as the *Secret History* recounts, he was on a hawking expedition and stole her from the Merkit, Chiledu, who was bringing her home as a bride from the Olkunu'ut, a minor tribe of the Onggirat. This story is recounted only in the *Secret History*; it is glossed over in the official historiographies.

The second wife known to us – about whose actual identity there is some controversy – is the mother of Temuchin's half-brothers Bekhter and Belgutei. The *Altan tobchi* names the mother of Temuchin's half-brothers as Suchikel (Suchikin); and although the same source also identifies that lady as the mother of Yisugei, Pelliot is nevertheless inclined to assume that Belgutei's mother was named Suchigu-eke. According to the *Secret History*, however, the mother of Bekhter and Belgutei would appear to be Ko'agchin, despite her words to the Merkit warriors: 'I was at the main tent for the sheep-shearing and am now on the way home to my own tent.' These words are ambiguous, possibly motivated by

5   *Genghis Khan's birthplace memorial. Dadal Somon, Khentei Province.*

a desire to conceal her identity and thus avoid being taken prisoner. Had Ko'agchin been a mere servant of Yisugei it would be difficult to explain her feeling of shame when given as wife to a commoner during her subsequent captivity.[95]

Hö'elun bore a son at the time Yisugei returned home from a campaign against the Tartars. The *Secret History* records the event in the following terms: 'As Yisugei-ba'atur returned with his captives, Temuchin-uge, Kori-buka and other Tartars, Hö'elun-uchin was in labour at Del'iun-boldok on the Onon River, where she gave birth to Genghis Khan. At birth he clutched in his right hand a blood clot the size of a knuckle bone.' (Later lamaistic sources claimed Temuchin was clutching the state seal – *kashbu*.) 'And thus his father named him Temuchin because he was born when Yisugei brought in Temuchin-uge.' This story of Temuchin's birth is found, with minor differences, in other sources.[96]

It is not known when the legend arose, nor who was responsible for spreading it, although Pelliot points to the foreign origin of the folkloristic motif. Other legends concerning Temuchin's birth also circulated among the Mongols. According to the Armenian chronicler Kirakos, the Mongols believed that Temuchin was not created from human seed, but by a ray of light which penetrated through the rooflight of the tent and announced to the mother: 'Conceive and you will bear a son who will be a World Conqueror.' The chronicler adds that this legend was related by Kutun-noyan, a Mongol of the highest position.

The 'Light Conception Motif' which Kirakos links with Temuchin's birth was widespread among the nomads. The *Secret History* tells how Alan-ko'a, the reputed ancestress of the Borjigid, explained the conception of her illegitimate son: 'Night after night a golden glittering man entered through the skylight of the *ger*. He stroked my stomach and his rays entered my womb, When he left he crawled away like a yellow dog on the sunbeam or moonbeam.' The *Liaoshi (History of the Liao Dynasty)* relates that the mother of Abaoji, founder of the Khitan dynasty, also became pregnant after she dreamed that the sun sank into her lap.[97]

In accordance with an old nomadic custom which, as Lattimore points out, was also known in ancient China, Yisugei gave the new-born child the name of the captured Tartar chieftain. Mongolian tradition offers the alternative explanation that Temuchin received his name because he was a smith – *temurchi* – or belonged to a family of smiths. This traditional explanation was widespread in the thirteenth and fourteenth centuries and both Munkujev and Rockhill report its survival into modern times. Although bLo-bzan comments that the choice of Temuchin's name is partly attributable to his cradle being made of iron, it is certainly striking that the names of Temuchin's brother, Temuge, and of his sister, Temulun, also derive from the root *temur* – iron.[98]

The year of Temuchin's birth is controversial. Rashid ad-Din relates that it was known to 'the Mongol princes, emirs and dignitaries and was made public' that Genghis Khan attained the age of seventy-two years. Since the year of his death (1227) has been firmly established by Pelliot, it would thus follow that Temuchin was born in 1155. This tradition was known to the Chinese Zhao Hong, who gives Temuchin's year of birth as the year *jiaxu* – 1154/5. In contrast, the *Yuanshi*, the *Shenwu* and the *Zhuogeng lu* record Temuchin's year of birth as 1162. There was also an early tradition, to which Pelliot has drawn attention, that Temuchin was born in 1167. Yang Weizheng – quoted by Tao Zongyi – offers the year *dinghai* (1167) as Temuchin's date of birth; and in the older version of the *Shenwu*, as in the *Lidai fozu tongzai* (*The Record of Successive Generations of Buddha*), Genghis is said to have died at the age of sixty. Without firmly committing himself, Pelliot expresses the view that 1167 ought to be considered as the year of Temuchin's birth, since this date is more compatible with the life history of Genghis Khan.[99]

The tradition that Yisugei had just returned from a battle against the Tartars offers no clues to the date of Temuchin's birth. The *Secret History* relates the story immediately after the campaign of vengeance which Kutula and Kadan led against the Tartars and most authors thus assume that Yisugei brought home his Tartar chiefs from that campaign. The Mongols were, however, unsuccessful in that particular campaign and there is no mention of Yisugei's participation in it, so one is clearly considering two different episodes.[100]

Acceptance of the earliest postulated date of 1155 would lead to the conclusion that Temuchin only became a father at the age of thirty,[101] most unlikely if one considers the early Mongol marriages; he would not have subjugated the peoples of Central Asia and begun to build up his empire before he was fifty; at sixty he would have undertaken his campaigns against the most powerful and civilized states of Asia; well into his sixties he would have undergone the strain of the western campaign, withstanding climatic conditions which the Mongols found very enervating; and at seventy-two he would have personally led the campaign against the Tanguts in 1227.

Cross-reference to the age of his sister Temulun also suggests a later date for Temuchin's birth. Temulun was, according to the *Altan tobchi*, nine years younger than Temuchin, and the *Secret History* relates that Hö'elun was carrying Temulun on her lap at the time of the attack by the Merkits. If we accept Temuchin's year of birth as 1155 then Temulun would have been eighteen years old at the time of that attack![102]

Such contradictions and improbabilities disappear if we assume that Temuchin was born about a decade later, although I believe that the date cannot be exactly calculated – and doubt whether Genghis himself knew it. The Chinese Zhao Hong reports in his travelogue that he often questioned Mongols about their age, whereupon they laughed at the question and answered 'We have never known it.' This was also true of the Jurchid. Even in the *Jinshi* (*History of the Chin*) it was noted that, before the Jurchid had a written language and an organized infrastructure of officials, they could not fix ages with any certainty; and Herbert Franke has since pointed out that the Jurchid celebrated their birthdays on any one of the Chinese feast days, because they did not themselves know when they were born.[103]

In the remainder of this work it is assumed that Temuchin was born around the mid 1160s.

Temuchin's youth

Hö'elun bore Yisugei three more sons in addition to Temuchin. These were Jochi-Kasar, Kachun and Temuge, and there was also a daughter, Temulun. The *Altan tobchi* provides the relative ages of these siblings: 'When Temuchin was nine years of age Jochi-kasar was seven, Kachun was five, Temuge-otchigin was three and Temulun was still in her cradle.' The family also consisted of two other sons, Bekhter and Belgutei, born of a second wife. The official histories do not mention Bekhter, thus enabling them to gloss over his murder by Temuchin. They also record Belgutei simply as a fifth son of Yisugei, listing him in order of rank rather than according to year of birth.[104]

Temuchin spent his childhood with his siblings by the River Onon, where Yisugei had his main camp. Like all Mongol children, he learned to ride at an early age and practised archery by shooting at birds. In winter he played on the ice of the Onon with his brothers and other youngsters, among whom was his youthful companion, Jamuka. These two boys were linked by a close friendship. The *Secret History* tells us that they made a compact of blood-brothership (*anda*) by exchanging knuckle-bones, and then, in spring, Jamuka gave Temuchin a whistling arrow which he had made and received an arrow whose head Temuchin had carved from juniper wood.[105]

The oath of blood-brothership was, according to Pelliot, taken by members of different clans and was regarded by the nomads as more binding than the tie of a direct blood relationship. The oath, to maintain eternal friendship, was strengthened by drinking from a beaker in which a few drops of blood of the new brothers had been mixed. Ye Longli relates how, when the founder of the Liao dynasty concluded a pact of blood-brothership with Li Cunxu, 'they both entered a tent where they drank and then squeezed each other's hands'. After the oath came the exchange of gifts. The *Secret History* recounts that when Temuchin and Jamuka renewed their pact after the defeat of the Merkits they exchanged girdles and horses which they had taken as booty from the enemy. The *Liaoshi* (*History of the Liao Dynasty*) points out that such exchanges of belts and horses were common among the Khitans, the exchange of articles of clothing being of particular significance – the Chinese term for blood-brothers was *paoge*, 'clothing-brothers'. It has been suggested by Doerfer that the conclusion of an *anda* relationship required at least a symbolic degree of communal life, but Vladimirtsov does not consider this to have been an absolute condition of such a pact.[106]

When Temuchin was eight years old (nine years according to Mongol calculations) Yisugei decided to seek a fiancée for him. The Mongols entered into marriage at an early age and this was, for the aristocratic families, a means of forming alliances and increasing the reputation of the family.[107] Yisugei intended to seek a fiancée among the Olkunu'ut, a branch of the Onggirat to which he was related as a result of his abduction of Hö'elun. There had in any case been, from time immemorial, marriage alliances between the Mongol ruling house and the Onggirat, one of the most important of the Mongol tribes whose lineage, according to the stories collected by Rashid ad-Din, could be traced back to Mongol warriors who, defeated by the Turks, took refuge in the Erkene-kun mountains.[108]

En route to the pastures of the Onggirat – which Pelliot locates east of Lake Buir – Yisugei was, however, invited to visit Dai-sechen, a member of the Boskur sub-tribe of the Onggirat, who had his main camp north-east of Lake Kulun. Dai-sechen's daughter, Börte, who was a year older than Temuchin had, according to the *Secret History* 'a lively face and flashing eyes'; Yisugei is said to have taken an instant liking to the girl and to have become very fond of her.[109]

The time-honoured betrothal negotiations commenced. According to Rashid ad-Din, Dai-sechen caused many difficulties and eventually gave his agreement only as the result of intercession by his young son, Alchi-noyan, who had felt drawn to Temuchin at first sight and who was later to win much renown and receive high honours in the campaigns against the Xi-Xia and the Muslims.[110] Dai-sechen, however, made a condition that, as a future son-in-law, Temuchin must live in his family.

The custom of leaving a son with the future parents-in-law was widespread among the early Turkic-Mongol nomads. Rashid recounts the tradition that the nine sons of the legendary Monolun nomadized for some time with the tribes from which they chose their brides; Juvaini draws attention to the fact that young Turkic bridegrooms might, out of respect for their parents-in-law, return to their homes only after a year.[111] The practice originated in matriarchal conditions but its significance changed in later times as economic factors became important. In China, as well as among the nomads, redeeming the bride's purchase price was the main reason for the continuing custom; the evidence of Plano Carpini and of Rubruck is that the bride-price was very high. Given that the spare horse which Yisugei left behind with Dai-sechen bespoke only modest means, compared with which Börte's dowry of a sable cloak was a princely ransom, economic considerations were therefore probably decisive in Dai-sechen's condition that Temuchin should remain, as son-in-law, in his household.[112]

This marriage agreement won for Yisugei a valuable alliance with the Onggirat, one of the most respected and most powerful of the Mongol tribes, whose role in the struggle for the mastery of the steppe should not be underestimated. Yet the trip was to prove Yisugei's undoing. On his way home Yisugei encountered some Tartars who had gathered for a meal. Since he was thirsty he dismounted and joined the group, availing himself of the time-honoured custom which required nomads to offer hospitality to strangers on the steppe. The Tartars, however, recognizing Yisugei as an enemy who had previously robbed them, mixed poison in his food.[113] Yisugei became ill while travelling homewards but, although he realized that he could not escape death, he succeeded in reaching his own camp. On his death-bed he entrusted Mönglik, one of his loyal retainers, with bringing home his eldest son, Temuchin. Mönglik faithfully carried out the task entrusted to him and Temuchin returned to the family camp.

Yisugei's death sealed the fate of his family. His followers lamented: 'The deep waters have dried up, the sparkling stone is shattered.' They refused to serve the widow, whose sons had not yet come of age, and the widows of the deceased Tayichi'ut tribal leader, Ambakai, no longer permitted Hö'elun to attend the ceremonies in veneration of their ancestors. The Tayichi'ut eventually deserted the widow's camp. Hö'elun, an energetic woman, attempted to prevent her own people from leaving, mounted on horseback and carrying the tribal banner[114] she temporarily succeeded in halting the exodus – 'but those she persuaded to return did not remain in her camp. They soon set out again to follow the Tayichi'ut.'[115]

The behaviour of the *nökhöd* is understandable since, with Yisugei's death, their expectations of rich plunder and military fame had been dashed. It is more difficult to understand the behaviour of Yisugei's own clan towards Hö'elun. Why did Yisugei's brothers not support the widow? According to Levirate law, which was accepted among the Mongols, the youngest brother, Da'aritai-otchigin, had a claim to the widow and a duty to protect her. Did Hö'elun refuse marriage to him – as Tolui's widow, Sorkaktani, later refused to marry Guyuk, son of Ögödei Kha'an, asserting that she wished to devote herself to bringing up her children?[116] Or does the author of the *Secret History* dramatize the situation of the bereaved family in order to enhance Temuchin's eventual rise to World Conqueror?

Such a hypothesis may have some foundation. According to Rashid ad-Din, Da'aritai-otchigin and his warriors stood by Temuchin when Yisugei's people left the widow's camp. Rashid also reports that, when Temuchin lost his father and his people defected to the Tayichi'ut, his cousin Kuchar, son of Nekuntaishi, an older brother of Yisugei, formed an alliance with Temuchin and served him in an honourable and praiseworthy fashion.[117]

If, however, we accept the account of the *Secret History*, Hö'elun and her children were deserted by all and suffered great deprivation. 'Her cap firmly on her head and her dress girt around her knees, she ran up and down the Onon River collecting rowans and bird cherries, feeding her chicks night and day.'[118] The boys too had to contribute to their sustenance. They used bow and hook to provide the daily food, these activities leading to an incident which is deliberately suppressed by the court historians.

The murder of Bekhter

There was no harmony in Hö'elun's family. Her sons were divided from their half-brothers by rivalry and envy, and the relationship took a dramatic turn for the worse when Bekhter and Belgutei refused to share hunting spoils with Temuchin and Kasar.

The division of spoils, sanctified by custom and tradition, was of prime importance in the life of the nomads. After one incident Temuchin and his brother, Jochi-kasar, informed their mother: 'We caught a splendid *sokosun* fish which our brothers Bekhter and Belgutei then took from us.' In vain their mother bade them remember that they had 'no companions except their shadows, and only a horse's tail for a whip', also that they must still seek revenge for the humiliation suffered at the hands of the Tayichi'ut. 'Recently they took from us a lark which we had shot with an arrow. Now they have robbed us again. How can we live with each other?' demanded the brothers. They then stormed out and crept up on Bekhter, who was sitting on a hillock tending the horses. Bekhter made no attempt to defend himself, nor did he seek to escape; he remained squatting on the ground, only beseeching them to spare his younger brother, Belgutei. 'Temuchin and Kasar', so goes the story, 'both shot him from in front at close range, as if at target practice. Then they went away.' After this deed the two were greeted by their mother with the words 'You murderers!' The *Secret History* adds that she showered them both with wild verbal abuse, 'quoting olden proverbs and citing the words of the ancestors as an example for her sons'.[119]

There is no reason to doubt the historicity of the murder. Many contemporaries, who certainly knew of the deed, would still be alive when the *Secret History* was compiled and the silence of court historians is explained by their desire to protect the reputation of

Genghis Khan. The *Secret History's* dialogue and its description of the circumstances in which the deed was perpetrated are literary tools, which permit the author to express his attitude towards the deed.

The motive for Bekhter's murder was undoubtedly more fundamental than the mere theft of a fish. Temuchin's acceptance as head of the family was at stake. The ages of the stepbrothers are not provided by our sources and although Wang Guowei and Pelliot regard Belgutei as younger than Kasar he must, as Tu Ji assumes, have been older.[120] The *Yuanshi* reports that Belgutei participated in the election of Möngke Kha'an in 1251, and according to Rashid ad-Din he died in 1255 at the age of 110! This is certainly exaggerated, but it does indicate that Belgutei reached an unusually ripe old age, perhaps between ninety and one hundred years. He could, therefore, have been born between 1155 and 1165 and thus, according to our chronology, have been older than Temuchin himself. Had the half-brothers been younger, Hö'elun's sons would never have allowed themselves to be robbed of their hunting spoils. Temuchin, the eldest son of the senior wife of the head of the family, regarded that act as an infringement of his privileges and exercised his right to pass judgement on guilty family members. Bekhter's behaviour indicated that he was conscious of his guilt and Belgutei did not seek to avenge his brother's execution. He remained a faithful follower of and received high honours from Genghis Khan, who is reported to have said: 'It is to Belgutei's strength and Kasar's prowess as an archer that I owe the conquest of the World Empire.'[121]

Temuchin in Tayichi'ut captivity

In the *Secret History* the account of Temuchin's capture by the Tayichi'ut follows directly on the episode of Bekhter's murder, but with no attempt to investigate any possible connection. Was there, perhaps, a relationship between Bekhter's murder and Temuchin's captivity? Had news of Temuchin's deed come to the ears of Tarkutai-kiriltuk, one of the leading princes of the Tayichi'ut, and was Temuchin to be punished for it? After his capture Temuchin was treated as a criminal prisoner in the

Tayichi'ut camp; he was placed in a cage and each day and night he was kept under guard by a different household (*ail*).[122]

The *Secret History* offers two differing accounts of the episode.[123] According to one version Tarkutai regarded Temuchin as a potential rival and as he left for Hö'elun's camp he called out: 'The evil brood is leaving the nest, the slobbering young have grown up!. Then, when the Tayichi'ut reached Hö'elun's camp and the family sought refuge in the forest – Belgutei building a defensive barrier, Kasar attacking the enemy with arrows and the small children hiding in the ravines – the Tayichi'ut announced: 'Your elder brother Temuchin must come forth! We do not need the rest of you!' Temuchin fled on horseback to a hillock in the woods, but the Tayichi'ut encircled the thicket where he had hidden, remaining there until hunger drove him out and he was captured.

Temuchin's imprisonment by the Tayichi'ut is presented quite differently in a later paragraph of the *Secret History*. In this version when Tarkutai, made prisoner by his own people, is about to be delivered over to Temuchin, his sons and brothers hasten to his assistance. Tarkutai, however, calls to them: 'Temuchin will not kill me! When he was young and lived in a leaderless encampment, yet had flashing eyes and a lively face. I brought him from there to my own camp in order to educate him. He was quick to learn, so I brought him up and trained him as one would a two or three-year-old horse . . .'

Do these words of Tarkutai refer to another incident? In his summary of the life of Genghis Khan, Rashid ad-Din writes that, after Yisugei's death, Temuchin suffered great tribulations at the hands of the Tayichi'ut and other senior and junior relatives, also from the Merkits, the Tartars and other tribes. 'Several tribes took him prisoner on many occasions but he always found some way or another of freeing himself.'

In his *History of the Tribes*, Rashid clearly combines elements from the Merkit attack and their abduction of Börte with elements from Temuchin's imprisonment by the Tayichi'ut, thus producing the following account. 'On one occasion Temuchin had ridden out on important matters when his saddle-girth became loose as he rode up a hill. This evil omen made him consider whether he should turn back, but he continued on his way. Suddenly a party of Merkits appeared, captured him and held him prisoner until a ransom of goods from Temuchin's camp were delivered to them and Temuchin was taken home.' Rashid also reports that, after the battle with Jamuka, when Temuchin was deserted by his people, he was captured by the enemy and befriended by Sorkan-shira – whose succour, however, the *Secret History* links with Temuchin's capture by the Tayichi'ut.[124]

Temuchin was obviously held prisoner on more than one occasion. The nomads were constantly exposed to such raids, young boys being carried off as servants or followers, either for political reasons or to extract a ransom. The *Secret History* informs us that Toghrul, ruler of the Keraits, was kidnapped twice in his youth, by the Merkits when he was seven years old and by the Tartars when he was thirteen; also that his brother, Jagambu, was captured by the Tanguts, but because of his intelligence and ability he achieved high office in the Tangut empire. Rashid reports additionally that Jamuka was a prisoner of the Merkits for many years.[125]

Even those sources which seek to prevent a loss of face on Temuchin's part by glossing over his periods of captivity do contain certain allusions to them, and the news spread beyond Mongolia. The Chinese Zhao Hong, who thus learned of this captivity, does not, however, write of capture by the Tayichi'ut, but that Temuchin was for ten years a slave of the Chin. Raverty offers, from Islamic sources, an exact date for Temuchin's imprisonment by the Tayichi'ut, citing year 584 of the Hegira (1187/8). This cannot, however, refer to the event portrayed in the *Secret History*, since the retaliatory campaign against the Merkits had taken place before this date.[126]

Our sources have at times transposed elements from one event to another, or combined two occurrences in one story. The motives ascribed to Tarkutai are controversial and the official Chinese historiography ignores the incident. Nevertheless, Temuchin's imprisonment by the Tayichi'ut can scarcely be doubted.

Temuchin's release from imprisonment is described as follows in the *Secret History*:[127] 'While, on the sixteenth day of the first summer month, the Tayichi'ut were celebrating the Day of the Red Moon, Temuchin was only guarded by a puny youth. Breaking loose from his gaoler, Temuchin struck him on the skull with the cangue and hid in the bed of the River Onon, lying on his back with only his face projecting from the water. He was discovered there by Sorkan-shira, a Suldu,[128] who did not betray him but advised that he wait for nightfall and then flee to his mother. Temuchin waited for the advent of darkness but, rather than flee to his mother, he made his way to the Suldu tents, remembering that when he spent a night there as a prisoner Sorkan-shira's sons had taken pity on him, loosened the cangue and permitted him to sleep – and now Sorkan had not betrayed him to the Tayichi'ut.'

Sorkan-shira was displeased by the arrival of the escapee, fearing the wrath of the Tayichi'ut, his masters. Initially he was unwilling to hide Temuchin but, yielding to the entreaties of his children, concealed the fugitive in a cart loaded with wool where the Tayichi'ut searchers failed to find him. Temuchin was saved, given a horse and supplies and set off to join his kindred.

Rashid ad-Din's version of Temuchin's escape with the assistance of Sorkan-shira is that the latter pulled Temuchin from the river during the night, released him from the cangue, brought him home and hid him in a cart packed with wool. The role of Sorkan's children is not mentioned; in their place appears an old woman who takes pity on Temuchin and cares for him, combing his hair and packing felt between his raw and bloody neck and the cangue. The Rashid text which follows this account of the escape contains anachronisms. It reports that Tolui was already born when Temuchin reached his family, also that, after Temuchin's flight, Sorkan-shira feared the discovery of his role and fled from the Tayichi'ut to enter Temuchin's service.[129]

The *Secret History*'s description of Temuchin's escape from captivity is certainly romantically embellished, yet the attributes ascribed to Temuchin by that source on this occasion are typical of his real character – although, as stressed in the preface, the author of the *Secret History*, a member of Temuchin's close circle, tended to criticize rather than idealize Genghis Khan. Temuchin does not act on impulse. He selects for his escape a Tayichi'ut feast day when they pay little attention to their captive; he does not take Sorkan's advice to flee that same night, knowing that a horseless nomad has little chance of escaping his pursuers or of surviving; in expecting to be saved by an *ötögu bo'ol* he exhibits the understanding of people which was to distinguish him in later life; and he exerts over young people that personal attraction which had already been tested in Dai-sechen's camp.[130]

Temuchin did not forget the experiences of his captivity. In the Tayichi'ut camp he had become acquainted with the lot of a commoner, the capriciousness of the *noyat*, the faithlessness of relatives who set their selfish interests above the duty of family and tribal solidarity. Young Temuchin drew his own conclusions from these experiences and put them to good use in his future struggle for power.

The *Secret History* enables us to place the incidents from Temuchin's youth in the following tentative order. Temuchin was eight or nine years old when he was brought home after Yisugei's death. He was probably some fourteen to fifteen years old when he murdered Bekhter and then became a captive of the Tayichi'ut. That period of captivity cannot have been a lengthy one since, according to the *Secret History*, when Temuchin was provided with a horse and supplies and left Sorkan's tent, he followed tracks and found his way back to the camp in which his family had entrenched itself. The position of the family had not improved; they still had to eke out their existence by hunting marmots and steppe rats.[131]

Horse rustling

Nomads who separated from their tribe and lived in isolation were prey to many dangers, especially the loss of their horses, the nomads' irreplaceable possession. Bodunchar's words when expelled from his family illustrate this nomadic dependence: 'If the horse dies, I die; if it lives, I survive'; and when Kutula fled from the Dörbets and his horse became bogged down in a marsh, his pursuers called out: 'What can a Mongol do if he loses his horse? Come back willingly!'[132] The *Secret History* provides the following apt anecdote from Temuchin's early life.[133]

In broad daylight robbers (Jurkin warriors according to the *Yuanshi*) appeared at Hö'elun's camp and in full sight of the family stole the eight geldings which were tethered in front of the tent. The family owned only one other horse, on which Belgutei had ridden out to hunt marmots. When he returned home in the evening Belgutei wanted to go in search of the stolen horses. Kasar also offered to do so but Temuchin rejected these offers. He was the eldest and, although no daredevil, would do his duty. He mounted Belgutei's horse and followed the tracks of the stolen horses. On the way he met young Bo'orchu, the thirteen-year old son of Nayan the Rich, a member of the Arulat tribe which had maintained friendly relations with Yisugei.[134] When Bo'orchu discovered the purpose of Temuchin's journey he 'simply threw his leather milk bucket and ladle down on the steppe' and joined Temuchin. They found the geldings and, thanks to darkness, evaded the pursuing enemy.

Temuchin sought to reward Bo'orchu for his assistance: 'Friend, would I ever have found my horses without you? Let us share them. How many do you wish?' he asks. But Bo'orchu rejects the offer: 'I joined you because I saw that you were in trouble and in need of help. Shall I now take a share as if this were booty? What sort of service would I then have rendered you? I require nothing!' This sealed a lifelong friendship between Genghis and Bo'orchu, who with Mukali was one of Genghis' main supporters in the struggle for leadership of the tribes.

Temuchin certainly had other adventures. In one adage preserved by Rashid ad-Din, Genghis Khan relates the following episodes from his youth. 'Before I ascended the throne I was riding alone on one occasion. Six men lay in ambush along the route, with evil intentions towards me. As I approached them I drew my sword and attacked. They, for their part, loosed arrows at me but these all flew past without one hitting me. I hacked the men down and rode on unscathed. On my return I passed close to their bodies. Their six geldings were roaming masterless in the area and could not be caught, but I drove them home before me.'

A second anecdote runs; 'I was riding with Bogurchi when twelve men lay in ambush against us on a hill. Bogurchi was riding behind and I did not wait for him but, relying on my own strength and energy. I attacked the ambushers. All twelve loosed their bows at me. Arrows flew around me, but I pressed home my attack. Suddenly an arrow struck me in the mouth. I fell and lost consciousness. In the meantime Bogurchi had hurried forward . . . he brought water. I washed out my mouth and spat out the blood which had run into my throat. I recovered consciousness and the ability to move. I rose and attacked them again. They were astounded by my strength, tumbled down the hill and breathed their last. The reason that Bogurchi and his descendants have been

6 *Landscape in the Orkhon River country of Central Mongolia.*

raised to the rank of *Darkhan* is the praiseworthy zeal which he showed on that occasion.'

Rashid ad-Din offers a variant of this last episode in his *History of the Tribes*: 'Temuchin was riding, accompanied by Bo'orchu and Boroghul, against some Tayichi'ut, when he was struck in the neck by an arrow. The three drew back, Boroghul heated a stone and poured water over it, forcing Temuchin to inhale the steam until the clotted blood in his throat dissolved. Because it was snowing heavily Bo'orchu stretched his blanket over Temuchin's head and held it there until morning, although the snow rose to his thighs.'[135]

Rashid's *biliks* are clearly an amalgam of several events. According to the *Secret History*, Temuchin was wounded in the neck on the battlefield of Köyitän, but it was Jelme rather than Bo'orchu who assisted him on that occasion; and when distributing rewards at the Khuriltai in 1206[136] Genghis made no mention whatever of the act attributed to Bo'orchu in the *bilik*. Rashid's stories contain innumerable exaggerations. It is difficult to believe that Genghis was capable of such boasting.

Temuchin seeks a protector

When Temuchin was fifteen, the age at which young Mongols were regarded as reaching their majority, he thought of the fiancée whom he had left with Dai-sechen and decided to bring her home. Accompanied by Belgutei, he set off for the camp of Dai-sechen, who was overjoyed to see the son-in-law whom he had given up for lost. He permitted the consummation of the marriage and then allowed Temuchin to take Börte-uchin home as his wife.[137] The bride was accompanied by her mother and took a black sable cloak as a present for her mother-in-law.

A new period had begun in Temuchin's life; he was no longer a boy. The privations of his childhood had toughened his body, his senses were tuned to the dangers which lay in wait on the steppe and his Tayichi'ut captivity had taught him the need for a patron if he was to remain protected from attacks by his enemies. But Temuchin was ambitious; he had inherited from his mother the determination to attain power and realized that, if this aim were to be achieved, he must not present himself as a helpless outsider. He was determined to enter the service of a patron as a leader (*noyan*), not as a mere follower (*nökhör*).

Single-mindedly Temuchin prepared to carry out his plan. He dispatched his brother Belgutei to summon young Bo'orchu, who had assisted him in recovering the stolen horses. Bo'orchu responded to this call and, without even bidding farewell to his father, quit his wealthy parental home to enter Temuchin's service.[138] Temuchin had not only this first follower but also his brothers, who had developed into capable warriors – the accurate archer Kasar and the powerful Belgutei, who could fell trees with one blow of his axe. Nor did Temuchin go empty-handed to offer his services. He had, after all, the sable cloak, Börte's wedding gift. Sable, regarded by the Mongols as the 'King of Furs' – a first-class sable cloak, Marco Polo noted,[139] cost 2,000 gold bezants, as much as 1,000 even when made of only second-class skins – would secure for Temuchin the favour and goodwill of his new patron. Thus prepared, Temuchin accompanied by his brothers, Kasar and Belgutei, sought out Toghrul, leader of the Keraits.

Toghrul was an important tribal chieftain, whose empire stretched from the Onon River in the west, across the homelands of the Mongols to the Chinese frontiers in the east.[140] The respect which he was accorded by the nomads was due, above all, to his relations with the Chin emperor, to whom Toghrul paid tribute but on whose assistance he could therefore rely.

Toghrul had an eventful youth. At seven years of age he was carried off by the Merkits, who set him to grind mortar, and when he was thirteen he and his mother were abducted by the Tartars, whose camels Toghrul was forced to tend.[141] On the death of his father, Kyriakus, Toghrul committed fratricide in order to gain the Kerait throne, but was driven out of the land by his uncle, the *Gurkhan*. In this plight he sought refuge with Temuchin's father, Yisugei, Kutula-khan warned Yisugei: 'It is not good to maintain friendship with him [Toghrul]. We have come to know his character. It would be better to seal an *anda* pact with the *Gurkhan*. He has a good and sensitive character, while Toghrul murdered his brothers and stained his honour with blood . . .' Yisugei did not heed this advice; he attacked the *gurkhan*, drove him to flight and reinstated Toghrul as ruler of his people.[142]

In the *Xixia shushi* (*The Historical Record of the Xi-Xia*), Wu Guangcheng notes under the eleventh year *dading* of the Chin (1171): 'The Kerait leader, *Ong-khan*, killed his brothers and attacked his uncle, the *Gurkhan*. The leader of the Mongol tribes, Yisugei, assisted him and the *gurkhan's* troops suffered defeat.' If this dating were accurate it would offer yet another argument for Temuchin's year of birth to be placed in the middle of the 1160s. But the chronological statements in this work are unreliable. It reports, for example, that Toghrul returned home after his second flight in the fourteenth in the year *dading* (1174)! If, however, we follow the chronology of the *Secret History*, Toghrul's appeal to Yisugei for help must have been before 1171, since by that date Kutula-khan was no longer alive.[143]

As Temuchin now stood before Toghrul he reminded him of the former friendship between Toghrul and Yisugei; 'In earlier days you swore friendship with my father, Yisugei. Accordingly, you are as my own father[144] and I bring you my wife's wedding gift (*emusgel*).'[145] With these words Temuchin handed Toghrul the sable cloak. Toghrul accepted the present with great pleasure and promised Temuchin: 'In gratitude for the black sable cloak I will reunite you with your people. In gratitude for the black sable cloak I will bring together again your dispersed people.'[146] Toghrul's pleasure was unlikely to be feigned. He stood in need of truly faithful followers because he could not trust his family, his own son Senggum as well as the *Gurkhan*, his uncle, having designs on the throne.[147]

By acknowledging Toghrul as his adopted father Temuchin entered into a vassal relationship which assured him the protection of a powerful leader. According to al-'Umari, Temuchin paid regular youthful visits to Toghrul 'and eventually the Unk-khan [Wang-khan] took him into his retinue and kept Temuchin close to him.'[148] This pact opened up a new phase of Temuchin's life. His reputation rose and he began to be a person of some account on the steppe. An Urianghai tribesman, for example, mindful of a promise made to Yisugei on the occasion of Temuchin's birth, presented his son, Jelme, to Temuchin as a servant.[149]

It was not long before Temuchin had an opportunity to put his new relationship with the Kerait leader to the test.

The Merkit attack

The steppe has keen ears. News spreads quickly among the nomads. The Merkits, learning that Temuchin had brought home a wife, decided that the time was ripe to take revenge for the abduction of Hö'elun. True, Chiledu, from whom Yisugei had stolen Hö'elun, was no longer alive; but revenge was a family obligation, handed down from one generation to the next. Retribution for the deed of the father, Yisugei, must be exacted from Temuchin. 300 Merkits attacked the camp of Temuchin and his family, who took flight, 'Temuchin mounted a horse, Kasar mounted a horse, Kachun mounted a horse, Temuge-otchigin mounted a horse, Belgutei mounted a horse and Jelme mounted a horse. Mother Hö'elun took Temulun on her lap and a pack horse was made ready – but there was no horse for Börte', reports the *Secret History*. Temuchin abandoned his newly married wife to her fate. Did he lose his head in panic or did he intentionally abandon Börte and Belgutei's mother in order to deflect pursuit by the Merkits? The Merkits did indeed halt their pursuit of Temuchin when they found Börte hidden in a cart and made her captive. 'We are carrying off your women as reparation for Hö'elun; we have our revenge', they shouted as they turned back.[150]

Temuchin was saved; that alone was important. He began to believe in his destiny and gave fervent thanks to Heaven for his escape from deadly danger. 'The Burkhan has preserved my life like that of a louse and I have conquered great fear. I will honour the *Burkhan-Kaldun* with sacrifices every morning and pray to it every day. My children and my children's children shall be mindful of this' he cried. The *Secret History* continues: 'With these words he turned towards the sun, his belt around his neck and his hat hanging over his hand, beat his breast and knelt nine times to offer a libation and prayer to the sun.'[151]

In the *Collected Chronicles* Rashid presents the incident differently. The Merkits plundered Temuchin's camp and led Börte, who was pregnant with Jochi, away into captivity, sending her to the leader of the Keraits, with whom they were then at peace. Toghrul treated her with every respect and when his nobles urgd him to marry her, he replied; 'She is my daughter-in-law. I cannot look upon her with the eyes of a betrayer.' When Temuchin received news that Börte was at the court of the Kerait leader he despatched Saba, a man of Jalair extraction, to bring her home. Toghrul released Börte with every honour. On the way home Jochi[152] was born. Because the route was dangerous and it was impossible to stop and construct a cradle, Saba kneaded a soft dough, wrapped the new-born infant in this and carried him carefully home. The infant was given the name Jochi because he was born unexpectedly.[153]

Rashid's version is implausible. It is improbable that the Merkits would, as Rashid suggests, have renounced their revenge for the abduction of Hö'elun, handing Börte over to the leader of the Keraits, the *anda* of their enemy. Rashid's intention as court historian, to save Börte's honour in order to preserve Genghis Khan's reputation, is all too obvious: Börte is already pregnant when she is abducted; emphasis is laid upon the respect with which Toghrul treats her and on the fact that she is unsullied by him. The version offered by the *Secret History* is more consistent; Börte is abducted by the Merkits as revenge for the abduction of Hö'elun and, in accordance with Levirate law, she is given as wife to Chilger, younger brother of the deceased Chiledu.

Temuchin never acted rashly and did not attempt any adventurous plan to rescue Börte. He had, after all, a patron from whom he expected assistance. Accompanied by his brothers, Kasar and Belgutei, Temuchin made his way to the Kerait ruler, who was an enemy of the Merkits. Toghrul, fully conscious of his obligations towards his new vassal, promised Temuchin: 'In gratitude for the sable cloak I will find your Börte for you, even if I have to destroy all the Merkits. In gratitude for the black sable cloak we will rescue your wife Börte, even if we have to massacre every Merkit!'[154]

Toghrul was ready to put 20,000 men into the field and another 20,000 were to be provided by Jamuka from the Jadarat.[155] Jamuka had personal reasons for taking part in the campaign against the Merkits. He, like Temuchin, had weathered difficult times and said of himself: 'As a small child I was deserted by my father and mother. I have no brothers. My wife is a shrew. I have untrustworthy companions.'[156] As we have already seen, when Temuchin was eleven years old (ten years by our reckoning) he and Jamuka played on the Onon ice together, exchanged knuckle-bones and arrows and swore eternal friendship. Rashid ad-Din relates how Jamuka was later attacked and robbed, losing all his belongings to Tokto'a-beki, the leader of a Merkit tribe. Jamuka then wandered around with thirty companions until, unable to rescue himself from this difficult situation, he was compelled to recognize Tokto'a-beki as his overlord and enter his service. There he was clever enough to insinuate himself into the favour of the leader's immediate retinue; then by a stratagem – exploiting the bodyguards' dereliction of duty, he forced his way with his thirty men into Tokto'a's sleeping quarters – Jamuka secured his release and the restitution of all his belongings.[157]

Like Temuchin, Jamuka had acknowledged Toghrul as his overlord, but unlike Temuchin's son-to-father relationship, Jamuka's relationship to Toghrul was that of a younger brother. Jamuka was an independent leader among his own people and was treated as such by the Kerait leader, who delegated to him command of the Merkit campaign. Jamuka laid down the order of march of the various units and determined the date of the military operation. Thus, when Toghrul and Temuchin were late at the rendezvous the Kerait leader said: 'Because we are three days late at the rendezvous Younger Brother Jamuka has the right to criticize and chastise us.'[158]

The allied attack on the Merkits was crowned with complete success. The *Secret History* tells in a dramatic passage how Temuchin is reunited with his beloved Börte; whereupon, on Temuchin's initiative, the pursuit of the Merkits is halted. 'I have found that which I had lost and which I sought. We should camp here rather than march through the night', is the message which he sends to Toghrul and Jamuka. Temuchin renounces the pursuit of Chilger-bökö to whom, as younger brother of the deceased Chiledu, Börte had been given.[159]

This campaign by Toghrul, Jamuka and Temuchin against the Merkits is not mentioned in either the *Yuanshi* or the *Shenwu qinzheng lu*. Pelliot surmises that the description in the *Secret History* is an amalgam of events which spread over a number of years, and that the description of Börte's release is completely fictitious. The reunion between Temuchin and Börte is certainly romanticized and should be regarded as literary embellishment, yet Börte's captivity at the hands of the Merkits probably conforms to historical fact. It would be difficult to explain the election of Ögödei as Genghis Khan's successor if there had been no doubts among the Mongols concerning the legitimacy of Jochi's birth.[160]

Our adopted chronology, based on Ögödei's date of birth, indicates that the campaign against the Merkits must have taken place around 1184 when Temuchin was seventeen or eighteen years old.

The break between Temuchin and Jamuka

After plundering the Merkit camp, Toghrul returned to his main camp in the Black Forest on the Tula River. Jamuka and Temuchin travelled and camped together, renewing the compact of blood-brothership (*anda*) which they had sworn in their youth and exchanging as gifts the girdles and horses looted from the Merkits. They showed great affection for each other, celebrated together in feasting and dancing, and at nights they slept apart from the others, under one blanket. 'Thus Temuchin and Jamuka spent a whole year and the half of another year together in peaceful harmony.'[161]

One day the two friends decided to move camp and, while riding together ahead of the carts, Jamuka uttered the following words, whose meaning Temuchin could not understand: 'If we camp close to the hill those who herd our horses will have their tents. If we camp beside the mountain stream those who herd our sheep and lambs will have [food for] their gullets.' Börte later interpreted these words to mean that Jamuka was weary of them and, acting upon her advice, Temuchin quit the joint camp. He and his people travelled on all night without making camp. During their night trek they passed the camp of the Tayichi'ut, who, alarmed, broke camp that night and moved, in utter confusion, to join Jamuka.[162]

The *Secret History*'s account of the events following the victory over the Merkits leaves many open questions.

The Russian historians Barthold and Vladimirtsov both regard Jamuka as the advocate of the interests of the common people and the pioneer of a democratic movement.[163] Jamuka's words certainly express the antagonism existing between the horse-breeders and sheep-breeders, an antagonism which played a significant role in the struggle for supremacy on the steppe. The horse-breeders were the aristocrats of the steppe, upholding the rigid organization of the tribal hierarchy. Temuchin, however, did not belong to this élite. He was a shepherd, whose family at the time of the Merkit attack possessed only nine horses.[164] He was also an outsider who had, apart from his brothers, only two followers, Bo'orchu and Jelme; and while Vladimirtsov somewhat revises his views in *Régime social* he still lays stress on Genghis Khan's aristocratic pretensions, although he has to acknowledge that, 'surprisingly'. no tribal leaders of any consequence joined Genghis Khan.

After the victory over the Merkits, Temuchin remained with Jamuka – an unusual occurrence because independent nomad groups always separated and returned to their own family camps after such campaigns. The *Secret History* presents the old friendship between Temuchin and Jamuka as having motivated them to remain together; but was it really so? When the victory over the Merkits had been won, Temuchin expressed his thanks to the Kerait ruler and to Jamuka in the words: 'I was accepted as a companion (*nökhöcekde-*) by [both] my Royal Father and by my Friend Jamuka.'[165] Do these words perhaps express Temuchin's acceptance that he was Jamuka's follower (*nökhör*)? One cannot believe that Jamuka's assistance to Temuchin was entirely altruistic. Jamuka was ambitious and hungry for power. Did he perhaps expect that, in return for his support. Temuchin would become his follower?

The *Secret History* reports that, for the attack on the Merkits, Jamuka raised a division from among the tribe of his blood-brother: 'Upstream on the Onon River are the people of the *anda*. With 10,000 men [which I will raise] from the *anda* and another 10,000 [which I will raise] here, this will make 20,000 . . .'[166] Does this refer to the dependants of Temuchin's relatives, Altan and Kuchar, who, as one learns from later events, were at this time with Jamuka? Did the fact that Jamuka could thus dispose of their people eventually cause Altan and Kuchar to desert Jamuka for Temuchin?

According to the main account in the *Secret History*, the initiative for the separation of the two blood-brothers came from Jamuka; yet, in a later paragraph, Jamuka accuses Altan and Kuchar of having engineered the separation.[167] Doubtless, Temuchin was not uninvolved in the break; he was no less ambitious than Jamuka and could not, in the long term, have been satisfied with a position which was subservient to Jamuka. The honeymoon period with Jamuka had not been one of mere festivities; Temuchin had made good use of that time to recruit his own following.

The road to power

The separation from Jamuka was a turning point in Temuchin's life. This step announced his intention of playing an active role in the struggle for supremacy over the Mongol tribes and it was certain to lead to conflict with Jamuka, who was pursuing a similar goal.

Jamuka was the legitimate ruler of the Jadarat tribe. He could thus rely both on the support of those conservative elements who upheld the tribal constitution, and also on the solidarity of the tribal princes. Although Temuchin's father had been of aristocratic lineage his tribe had defected after his death; the people Temuchin was now gathering around him came from other levels of society. They were men who challenged the legitimacy of the tribal hierarchy and tribal constitution, who left clan and tribe to enter the service of a leader who would, they hoped, offer them a freer and better life; and above all there were the serfs (*ötögus bo'ol*), who sought freedom from exploitation by their current masters. Temuchin had to win the loyalty of these people by cultivating a reputation as a just and liberal master.

The story is told that on one occasion, when out hunting near the Jeuret tribe,[168] Temuchin suggested that they should camp together overnight. Since these people lacked food supplies he ordered help to be given them; on the following day, during the hunt, he had animals driven towards the Jeuret, allowing them to kill a great number. The Jeuret then said to each other; 'Although the *Taichiwu* [Tayichi'ut] are our brothers, they have often robbed us of our carts and our horses, even taken away our food supplies. Is this man here not the one who shows us much kindness?' After the hunt Temuchin sent a messenger to the Jeuret, inviting them to conclude a treaty with him. The tribal prince did not accept this proposal but two Jeuret leaders and their people did join Temuchin.[169]

The generosity with which Temuchin treated his own people became widely known. The *Yuanshi* relates that tribes subject to the Tayichi'ut saw how Temuchin showered his people with horses and furs.[170] Suffering under the lawlessness of their own masters, these feudal serfs said to each other: 'The Prince [Temuchin] dresses his people in his own clothes, he permits them to ride his own horses; this man could certainly bring peace to the tribe and rule the nation'.[171]

Temuchin's policies brought him success and his following increased. After he separated from Jamuka, people came individually or in groups from other tribes to enter his service. They came from the Jalair and from the Tarkut; Önggur came with his Baya'uts and Changsi'ut with his clan;[172] two brothers from the Barulas and two from the Mankut joined him; Bo'orchu's younger brother left the Arulat and Jelme's brothers the Urianghai; people also came to join Temuchin from the Besut, the Suldu, the Qongqotan, the Olkunu'ut and the Korolas; a carpenter came from the Dörbets, individuals arrived from the Ikires, the Noyakin and the Oronar; fathers and their sons came from the Barulas and a whole camp from the Ba'arin; one man even came from the Jadarat, Jamuka's own tribe.[173]

This enumeration is informative. With the exception of the Kiyat leaders, Changsi'ut and Önggur, both relatives of Temuchin, the tribal rulers stood by Jamuka. Individuals from different tribes, however, made personal decisions to break with Jamuka; many of these were *ötögus bo'ol* such as the Jalair, the Suldu and the Baya'ut.[174]

After the victory over the Merkits Temuchin became a serious contender in the struggle for mastery of the Mongol tribes. He had once more a tribal following of his own and had enriched himself from the Merkit booty. The Mongol people began to regard him as their champion in the struggle to unite the Mongol tribes and re-establish their former power.

Tales began to spread that Temuchin had a heavenly mandate and was destined to become lord of the steppe. When the Ba'arin, Korchi, came to join Temuchin, he declared; 'Jamuka and I are from the same womb. We would never have deserted Jamuka but for the appearance of a heavenly omen. A snow-white cow appeared, circled round Jamuka, butted his tent cart and then butted Jamuka ... And then a hornless white ox appeared, trailing a large tent post which was harnessed to its back ... and it came up behind Temuchin, bellowing again and again: "Heaven and Earth have agreed that Temuchin shall be Lord of the Empire. I bring him this Empire."[175] Later, at a location on the Korkonar River where Kutula-khan used to hold festivities, Mukali made known a similar omen which he claimed to have received from Heaven.[176]

The shamans took care to spread these stories. Mönglik's son, the shaman Kököchu (Teb-tengri) related how God had told him: 'I have given the whole surface of the earth to Temuchin and to his sons.'[177] Such prophecies did not fail to influence the superstitious Mongols and, whether he was responsible for instigating them or not, Temuchin well understood how to exploit them as propaganda; after the victory over the Merkits, he may perhaps have begun to believe in his 'mission'. Thanking Toghrul and Jamuka for their support, Temuchin proclaimed at the same time: 'My strength was fortified by Heaven and Earth. Foreordained [for this] by Mighty Heaven, I was brought here by Mother Earth.'[178]

2

Rise to Supremacy on the Steppe

Temuchin's election as khan

The breach between Jamuka and Temuchin drew the battle-lines. Some Mongols declared for Temuchin, a conflict between the two rivals became inevitable and nomadic custom required that a khan be elected before the forthcoming struggle.[1]

After the breach with Jamuka, Temuchin set up camp by the Kimurka Stream.[2] There he was joined by Sacha-beki and Taichu, the two sons of Sorkatu of the Jurkin, a tribe related to the Borjigid, both tribes being descended from sons of Kabul-khan. To the Kimurka camp came also Kuchar-beki, the son of Yisugei's elder brother Nekun-taishi, and Altan-otchigin, a son of Kutula.[3] All these relatives were senior to Temuchin in the family hierarchy and had a greater claim than himself to the title of khan; as Temuchin reminded them in a later message, they were all initially offered the khanship and he, Temuchin, was only elected after they had rejected the title.

Although Temuchin belonged to a cadet branch of his family, he was now in a very strong position. He had proved his military ability in the campaign against the Merkits and he had enriched himself with followers and herds; above all, he enjoyed the favour and the protection of the powerful leader of the Keraits.

Having broken with Jamuka, Altan and Kuchar found themselves in a quandary. Dependent only on their own forces they could not hope to withstand any attack by Jamuka; their only alternatives were to seek protection from Temuchin or from the Keraits. As Vladimirtsov suggests,[4] they thought that Temuchin, being their relative, would prove a malleable tool in their hands and that through him they could most readily achieve their personal interests. Later, realizing that in electing Temuchin they had chosen a leader who was determined to use an iron fist to enforce his own will, they both allied themselves with Wang-khan in his struggle against Temuchin.

It is more difficult to explain the stance of Sacha-beki, descended from a more senior branch than Temuchin and himself eager for power. Although other factors may also have influenced him he too, like Altan and Kuchar, probably underrated Temuchin's strength of will and ambition – and he eventually refused to serve under Temuchin.

After consulting with and obtaining the consent of Sacha-beki, Altan and Kuchar agreed to elect Temuchin. They declared: "We wish to make you khan", and they swore the following oath of allegiance: "When you are khan, Temuchin, we will ride as your spearhead against the multitudinous enemy and bring back their beautiful women and maidens and their ceremonial tents;[5] and from the foreign tribes[6] we will bring comely women and maidens, also their fine-limbed geldings at a trot, and present them to you. When we hunt the wild animals, we will be in the van of the hunters[7] and will give you [the slaughtered animals]. We will drive the steppe animals towards you in such numbers that their bellies touch, the mountain animals in such numbers that their rumps touch. If, on the day of battle, we do not obey your commands, separate us from our belongings,[8] from our wives and our women and throw our black heads away on the empty steppe. If, in time of peace, we break our word to you, separate us from our servants, from our women and children and banish us to a leaderless land." Having sworn this oath they made Temuchin Khan, naming him Genghis Khan.'[9]

It is generally, and correctly, assumed that the title of Genghis Khan was not conferred on Temuchin until after the subjugation of the nomadic tribes and that the *Secret History* text thus contains an anachronism. Elevation to the rank of Khan was, however, of great significance to Temuchin. A dream, which years ago would have seemed unattainable, had been realized; Temuchin was now an equal partner of the Kerait leader. True, the khanship was as yet only titular; the majority and the most powerful of the Mongol tribes, such as the Tayichi'ut, the Onggirat, the Seljiut and the

Arulat, continued to support Jamuka. This election, however, legitimized Temuchin's claim to rule the Mongols; the measures which he took after this election indicated his intention of creating the basis necessary to make that claim a reality.

The Mongols lacked even the most basic administrative system and any formal organization of services. Temuchin organized his followers into groups of Quiver Bearers and Sword Bearers, making some responsible for beverages, some for victuals; others were made responsible for the sheep or the horses on the pasturelands, or for the maintenance of the tent wagons.[10] Having made these arrangements for the running of the camp and appointed his first two followers, Bo'orchu and Jelme, in overall charge, Temuchin hastened to send messages to the Kerait leader and to Jamuka, informing them of his election.

Toghrul was delighted with the election of his vassal as khan. Believing that Temuchin was his loyal ally, he responded: 'It is right and proper that you have elected my son Temuchin as your leader. How could you Mongols be without a leader? Do not go back on your decision. Do not break your decision or your agreement. Do not rend the collar of your cloaks.'

Toghrul's behaviour has been interpreted as evidence of political myopia. He had, however, no cause to doubt Temuchin's loyalty; and a young Temuchin, bound in gratitude to him, offered Toghrul greater certainty of maintaining dominance over the Mongol tribes than would the intriguing and unreliable Jamuka or the ambitious Sacha-beki of the Jurkin.

'Clever' Jamuka (*Jamuka-sechen*) had no illusions about the consequences of the election of his *anda* as khan. He did not conceal his suspicion and sent a message to Altan and Kuchar, reproaching them: 'Altan and Kuchar! Why have you caused a breach between my *anda* Temuchin and myself . . .? Why did you not elect *anda* Temuchin as khan while we were together? What thoughts have motivated you to elect him khan now?'[11]

The struggle between Temuchin and Jamuka

A clash between Temuchin and Jamuka had become inevitable. Actual hostilities were provoked by Jamuka, using the following incident as a pretext. One of Jamuka's tribesmen, Taichar, stole

7   *Herdsman and family in front of Ger.*

horses from Jochi-darmala of the Jalair, a tribe which from time immemorial had been subject to Temuchin's forefathers. Jochi-darmala pursued the thief, killed him and repossessed the horses, a not unusual steppe occurrence which the nomad normally expiated by a simple fine.[12] In order to explain subsequent events the *Secret History* suggests that Taichar was Jamuka's brother; but this is contradicted by Jamuka's speech immediately before his death, in which he remarks that he had no brothers, also by other sources which refer to Taichar as a dependant or a relative of Jamuka.[13]

Political considerations, rather than any relationship to the horse thief, underlay Jamuka's reaction to the incident. As soon as Temuchin was elected khan Jamuka decided to do battle. Using Taichar's murder as a pretext, he formed a coalition against Temuchin. Temuchin's actions within his *ulus* after his election had resulted in some followers enjoying greater prestige than his noble relatives, thus arousing the suspicions of the tribal chieftains. They declared for Jamuka, who advanced against Temuchin at the head of 30,000 warriors drawn from the Jadirat and thirteen other tribes.[14] Temuchin, alerted to the impending danger by messengers sent by an Ikires tribesman, took the field against Jamuka with a force of thirteen 'camps'[15] and battle was joined at Dalan Balzhut. Temuchin was defeated by Jamuka and, perhaps because his escape route towards eastern Mongolia was barred, sought refuge in the narrow Jerene Pass on the upper reaches of the Onon River. Jamuka did not pursue him but, according to the *Secret History*, turned back, had the Chinos princes boiled in seventy cauldrons and then rode off with the heads of Ne'uder and Chaka'an tied to his horse's tail.[16]

Rashid ad-Din offers a different account of these events. He relates that Jochi-darmala killed Taichar with an arrow as the latter crept up to steal the horses. Thereupon, Jamuka joined the Tayichi'ut, with whom several other tribes (the Ikires, a branch clan of the Onggirat, the Korolas[17] from the Mongol-Darlekin, as well as the Uru'ud and the Noyakin from the Nirun-Mongols) also allied themselves. This coalition rebelled against Temuchin and fought against him for a long time, until he was defeated and deserted by his followers. Temuchin then fell into the hands of his enemies, but was freed from captivity by Sorkan-shira of the Suldu. Rashid explains that, during the following years, Temuchin re-established his power base and that finally the Tayichi'ut and their allies rode against him with 30,000 men. Temuchin, forewarned of the impending attack, drew up his forces in thirteen divisions and fought the coalition at Dalan Balzhut, where he won the day and had the enemy prisoners boiled in seventy cauldrons.[18]

It is clear that Rashid ad-Din's description confuses events. He relates the story of Taichar's horse-stealing immediately following the death of Yisugei and links it to Temuchin's captivity with the Tayichi'ut while, at that point in time, there was no need of any coalition to overcome Temuchin. It is important to note, however, that Rashid ad-Din was aware of Temuchin's defeat in the struggle against the coalition; but as court historian he, like other official historiographers, ascribes the victory at Dalan Balzhut to Temuchin, although this places on Temuchin the blame for the heinous execution of the Chinos princes – and also ignores Rashid's own statement that the Chinos princes fought alongside Temuchin.

Executing enemies in this manner was designed to prevent the survival of their spirits which might, from beyond the grave, exercise revenge on the clan and tribe. Boiling in a cauldron was mentioned in early Chinese records as one form of carrying out an execution,[19] and there are many references to it in Siberian folklore. The destruction of clan enemies was carried out in this way by the Western Evenke.[20] The method of execution was also known among the Mongols and al-'Umari reports that Eljigidei suffered such a death during the empire period.[21]

The anecdote regarding the boiling of the Chinos princes offered a link with the word *chinos* (wolf) and thus presented the bards with an opportunity to spread the story; indeed the *Shenwu* does not speak of Chinos princes, but rather of wolves which were cooked in seventy-two vessels and then eaten.[22] In our context the anecdote is thus almost certainly folkloristic. Jamuka would, as the *Secret History* recounts, have ridden off with the heads of the Chinos princes Ne'uder and Chaka'an-uwa tied to his horse's tail.[23]

Grousset and Pelliot share the view that Jamuka was victorious at the Battle of Dalan Balzhut, a victory which had far-reaching consequences.[24] Temuchin never forgot that defeat and he later reproached Jamuka with it before having him executed. On that occasion he reminded Jamuka: 'When those two, Jochi-darmala and Taichar, were stealing each other's horses, you *anda* Jamuka used that pretext to beget treachery and to attack me; and, when we fought at Dalan Balzhut, did you not force me to flee to a ravine near Jerene and thus cause me great distress?'[25]

The quarrel with the Jurkin

If we accept the presentation of the *Secret History*, the Mongols were shocked by the cruelty with which Jamuka treated his Chinos prisoners. Jurchedei of the Uru'ud and Kuildar of the Mankut, with their tribesmen, deserted Jamuka and joined Temuchin. Mönglik of the Qongqotan and his seven sons also rushed to ally themselves with Temuchin.[26] The *Secret History* recounts that Temuchin was delighted that so many tribes deserted Jamuka to join him and it was agreed with Sacha-beki and with Taichu of the Jurkin to hold a banquet in the Onon forest.

This amity was to be destroyed during that banquet. A servant, Shiki'ur, offended against protocol by pouring *kumis* for a secondary wife of Sacha-beki in precedence to his senior wife; thereupon the latter attacked and belaboured Shiki'ur. The ensuing tension exploded into open fighting when a snaffle was stolen by one of the Jurkin followers.[27] Belgutei, who was the Borjigid steward responsible for maintaining order at the banquet, seized the thief. Buri-bökö, a cousin of Yisugei, who was the Jurkin steward, intervened in defence of his fellow tribesman.

In accordance with Mongol custom Belgutei and Buri then entered into a wrestling match, regarded by the Mongols as a form of trial by ordeal and designed to settle such quarrels. It is suggested that, even before the wrestling match began, Buri-bökö injured Belgutei with a sword-stroke; such an allegation may well have been invented in order to justify the later revenge on Buri-bökö. Buri was the athletic champion of his tribe and had no need to resort to sword-play in order to turn a wrestling match in his favour. Indeed, the *Secret History*, possibly referring to this wrestling match, reports: 'When Buri-bökö was with the Jurkin he grasped Belgutei with one hand, tripped him with one foot and so secured a fall.'[28]

Whatever the facts of the wrestling bout, a hand-to-hand scuffle ensued among the guests. The *Secret History* describes in epic fashion how Temuchin and the other participants in the banquet, clearly intoxicated by imbibing *kumis* too freely, 'broke branches from trees, wrenched the beaters from the leather milk buckets and fell upon each other'. Temuchin, normally so self-controlled, allowed free rein to his passionate nature, refusing to listen to Belgutei's advice that revenge should be postponed and that they should not allow the recently concluded treaty with the Jurkin to be broken on account of a matter of such small import. Not until Temuchin, doubtless sobered by the fighting, realized the full consequences of the quarrel, was a decision taken to return the Jurkin princesses, who had been taken prisoner, and to despatch messengers to effect a reconciliation with the Jurkin.[29]

Belgutei's words as reported by the *Secret History*: 'You must not quarrel with your brethren on my account . . . when you have just become reconciled to them again', might be interpreted as indicating that the purpose of the Onon banquet was to **renew** friendship with the Jurkin; yet, as we have seen, the Jurkin princes were among those who had elected Temuchin as khan and they had fought alongside him against Jamuka's coalition.[30]

The *Secret History* relates the incident of the Onon River banquet immediately after the Battle of Dalan Balzhut, but adds that the Tartars, pursued by the Chin chancellor Ongging (Wanyen Xiang), were at that time pushing along the Uldza River. Rashid ad-Din also reports that the news of the Chin pursuit of the Tartars arrived during the negotiations which followed the quarrel between the Mongols and the Jurkin.[31] It is thus evident that the episode as reported actually spans a long period of Temuchin's life.

A gap in Temuchin's life history?

The campaign against the Merkits took place around 1184. Temuchin's election as khan followed some eighteen months later. Reacting to that election, Jamuka made preparations for a counter-attack and this led to the Battle of Dalan Balzhut, at latest in the year 1187. It is known from the official *History of the Chin*, however, that the campaign against the Tartars did not take place until 1196;[32] the Battle of Dalan Balzhut and the Tartar campaign are thus obviously separated by about ten years. Rashid ad-Din comments that from 1168 to 1194 Temuchin experienced great difficulties and suffered tribulations of many kinds, and that events were thus not recorded in detail, nor for every year of that period.[33] Clearly, something in Temuchin's life has been concealed, which, whatever it may have been, was taboo not only for contemporaries but also for later historians, because it was detrimental to the prestige of the World Conqueror.

The frontiers between the nomads and adjoining states were not closed in time of peace; political refugees would seek shelter with neighbouring tribes after an unsuccessful rebellion or a defeat. Toghrul fled to Kara-Khitai; some Chin rebels took refuge with the nomads while others sought nomad assistance to exact revenge for wrongs which they claimed to have suffered.[34] The victory of the coalition led by Jamuka caused a crisis in Mongolia. Temuchin's defeat undermined the strength of the Kerait ruler, and his brother Erke-kara seized the opportunity to intrigue against and finally drive Toghrul from his kingdom. Toghrul's uncle, Jagambu, also left Mongolia and sought refuge with the Chin.[35] There is also every reason to believe that, after the defeat at Dalan Balzhut, Temuchin himself fled from Mongolia and sought the protection of the Chin.

Rashid ad-Din's version of Temuchin's famous message to Wang-khan cites as Temuchin's second greatest service to Wang-khan the fact that Temuchin brought Jagambu back from the land of the *Jaukut* (Jurchid) in China,[36] where Jagambu was living, 'by stern warnings and gestures' – which according to Rashid actually led to fighting between Temuchin and Jagambu.[37] Obviously, such activities by Temuchin on Chin territory would only have been possible with the agreement of or on behalf of the Chin government; but, as we shall see, the Chin did have an interest in re-establishing Toghrul's power and Temuchin and Jagambu were to be instrumental in this restoration.

Rashid ad-Din's datings of the events are contradictory. According to Rashid's main text, Temuchin's campaign against Jagambu is said to have taken place following the destruction of the Jurkin, thus after the attack on the Tartars, while in Rashid's Chronological Summary Temuchin had already returned to Mongolia in 1195. I subscribe to the latter dating, which indicates that Temuchin fought in Mongolia after his victory over the Tartars.[38]

Such an interpretation imparts a degree of credibility to Zhao Hong's assertion that Temuchin spent ten years as a slave of the Chin.[39] Zhao Hong, a Southern Chinese, was bound by no taboo, his travelogue was a personal account and he was free to report matters which the official historians concealed. Zhao Hong's assertion has been treated lightly by many, regarded as an expression of the national arrogance of the Chinese author. The assertion should certainly be given the most careful consideration. It is the key to the ten-year gap in the life of Temuchin and, taken together with Jagambu's flight, explains Toghrul's banishment from Mongolia.

Toghrul flees to Kara-Khitai

Toghrul ruled the greater part of Mongolia, exercised supremacy over the Mongolian tribes and could rely upon the support of the *Altan Khan* (Golden Khan), the nomadic name for the Chin emperor. Toghrul's rule was, however, constantly threatened by internal family strife and by the enmity of the Naimans.

Toghrul had ascended the Kerait throne by committing fratricide[40] and he mistrusted his closest relatives. Erke-kara – Toghrul's uncle rather than his younger brother, according to Pelliot – who had participated in the fratricide and retained regal aspirations, sought assistance from Inanch-khan of the Naimans, who drove Toghrul from his country and placed Erke-kara on the throne.[41] Toghrul fled to Kara-Khitai but had been there little more than a year when he rebelled against the *Gurkhan* of that country. In dire distress, he plundered his way through the lands of the Uighurs and the Tanguts and then, having heard of Temuchin's resurgence of strength, appeared by Lake Guse'ur and sent two of his companions to Temuchin with news of his arrival.[42] The *Secret History* reports that, in recognition of the earlier friendship between Toghrul and Yisugei, Temuchin came from the source of the Kerulen to meet Toghrul, imposed a special levy on his own tribe to support Toghrul, took him into his camp and fed him.[43]

Most sources report this occurrence in connection with Toghrul's first banishment at the time of Yisugei and thus offer no evidence which enables us to date the actual event. The dating, eleventh year *dading* (1174), offered in *Xi-Xia shushi*,[44] is quite out of the question since at that time Temuchin was in no position to offer support to the Kerait ruler. Rashid ad-Din offers an exact date for the meeting by Lake Guse'ur – February/March 1196. This would place the meeting immediately before the campaign against the Tartars, the date of which can be accurately ascertained from the Chin records as May/June 1196. Since, however, in an earlier passage Rashid incorrectly asserts that the Tartar campaign began in 1194, it is clearly his interpretation that the Kerait leader returned to Mongolia only after Temuchin's victorious attack on the Tartars.[45]

Toghrul's absence was a relatively long one. He spent a year in Kara-Khitai, returning to Mongolia only when he learned of the improvement in Temuchin's fortunes, presumably after the Tartar campaign. Such a hypothesis excludes any participation by Toghrul in that campaign and it must now be considered to what extent this can be supported by the texts.

The attack on the Tartars

The role of the Tartars in the traditional policies of the Chin emperors was that of gendarmes, whose duty it was to ensure that no East Mongolian tribe became sufficiently powerful to pose a threat to the Jurchid. Yet the avaricious and quarrelsome Tartars were not completely reliable and had often carried out plundering raids into northern China or instigated rebellions against the Jurchid. During a Jurchid campaign against the Onggirat in autumn 1195 a Tartar chieftain, Sechu, rebelled because of a dispute over the division of spoils. The Jurchid commander, Wanyen Xiang (Ongging-chingsang of the *Secret History*), made a surprise attack on the Tartars and forced them to flee northwards, although the Chinese forces were so weakened by the loss of the Tartar rebels that in February 1196 the Onggirat were able to attack one Chinese unit and kill its commanding officer.[46]

Rashid ad-Din reports that when Temuchin learned of the Tartar retreat he sent messages to the Jurkin suggesting that they join forces with him against the Tartars. Having waited six days in vain for the Jurkin response he then took a small troop of his forces and (in May/June 1196) attacked the Tartars, who were moving up the Uldza Valley. The Tartar princeling, Muzhin-sultu (Meguzhin se'ultu of the *Secret History*), was killed and Temuchin carried off his golden cradle and pearl-encrusted quilt. The Chin commander, Wanyen Xiang, rewarded Temuchin with the title *cha'ut-kuri* and at the same time bestowed upon Toghrul the title of Wang-khan.[47]

The *Secret History* text differs in important aspects from Rashid's presentation of events, recording in particular that the Chin Commander-in-Chief, Ongging-chingsang, sought Temuchin's support in pursuing the Tartars. Temuchin is then said to have sent messengers to Toghrul, who came with his army to Temuchin's assistance. When the two armies had united they called upon the Jurchid princes to join with them, but the latter did not respond to the invitation.[48]

Toghrul's participation in the Tartar campaign does not accord with Rashid's chronology, in which Toghrul only regains control of his kingdom and army in 1197. His presence would also make it difficult to explain why the Chin Commander-in-Chief would have sought support from Toghrul's vassal, Temuchin, rather than from the Kerait ruler himself. Toghrul was, quite clearly, not in Mongolia at this time and Rashid comments that he set off home to Mongolia only after learning of Temuchin's return to power.

Against this the objection may be raised that there could therefore be no reason for granting a princely title to the Kerait ruler, but one cannot accept Rashid's assertion that this title was granted by the Chin army commander, Wanyen Xiang. The grant of the royal title, *Wang*, could only be conferred by the Chin emperor and the dispersal of one unit of fugitive Tartars was too insignificant to justify such an honour. The Chin government must certainly have had other grounds for conferring such a distinction on Toghrul and, as Pelliot remarks, the texts do not necessarily exclude the possibility that the title was awarded to Toghrul on a different occasion.[49]

The Jurchid had indeed a vital interest in maintaining the balance of power in eastern Mongolia. Toghrul was an elderly and obedient man, constantly preoccupied with protecting his throne from the machinations of his relatives; he was not dangerous to the Chin empire, whose government, therefore, supported his restoration. This princely title was intended to enhance Toghrul's authority in the eyes of the nomads and thus assist him to regain his position as ruler.

Although Temuchin had to content himself with a modest title, equivalent to commander of a squadron, the balance of power between himself and Wang-khan – as I shall henceforth refer to Toghrul – had fundamentally changed. Temuchin still needed Wang-khan, and for this reason alone restored him to his people. The political initiative had, however, passed into Temuchin's hands and, with Wang-khan's assistance, he intended to realize his ambitious plans, encompassing the destruction of all potential rivals and enemies who might stand in his way. Temuchin no longer felt himself to be Wang-khan's vassal, but rather his equal partner; he did not, as some historians suggest, act disinterestedly when the Kerait ruler sought his assistance. As later events make clear, Temuchin exploited Toghrul's plight to wring from him promises and concessions.[50]

Temuchin was not the only one who sought to achieve mastery over the tribes of eastern Mongolia. According to Rashid ad-Din, however, the prospects of the other contenders in this struggle were assessed as follows by the Baya'ut, Sorkan: 'Sacha-beki of the Kiyat-Jurkin aspires to supreme leadership, but it is not for him. Neither will Jamuka-sechen, who constantly incites one person against the other and pursues his aims with flattery and guile, be successful. Jochi-bara [Jochi-kasar, Genghis Khan's brother] has the same aim and counts on his strength and his skill as an archer, but he will not succeed. Although Alak-udur of the Merkits has a certain power and dignity he will not achieve the supreme position he covets. But Temuchin has the presence, mode of behaviour and ability to rule and govern – and he will certainly attain the title of Emperor.'[51]

The struggle against Sacha-beki

Temuchin's first move was to attack his clansman, Sacha-beki. According to the *Secret History*, Sacha-beki had not complied with Temuchin's demand to join him in the attack on the Tartars; indeed, some of his people had taken advantage of Temuchin's absence to plunder the latter's main camp and kill ten of his men. The *Yuanshi*, on the other hand, reports that in Temuchin's absence his camp was attacked by the Naimans and that, when Temuchin then sent sixty men to Sacha-beki to seek military support in a campaign of vengeance against the Naimans, ten of these men were killed, while the remaining fifty were stripped of their clothing and sent back to Temuchin.[52]

Whatever the *casus belli*, Temuchin attacked the Jurkin camp and carried off many prisoners. Sacha-beki and Taichu were actually able to save themselves, their wives and children and some of their people, but were pursued, captured and killed by Temuchin several months later. According to the *Shenwu*, the Jurkin princes were pursued and killed in the winter of the same year; the same source also reports that this pursuit was preceded by a meeting between Temuchin and Wang-khan, at which these two renewed their *anda* oath.[53]

Attacking or executing clansmen offended against tribal custom and the court historians again seek to justify Temuchin's actions. Rashid ad-Din relates that, after the attack on the Tartars, Temuchin wished to present some of the spoils to the Jurkin in order to win their friendship; but while he was *en route* to the

Jurkin they killed ten of his men, stealing the horses and the clothes from another fifty. Thereupon Temuchin was 'unwillingly' compelled to take measures against them.[54]

Rashid's story is tendentious. One cannot believe that Temuchin intended to present part of the spoils to the Jurkin, who had, after all, refused to participate in the Tartar campaign. Little credence can be given to the assertion that Temuchin carried out the deed in Wang-khan's interests, as is suggested in Rashid's version of Temuchin's famous message to Wang-khan: 'For you I killed my Elder Brother and destroyed my Younger Brother! If anyone asks who these were, they were Sacha-beki, my Elder Brother and Taichu-kuri, my Younger Brother.'[55]

Wang-khan may, because of Sacha-beki's ambition, have agreed to the elimination of the Jurkin princes, but the motivation for Temuchin's actions was certainly personal and political. The execution scene as recounted in the *Secret History* may emphasize the guilt of the Jurkin princes: when Temuchin accuses them of having broken their oath to him they accept their guilt, stretch out their necks and await their just sentence, whereupon Temuchin 'makes an end of them and casts their bodies on the steppe'; nevertheless, the author of the *Secret History* cannot hide his personal disapproval of the deed. He reminds his readers that the Jurkin were the descendants of Sorkatu-jurki, himself a descendant of Kabul-khan: 'The cleverest, the strongest, the most powerful men were selected' and as 'strong, brave, proud and invincible men' were named Jurkin after him. The author's disapproval is manifest in the final sentence: 'When Genghis Khan broke these proud men, he destroyed the leadership of the Jurkin clan and made the Jurkin people his own servants.'[56]

Political considerations motivated Temuchin's execution of the Jurkin leaders but lust for revenge led him to settle an old score after the victory over the Jurkin. Temuchin had not forgotten the incident at the banquet which led to the wrestling bout between Buri-bökö and Belgutei. The time was now ripe to take revenge on Buri-bökö; Temuchin ordered that Buri and Belgutei should wrestle again in order to expiate the guilt.

Buri-bökö was the athletic champion of his people; he had never been defeated in wrestling and had previously defeated Belgutei. On this occasion he allowed himself to be thrown, knowing that his fate was thus sealed. Belgutei broke his back.

Buri's last words were: 'Belgutei could never have beaten me. For fear of the Khan I intentionally held myself in check and allowed myself to be thrown; thus I have forfeited my life.' Buri-bökö was a Borjigin, indeed a cousin of Yisugei. He was a famous wrestler and his death in such tragic circumstances must have diminished Temuchin's popularity and reputation. The court historians suppress the incident, but the author of the *Secret History* does not conceal with whom his sympathies lay. He writes: 'He [Buri] left the sons of Bartan-bagatur [Yisugei's father] for the brave sons of Barkak [from whom the Jurkin were descended] and became their companion and the nation's athletic champion. He was forced to allow Belgutei to break his back and thus he died!'[57]

The events which followed the execution of the Jurkin princes and the death of Buri are confused, their dating is doubtful and the many contradictions between the texts emphasize the problematical character of the chronology. Thus, for example, the *Secret History* states that Wang-khan's campaign against the Merkits, the battle against Buiruk-khan of the Naimans, the Tartar and Tayichi'ut campaigns, all took place in the Year of the Dog (1202);[58] Rashid ad-Din, on the other hand, places these events respectively in the Year of the Horse (1198), the Year of the Sheep (1199) and 'before the election of Jamuka as Gurkhan in 1201'.[59] Rashid's chronology is, in general, followed by the *Shenwu* and the *Yuanshi*.

The *Secret History* continues its story with the election of Jamuka as *Gurkhan*. The execution of the Jurkin princes took place, as we have seen, in winter 1196–7 but Jamuka was not elected until 1201.[60] The *Secret History* thus has a gap of four or five years; Rashid's chronology of the events appears more reliable. According to the *Collected Chronicles*, Temuchin's next moves were directed towards restoring Wang-khan's rule over the Keraits. The first step was to force Jagambu into submission and bring him, together with the Tonkait,[61] a vassal tribe of the Keraits, back from China to join and support Wang-khan.[62] In the autumn of the Year of the Snake (1197)[63] Temuchin together with Wang-khan and Jagambu – the latter later deserted to the Naimans[64] – then undertook a successful campaign against Tokto'a-beki of the Uduit-Merkits.[65] After the campaign Temuchin presented the whole of the spoils to Wang-khan and his retinue.[66]

Pelliot points out that neither the *Secret History* nor the *Shenwu* makes reference to this 1197 campaign; he infers from this and the coincidence of campaign names that both incidents refer to the Merkit campaign following the abduction of Börte.[67] But the *Secret History* does mention Toghrul's participation in a Merkit campaign after his return from Kara-Khitai and in a second passage states: 'Then Jaqa-gambu of the Kerait came to join Genghis Khan, who was camped at Tersut. When, following this arrival, the Merkit came to do battle, Genghis Khan and Jaqa-gambu fought and repulsed them.'[68] The mention of Tersut indicates that the *Secret History* is here referring to the 1197 campaign. The *Yuanshi* virtually repeats the text in the *Collected Chronicles*, but adds that the 'Emperor' (i.e. Genghis Khan) presented to Wang-khan all the goods and the provisions plundered from the Merkits and that because of this Wang-khan's tribal dependants gradually rallied to him.[69]

Wang-khan now felt strong enough to act independently. In the Year of the Horse (1198), without informing or consulting with Temuchin, he attacked the Merkits, killed Tokto'a-beki's son, taking prisoner his two daughters and two brothers as well as other household members and servants. Moreover, Wang-khan retained all the spoils for himself, offering no share to Temuchin.[70] Temuchin was enraged by Wang-khan's behaviour, but suppressed his displeasure. He had used Wang-khan as a stepping-stone to power and would continue to support him. Temuchin set off, together with Wang-khan, to fight the Kerait leader's arch-enemy, Buiruk-khan of the Naimans.

The battle with Buiruk-khan

Inanch-khan, who deposed Wang-khan, had died, dividing his empire between his two sons, Buiruk-khan and Tayang-khan. The brothers were sworn enemies, perhaps on account of a love affair, although Pelliot surmises that the real cause of the enmity was the nomination of the younger son as Inanch-khan's successor.[71] Buiruk ruled only the mountainous area of the Altai, while Tayang had received the steppe area on the Black Irtysch.

Temuchin and Wang-khan took advantage of the discord between the brothers and, according to Rashid ad-Din, attacked

Buiruk-khan in 1198/9,[72] possibly with the connivance of
Tayang. They reached the camp of Buiruk-khan, who, clearly not
anticipating the attack, took flight and was pursued across the
Altai Mountains. Returning from this pursuit Temuchin and
Wang-khan were confronted by a Naiman army, commanded by
Kökse'u- sabrak. Temuchin and Wang-khan drew up their troops
ready for battle the following morning; Wang-khan, however,
pulled out secretly during the night. The *Secret History* attributes this decision to the intervention of Jamuka, who accused
Temuchin of treason. 'My *anda* Temuchin has for a long time
had diplomatic relations with the Naimans', Jamuka persuades
Wang-khan. 'Now he has not come with you. My Lord! My Lord!
I am a constant, white-feathered bird. My *anda* is a lark, a bird of
passage. He will have joined the Naimans. He has remained
behind in order to submit to them.'[73]

The following morning, when Temuchin realized that Wang-
khan had deserted and left him in the lurch, he also retreated.
Kökse'u-sabrak did not, however, attack Temuchin. He pursued
Wang-khan, carrying off the wife, children and followers of
Senggum,[74] Wang-khan's son, as well as half of Wang-khan's
people and also his herds and food supplies. Thereupon Wang-
khan sent a messenger to Temuchin with an appeal for help, an
appeal to which Temuchin responded, dispatching to Wang-
khan's assistance troops under his four most stalwart commanders. These saved Senggum from capture and rescued his followers,
wife and children.[75]

This account in the *Secret History* raises many questions,
especially that of Temuchin's puzzling behaviour. Wang-khan
had betrayed him, deserting secretly on the eve of battle and
leaving Temuchin to his fate. Despite this, Temuchin sends his
most devoted companions to rescue Wang-khan's son from a
desperate situation.

An ingenious solution to this question is offered by Gumilev,[76]
who suggests the following interpretation of the events. During
the night before the battle Temuchin makes several demands of
Wang-khan. The latter rejects these and immediately leaves the
battlefield. When, however, the Keraits have been defeated by
Kökse'u-sabrak, Wang-khan is compelled to accept Temuchin's
conditions. Temuchin, interpreting the appeal for help as an

indication of such an acceptance, sends his 'Four Warriors' to the assistance of Wang-khan and Senggum.

Gumilev's hypothesis offers a plausible explanation for Temuchin's otherwise incomprehensible behaviour. It seems certain that, when the deposed Wang-khan sought Temuchin's assistance, the latter made several demands of Wang-khan. In that hour of need, Wang-khan found himself constrained to agree to Temuchin's conditions but later, having reasserted control over his tribe, regretted his promise and deserted with his forces.

The author of the *Secret History* alludes to the possibility that Temuchin's demands concerned the succession to the Kerait throne. 'When Wang-khan learned of his son's rescue, he exclaimed: "My *anda* Yisugei-bagatur initially rescued my lost people and now his son, Temuchin, has again rescued my lost people. When these two, father and son, reunited me with my lost people, for whom did they take such trouble to assemble them?" Having posed this question, Wang-khan thought: "I am now an old man. When I grow older, when my life is spent and I am at rest on the Heights — when my life is spent and I ascend the Mountain Cliffs, who will rule my people? My younger brothers have no ability. My son Senggum is a nonentity, and he is my only son. I will make my son Temuchin Senggum's elder brother so that, having two sons, I can then rest in peace." ' The *Secret History* then relates that, as a result of this decision, Wang-khan and Temuchin met in the Black Forest on the Tula River. There they renewed their *anda* accord as father and son, agreeing to fight their enemies together, to hunt together and to give no credence to the words of envious persons or enemies until they had talked face to face. Thereafter they lived together in closest friendship.[77]

The version which comes to us through Rashid ad-Din is quite different. Rashid reports that in the spring of the Year of the Monkey (1200) Temuchin and Wang-khan met and held discussions in the vicinity of Sari-kähär. Rashid also recounts the story that Wang-khan intended to take Temuchin prisoner on this occasion, but that the attempt was frustrated because Asu-noyan of the Ba'arin became suspicious during the feast — Asu's vigilance was later rewarded with the command of a Ba'arin division.[78]

8   *Hill landscape with Tula River.*

Rashid's text accords with my own interpretation of the events. When Wang-khan's departure from the battlefield did not have the expected result he attempted to take Temuchin prisoner and thus render the latter harmless. Rashid's account is also preferable because Jamuka's allegation – possibly a stratagem designed to divide and thus weaken his two rivals – that Temuchin sought to betray Wang-khan is in direct contrast to Temuchin's actions before and after Wang-khan's furtive withdrawal. Temuchin's plan was, with Wang-khan's assistance, to gain the Kerait throne. This claim by Temuchin to succeed to the Kerait throne, rather than any fear of treachery on Temuchin's part, was the real reason for Wang-khan's behaviour. Temuchin would certainly not have rushed to the aid of Senggum, Wang-khan's son, if he had nursed the treacherous intentions ascribed to him by Jamuka.

According to Rashid's text, Temuchin and Wang-khan moved from Sari-kähär to attack and defeat the Tayichi'ut, killing the princes Tarkutai and Kududar.[79] This campaign is not mentioned in the *Secret History*, which, we must note, also recounts the campaign against Buiruk-khan after reporting Jamuka's election as *Gurkhan*. Such a chronology is refuted by Jamuka's presence in Wang-khan's camp during the Naiman campaign, since this would not have been possible after the coalition led by him attacked Wang-khan. In addition, the participation of Tokto'a's son Kutu in the coalition cannot be reconciled with the chronological order of the *Secret History*; that source itself maintains that Kutu, captured by Wang-khan during the campaign against the Merkits, only succeeded in escaping and rejoining his father after the attack on Senggum by Kökse'u-sabrak.[80] Finally, it was Temuchin's very victories over the Naiman and the Tayichi'ut which led to the formation of the broad-based coalition of tribal leaders against him.

The chronology of the *Secret History* is unreliable because the author considers the individual episodes of his epic to be more important than either their interrelation or correct chronological order.

The election of Jamuka as Gurkhan

The aims pursued by Temuchin had now become obvious, sparking off a reaction among the tribal leaders, who realized that unless they submitted to Temuchin, thus renouncing their independence, they could expect to share the fate of the Jurkin princes. The *Yuanshi* records: 'When the Hadajin [Katagin], Sanjiwu [Seljiut], Doluban [Dörbet], Dadaer [Tartar] and Hongjila [Onggirat] tribes learned that the Naiman and the Taichiwu [Tayichi'ut] had been defeated they became very fearful and could not settle down.'[81] They concluded a treaty of alliance, sealing it by sacrificing a white horse[82] and swearing an oath that they would attack Temuchin and the Wang-khan. Dai-sechen, Temuchin's father-in-law, incorrectly described in the Chinese text as chief of the Onggirat, sent warning of the coalition's hostile intentions to Temuchin, who then took the field together with Wang-khan against the coalition. The armies clashed near the Onon River, where, according to Rashid ad-Din and other sources, the coalition was defeated after a bitter battle.[83]

A victory by Temuchin is not easy to reconcile with the fact that Wang-khan spent the following winter in Kuba-kaya on the Manchurian border, east of Lake Kulun,[84] while Temuchin was actually in China – neither the first nor the last occasion on which he sought refuge near the Chinese frontier after a defeat![85] The defection and flight to the Naimans by Jagambu and four of Wang-khan's highest dignitaries is also most readily explained by a defeat of, rather than a victory by the Kerait leader.

Wang-khan's reverse was exploited by the allies. A group of tribal princes assembled by the Alghui Spring between the lower Kerulen and the Argun rivers, near the Buir and Kulun lakes,[86] where they renewed their alliance by sacrificing a gelding and a mare and swearing another oath. Thereafter, according to the *Secret History* – which makes no mention of the first campaign by the coalition – the allies moved down the Ergi River to the confluence of the Gen and Argun rivers where, in the Year of the Cock (1201), they elected Jamuka as *Gurkhan*, Khan of all the tribes.[87] After the election they resolved to take the field once more against Temuchin and Wang-khan.[88]

There was a social background to the impending struggle. The old steppe order hung in the balance and the tribal princes, concerned to preserve their independence, were solid in their opposition to Temuchin. Buiruk-khan of the Naimans, Kutu the son of Tokto'a-beki of the Merkits, Kuduka-beki of the Oirats, the Tayichi'ut princes Tarkutai-kiriltuk, A'uchu-bagatur and others adhered to Jamuka's coalition. Temuchin, warned by a Korola tribesman of the coalition's decision to take the field against him, immediately sent a messenger to Wang-khan, who mobilized his levies and hurried to join Temuchin. Wang-khan's fate was bound to Temuchin's; he had slipped into dependence on the latter and the coalition had decreed his destruction. The opposing armies met at Köyitän near the Khalkha River[89] but because of the rapidly approaching dusk the battle was delayed until the following day. The *Secret History* reports that when hostilities recommenced Buiruk-khan of the Naimans and Kuduka-beki of the Oirats attempted to use their powers to confuse the enemy by magical weather conjured up using a *Jada* stone.[90] The magical rainstorm, however, changed direction. 'They could not move forwards, but fell into the ditches! And they said: "Heaven does not favour us", and their forces broke up.'[91] The Naimans, Merkits, Oirats and the Tayichi'ut left the field and Jamuka himself fled home – but not before robbing those who had elected him, an action which ended for ever his short-lived leadership.

Rashid maintains that after the battle Wang-khan and Temuchin set up a joint winter camp and that Jamuka came there and submitted to the latter;[92] the *Secret History*, however, relates that Wang-khan pursued Jamuka from the battlefield while Temuchin set off in pursuit of A'uchu-bagatur of the Tayichi'ut in the direction of the Onon River. As soon as his troops were over the river in good order, A'uchu turned to fight. The resistance was bitter; the battle swayed hither and thither until the onset of darkness and the opponents spent the night in their positions. During the night the Tayichi'ut troops fled in all directions. They left to their fate their dependants, who had taken refuge in the wagon laager, and on these Temuchin exacted a terrible revenge for the humiliation which he had suffered in his youth. The *Secret History* reports: 'Temuchin slaughtered all the males of Tayichi'ut lineage, even the sons and grandsons, so that they wafted away as the ash [from the hearth], but he took their women and servants with him.'[93]

In connection with these events the *Secret History* relates certain anecdotes which merit introduction here since, even if the occurrences were not quite as described, or are imaginary, they do highlight some of Temuchin's typical traits of character.

According to the *Secret History*, Temuchin was wounded in a neck vein by an arrow during the battle. The nomads were in the habit of using poisoned arrows and Temuchin was in a critical condition. Jelme saved his life by sucking the clotted blood from the wound and at midnight Temuchin regained consciousness. In order to still Temuchin's fevered thirst Jelme then, wearing only breeches, made his way into the enemy camp to find milk and was able, undetected, to take a dish of yoghurt from a cart. When Temuchin recovered he was distrustful and demanded to know why Jelme had undressed before entering the enemy camp. Only when Jelme had explained his action did Temuchin find words of thanks and praise for the deed. 'You have saved my life', he said to Jelme, '. . . I will never forget the three services you have rendered.'[94] Temuchin kept his word. When honours were distributed at the Khuriltai in 1206 Jelme was not only appointed to command of a regiment but also received the privilege of the 'Ninefold Pardon'.

Temuchin must have made a very quick recovery, because the following morning, according to the *Secret History*, he was pursuing fugitives from the battle when he heard a woman calling his name loudly. He sent a messenger to her and learned that she was Kada'an, the daughter of Sorkan-shira, and that she had called to him because her husband had been captured by Temuchin's troops. Thereupon Temuchin galloped to her, dismounted, 'and they fell into each other's arms'. The soldiers had, alas, already killed her husband, but when Temuchin and his army camped on the battlefield overnight he had Kada'an brought to his camp and seated beside him.[95] Such actions served to increase Temuchin's popularity among the ordinary people. The following day Sorkan-shira appeared with his sons and entered Temuchin's service.

Temuchin's sense of justice was well known to the Mongols and he valued courage and honesty even among his enemies. During the battle Temuchin's horse was killed by an arrow. When Temuchin demanded to know the identity of the archer a Besut tribesman, a serf of the Tayichi'ut leader, Tödöge, stepped forward and admitted responsibility. Temuchin's response was: 'A person who has been an enemy shrinks from admitting this and personally conceals whom he has killed or what damage he has caused, saying nothing about it. This man, however, does not conceal whom he has killed and what damage he has done, but freely admits it. Such a man is worthy of being a companion.' In memory of the incident he named the man Jebe ('Arrow').[96]

Rashid ad-Din offers a perhaps more realistic account of the Jebe incident, according to which Jebe escaped after the battle but found himself encircled one day in a ring of beaters when Temuchin was hunting. Temuchin recognized Jebe and wanted to fight him but Bo'orchu volunteered to do so and Temuchin gave him his own horse. Bo'orchu attacked, firing an arrow which failed to hit Jebe, whose own arrow, however, hit Temuchin's horse, which collapsed and died. Jebe fled, but a few days later, driven by necessity, he appeared before Temuchin and threw himself on the latter's mercy. Temuchin, in recognition of his courage, appointed him to command a troop. Jebe distinguished himself in Temuchin's service, was promoted to command a squadron, then later given command of a regiment and finally of a division. Temuchin was a good judge of people. Jebe became one of the most brilliant of the World Conqueror's generals.[97]

Temuchin regarded disloyalty towards a legitimate leader as meriting the death penalty, even if such treason were to his personal advantage. Thus, for example, the followers who surrendered Jamuka to Temuchin were executed; the groom who abandoned Senggum in his time of need was beheaded; but Kadak-bagatur of the Jirgen was pardoned and praised for his stubborn resistance which made it possible for his leader, Wangkhan, to flee.[98]

The *Secret History* also recounts how, after the defeat of the Tayichi'ut, Tarkutai-kiriltuk, the tribal leader who had held Temuchin captive in his youth, was able to escape the slaughter and hide in the woods, where Shirkutu of the Naked Ba'arin – a tribe which was subject to the Tayichi'ut – and his sons took him prisoner. They were on their way to Temuchin when Tarkutai's sons and brothers came to rescue him, but withdrew when Shirkutu threatened to kill Tarkutai. It was on this occasion that Tarkutai himself expressed the strong conviction that Temuchin would not kill him; Shirkutu's son Naya'a, however, thought of the fate which awaited those who betrayed their master, and on his entreaty Tarkutai was released. When Shirkutu and his sons appeared before Temuchin the father spoke as follows: 'We had taken Tarkutai prisoner and were on our way to you. But we could not betray him. We thought: "How can we, having accepted him as our lawful master, deliver him up to death?" So we released him and have now come to offer our services to Genghis Khan.' The latter answered: 'Had you appeared here with your hand on your own master, Tarkutai, then as men who had done violence to their lawful master you would have been beheaded. Your feeling that you should not betray your lawful master was correct.' Genghis rewarded Naya'a, who was later to rise to command a division – the highest military rank, which he shared with Mukali and Bo'orchu.[99] Whether or not it is invented the anecdote quoted from the *Secret History* is a clear expression of Temuchin's attitude towards the duty of loyalty which every follower owed to his master.

Tarkutai did not, however, escape his fate. Rashid reports that he was killed after the defeat of the Tayichi'ut and specifies in the *History of the Tribes* that he died in a hand-to-hand fight with one of the sons of Sorkan-shira.[100]

The extermination of the Tartars

Victory over the tribal coalition and the destruction of the
Tayichi'ut awakened a new ambition in Temuchin. He would not
only inherit the leadership of the Kerait but would also extend his
rule over all the peoples who lived on the Mongolian steppe.
Single-mindedly he prepared the destruction of those enemies who
might stand between him and this goal.

From time immemorial the Tartars had been claimants to
hegemony in Mongolia. Although disunited, they were a dangerous enemy, greatly superior to Temuchin's hordes in numbers,
wealth and civilization. These arch-enemies of the Mongols had to
be defeated, but Temuchin was well aware that he could not
achieve that aim with undisciplined forces. In the Year of the Dog
(1202),[101] before he forced the encounter with the Tartars at
Dalan-nemurges near the Khalkha River,[102] Temuchin therefore
promulgated the following order: 'When we rout the enemy we
will not halt to take booty. When the victory is decided the booty
belongs to us collectively and I will then distribute it. If we are
repulsed by the enemy we will reform on the spot from which we
launched our attack. Any man who does not reform on the spot
from which we attacked will be executed.'[103]

This order violated an ancient custom of the nomads, who only
fought because of booty, and whose chieftains had the right to
dispose of whatever spoils they took, setting aside a portion for
their khan. Now Temuchin claimed all the spoils for himself, with
the right to distribute it as he thought fit. Temuchin knew full
well that his order would give rise to discontent among his
chieftains; but he also knew that he could defeat the superior
enemy only by having a disciplined army. He thus allowed the
situation to develop into a trial of strength. Altan, Kuchar and
Da'aritai, who thought that they could set themselves above this
order, halted when the booty was reached. These were the
aristocrats who had raised Temuchin to the khanship; they were
his relatives and held, in their opinion, a higher position in the
tribal hierarchy than he did – but an example had to be made of
them. Temuchin despatched Jebe and Khubilai to these princes
and 'deprived them of the plundered herds and all other spoils
they had taken'.[104]

Although these three princes later deserted to Wang-khan and, according to Rashid ad-Din,[105] contributed to the quarrel between Temuchin and Wang-khan, Temuchin's measures proved themselves. The Tartars were defeated. Temuchin and his dependants held a 'Grand Council' in an isolated tent, where the family jointly decided upon the complete eradication of the defeated Tartar tribe 'as revenge and retribution for our forefathers and fathers', i.e. for handing Ambakai over to the Chin and for poisoning Yisugei.[106] The women and children were made slaves and divided among the warriors. Temuchin took for himself the sisters Yisugen and Yisui, the latter eventually to become one of his favourite wives.

The extinction of the Tartars provided Temuchin with a hinterland, guaranteeing him greater freedom of movement in the impending battles.

The breach in the alliance between Temuchin and Wang-khan

After his victory over the Tartars, Temuchin considered the time ripe to strengthen his claim to the throne of the Kerait ruler by a marriage alliance. Temuchin's eldest son, Jochi,[107] would receive Wang-khan's daughter as wife; in return Temuchin would promise one of his daughters to the son of Senggum. The marriage proposal was rejected by an indignant Senggum. 'When one of our women goes to you she is left standing by the door, constantly looking towards the place of honour. When, however, one of your women comes to us she sits in the place of honour, looking towards the door.' This was Senggum's reply, according to the *Secret History*, which adds: 'These words caused Genghis Khan to lose his heartfelt affection for Wang-khan and Nilka-senggum.'[108]

It had become obvious that the succession to the Kerait throne was at stake. The steppe aristocrats supported Nilka-senggum; the *Secret History* comments that in the Year of the Pig (1203) Jamuka, Altan, Kuchar and other tribal leaders came together and moved to join Senggum. Once again it is Jamuka who attempts to force immediate action. 'Can you trust him [Temuchin]?' he asks. 'If you do not strike at once what will become of you? If you move against *anda* Temuchin then I will attack him on his flank.' Altan and Kuchar promise: 'For you we will kill the sons and the elder brothers of Mother Hö'elun and throw their younger brothers on the steppe.' Others made similar promises and Senggum then sent messengers to his father to inform him of the agreement which had been concluded.[109]

Wang-khan was irresolute; he was in a difficult position. Until now Temuchin had always been his support, and Wang-khan did not trust Jamuka. Senggum then went personally to his father and said: 'Even now, while you are still alive, he [Temuchin] leaves us no power. When, my Lord and father, you are very old,[110] will he permit us to rule your people which your father Kyriakus-buiruk-khan united with such difficulty? By whom and in what fashion will he have our people ruled?' Wang-khan was bound by his promises to Temuchin and knew that he could not even trust his son, whom, in his message, Temuchin had accused of lusting after the Kerait throne even during the lifetime of Wang-khan. He must manoeuvre in order to maintain his supremacy. 'How can I reject my Child, my Son? Is it right to plan mischief against him when we have until now [always] looked to him for support?' he asks. This infuriated Senggum, who stormed out, slamming the door behind him. Eventually, in order to avoid a breach with his son, Wang-khan allowed Senggum freedom of action.[111]

The *Secret History* places the blame for the breach with Temuchin squarely on Senggum, but although the initiative for the break doubtless originated with Senggum, Wang-khan also sought to rid himself of his ambitious vassal. As we have already seen, Rashid ad-Din has highlighted Wang-khan's attempt to capture Temuchin, also the desertion before the battle against the Naimans. Oral tradition, reported by Marco Polo, also attributes to Wang-khan responsibility for the failure of the marriage alliance proposed by Temuchin. Temuchin's message is said to have caused Wang-khan to erupt in rage. 'How dare Genghis Khan seek the hand of my daughter?', he exclaimed. 'Does he not recognize that I am his liege, that he is my vassal? Go back and tell him that I would rather burn my daughter than give her to his family in marriage.'[112]

Wang-khan did not, however, seek open conflict. A plan was therefore hatched to capture Temuchin by a stratagem. Senggum sent a message to Temuchin, agreeing to the proposed marriage alliance and inviting him to a betrothal feast.[113] Joy at the fulfilment of his wishes caused Temuchin to forget his customary caution and suspicion and he set off, apparently accompanied by ten men – although Rashid speaks only of two companions. Only when he spent a night *en route* with Father Mönglik and the latter warned him not to trust Senggum's sudden change of mind, did Temuchin recognize the trap which was being set for him and return home.

Senggum once again decided to take the field with his allies against Temuchin but two horse-herders, Badai and Kishlik, learning of the plans from a secretly overheard conversation, hastened to warn Temuchin. Temuchin did not forget their deed. At the Khuriltai in 1206 they were appointed to command divisions and raised to the rank of *Darkhan*. 'Badai and Kishlik were Tseren herdsmen. Now you shall both, my supporters, rejoice that I create you Quiver Bearers and Cup Bearers', were Genghis Khan's words to them.[114]

Rashid ad-Din, however, offers a differing version of this incident in *The History of the Tribes*. According to this account, Wang-khan suggested to the shaman Teb-tengri, son of Mönglik, who had married a girl from a Kerait sub-tribe, that they attack Temuchin on two fronts. Teb-tengri, it is claimed, informed Temuchin of this plan, and this was one reason for Wang-khan's defeat.[115]

Temuchin was unprepared for an attack; the *Secret History* reports: 'During the night Temuchin warned those of his immediate entourage whom he could trust. In order to facilitate their escape they disposed of all their goods and fled that very night.' Temuchin was pursued to the frontier of China and was forced to fight at Kalakalzhit-elet, which, as Poppe suggests, must be near Dalan-nemurges, in the vicinity of the Khalkha and Ulchin rivers, on the frontier of Manchuria.[116] Once more, as after the defeat at Dalan Balzhut, Temuchin fled to the furthest frontiers of Mongolia, in the expectation of receiving reinforcements and building up his supply of weapons – or, if necessary, seeking refuge with the Jurchid. And as so often after such a defeat, the Mongols rallied to his support. Kuildar with the Mankut and Jurchedei with his Uru'ud deserted Jamuka and, as they had both done after the battle of Dalan Balzhut, hastened to Temuchin's assistance and attacked the Keraits who were on his heels.

Those sources which describe this battle as a victory for Temuchin present it in tendentious terms.[117] Rashid's report is much more acceptable, reporting that, despite Kuildar's heroic breakthrough, Temuchin's complete defeat could not have been prevented had not Senggum been struck in the head by an arrow.[118] This interpretation is supported by Temuchin's own words when, rewarding Jurchedei for this deed, he acknowledged: 'What, in truth, would have become of us if you had not wounded Senggum?'[119]

Wang-khan did not pursue the defeated army. As one of his dignitaries stressed, Temuchin was no longer a serious opponent: 'The majority of the Mongols are with Jamuka; Altan and Kuchar are on our side. Where will those Mongols go who have ridden off with Temuchin? They have only one horse [each] and only the trees as a shelter. If they do not return we can ride out, collect them like horse droppings and bring them back.'[120] In fact Wang-khan was not interested in the complete destruction of Temuchin. He had to prepare himself for the onslaught of more dangerous enemies.[121]

It is also clear that even Jamuka did not plan to encompass Temuchin's complete destruction. He was playing a double game; according to the *Secret History*, he had before the battle informed Temuchin of the composition and the plan of battle of the Kerait forces.[122] When his two rivals, Temuchin and Wang-khan, had been divided and weakened in battle the time would be ripe for Jamuka to put his ambitious plans into action and assume supreme leadership.

Temuchin's position was critical after the battle of Kalakalzhit-elet; Rashid reports that he lost most of his troops as he retreated from the battlefield. His forces had suffered severe losses. Kuildar was fatally wounded; Ögödei, Boroghul and Bo'orchu were missing.[123] But despite the danger Temuchin was determined to wait for them; he and his men spent the night by their horses, snaffles in hand, because Temuchin decreed: 'If the enemy follow us, we will fight.' At daybreak they saw a man approaching. It was Bo'orchu. His horse had been killed during the attack and he was thus compelled to flee on foot until the Keraits halted on joining up with Senggum, and he was able to steal a spare horse and set off on the trail of the Mongols. Temuchin was deeply moved, striking his breast and calling on Eternal Heaven to bear witness to his emotion.

Soon thereafter another person was seen approaching. It was Boroghul, bringing with him Ögödei, who had been wounded in the neck. Boroghul had sucked out the wound and blood was dripping from the corner of his mouth. When Temuchin saw this 'he wept tears and his heart was sore'. He immediately caused a fire to be lit and the wound to be cauterized, lamenting again: 'Had the enemy come we would have fought them.' Only then did Temuchin withdraw towards Dalan-nemurges,[124] accompanied by a very small body of warriors – at roll-call a mere 2,600 according to the *Secret History*, some 4,600 according to Rashid.[125]

There have been many attempts to identify the famous Baljuna, the swamp area in which Temuchin eventually took refuge, originally identified by d'Ohsson as a tributary of the Ingoda River. Later researches identify the Baljuna with the small Lake Balzino, the source of the Tura River – but while Hong Jun comments that this wooded area is certainly regarded by the Mongols as the place where Temuchin took refuge on this occasion, this localization is, with some justification, rejected by Pelliot as being both historically and geographically unacceptable. Despite this refutation the traditional theory has been revived by Poppe, who firmly identifies Lake Balzino, some 50 miles west of the town of Aginskoe in the Buriat Autonomous Republic, with the historical Baljuna. Perlee locates Baljuna further south, at Balzh Bulak (43N 119E), the source of the Mogoit, a tributary of the Khalkha River; this is regarded by de Rachewiltz as geographically the most plausible identification. Temuchin's Baljuna camp should certainly be sought in the south-east of Mongolia on the frontier of the Chin empire.[126]

Temuchin's position was critical but the defeat had not disheartened him. He required time to gather reinforcements; our sources indicate that he spent quite a long period on the Baljuna, during which he initiated brisk diplomatic and recruitment activity. In a message to the Onggirat, reminding them of the marriage alliance which existed between their two peoples, Temuchin called on them to join him. The Onggirat were not hostile to Temuchin – they had deserted him only when, as we have seen, Kasar unleashed an unexpected attack on them – so they responded to his overtures and became his subjects.[127] Other tribes then followed their example. Rashid reports that after an attack on them by the Korolas the Ikires moved to the Baljuna and joined Temuchin; and in 'The History of Genghis Khan' Rashid comments that Da'aritai-otchigin and his followers, a clan of the Nirun Mongols, the Sakait clan of the Keraits and the Nunjin clan all joined Temuchin on this occasion, while Altan, Kuchar and the Tartar prince Kutu-temur fled to join the Naimans.[128]

In the struggle against the Kerait leader Temuchin represented the national interests of the Mongols, but he also understood how to win over to his cause the members of other tribes. It was certainly not only his imposing figure which caused the members of the former ruling house of the Khitans, the brothers Ila Ahai and Tuka, to declare for Temuchin – if he was victorious they expected strong support from him in their fight against the hated Jurchid. The Muslim merchants Ja'far and Hasan – the latter came from the Onggut with 1,000 sheep which he sought to barter for sable and squirrel skins – entered Temuchin's service because they expected from his victory favourable terms in trading with the nomads and protection for their trade caravans to China.[129]

Temuchin, as we have just seen, even succeeded in recruiting dependants of the Kerait tribe. 'Whoever deserted the *Unk khan* in order to join and support *Jinkiz khan* was showered with signs of the latter's favour. He showed them such favour, bestowing on them such honours and distinctions, that they flocked to him, individually or with companions.' Thus, according to al-'Umari, '*Jinkiz khan*'s power and influence multiplied and his eminence and reputation increased.' Among these Kerait defectors was Chingai, who became one of Genghis Khan's closest advisors and who, under Ögödei Kha'an, was later to play an important political role.[130]

The stakes were high. Everything which had been achieved up to this time was at risk in the impending battle; those who now supported Temuchin must have realized that they were, for better or for worse, inextricably bound to his fate. Temuchin swore an oath: 'When I have completed this great task I will share the bitter and sweet fruits with you. If I break my word, may I become as the waters of the Baljuna.' To reinforce the oath he and his trusty followers then drank of the muddy waters of the Baljuna.[131]

The historicity of this covenant is questioned by Pelliot. It is certainly astonishing that it is not reported, merely hinted at in the *Secret History* or later Mongol chronicles. The incident was, however, well known and those who took part in the Baljuna Covenant were later distinguished by the highest honours. Reference is always made to the event in their biographies and, as late as the fourteenth century, they were widely known as *Baljuntu* or 'Muddy Water Drinkers'.[132]

One must accept Cleaves's opinion that the Baljuna Covenant actually took place, but it is more difficult to determine when the covenant was sworn. Cleaves assumes that it took place during the flight from the battlefield, pointing out that Ja'far-khwaja's biography lists only nineteen persons as having sworn the Baljuna Oath. The number quoted does not, of course, indicate that this was the total of Temuchin's followers. Only the leaders (*noyat*), not all the warriors took the oath, and Rashid comments that after the defeat of Kalakalzhit-elet, the numbers of men with Temuchin was not large.[133] That the covenant was sworn after the battle of Kalakalzhit-elet (the *Shenwu* and *Yuanshi* actually claim that it took place after Temuchin had sent his messages to his opponents) is supported by our sources, which indicate the presence of Khitans, Keraits, Tanguts and the Muslims, as well as the absence of the hero of the battle, Kuildar, who died of wounds received on the field.[134]

It was customary among the nomads that, when unrelated tribes united in an enterprise, such an alliance was sealed by an oath. Temuchin's words and the participation of representatives of non-Mongol peoples and tribes are evidence that an alliance was sealed on the Baljuna with the aim of overthrowing Kerait supremacy.[135]

Temuchin's messages to his opponents

Temuchin's political activity had brought him significant reinforcements. He now made an attempt to split his opponents before the impending battle.

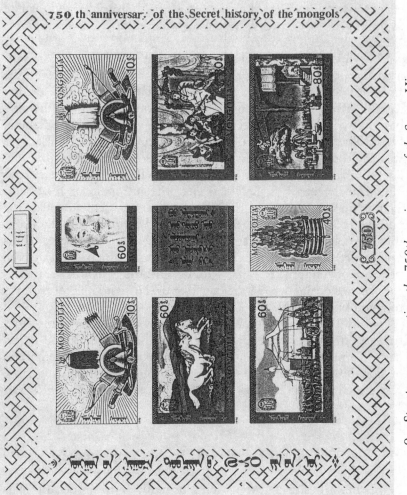

9 Stamps commemorating the 750th anniversary of the Secret History.

Temuchin was well aware of Wang-khan's difficult position and in his famous message he sought to convince the latter that only in alliance with himself could Wang-khan continue to exercise his role as leader. He accused Wang-khan of having broken their agreement. Wang-khan, he asserted, had allowed himself to be provoked and incited by an outsider (Jamuka) and, contrary to their agreement, had not attempted to clarify the matter by a face-to-face discussion. Temuchin warned Wang-khan: 'If a two-shafted cart has a broken shaft the ox cannot pull it. Am I not your second such shaft? If a two-wheeled cart has a broken wheel it can travel no further. Am I not your second such wheel?' Temuchin's services to Wang-khan were not inconsiderable. His father Yisugei had already assisted the fratricidal Wang-khan in his hour of need and returned his people to him; then, when Wang-khan fled for the second time, it was Temuchin who gave refuge to the solitary, wandering and starving victim and provided protection for his people. The following year Temuchin plundered the Merkits and presented the booty to Wang-khan. When Kökse'u-sabrak of the Naimans captured Senggum's wife and his people, Temuchin responded to Wang-khan's plea for help and sent troops under his four great commanders to recover Senggum's wife and people. 'My King and Father, what cause do you now have to reproach me?' Temuchin demands of Wang-khan.[136]

Rashid's version of this message sets out Temuchin's services in much greater detail. Temuchin had brought Jagambu back from China in order to assist in restoring Wang-khan to the throne; he had, at Wang-khan's behest, killed the Jurkin princes Sacha-beki and Taichu.[137] He had helped Wang-khan when the latter was in dire distress and had presented him with all the booty taken from the Merkits, while Wang-khan had undertaken alone, without waiting for Temuchin, a jointly planned attack on Tokto'a of the Merkits — and had retained all those spoils for himself. Temuchin had done Wang-khan a further service when he sent his four great warriors to save him and return to him the people captured by the Naimans. Finally Temuchin had, on Wang-khan's behalf, subdued the Dörbets, Tartars, Seljiut and Tonkait, the tribes with which Wang-khan now threatened him. 'What have you done which was to my advantage?' Temuchin demands of the Kerait ruler. He reminds Wang-khan: 'I have valid claims upon you. I

have often been useful to you'; and he ends his message with the
parable of the two-shafted cart.[138]

This message did not fail to have an effect on Wang-khan.
Temuchin had until now loyally fulfilled his obligations; the cause
of the break between the two lay exclusively with Wang-khan,
who also felt threatened by those around him and was thus
susceptible to Temuchin's warning. The *Secret History* records:
'Wang-khan acknowledged: "I have deviated from a duty from
which one ought not to stray." He then swore: "If henceforth I
look upon my Son with evil thoughts, may my blood be shed as
this blood is now shed"; and to strengthen this oath he cut the
tip of his little finger with a knife, allowed some blood to flow
and sent it to Temuchin in a capsule of birch bark.' Rashid, by
contrast, reports that, while acknowledging guilt, Wang-khan
allowed Senggum to decide what response should be sent to
Temuchin's message.[139]

Temuchin also sent a message to Altan and Kuchar who, as
we have already seen, deserted him for Wang-khan because
Temuchin deprived them of the booty which, infringing his orders
against looting, they took from the Tartars. This communication
was obviously an attempt to change their attitude and win them
over to his cause. The version in the *Yuanshi* reads: 'Our land had
formerly no leader. It was suggested that we place both *Xiechi*
[Sacha] and Taichu, legitimate descendants of my grandfather,
Balaha [Barkak], on the throne, but they declined to accept; then
you *Huochaer* [Kuchar], son of my uncle *Niekun* [Nekun], were
proposed as leader, but you also firmly rejected the offer; the
matter could not simply be left unresolved and so the throne was
then offered to you *Andan* [Altan], as son of my ancestor *Hudula*
[Kutula], but your refusal was also firm. Thereupon you put
pressure upon me to become your leader. Was it thus initially my
personal desire? It was not egoistic motivation which brought
me to this [position]. The Land of the Three Rivers, founded by
our ancestors, must not become the possession of strangers. You
choose to serve Wang-khan, whose fundamental convictions are
not steadfast. If he has treated me as he has done, will his
behaviour towards you not be worse? I now withdraw from you.
I withdraw.'[140]

The last sentence contradicts the overall content of the message.
Temuchin is appealing to the national pride of his relatives from

whom he had accepted the dignity of Khan in order to preserve the Land of the Three Rivers from strangers. Now he calls on Altan and Kuchar to set aside their resentment and serve him once again for the sake of the Mongol cause.

The version in the *Secret History* emphasizes the duty of vassals towards their elected leader: 'If you had been elected Khan, then I would . . . have brought you the rosy-cheeked girls and women and the sturdy geldings. If ordered to a hunt I would have driven the mountain animals to you in such numbers that their thighs would rub together.' With these words Temuchin reminded Altan and Kuchar of their own oath sworn to him.[141] Again, the end of this message as reported by the *Secret History* seems at first glance equally strange: 'Let people now say that you are faithful followers of my Master and Father, rather than that you are the supports of the Cha'ut-quri [i.e. Temuchin]. And allow no one, whoever they may be, to set up camp by the sources of the Three Rivers.' The corresponding passage in Rashid – it is completely missing from Berezin's translation, while the beginning of the message is not given by Smirnova – is no less puzzling. It runs: 'Do not allow it to be said that the planned enterprise was brought to a successful conclusion as the result of negotiations by the Cha'ut-quri. Do not act in such a way that I will be mentioned in the event of failure. Since you are now with him, remain with him this year. Spend the coming winter there.'[142]

The message is obviously in code because it would be delivered to Altan and Kuchar in the presence of Wang-khan.[143] Between the lines it is possible to read an invitation to rebel against Wang-khan, or at least an indication that Temuchin was anxious to recruit the two Mongol leaders as agents who would remain for another year at Wang-khan's court. Temuchin did not yet feel strong enough to make an immediate attack but planned one for the following year; in the meantime Altan and Kuchar were to keep him informed of Wang-khan's activities and plans.

The message to Jamuka, reported only in the *Secret History*, is couched in a quite different tone. In it Temuchin expresses his opinion of Jamuka in blunt terms: 'Because you hate me, you have caused a breach between myself and my King and Father. It was our custom that whichever of us rose first drank from the blue goblet of my King and Father. You were distressed when I was the first to rise and drank from it. Now, empty the blue goblet of my King and Father! How much will you spill in so doing?' This is Temuchin's threatening message to Jamuka.[144]

With Senggum, as with Jamuka, there could be no question of any pact; Temuchin informed 'the naked-born son' (the natural son of Wang-khan): 'Our King and Father sought to care for us equally but, fearing that I might come between you, you have pursued me with your hate . . . Do not cause our King and Father to grieve; do not estrange yourself from him by holding to your earlier thoughts and continuing to contemplate becoming ruler while our King and Father still lives.'[145]

The challenge was unambiguous; the *Secret History* records that when Senggum received the message he exclaimed; 'It is clear to me what lies behind these words. They are the opening words of the battle. Bilge-beki and Todoyan, raise the war banner and see to it that the geldings are well fed. There can be no more hesitation!' Senggum knew that the impending battle would be decisive. Rashid reports him as saying: 'If he [Temuchin] is victorious then our *ulus* will be his. If we are the victors his *ulus* will belong to us.'[146]

The end of the Kerait empire

Temuchin was determined to go over to the offensive but Jamuka and his supporters were also preparing for action, anxious to exploit the favourable circumstances resulting from the break between Wang-khan and Temuchin in order to seize power for themselves. Rashid ad-Din reports: 'Da'aritai, Altan, Kuchar, Jamuka of the Juirat, the Ba'arin and others had united and made the following agreement: "If we attack Wang-khan unexpectedly then we will ourselves become the leaders, joining neither Wang-khan nor Temuchin and paying no respect to either".'[147] Wang-khan was able to frustrate these traitorous intentions but a number of his supporters deserted him. Jamuka, Altan and other tribal leaders fled to the Naimans while Da'aritai, together with some Mongol and Kerait tribes, joined Temuchin, who was still encamped on the Baljuna. Temuchin did not plan an attack on Wang-khan before the following year but a fresh development caused him to alter these plans and initiate immediate action.

Kasar lived apart from Temuchin and his loyalties may have been divided. According to Rashid ad-Din, Kasar's wives and children were abducted by Kerait warriors; Kasar, in attempting to fight his way through to Temuchin, suffered the greatest distress and was in a state of complete exhaustion when he reached Temuchin's camp on the Baljuna.[148] The *Secret History* mentions no such attack by Kerait warriors but, hinting that Kasar might have thrown in his lot with Wang-khan, recounts that only by leaving behind his wife and three sons was Kasar able to escape from Wang-khan and, with a few followers, set off to rejoin Temuchin. On the way he suffered great deprivation, being forced to feed on raw hides and sinews before stumbling across Temuchin at Baljuna. 'Genghis Khan was greatly pleased by Kasar's arrival', comments the author of the *Secret History*.[149]

Temuchin took advantage of Kasar's arrival to launch a stratagem. He despatched two messagers to Wang-khan to present the following message in Kasar's name: 'I sought my elder brother but lost sight of him. I followed his tracks but could not find his route. I called to him but my voice was not heard. I now sleep with only the stars above me and the earth as a pillow. My wife and child are with my King and Father. If I had hope and a guarantee from you I would rejoin my King and Father.'[150]

Wang-khan allowed himself to be deceived. He suspected no evil intent and sent a guarantor as a sign of his agreement. Temuchin had, however, set off with his forces to follow his messengers and intercepted the guarantor, Iturgen, who attempted to turn back when he saw Temuchin's military preparations. Temuchin handed Iturgen over to Kasar for execution – thus, perhaps, ensuring that Kasar could never return to Wang-khan.[151] Informed by his messengers that Wang-khan was unprepared and was feasting unconcernedly, Temuchin decided to attack immediately and rode with his troops through the night to Wang-khan's encampment on the Checher Heights on the lower reaches of the Kerulen River.[152] Although taken by surprise the Keraits put up fierce resistance and the battle raged for three days and three nights before they surrendered.[153] Wang-khan fled during the night and was killed by a Naiman, who failed to recognize him. Senggum fled to Tibet, and from there to the Khotan and Kashgar areas, where he was later captured and killed.[154]

Such was the inglorious end of the ruler of the mighty Kerait empire, of whom even the West had heard through the legend of Prester John. Wang-khan had borne the stigma of fratricide throughout his reign and his indecisiveness and character weaknesses had ensured that, at the end of the day, he stood alone, surrounded by internal and external enemies. He had given Temuchin his trust, had supported him and assisted him to power – even while fleeing Wang-khan had doubts whether he had treated Temuchin correctly in turning his back on him. 'Have I broken with a man who may have deserved that I should not desert him? Or have I distanced myself from someone who has deserved such estrangement? Everything I suffer – alienation, distress, grief, misery, wandering and helplessness – is the fault of the man with the swollen face', meditates Wang-khan as he places the blame firmly on his son, Senggum.[155]

Temuchin did not destroy the Keraits as he had the Tartars and the Tayichi'ut. He pardoned the Kerait Commander-in-Chief who had offered such bitter resistance, praising him for his bravery and his loyalty towards his ruler. 'This is someone fit to be a companion', said Temuchin and then decreed: 'In recompense for the life of Kuildar, Kadak-bagatur, together with one hundred Jirgid, shall devote himself to the widow and the children of Kuildar.' Temuchin also showed mercy to Jagambu, who, he decreed, 'with those servants and people subject to him, shall as one group be our second shaft'.[156]

The Kerait princesses were married off. Temuchin took for himself Jagambu's elder daughter, Ibaka – although he later separated and gave her in marriage to Jurchedei – to whom he also entrusted the killing of Jagambu when the latter, unhappy with the role allocated to him, began to conspire against Temuchin.[157] The younger daughter, Sorkaktani, later to play an important political role during the reign of Ögödei Kha'an, was given to Temuchin's son, Tolui, who also received the Wang-khan's granddaughter, Dokuz-khatun. After Tolui's death the latter was, in accordance with Mongol custom, married to his son, the Il-khan Hulegu, and she exercised great influence on his religious policies.[158] According to the *Secret History*, Jochi was given Wang-khan's daughter Cha'ur-beki, but Berezin maintains that Temuchin kept her for himself.[159] The Kerait people were plundered and enslaved by the victors.

Temuchin had achieved his long-sought goal. He now sat on the throne of Wang-khan, his master and protector for many years. Those who had assisted Temuchin in this victory were generously rewarded, especially the two herdsmen, Badai and Kishlik, who, by giving warning of Wang-khan's impending attack, had saved Temuchin's life. 'To Badai and Kishlik', decreed Temuchin, 'I give the golden palace tent of Wang-khan together with the golden wine bowls and beakers and the servants who have had charge of these – also the Kerait and Ongqoyit as bodyguard. I give you both also', he continued, 'the right to bear the quiver and drink from the cup [i.e. Temuchin appointed them Quiver Bearers and Cup Bearers]. You, your children and grandchildren, shall enjoy all the privileges of a *Darkhan*. When you defeat the enemy you shall retain all the spoils you capture and when you hunt the steppe animals you shall keep all you kill.'[160]

Juvaini defines the privileges of *Darkhan* as follows: 'The *Darkhan* are freed from compulsory taxation and receive a share of booty from each campaign. They also enjoy the right of entrée to their master's palace at any time.' Juvaini adds that Genghis Khan also gave the two herdsmen troops and servants and showered them with cattle, horses and equipment; he also decreed that they should be exempt from punishment for whatever crime and that this exemption should apply to their descendants, to the ninth generation.[161]

Additional privileges were usually associated with the title of *Darkhan*. When Genghis Khan rewarded Sorkan-shira and his sons at the Khuriltai in 1206, he decreed: 'You shall hold the Kerait lands, free of all taxes, for your grazing. Furthermore I appoint you and your heirs Quiver Bearers and Cup Bearers; and you shall also benefit from the Ninefold Pardon.' Genghis Khan also granted Sorkan-shira's two sons a further boon: 'If you, Chila'un and Jimbai, have any thought which you wish to express or any request to make, then do not express these to any intermediary; tell me personally what you think and request of me personally whatever you may require.' Genghis Khan also said on the occasion of this Khuriltai: 'The bestowal on you, Sorkan-shira, Badai and Kishlik, of the title *Darkhan* means that you have the right to retain all the booty you capture on a plundering raid against the enemy and to keep all the animals you kill when we hunt on the steppe.'[162]

In early times the *Darkhan*'s most important privilege was his right to retain the spoils of war and of the hunt but this was later equated, as Juvaini notes, with freedom from taxation. Ibn Battuta comments as follows: 'The word *tarkhan* indicates among the Turkic peoples an area [*sic*] which is exempt from all imposts.'[163] With his elevation to the status of a freed man the *Darkhan* was also usually presented with servants; at the Khuriltai of 1206 Badai and Kishlik received both warriors and servants since they, like Sorkan-shira, were appointed to command regiments.[164] In later times a newly appointed *darkhan* often received a personal apanage[165] and Tao Zongyi actually glosses the word *dalahan* (*darkhan*) as 'a ruler who enjoys free adminis- trative control within his enfeoffed state'.[166]

The title *Darkhan* was originally granted for military services, but even in the days of Genghis Khan it was sometimes bestowed on religious dignitaries. In 1219 Genghis Khan raised the young seventeen year-old Buddhist monk Haiyun to the rank of *Darkhan* and in 1223 the Taoist sage Changchun was granted exemption from all taxes.[167] During the Yuan dynasty the title *Darkhan* was bestowed mainly on government officials.[168] The institution continued among the Mongols after the collapse of the Yuan dynasty and the title was bestowed not only on many religious dignitaries but also on persons of low birth.[169] In 1665, for example, Lubsan-taishi bestowed the title on a Russian interpreter and requested the Tsar to exempt the interpreter from all tax obligations.[170]

Despite Temuchin's successes which led to the bestowal of these honours in 1203–4, the Mongol tribes were by no means united and Temuchin now called on them to submit to him. Al-'Umari reports that he sent messages 'to the individual tribes and sub-tribes, informing them of his views, his justice, laws and generosity, stressing also that they would be held in great respect if they joined him and that their rights as rulers would be confirmed if they supported him'.[171] The Oirats and Onggirat, the most important tribes to respond to his call, were incorporated into the Mongol army and treated with favour and clemency. Those tribes which resisted were, however, annihilated until all declared their submission.

Temuchin set himself wider aims than any of the Mongol khans before him. A new order was to regulate steppe life and at an

assembly Temuchin laid the basis of a legal system by promul-
gating laws which did not simply concern themselves with
military organization, but affected the very life and customs of the
Mongols. As Juvaini remarks: 'He [Genghis] abolished traditions
which were repugnant, such as theft and adultery.'[172]

When Temuchin had promulgated his laws he was raised to the
[Kerait] throne.

War against the Naimans

The Naimans were now the only Central Asian nomadic people in
a position to challenge Temuchin's rise to power. Temuchin's
old enemies, Jamuka, Altan and Kuchar, also Alin-taishi of the
Keraits had, after the defeat of Wang-khan, fled to join Tayang-
khan. They could count on the support of Tokto'a-beki of the
Merkits, of Kuduka-beki of the Oirats and of many other Mongol
tribal leaders – and they all clamoured for the opening of hostilities against Temuchin.

Power among the Naimans was exercised by Khatun-gurbesu,
described by the *Secret History* as the mother of Tayang-khan,
while Rashid maintains that she was his favourite wife on whose
account Tayang quarrelled with his brother Buiruk-khan. There
is only an apparent contradiction between these two important
sources. Khatun-gurbesu, the wife of the late Inanch-khan, was
the stepmother of Tayang-khan and, in accordance with Levirate
law, was married to Tayang-khan after his father's death.[173]
Gurbesu was an energetic and arrogant woman who spoke of the
Mongols with utter contempt. 'The *Mangqol* have an unpleasant
scent and wear black clothes. They live far away and long may
they remain distant! We could, however, abduct their aristocratic
daughters and step-daughters and, once we had washed their
hands, use them to milk our sheep and cows.'[174]

Tayang-khan – or Baibuka as he was known before the Chin
conferred on him the title *taiwang* (Great King)[175] – was completely under his wife's influence, and had no personal authority
among the aristocrats of the Naiman empire. Bowing to the
wishes of the war faction, he sent messengers to Alakush-
teginkuri, the tribal prince of the Onggut – a tribe which, being of
Turkic descent and of Nestorian persuasion, had racial and

religious ties with the Naimans[176] – inviting him to participate in
the campaign against Temuchin. The plan miscarried. Not only
did Temuchin have friendly relations with the Onggut prince, to
whose son he had presented a Kerait princess,[177] but Alakush also
served the Altan Khan (the Chin emperor). It was not in the
interests of the Chin government to assist the obviously stronger
party, the Naimans, and thus upset the balance of power in
Mongolia. Alakush therefore informed Temuchin of the Naiman
preparations for war.

As a result of his warning Temuchin took some prudent
military measures before setting out for battle. He introduced a
strict organization of his forces. The army was divided into units
of Thousands (Regiments), Hundreds (Squadrons) and Tens
(Troops). A bodyguard was created, consisting of eighty night
guards and seventy day guards, and Temuchin appointed to the
bodyguard not only sons of commanders of regiments and
squadrons who were personally known to him, but also the sons
of ordinary tribesmen.[178] In addition, following the Kerait
pattern, one regiment was created, composed of élite troops, who
fought in front of and protected Temuchin in wartime and
provided the day guard in times of peace. When Temuchin had
completed these organizational measures he consecrated the war
banner on the day of the Feast of the Moon in the Year of the Rat
(1204) and took the field against the Naimans.[179]

The Naimans, supported by the Merkits under Tokto'a-beki,
the Jadirat under Jamuka, and the tribes of the Dörbet, Tartars,
Katagin and Seljiut, enjoyed overwhelming superiority of forces;
Temuchin's horses were exhausted from the long march.[180] He
therefore employed a stratagem, suggested to him by one of his
commanders, Dodai-cherbi, setting up dummies and lighting
innumerable camp-fires.[181] Deceived as to the strength of the
attacking Mongol forces, Tayang-khan decided to withdraw
his army in good order across the Altai Mountains, entice the
Mongols into the interior, then turn and fight. It was a sensible
and promising plan to employ the 'dogfight' (*nokhai kerel kere-*),
the well-known nomad tactic of using a feigned withdrawal to
entice the enemy into pursuit, then suddenly to turn on the
exhausted pursuers;[182] this tactic did not, however, accord with
the mood of the Naiman army. When Tayang-khan sent a
messenger to inform his son Kuchlug of his plan, the latter

exclaimed: 'Old Woman Tayang again! He must have lost his courage to utter such words! Where could such a horde of Mongols have sprung from? The majority of the Mongol tribes are here with Jamuka. Has Old Woman Tayang not sent us this message because he is afraid? Tayang, who has never dared venture further afield than a pregnant woman would go to urinate, nor even a calf to graze!'[183] These words of Kuchlug expressed the general view of the Naiman military commanders. One senior Naiman commander took his leave with the words: 'Had we suspected that you were such a coward, we would have done better to send for Mother Gurbesu and, although she is only a woman, given her command of the army.'[184]

Tayang-khan was forced to bow to the will of the army and march against the enemy, but before the armies clashed Jamuka had left the field. The author of the *Secret History*, whose sympathies clearly lie with Jamuka, presents Jamuka's behaviour as being in support of Temuchin. Jamuka is said to have attempted, by his description of the might of the approaching Mongol forces, to instil fear in Tayang-khan; he is also said to have informed Temuchin by messenger of his actions and reported that Tayang-khan, at his wits' end, was so terrified that he could be defeated by words alone. According to the *Secret History*, Temuchin acknowledged this service in his last argument with Jamuka.[185]

This account does not merit serious consideration and the role ascribed to Jamuka during the battle by the author of the *Secret History* belongs to the realm of fables. Jamuka, the ambitious rival who was always instigating conspiracies and creating coalitions against Temuchin, who had earlier sought to convince Wang-khan that Temuchin maintained relations with the Naimans, is supposed to have assisted him to victory in this decisive battle? If this were so, why did Jamuka not rejoin Temuchin after the victory over the Naimans? Rashid's explanation, that Jamuka lost faith in a Naiman victory when he saw Temuchin's new battle order, is perhaps nearer the truth, although considerations other than a belief in Temuchin's military superiority also influenced Jamuka's decision to flee the field. The racial and religious contrasts between the Naimans and the Mongols were too great and Jamuka could not trust his followers and warriors to fight with him on the side of the Naimans. Jamuka's actions were forced upon him.[186]

The defection of his Mongol allies sealed Tayang-khan's fate, but the battle was bitter. The 'cowardly' Tayang fell in battle, brought down by many wounds, and his companions fought until all were killed. Temuchin, who had sought to take them alive, expressed astonishment at their heroism and loyalty. 'He who has such companions need not grieve', he exclaimed. The warriors who attempted to escape down the steep cliffs during the night fell to their deaths. 'They died, packed close together like felled trees', comments the author of the *Secret History*.[187] The victory was absolute. Only Kuchlug with a few others succeeded in escaping and fled to his uncle, Buiruk-khan, who had clearly not recovered from his defeat by Temuchin and Wang-khan and, having received no assistance from Tayang-khan against Temuchin, had taken no part in this latest campaign.

'Thus, in the foothills of the Altai, Genghis Khan put an end to the Naiman nation and made it his own.' The Juirat, Katagin, Seljiut, Dörbet, Tayichi'ut and Onggirat tribes submitted to Temuchin, who took possession of Tayang's wife. Gurbesu, mocking her with the words: 'Did you not say that the Mongols had a bad scent! Why then have you come to me?'[188]

The Merkits fled the field rather than submit. In autumn in the same Year of the Rat (1204) Temuchin therefore once more took the field against their leader, Tokto'a-beki, defeated him and captured his whole tribe. Only Tokto'a, his sons and a few followers managed to escape with their lives and fled to join Buiruk-khan.[189] Those Merkits who went to ground and then continued the struggle were decimated. Kutulkan-mergen, the youngest son of Tokto'a-beki, who escaped and attempted to fight his way through to the Kipchaks, was captured by Jochi, who had been despatched in pursuit. Because Kutulkan was a renowned archer Jochi begged Temuchin to spare his life. Temuchin's response to Jochi's intercession was: 'There is no tribe more wicked than the Merkit. How often have we fought them? They have caused us much vexation and sorrow. How can we spare his life? He will only instigate another rebellion. I have conquered these lands, armies and tribes for you, my sons. Of what use is he? There is no better place for an enemy of our nation than the grave!'[190]

Jamuka's end

Recognizing the hopelessness of the Naiman position, Jamuka deserted his allies and fled. His people did not follow him; with only a few companions he hid himself, an exile, in the Tannu Mountains.[191] Jamuka had betrayed the national cause by allying himself with the Naimans, the enemies of the Mongols. Thus, on an occasion when they had just killed a wild sheep and were sitting down to eat it, Jamuka's companions took him prisoner and handed him over to Temuchin. The latter had always pitilessly punished treachery against a legitimate master. At Jamuka's request, Temuchin now had those companions who betrayed Jamuka to him beheaded in the presence of their former leader.

Temuchin always treated his rivals mercilessly. Jamuka, however, was a close friend of his youth, also his *anda*; and in Mongol eyes the killing of an *anda* was more heinous than fratricide. According to the *Secret History* Temuchin hesitates and the final discussion between the two friends is described in a highly dramatic passage.[192] Temuchin lists the many services which Jamuka has rendered him: before the battle with Wang-khan Jamuka informed him of the Kerait battle order; on the eve of the battle against the Naimans Jamuka had put the fear of death into Tayang-khan. Temuchin begs Jamuka to be once more his companion.[193]

Jamuka knew his friend well enough to realize that his fate was sealed. 'When I should have been a good companion. I was no companion to you', he answered. 'Now, my friend, you have pacified the peoples of this region and have united alien lands. The supreme throne is yours ... I am your subject, my friend.' Jamuka had only one request: 'If, my friend, you are pleased to kill me, do so without shedding my blood. Then, when I am dead and if you place my corpse on a high place, I will watch over you, your grandsons and their grandsons, into the distant future. I will be your eternal spiritual protector! I am of noble, of special birth.' According to the *Secret History*, Temuchin granted this last wish of his *anda*.[194]

This presentation in the *Secret History* is romanticized. Rashid reports in one passage of the *Collected Chronicles* that Temuchin presented Jamuka and his followers to a cousin, Eljigidei, who, it is said, caused Jamuka to suffer an agonizing death by dismemberment a few days later. Yet, in a later passage, Rashid maintains that Temuchin handed Jamuka over to Otchigin-noyan for execution, and also that the one hundred Jadirat warriors who accompanied Jamuka were assimilated into Otchigin's army.[195]

Temuchin was rid of his most dangerous rival. Jamuka was clever, gifted and intuitive, but he was scheming and disloyal – such is Rashid's judgement. Jamuka believed that political intrigues would help him to achieve power and, while Temuchin was still an unimportant vassal of Wang-khan, Jamuka supported him. As soon, however, as Temuchin's power and prestige increased, Jamuka sought to drive a wedge between him and Wang-khan, with a view to undermining them both. During the battle with the Naimans Jamuka's behaviour was dictated by factors over which he had no control, since his followers and his people refused to fight on the side of the Naimans against Temuchin. As the *Secret History* comments, Jamuka lost because, with the exception of a few aristocrats, the Mongol nation declared its support for Temuchin.[196]

3

Genghis Khan, Ruler of the Mongol Empire

The Khuriltai of 1206

The defeat of the Naimans made Temuchin ruler of the peoples of Central Asia. A Grand Assembly was summoned to meet and celebrate this event at the source of the Onon River in the spring of the Year of the Tiger (1206). The white standard[1] symbolizing the protective spirit of the nation, tribe or army – its nine points representing the Mongol tribes – was raised and Temuchin was enthroned as emperor, receiving the title Genghis Khan.[2]

The etymology and meaning of the word Genghis (*Chinggis*) are still a subject of controversy. The word has been variously interpreted as 'firm', 'strong', 'righteous', 'loyal', 'hard' or 'cruel', depending upon the meaning attributed to the word *ching* by different Mongol tribes. In general such attributions seek to stress the quality of a 'firm and strong khan' rather than exhibiting any desire to vie with the title of *Gurkhan* ('Universal Ruler') which had been bestowed on Jamuka.[3]

An alternative and probably sounder derivation, advanced quite independently by von Ramstedt and Pelliot, is from the Turkic *tängiz*, 'sea or ocean.'[4] This interpretation is supported by the Mongolian equivalent *dalai-yin khan* on the seal of the Great Khan and the Turkic formal preamble *tailai-nung han* in Guyuk Kha'an's letter to Pope Innocent IV.[5] In *dalai lama*, the Mongolian rendering of the Tibetan lamaistic title, *rGyamts'o blama*, meaning 'Ruler of the Seas' or 'Ruler of the World', *dalai* is used as a concept for 'universal' or 'all-embracing'; this is clearly exhibited by the juxtaposition of *dalai* and *yeke* ('great') in the

Juyongguan Inscription.[6] The title 'Oceanic Ruler' is very old. In Uighur legend *Tengiz* (*Dengiz-khan*) is the name of the youngest son of the Uighur Oguz-khan[7] – and, despite Pelliot's phonetic objections, it may even be identified in the name of one of the sons of Attila the Hun.

Although in Rashid ad-Din's day the Mongols had forgotten the original tradition and the title was simply equated with the Mongolian word *ching* ('firm' or 'strong'), Rashid uses the wider interpretation of the title when he compares it with the Persian *shah-an-shah*. Nasir ad-Din also gives Hulegu the title *padshah-i jahan* ('Universal Ruler'), a non-Islamic title which, as Minorsky comments, must be a rendering of *dalai-khan*.[8] The Genghiside imperial family retained this tradition into the seventeenth century, when a son of Dayan-khan bore the title *erdeni dalai khan*.

Temuchin owed his victory to the steadfastness, loyalty and sacrifice of his followers and his first act on ascending the throne was to reward his comrades-in-arms. 'Bo'orchu and Mukali have brought me to this high office', he declared. 'They shall now enjoy a position above all others and be granted the "Ninefold Pardon".'[9] The *Secret History* devotes twenty-one paragraphs to an account of the services of those who assisted Temuchin to power and to the rewards which Genghis Khan bestowed on them.[10]

Having thus generously fulfilled his obligations towards his comrades-in- arms, Genghis Khan devoted himself to the task of creating a new order on the steppe. The states hitherto created by the nomads had crumbled after brief periods as the result of internal squabbles and they had been unable to withstand external attacks; his empire was to exist for ever. Two considerations formed the basis of the measures which Genghis now introduced: the power of the tribal chieftains must be reduced and a core unit must be created which would be unconditionally loyal to the ruler and would carry out his policies, whatever these might be.

The population was divided into units based on the military organization and general conscription was introduced for all males. According to the *Yuanshi*, conscription was initially from the age of fifteen to seventy, irrespective of the number of males in a household;[11] Abu'l Faraj maintains that twenty years of age was the lower limit. The conquered nations were subject to special military service regulations. In the Five Section Legal Code the age

10   *The enthronement of Genghis Khan at the 1206 Khuriltai.*

for the conscription of Chinese subjects is specified as fifteen to seventy, although during the Yuan dynasty the lower limit was twenty years of age for the sons of officers who were to inherit parental appointments as commanders.[12] Khitan men were liable for military service from fifteen to fifty years of age.[13]

The ninety-five 'Thousands' thus created were placed under the command of Temuchin's old comrades-in-arms, selected not because of birth or position in the tribal hierarchy, but on account of the services which they had already rendered.[14] The commanders included persons of humble origins: the shepherd Degei, the horse-herders Kishlik and Badai, the carpenter Kuchugur, the sons of blacksmiths, Jelme, Subodei and Cha'urkan. Many were members of vassal clans (*ötögus bo'ol*): the Jalair, Sunit and Baya'ut, and Genghis stressed the earlier status of such men when announcing their appointments and rewards, 'Sorkan-shira belonged to Tödöge of the Tayichi'ut and both Badai and Kishlik were horse-herders belonging to Tseren, one of Wang-khan's nobles. But now, my supporters, you shall rejoice that I appoint you Quiver Bearers and Cup Bearers.'[15]

The Russian historian Vladimirtsov maintains that Genghis introduced an aristocrat-based military reorganization in order to prevent the dissolution of the tribal system. The examples quoted above indicate that, on the contrary, this was not so. In making senior appointments designed to weaken the power of the tribal chieftains Genghis specifically drew attention to the lowly social status of such persons as Sorkan-shira, Badai and Kishlik. The latter were simple horse-herders (*aduchi*) not, as suggested by Doerfer's translation of *aktachi*, 'Masters of Horse'. The *aktachi* belonged to the imperial bodyguard, from which élite corps many senior commanders were later appointed.[16]

The 'Thousands' were not created on the basis of tribal affiliation and in distributing tribal members under the command of men from other tribes Genghis was obviously pursuing his aim of weakening the power of the tribal leaders. He ordered the shepherd Degei to create and command a regiment composed of unregistered males; the carpenter Kuchugur collected his thousand men from here and there; Jebe and Subodei were to command regiments composed of warriors whom they themselves had captured. Korchi gathered a regiment together from the 3,000 Ba'arin whom he had been awarded as a special favour, adding to these Chinos, To'olas and Telenggut from the Adarkin tribe. Tribal unity was only preserved in those few cases in which Genghis was sure of their loyalty. This privilege was extended to the Oirats and the Onggut, who had voluntarily allied themselves with Genghis. Two further such exemptions were granted, in both cases to *ötögus bo'ol* clans who had supported Temuchin and whose loyalty he could thus trust. In recognition of the valour of Chaghan-ko'a, a valiant warrior who died in the battle of Dalan Balzhut, his son To'oril was granted the privilege of uniting in one unit all his Negus tribesmen who had been dispersed among various tribes; similarly, Önggur, a respected man who had been Genghis Khan's cupbearer (*ba'urchi*), and who after the fall of Zhongdu was, together with Shigi-khutukhu and Arkai, entrusted with drawing up the inventory of the booty taken from the Chin emperor, was granted the privilege of commanding a regiment composed exclusively of the dispersed Baya'uts. The 2,000 Ikires who were permitted to form one unit represented a special case; their commander, Botu-guregen, was Genghis' son-in-law and was able to claim privileged treatment.[17]

This military reorganization carried out by Genghis Khan had a far-reaching influence on the social structure of the Mongol nation. Men were not permitted, on pain of death and the punishment of their commanders, to leave the units to which they had been assigned; their families, who were responsible for providing their military equipment, were also subordinated to the unit's military commander.[18]

These measures created a new military nobility which owed its rise to the ruler and was thus absolutely loyal to him. Their posts as commanders were hereditary, but any commander who failed to measure up to his tasks could be removed from office. A *bilik* recorded by Rashid states: 'If a troop commander is unable to keep his troop ready for battle, he, his wife and children will all be arraigned and another leader will be selected from within the troop. Commanders of squadrons, regiments and divisions will be dealt with in similar manner.'[19]

Genghis demanded from his most senior military commanders the same blind obedience which he exacted from the ordinary soldier. In order to prevent possible conspiracies he forbade the army commanders to associate with each other and in many cases supervision was exercised by dividing responsibility between two joint commanders. Thus, for example, Genghis decreed that Kuchugur and Mulkalku should be joint commanders of their regiment, a principle of collective leadership later to become the basis of the administration of the conquered lands.[20]

The brothers and sons of military commanders were incorporated as hostages into the bodyguard. This élite corps was expanded to 10,000 men and the members of the bodyguard enjoyed special privileges, ranking above the ordinary regimental commanders, their household members (*kötöchin*) above the ordinary squadron and troop commanders. Genghis Khan decreed: 'If an ordinary regimental commander claims equality with a member of my bodyguard and quarrels with him on this score, I will punish the relevant regimental commander.'[21] The bodyguard became an instrument of power on which Genghis Khan could rely implicitly and from which the cadres entrusted with the administration of the empire were later selected.

These basic principles of military reorganization were to give the Mongol army complete superiority over the armies of some of the most powerful and civilized states of that era, creating both fear and wonder. Juvaini writes: 'From the days of Adam to the present there has been no army comparable to that of the Tatars.'[22]

Genghis did not limit his reorganization to the army; peace and order had to be established within the family and the clan. Draconian laws were promulgated in order to put an end to continual robbery and blood feuds; the death penalty was imposed for robbery and adultery. Genghis learned state administration from the Naimans. He was taught administrative methodology by the former Naiman chancellor, Tata-tonga, who persuaded him that royal orders should in future be legalized by a seal – Tata-tonga was entrusted with the post of Keeper of the Great Seal. The illiterate Genghis Khan was also quick to grasp the importance of the written word, which would ensure that his wishes and his laws would be preserved accurately and without alteration for future generations. He gave orders that the Genghiside princes were to learn the Uighur script used by the Naimans.[23]

Genghis was well aware of the quarrelsome nature of the Mongols. The distribution of the subjugated tribes between the royal family and his comrades-in-arms had not been possible without displays of envy and resentment. Mother Hö'elun and Otchigin had jointly received 10,000 souls; the *Secret History* reports: 'Mother Hö'elun felt that she had been disadvantaged – but said nothing.' Genghis' adopted son Shigikhutukhu, however, was unable to control himself when Bo'orchu and Mukali were designated to the top posts. He protested: 'Have Bo'orchu and Mukali rendered greater service than others? Have they given more of their strength than others? When it comes to distributing rewards I appear to have rendered less service [than they]! So I have given less of myself!'[24]

In order to avoid any future challenges, Genghis Khan instructed his adopted son: 'Write down the details of the distribution of rewards and of the legal decisions made for the nation and bind these in a Blue Book (*köke debter*). Until the days of my most distant successors', thus declared Genghis Khan, 'no one shall alter whatever, after consultation with myself, Shigi-khutukhu shall decide and set down in blue writing on white paper.'[25]

Realizing that the empire could not be ruled by one person, Genghis Khan appointed his half-brother Belgutei to be Minister of State and Supreme *Yarghuchi*[26] and entrusted his adopted son Shigi-khutukhu with jurisdiction throughout the empire. 'Punish robbery within the nation and clean up deception. Execute those who have deserved death and impose fines on those who deserve such fines', declared Genghis Khan, thus laying the groundwork for the civil administration of the future empire. The modern Japanese historian Tamura offers for discussion three dates for the beginning of the written record of Genghis Khan's decrees – 1189, 1204 and 1206. Since the Uighur script was only adopted by the Mongols after the defeat of the Naimans, the written record could not have begun before 1206. From that date all decrees, orders and directives for the administration of the empire were set down in writing and collected in a book which has become famous as the *Great Yasa* (*Yasak*). This collection of laws was constantly expanded, but the basic principles on which the empire was established and governed were laid down at the Khuriltai of 1206.[27]

The measures instituted by Genghis Khan introduced a completely new order into nomadic society. Interference in the rights of the tribal chiefs, the subordination of aristocrats to the orders of commoners, the division of the nation into military units and the

Chinese	Khitan	Jürched	Hsi Hsia	'Phags-pa	Syriac	Uighur	Mongolian	Manchu

11 Example of old Mongol script.

introduction of compulsory military service offended against the traditional nomadic way of life and could not but arouse discontent and resistance among the mass of the Mongol people. After the feeling of intoxication engendered by his rise to power Genghis Khan was soon to learn the sobering fact that it was easier to seize control than to maintain it.

The shaman and the emperor

In the magical world inhabited by the Mongols the shaman was no less respected nor less influential than the tribal leader. Among the forest peoples, such as the Oirats and the Merkits, the shaman was the ruler and bore the title *beki*. Among the cattle-breeders the shaman could also dispute the leadership with the tribal chieftain; and although these leaders were selected mainly for their military prowess they did also have a shamanist role. The Naiman rulers had the reputation of associating with spirits and demons; even Genghis Khan held converse with Heaven and fell into trances.

The Mongols turned to their shaman on all important occasions. He was called in to foretell the future of new-born children; in cases of illness he pacified the evil spirits; in the event of death he compelled the spirit of the departed to quit the house and he purified the householders and their belongings with fire; he was master of ceremonies at feasts and would use his powers to prevent

SHAMAN TEBTENGRI, THE MONGOL WIZARD.
From an old French Work on Tatary.

12   *The Mongol shaman Teb-tengri.*

drought or storms or to achieve military success; no Mongol would undertake a journey or begin any venture without a felicitous prophecy by the shaman. Moreover, the shaman came in contact with many tribes in the course of his wanderings and could, through the stories which he peddled, exercise an influence on tribal politics.[28]

The most influential shaman among the Mongols was Kököchu, the son of Mönglik, Yisugei's servant who, as we have seen, brought Temuchin back from the camp of Dai-sechen when Yisugei died and was later responsible for saving Temuchin's life by drawing attention to a plot by Senggum. According to Rashid ad-Din, Mönglik stood in great favour with Genghis Khan, was given Yisugei's widow, Hö'elun, as his wife and granted the privilege of sitting on Genghis' right hand.[29] Kököchu – or Teb-tengri (Most Heavenly) to give him his shamanist title – who was known even to the Uighurs and was said by the ordinary Mongol to ride to Heaven on a white charger, had supported Temuchin in the latter's struggle for supremacy. Juvaini relates that during the bitter cold which prevailed in the area Teb-tengri wandered naked through the barren steppe and the mountains, returning to proclaim: 'God spoke to me, saying: "I have given the whole Earth to Temuchin and his sons and I have named him Genghis Khan. See that he rules justly!" ' Temuchin realized that such stories had a powerful effect on the superstitious Mongols. He therefore trusted Mönglik's son completely and was in the habit of adhering strictly to the shaman's advice. Rashid comments that, aware of the influence which he exerted over Genghis Khan, the shaman became arrogant and spoke boldly to him – but the latter, conscious of the value to himself of the shaman's prophecies, still retained affection for him.[30]

Kököchu was ambitious and gathered around him many who were dissatisfied with the reforms introduced by Genghis Khan; even Wang-khan attempted to win his support in the struggle against Temuchin. Rashid and Juvaini both report that Kököchu was hungry for power, 'He was eager to become the ruler himself.' Teb-tengri's chosen method of achieving his aim was to sow dissension within Genghis Khan's family. He fanned the flames of Genghis Khan's suspicions regarding Kasar and, by humiliating Kasar, sought to diminish the reputation and authority of the ruler. The *Secret History* tells how Mönglik's seven sons banded

together to assault Kasar. In answer to Kasar's complaint,
Genghis Khan replied: 'You have never before allowed any
person to get the better of you; how could you now permit them
to triumph over you?' – and Kasar was so bitter at this response
that he did not appear for three days. Teb-tengri then informed
Genghis Khan: 'The King of Heaven has made several prophecies
to me. On one occasion he said: "Let Temuchin hold the nation in
his hands", but on other occasions he said the same of Kasar. Who
knows what will happen if you do not anticipate Kasar's actions.'
That same night, according to the *Secret History* , Genghis Khan
rode out to take Kasar prisoner.[31]

Genghis doubtless had reason to believe the words of Teb-
tengri; had not in earlier times a wise old man of the Baya'ut tribe
mentioned Kasar, along with Sacha-beki, Jamuka and Alak-udur
of the Tartars, as a pretender to the throne?[32] Kasar's role during
the struggle with Wang-khan had also been ambiguous. He had
broken with Temuchin; his wife and children had been with
Wang-khan and it is doubtful whether they were abducted by
the latter. Temuchin may, in order to bind Kasar to him, have
compelled Kasar to behead Wang-khan's envoy; and Pelliot, we
have noted, reads a similar intention into the letter sent by
Temuchin to Wang-khan in Kasar's name.[33]

The disagreements between Temuchin and his brother were
well known and are repeated in later Mongol accounts – Sagang-
sechen even speaks of a conspiracy by Kasar and Belgutei against
Genghis Khan.[34] According to Rashid ad-Din, Kasar had certainly been blameworthy on several occasions. After the defeat of
the Tartars he had, because his wife was of that tribe, flouted
Temuchin's order to kill a thousand Tartar prisoners; and it was
Kasar who attacked the Onggirat as they were moving forward
peacefully, thus causing them to join Jamuka. Despite this,
Genghis had appointed Kasar in overall command of the army in
the battle against the Naimans but now, as the result of Heaven's
ambiguous prophecy conveyed by Teb-tengri, Kasar would not be
forgiven. Genghis was about to arraign Kasar when Mother
H'o'elun, warned of his intention, set out to rescue Kasar. When
she arrived at daybreak Genghis was commencing Kasar's
interrogation and, surprised by her arrival, trembled and shook
before his mother. The *Secret History* relates how Hö'elun
dramatically secured Kasar's freedom but also reports that

Genghis, without his mother's knowledge, deprived Kasar of all but 1,400 of his people. It is said that when Hö'elun learned of this she took the deed very much to heart and quickly slipped into a decline.[35]

Genghis Khan's mother had saved him from the stigma of fratricide but the incident brought about the result desired by Teb-tengri: the number of deserters from Genghis to Teb-tengri steadily increased. The *Secret History* comments: 'After this incident peoples of nine languages assembled under Teb-tengri.' Among the many who elected to leave Genghis' camp were people belonging to his youngest brother, Temuge-otchigin, who sent a messenger to Teb-tengri, demanding the return of his people. The messenger was severely beaten and sent back on foot carrying his saddle; and, when Temuge-otchigin personally visited Teb-tengri the following morning, he was surrounded by Mönglik's seven sons and made to kneel in humble supplication before Teb-tengri.[36]

It was clear that Teb-tengri sought a trial of strength with Genghis. As on other occasions, the *Secret History* attributes Genghis' decisiveness to the influence of his entourage, this time the appearance of a weeping and wailing Börte: 'How will these people who secretly attack your younger brethren, who are as strong as firs and cypresses, ever allow my three or four little sons to rule?' There is no doubt that Genghis Khan was, in any event, determined to rid himself of this dangerous shaman, but it was certainly not easy for him to overcome his superstitious awe of the shaman's supernatural powers. In matters touching on his own power and authority, however, Genghis never hesitated; he stood firm and a trap was prepared for Teb-tengri. It was declared that the quarrel between Teb-tengri and Temuge-otchigin should be settled by the traditional wrestling bout. Otchigin then stationed three strong men outside the Khan's tent and, as the contestants went out to the ring, these seized Teb-tengri and broke his spine.[37]

When Otchigin re-entered the tent it was clear to Mönglik and his sons what had happened. The sons took up a threatening posture and grasped the sleeves of Genghis Khan's cloak. Genghis, although in fear, managed to shake them off and withdrew from the tent under the protection of his bodyguard. He then announced that the deed was the will of Heaven: 'Because

Teb-tengri beat and kicked my brethren and because he spread slander about my brethren, Heaven was displeased with him and took his life and body', he declared. For Mönglik, who had stood by him since the death of Yisugei, Genghis had other words: 'You failed to moderate the character of your sons and they sought to make themselves my equals', Genghis accused him. 'Had I realized the nature of your characters you would all have been dealt with as were Jamuka, Altan, Kuchar and their companions!' Now, however, that the danger was over Genghis was prepared to show mercy and declared: 'What happened is now history. In consideration of that fact I moderate my wrath and pardon you. But if you had held your immoderate characters in check who could have ever equalled Mönglik's descendants?' The author of the *Secret History* concludes this tale with the comment: 'from that moment, however, the standing of the Qongqotan was reduced'.[38]

Genghis appointed an arch-shaman who was devoted to him, Usun of the Ba'arin. 'You are a scion of a Ba'arin chieftain. Usun the Old shall be the senior in our *beki* hierarchy. When he has been appointed a *beki*, he shall be clothed in a white robe, given a white gelding to ride, be seated in a position of honour and shown every respect. He shall designate the favourable months and years', decreed Genghis. Thus did Genghis Khan enforce the primacy of imperial power over that of the priests.[39]

The consolidation of the empire

The years between the victory over the Naimans (1204) and the campaign against the Tanguts (1209) was the only period of Genghis Khan's life during which his energies were devoted to organizational tasks rather than war. It was a period during which he left military matters to his generals, while he himself created the basis for the internal structure of his empire and the consolidation of the power of the ruling family.

He did, however, make one exception. At the end of the Khuriltai in 1206 he decided to take the field against Buiruk-khan, who, following the defeat inflicted upon him by Wang-khan and Temuchin, had withdrawn to the Black Irtysch. Buiruk-khan had not participated in his brother's struggle with

Genghis, but his camp had become a rallying point for Genghis' enemies, including Tayang-khan's son, Kuchlug, and Tokto'a-beki. Buiruk-khan had no suspicion of Genghis' intentions and was hawking when the Mongols attacked, captured and killed him, abducting his wives, children, cattle and household.[40]

Following this victory the Kirghiz submitted to Genghis Khan in the Year of the Hare (1207), sending ambassadors with beautiful white falcons as a sign of their homage.[41] The Oirats followed this example in 1208, when, meeting by chance with the vanguard of the Mongol forces sent against Tokto'a-beki of the Merkits and Kuchlug, the Oirats directed them towards the enemy, who had taken refuge with Buiruk-khan. Tokto'a and Kuchlug were surprised by the Mongol force and prepared to do battle on the Irtysch. Tokto'a was killed by a stray arrow; since his sons had no opportunity to bury him or to take the corpse with them, they cut off his head and the combined Naiman and Merkit forces retreated with it. Most of their troops were drowned crossing the Irtysch and the few survivors scattered. Kuchlug fled to Kara-Khitai; the Merkits and Tokto'a-beki's sons joined the Kipchaks.[42]

The fame and reputation of Genghis Khan spread throughout Central Asia and news of his victories and rise to power reached Barchuk, the ruler of the Uighurs. The *Idikut* – the title is Turkic and means 'Sacred Majesty' – who paid tribute to Kara-Khitai, sought to free himself from this vassalage[43] and hoped to win the support of Genghis Khan. In spring in the Year of the Snake (1209) he dispatched a mission to Genghis Khan, offering the latter suzerainty over the Uighurs. 'If you, Genghis Khan, show me favour, I will be your fifth son and will place all my strength at your disposal.'[44] Genghis Khan reacted positively to this mission and was ready to give his daughter, Altun, in marriage, but he made it a condition that the *Idikut* should appear personally before him. 'Idu'ut shall come here, bringing gold and silver, small and large pearls, brocade, damask and silks' was his message. Barchuk did not hurry to respond, waiting to see how matters would develop. In summer 1209 Genghis dispatched a second mission to the *Idikut*, and in the Year of the Sheep (1211) Barchuk complied with Genghis Khan's demand and came to the latter, camped by the Kerulen after his victorious campaign against the Tanguts.[45]

The Uighurs were the first people outside the Mongol nation to acknowledge Genghis Khan's suzerainty. It was a political event of far-reaching importance and one which, from a military point of view, freed the Mongols from worries about defending their south-west flank. The example of the *Idikut* was followed in the same year by the appearance of Arslan of the Karluk to do homage to Genghis Khan, who, because of this peaceful submission, gave Arslan one of his daughters in marriage.[46]

War with the Tanguts

The Mongol tribes were united, the nomadic peoples of Central Asia had been brought to heel and Genghis Khan's leadership was assured. The economy of the pastoral peoples of Mongolia had, however, suffered grievous losses. The constant battles, and perhaps also climatic changes, had decimated their flocks.[47] The stock of animals had to be increased and this was one of the principal reasons for the initial attacks by the Mongols on the territory of the Tanguts.

The Tangut empire, whose northern frontier from the southern Gobi to the Kami Oasis was contiguous with the lands inhabited by the Mongols, had developed in the eleventh century into one of the strongest military powers of Asia and had extended its domains to include Ningxia, the Ordos and parts of Gansu. The main occupations of the population, consisting of Tanguts, Tibetans, Yellow Uighurs and Chinese, were agriculture, cattle-breeding and trade. The Tanguts had a large army and fortified towns which the Mongols did not understand how to attack. Initial Mongol campaigns against the Tanguts were thus in the nature of mere raids. As early as 1205, before the Great Assembly, Mongol forces under Ila Ahai had attacked Tangut territory and returned with rich hauls of camels and other animals.[48] The second campaign in autumn 1207 was also concerned only with plunder and after the Mongols had taken the town of Wolohai (in the Alashan area, near the present town of Tingyuan) they plundered the area and returned home in spring 1208. The *Yuanshi* suggests that this was in order to avoid the heat of summer, but it was probably because the Tangut ruler, Li Anquan – who came to the Tangut throne and was recognized as ruler of Xi-Xia by the Chinese in 1207, after his predecessor, Li Chunyu, had been deposed in a palace revolution because of his proven inability to defend the empire – had assembled a numerically superior military force.[49]

The relatively passive attitude of the Tanguts, the readiness with which the Uighurs recognized Mongol suzerainty, and pressure from Khitan and Chinese deserters to attack the Jurchid, influenced Genghis Khan to launch a new campaign against the Tanguts, this time with the aim of completely defeating the Tangut empire and thus opening the way for an attack on China. In 1209, after a march of some 650 miles – 200 of these through the sandy wastes of the Gobi – the Mongol forces under the personal command of Genghis Khan penetrated into the Tangut empire.[50] After storming Wolohai in May the Mongols suffered a reversal near a mountain pass at the hands of the Tangut army commanded by Weiming-linggong.[51] The Tanguts did not, however, exploit this victory and the two armies remained in their positions for two months.

In August reinforcements arrived from Mongolia and the Mongols went over to the attack. Employing their proven tactic of feigned withdrawal, they coaxed the enemy out of their fortified camp, then turned on their pursuers, inflicting a crushing defeat on the Tanguts and taking prisoner the Tangut commander, Weiming. The way stood open towards the Tangut capital and its siege began. The Tanguts put up a stiff resistance and the Mongols were still relatively inexperienced in besieging fortified cities. In October Genghis ordered the construction of a large dam which directed the floodwaters into the town. The position of the capital was one of despair and the Tangut ruler sent an express messenger to the Chin emperor with a request for assistance. The emperor's councillors, more far-seeing than the emperor himself, recommended that he should act on the Tangut request. 'If Xi-Xia falls, the Mongols will certainly attack us', said one councillor. The emperor was, however, not prepared to listen, 'It is advantageous to my state if its enemies attack each other. What grounds do we have for concern?' he responded.[52]

The fate of the Tangut capital appeared to be sealed, but the unexpected happened. In January 1210 the waters from the dam – breached, it is suggested, by the Tanguts – flooded the Mongol camp and peace negotiations were commenced.[53]

Genghis demanded that the Tanguts provide him with auxiliary troops but the Tangut ruler replied: 'We are a nation of town-dwellers. We would not be in a state to fight as auxiliaries in the event of a long march followed by a heated battle.' He promised, however, to offer rich tribute: camels with their herders, woollen goods and silk cloth, trained falcons and, finally, as a token of his submission, one of his daughters as wife to Genghis Khan.[54] In his current position Genghis had to be satisfied with this offer, but he never forgot this Tangut refusal to provide auxiliary troops. After his victorious western campaign Genghis, although in ill health, undertook a final campaign against the Tanguts and wreaked terrible vengeance on the Tangut people.

The Tanguts, outraged by the behaviour of the Chin, broke the peace which had existed since 1165, attacking and plundering the Chin frontier areas. Hostilities between the Chin and the Tanguts continued until 1225, when a fresh alliance was concluded against the common enemy, the Mongols.

The war in China

China had always been the target of attacks by the nomads, who were attracted not only by the immeasurable riches of that land but also by the prestige enjoyed throughout Asia by conquerors of that ancient and civilized people. The nomads, however, were usually satisfied with plundering forays over the frontier. Genghis Khan shared the nomadic fear of the power of the 'Golden Khan'. He had recognized the suzerainty of the Chin emperor, paid him tribute and had for his services been rewarded with the title *cha'ut-kuri*. That decoration had, however, been bestowed on the vassal of Wang-khan; now that Genghis Khan had become leader of all the Mongols he had to expect that the Chin emperor might find it difficult to accept the new concentration of power in Mongolia. A powerful leader on the frontier was a constant threat to the Chin and although they had not reacted in 1206 this was because war had just broken out with the Sung; but peace had been reached in 1208, the Sung being forced to pay double tribute and recognize the Chin emperor as their overlord.[55]

There were also other considerations. Temuchin's followers had elected him Khan in the expectation of fresh victories and rich booty; he would alienate them if he did not satisfy that expectation. War against the Jurchid would also strengthen the Mongol feeling of unity since it was a national duty to exact revenge for past humiliations; and although Genghis Khan had taken steps to ensure that when at the head of his army he could rely implicitly on his soldiers, even if these were from subject tribes, it was potentially dangerous to allow the latter to remain idle at home.

Crucial for his decision to attack the Chin empire was the information which Genghis received from that country. The thought of attacking the Chin probably arose as early as his meeting with the Khitan Ila Ahai, who, because of his linguistic abilities, was sent as Chin ambassador to the court of Wang-khan. Ahai was so impressed by the fine appearance of Genghis Khan at their first meeting that he immediately offered him his services. As a pledge of his loyalty Ahai brought with him the following year his brother Tuka, who entered the Mongol bodyguard as a hostage. Both brothers took part in the Baljuna Covenant and in the campaign against Wang-khan. Despite Chin suspicions concerning Ahai's long absence and the consequent imprisonment of his wife and children, Ahai remained with Genghis, commanded Mongol troops in the campaign against the Tanguts and the advance guard for Jebe's invasion of China. Although Ahai also took part in the siege of Wusha in 1211 he must have been despatched on a reconnaissance to the Jurchid in that year, since the *Yuanshi* reports: '. . . in autumn 1211 Yelu Ahai "submitted" and sought out Genghis Khan in the latter's field camp'. Ahai and his brother jointly commanded the Khitan troops at the siege of Zhongdu and were generously rewarded and accorded high titles after the fall of that city.[56]

At their first meetings Ila Ahai informed Genghis Khan that Chin preparations were insufficient for effective military defence, their morale was low and their end could be near.[57] Genghis Khan did not, however, seriously consider an attack on the Chin until after his election as Khan in 1206, when information provided by further defectors from the Chin strengthened his resolve. In 1206 a delegation from Liaodong informed him that Prince Ai had attempted a coup and they accused the Chin government of cruelly persecuting members of the ruling house.[58] In 1208 four senior Chin officials, Li Zhao, Wu Fengchen, Bai Lun and Tian Guangming, fled to the Mongols. They had addressed a memorial to the throne urging hostilities against the Mongols, but the emperor suspected that they were motivated by personal ambition and sentenced them to one hundred strokes. They now also urged Genghis Khan to attack the Chin.[59]

The *Yuanshi*[60] describes the situation in 1206 as follows: 'Prisoners [i.e. the Liaodong delegation] from China informed Genghis Khan of the despotism and cruelty of the Chin ruler but, although he decided to bring the emperor to justice, Genghis Khan did not yet dare put this decision into action.' He was not prepared to be drawn into a hasty attack against the Chin until the Tangut empire had been conquered and his rear protected from enemy attacks. The victory over the Tanguts, the readiness of the *idikut* to accept Genghis's suzerainty, also the friendship of the ruler of the Onggut, created the prerequisites for the Chin campaign and Genghis began to make his preparations for war. In these preparations he was not dependent only on defectors for information about the situation in China; he had his informants and agents – such as Ila Ahai – and he was also the recipient of intelligence from Muslim merchants such as Ja'far.[61]

The Chin empire was no longer the power it had been when the Jurchid originally conquered Northern China. The estrangement between those Jurchid leaders who remained in the tribal home-lands and the sinicized upper class at court, the dissatisfaction of the tribal leaders and the generals with the centralized policies of the Chin emperor, all led to constantly increasing tension. The Khitans who remained in Northern Mongolia regarded the racially and linguistically related Mongols as their allies and awaited an auspicious opportunity to rise against the hated Jurchid. In the biography of Ila Nieers the *Yuanshi* offers us eloquent evidence of the morale of the Chin. 'When Ila Nieers learned that Genghis Khan had assembled an army to attack the Jurchid he informed his relatives: "Now the time has come to take revenge for our people", and taking with him more than a hundred of his clansmen he joined Genghis Khan, who appointed him general (*yuanshuai*) of his home area, Jizhou.'[62]

The native Chinese also regarded the Jurchid as their enemies and were interested in bringing about a weakening of their power. Although the Chin had thus to reckon with war on two fronts, protecting the southern front from possible attack by the Sung and defending themselves against incursions by the Tanguts in the north-west, any Mongol attack on them was still a gamble. The Chin had a numerically superior army and a virtually inexhaustible supply of reserves. When Genghis Khan launched his attack the Chin army had a nominal strength of 600,000 – some 120,000 mounted archers, which were the equal of the Mongol cavalry, and almost 500,000 infantry; Genghis Khan had probably no more than 65,000 of his own troops and an auxiliary Onggut force of 10,000. Moreover, Genghis' position in Mongolia was not yet so secure that an uprising by the more recently subjugated tribes could be discounted.[63]

Genghis took the gamble. He had decided on war and in 1210 he refused the annual tribute which he probably owed the Chin emperor as a relic of that paid by the Kerait leader Wang-khan, whose tribe he now ruled. The *Yuanshi* describes this event as follows: 'The Chin emperor sent the Prince of Wei, Yunji [Yungi], to receive the tribute at Jingzhou [north of Guihuacheng]. The emperor [Genghis] received the prince but declined to offer the full ritual ceremony of greeting. Thereupon Yunji returned to court and sought troops in order to attack Genghis Khan, The Emperor Zhaozong died at this time and was succeeded as Chin emperor by Yunji, who sent news of his accession to Genghis Khan by hand of an ambassador, to whom Genghis should have kotowed on accepting the message. When Genghis learned the identity of the new Chin emperior, he made offensive remarks about him, faced the south, spat, mounted his horse and rode off to the north.[64]

This challenge meant war. In March in the Year of the Sheep (1211) Genghis held a Khuriltai on the Kerulen River at which the *Idikut* of the Uighurs, Barchuk, and Arslan, King of Karluk, formally recognized him as their overlord. The western frontier was now protected from hostile attack, but Genghis was concerned about the hinterland, where there had not yet been time to eliminate the desire of the conquered tribes for independence. The expectation of boundless booty was now to unite them but, in order to secure himself against any possible rebellion by Mongol clans, the Keraits, Naimans or others, Genghis Khan left behind in the homeland a corps of 20,000 men under command of the Onggirat Takuchar.[65]

Genghis also appealed to the national spirit of the Mongols, elevating the struggle against the Jurchid to a war of vengeance for past humiliations suffered by the Mongols. Rashid recounts how, before taking the field, Genghis Khan withdrew to the summit of a mountain and called for the assistance of Heaven with the words: 'O Eternal Heaven. You know and accept that the "Altan Khan" is the wind which has fanned the tumult, that it is he who began this quarrel. He it was who, without cause, executed Ökin-barkak and Ambakai-khan, captured and delivered over to him by the Tartars. These were the elder relatives of my father and grandfather and I seek to avenge their blood.'[66]

Juzjani also reports this event, recounting that Genghis Khan withdrew to a felt tent on the mountain and there, his belt hanging round his neck, communed with the Eternal Heaven. Meanwhile, obedient to his orders, the Mongol families – men and women in separate groups – spent three days and three nights, bareheaded and fasting. On the morning of the fourth day Genghis Khan emerged from his tent and proclaimed to his people: 'Heaven has promised me victory. Now we must prepare ourselves to take vengeance on the Altan Khan.'[67]

The Mongol armies set out in May; in June they reached the outer defence ring, said to extend for some 3,000 *li*, which the Chin emperor, Zhangzong, had constructed towards the end of the twelfth century some distance in front of the Great Wall.[68] These defences were held by Onggut forces, who offered no resistance; indeed their leader, Alakush, placed a corps of auxiliaries at Genghis Khan's disposal. According to Rashid ad-Din this action was resisted by the Onggut emirs, who murdered Alakush. Genghis sought to bring all the conspirators to justice but this was opposed by the nephew and heir of the victim, who made clear that the murder had taken place with the agreement of the whole Onggut tribe. 'If they are all killed, what will it serve you?' he asked Genghis, who contented himself with executing only the actual killers and their families.[69]

The Mongols pressed forward into Chahar, capturing the towns of Xuande fu and Fouzhou near Kalgan. Liu Bailin, the Chin commander of Weining, surrendered that town and joined the Mongols as commander of a regiment, serving in 1213 as Mongol commandant of the western capital, Xijing, and later taking part under Mukali in the fall of Yenjing.[70] The Chin emperor now made an offer of peace but this was rejected by Genghis Khan. Terror gripped the population and the Chin court. The Jurchid general, Jiujin, despatched to strengthen the frontier forces, attempted to dissuade Genghis Khan from any further fighting, sending forward as negotiator the Khitan Shimo Ming'an, a linguist who knew Genghis Khan personally from an earlier visit to the Mongols. Ming'an promptly defected and entered Genghis Khan's service, being given command of Mongol and Han troops. He distinguished himself at the storming of the city of Zhongdu and died of an illness in 1216, aged fifty-three.[71]

In autumn Jebe captured the strategic Juyong Pass either, as suggested by the *Yuanshi*, because of treachery by the Jurchid general or, according to the *Secret History*, by Jebe enticing the defenders from the pass and then attacking them. This allowed Genghis Khan, who was following close behind with the main Mongol army, to destroy the Khitan and Jurchid élite troops. This defeat was followed in November/December by a further serious blow for the Chin; Ila Ahai swept down on the imperial pastures and drove away the horses, thus depriving the Chin of the main source of remounts for their cavalry.[72]

The exploitation of these successful military operations was, however, delayed by an unforeseen incident. Genghis was wounded by a stray arrow at the siege of the western capital Xijing (Dadong). He entrusted the command of the armies to his son, Tolui, but the Jurchid were able to retake the defensive positions which the Mongols had captured. The *Yuanshi* records that when hostilities resumed in 1213 the Juyong Pass defences had been rebuilt and strengthened by the Chin and were now manned by élite forces. Approaching the mountain passes, Genghis Khan was nonplussed, but sent for the Muslim merchant Ja'far. Ja'far, who had joined Genghis at the Baljuna, had been sent as an ambassador to China but, rightly suspected as a Mongol informant, had been rejected by the Chin court. He possessed an excellent knowledge of the country and knew a lonely path which led through thick forests and over the mountains. At dead of night, mouths gagged, the Mongol army was led over this pass by Ja'far. The carefree Chin garrison, trusting in the strength of the fortifications, was asleep and, taken by surprise, massacred in cold blood.

This event is also recounted by Juzjani, who reports that Genghis Khan sent a Muslim, Ja'far by name, to the Chin troops under the pretence of trading with them. Ja'far was imprisoned and it was a considerable time before he succeeded in gaining his freedom and rejoining Genghis Khan, to whom he made a report which brought this path to Genghis' attention. Genghis Khan, according to the *Yuanshi*, valued Ja'far's services highly and Ja'far conducted the Mongol peace negotiations with the besieged city of Zhongdu (1214). After the capture of that city in 1215 Genghis is said to have declared to those around him: 'It is largely thanks to him that I have come this far', and turning to Ja'far he bade him shoot an arrow. 'The land covered by the flight of your arrow will be yours', he promised; Ja'far was appointed *darughachi* of the lands between the Yellow River in the south and the Iron Gate in the north, receiving a personal apanage of one hundred families.[73]

The victories of the Mongols, the defections and the treachery of the Khitans and of the Han Chinese, the peasant unrest caused by the prevailing famine, all spread uncertainty and mistrust among the Jurchid. The suspicion-ridden policies of the emperor, who had instigated colonization of the areas previously inhabited by the Khitans, resulted in open rebellion. A member of the former ruling Ila family, Liuge, amassed an army of 100,000 men and in spring 1212 proclaimed himself supreme commander (*du yuanshuai*) of Liaodong. He concluded an alliance with Genghis

13   *Genghis Khan in pursuit of his enemies.*

Khan, and with Mongol assistance inflicted a serious defeat on the able Jurchid commander sent against him. Liuge was officially recognized as King of the Liao Empire – but a Mongol co-regent was appointed.[74]

Signs of disintegration became evident in the Jurchid camp. The Jurchid general, Hushahu (Zhizhong), a member of the Jurchen family of Hilue, had distinguished himself in the war with the Sung and, after the peace treaty with the Sung, had in 1208 been appointed to command the frontier troops as commandant (*liushou*) of the western capital of Xijing. Hushahu, who commanded his own army, was an ambitious and power-hungry person, whose high-handedness and presumption knew no bounds following the accession of Weishao Wang – but he had many friends at court and the new emperor confirmed him in his appointments. In autumn 1213 he deserted his post at Xijing, thus allowing Genghis to force the Jijing Pass and defeat the Jurchid troops under General Wayen Gang near Yizhou. Wayen Gang, who accused Hushahu of accepting bribes from the Mongols then allowing them through the pass, was killed by Hushahu, who, untroubled by the advances of the Mongols, pursued his own egoistic aims. He made his way to the capital, where in August or September he carried out a palace revolution. He first murdered the governor of the city and then Emperor Chunghei, setting the Prince of Udabu on the throne as Emperor Xuanzong. Hushahu was loaded with honours by Xuanzong but did not long enjoy his moment of power. Shuhu Gaoqi, an army commander threatened by Hushahu, ringed the latter's residence with troops and Hushahu, who sought flight, was captured and executed.[75]

The Chin position was critical. With the exception of seven towns the whole area north of the Huanghe River was now in the hands of the Mongols. In spring 1214 Genghis Khan established his headquarters in the northern suburb of Zhongdu. The troops of the left wing under command of Kasar and Otchigin (Wochen nayan) and those of the right wing under Genghis' sons, Jochi, Chaghatai and Ögödei, were drawn up in front of Zhongdu and the Mongol generals urged Genghis Khan to exploit the situation and make an end of the Jurchid. Genghis did not take their advice; instead he put Ja'far in charge of peace negotiations which he instituted with the Chin emperor.[76]

Serious considerations led Genghis Khan to take this step. Carpini reports: 'The siege was so extended that the armies' provisions were completely exhausted; because they had nothing left to eat Genghis Khan had to order the sacrifice of every tenth man in order to provide sustenance for his comrades.'[77] Although Carpini undoubtedly exaggerates in ascribing such an order to Genghis, there are several such reports that, in an emergency, the Mongols would eat human flesh. Archbishop Peter of Russia reported to the Council of Lyons in 1245: 'The Mongols eat horse and dog flesh and other disgusting things and will, in emergency, even eat human flesh.'[78] Rashid ad-Din reports in his account of the privations suffered by Tolui's army during Ögödei Kha'an's campaign in China: 'Things were so bad that they ate the corpses of their dead companions and of fallen horses; they even ate hay.'[79] There are also assertions that Khitan troops who had been defeated by the Jurchid and whose provisions were exhausted 'slaughtered several thousand persons for every meal'.[80] The allegation of Yves de Narbonne – 'The Tartars feed on human flesh as if it were the most exquisite of dishes, the breasts of virgins being regarded by their chiefs as special delicacies . . .'[81] – is not elsewhere documented, but culinary cannibalism was not un-known to the Chinese.[82]

Apart from famine, an epidemic was spreading through the Mongol armies and, although the Chin emperor could not make up his mind to accept the advice, the suggestion was made by one Chin commander during a discussion of the beleaguered city: 'The Mongol troops are all ill because of the unaccustomed heat and the time has come to go over to the attack.' Although, contrary to the assertions of some sources, peace overtures were undoubtedly initiated by Genghis Khan – the *Jinshi* lists four Mongol embassies to the Chin court in the second month of 1214 – he gave no indication of his predicament. In his message to the Chin emperor he declared: 'Your districts and counties in Shandong and Hebei are now in my possession, leaving you with only Yendu [Yenjing]. Heaven has so weakened you that, if I were also now to attack you in your distress, what would Heaven think of me? I therefore intend to turn back with my army. Might you not provide some supplies for my troops, thus lessening the resentment of my generals?'[83] The negotiations conducted by Ja'far were brought to a successful conclusion. An imperial princess was presented to

Genghis Khan as a wife; gold and brocade, 500 boy and girl slaves and 3,000 horses were delivered to the Mongols as a gift from the Jurchid emperior. The *Secret History* comments that unlimited quantities of gold, silver, silk and valuables were handed over to the Mongol troops. 'They took away from Zhongdu as much as they could carry.'[84] Genghis Khan left the battlefield and withdrew to a summer camp in Mongolia.

In summer 1214 the Chin emperor decided to move the imperial residence to the southern capital, Nanjing (Kaifeng); the Crown Prince followed quickly on his heels. This transfer of the capital had disastrous consequences. The emperor's action was regarded as a sign of cowardice and weakness. Mutinies broke out among the Jurchid troops; the Khitan troops rebelled and joined the Mongols. At the Sung court a ministerial council was convoked, but opinions differed. Some recommended exploiting the Chin weakness, others pointed to the potential Mongol threat. 'The Chin have been our enemies, but now they are our bulwark against the Mongols', warned one councillor. The Sung emperor could not bring himself to take a decision, but Sung tribute to the Chin was discontinued.[85]

Genghis Khan was furious when he heard that the Chin capital had moved south, regarding the decision as a cunning manoeuvre by the Chin to gather their strength in the south and then attack the Mongols. In winter 1214 hostilities were reopened; an army commanded by Samuka and the Khitan Shimo Ming'an reinvested the city of Zhongdu; that same winter Mukali was ordered to advance into the province of Liaodong. Shimo Yexian (Yesen), a Khitan who joined the Mongols as soon as he learned that Genghis Khan had sent an army against the Jurchid, had drawn attention to the significance of capturing the northern capital in Liaoyang, the initial centre of Chin dynastic power.[86] Yesen was attached to Mukali's army and a daring escapade by him led to the capture of the northern capital in 1215. Learning that a new commandant was to assume defence of the city, Yesen lay in wait with a few horsemen on the road to the city and captured and killed the new commandant. Using the commandant's commission of appointment. Yesen made his way to the military headquarters, announced himself as the new commandant sent by the court, ordered the disbandment of the city guard and appointed new officers. Three days later Mukali forced his way into the city 'without firing a single arrow'. 108,000 households, 100,000 soldiers, food supplies and weapons fell into his grasp. General Yindahu and forty-seven other senior officers, plus thirty-two cities surrendered to him. 'The Chin mourned the loss of their homeland', comments the author of Yesen's biography. Yesen, who was appointed *darughachi* of the city, later took part in other campaigns and died at the age of forty-one during the siege of another city.[87]

The situation in the beleaguered capital of Zhongdu was one of despair and the population was reduced to eating human flesh. When a relief force dispatched with supplies was defeated by the Mongols, the commandant of the city, Wayen Fuxing (Chenghui), took poison, and the Khitan defector Shimo Ming'an forced his way into the capital.[88] The imperial treasury fell into the hands of the Mongols; Genghis Khan, who was passing the summer in Huan-zhou, sent his adopted son Shigi-khutukhu and two other *noyat* to undertake its inventory, an event which inspires the *Secret History* to recount a tale testifying to the uncompromising honesty of Shigi-khutukhu.[89]

Zhongdu was delivered over to a month of plundering, thousands of inhabitants were massacred and a large part of the city was destroyed by searing fires. Juzjani notes: 'When a few years later Baha ad-Din, leader of a mission from Sultan Muhammad of Khwarazm, approached the capital he saw a white hill and in answer to his query was told by the guide that it consisted of the bones of the massacred inhabitants. At another place the earth was, for a long stretch of the road, greasy from human fat and the air was so polluted that several members of the mission became ill and some died. This was the place, they were told, where on the day the city was stormed 60,000 virgins threw themselves to death from the fortifications in order to escape capture by the Mongols.'[90] Although the story contains serious exaggerations, there can be no doubt that the number of victims in the Zhongdu blood-bath was very high.

The campaign against the Jurchid was begun by the nomads as one of plunder and revenge. The acquisition of slaves, animals and riches rather than of territory was their aim, since fiefs were calculated in households rather than land.[91] Now, influenced by his Khitan and Chinese advisors, Genghis Khan changed his war aims and demanded that the Chin emperor cede the conquered territories. He ordered the emperor to offer as a gift to him all those habitations in Hebei and Shandong which had not yet fallen to the Mongols, to abdicate as emperor and to retain only the title of King of Henan.[92]

When these demands were not met Genghis Khan ordered the commencement of a southern campaign, command of which was given to a Chinese defector, Shi Tianni, whose father had in 1213 joined the Mongols with several thousand men. Tianni, who at his father's request was appointed to command a regiment, took part under Mukali at the siege of the Liaoyang capital and later raised his own army to follow Mukali in further campaigns. Cited by Mukali on many occasions for his services, Tianni died at the early age of thirty-nine. He had been responsible for exterminating a nest of rebels who were acting in collaboration with General Wu Xian, a Chinese who had submitted to the Mongols. Wu Xian, furious when he learned of this event, invited Tianni to a banquet. Despite every warning, the latter accepted. He was killed on his way back from the banquet.[93]

Genghis Khan returned to Mongolia as early as spring 1216.[94] In 1217 Mukali was appointed Viceroy (*guo-wang*) and Supreme Commander in Northern China – with local administration entrusted to Khitans and Chinese, who were responsible for raising auxiliary forces.[95] Genghis had good grounds for concern about the situation at home. He had learned that Kodu,[96] the brother of his arch-enemy Tokto'a-beki of the Merkits, had gathered a following around him and was preparing to attack. In 1217 an expedition was equipped and its commanders, Subodei and Tokuchar, were ordered to destroy the Merkits to the last man. The Merkits were defeated and massacred, even Kodu's youngest son, whom, when he was captured and brought before Jochi, the latter wished to pardon because of his skill in archery. Genghis answered Jochi's appeal thus: 'It is for you that I have conquered so many empires and armies. Why do we require him?' The last of the Merkits was then killed.[97]

The campaign against the Kori-Tumat forest tribes was less successful. Korchi of the Ba'arin, who as a reward for his prophecy in favour of Temuchin had been given the privilege of selecting thirty beautiful maidens from the Tumat tribe,[98] was taken prisoner when he appeared among the Tumat. Genghis thereupon dispatched to the Tumat the Oirat chief Kuduka, who understood the customs of the forest peoples; but he too was made prisoner and, when illness caused Naya'a to withdraw from command, Boroghul was dispatched against the Tumat in the Year of the Ox (1217).[99] The *Secret History* recounts how Boroghul, riding with two others in front of the main troops through a thick wood at dead of night, was captured and killed by Tumat scouts. Boroghul, a member of the Hushin tribe, had been found as a child in the sacked Jurkin camp and presented to Mother Hö'elun. He became Genghis Khan's Cupbearer and High Steward, was given command of part of the imperial bodyguard and then appointed to command a regiment.[100] Genghis Khan was enraged when he learned of Boroghul's death; he wanted to take personal command of the troops which would avenge the deed and only desisted from this intention on the urgent entreaties of Bo'orchu and Mukali. A Dörbet general was selected to lead the punitive expedition, the strictest discipline was ordered and, after prayers had been offered to the Eternal Heaven, the corps set out. The Tumats were taken by surprise while they were feasting and were defeated. Korchi and Kuduka, held prisoners by the chieftainess of the Tumat, were released. Korchi received his thirty beautiful Tumat maidens and Kuduka was presented with Bodokui-tarkhun, the Tumat chieftainess. One hundred Tumats were sacrificed to Boroghul's corpse. Genghis himself accepted responsibility for the children of the dead Boroghul. Rashid ad-Din reports his words: 'They must not grieve; I will care for them'; he also relates that Genghis Khan did later show them great favours and always took an interest in them.[101]

On the occasion of the campaign against the Tumats, the Kirghiz declined to make auxiliary troops available to the Mongols. This decided Genghis Khan to put an end to the independence of the forest peoples; his son, Jochi, was entrusted with this task.[102] Kuduka-beki of the Oirats was, according to the *Secret History*, the first to submit and he then guided the Mongols to his 10,000 Oirats, who were compelled to submit at Shikshit. When Jochi had subjugated the Oirat, Buriat and other forest peoples he reached the 10,000 Kirghiz and these too came to submit, their chiefs bringing white falcons, white stallions and black sables as gifts. Accompanied by the Oirat and Kirghiz chiefs Jochi returned home. Kuduka-beki was rewarded for his services to the Mongols with royal Mongol princesses for his sons. Jochi was praised by his father: 'You, the eldest of my sons, have now left home and have made a name for yourself. You have returned home from the subjugation of the 'fortunate'[103] forest peoples without causing injury or over-exhaustion to man or horse. I give these peoples to you!'[104]

The expedition against Kuchlug

Only one of Genghis Khan's enemies was still alive – Kuchlug, son of Tayang-khan of the Naimans. After the defeat on the Irtysch River he had succeeded in fleeing from Genghis Khan's implacable revenge and taken refuge with the *Gurkhan* of Kara-Khitai, whose favour and trust he succeeded in winning. Kuchlug married one of the daughters of the *Gurkhan* and under her influence he abjured his Christian faith and became a Buddhist convert. As his influence increased at the Kara-Khitan court, so Kuchlug's ambition grew and he extracted from the elderly *Gurkhan* permission to gather together his fellow Naiman tribes-men who were scattered throughout Mongolia.

Kuchlug's ambitious plans received support from Sultan Muhammad of Khwarazm, who paid tribute to Kara-Khitai. The sultan, who had expanded his empire by the conquest of the sultanates of Ghur and Ghazna, Khorasan, Iraq and part of Turkestan, was no longer willing to acknowledge the suzerainty of and pay tribute to Kara-Khitai. A secret agreement was reached between Kuchlug and Muhammad to make a simultaneous attack on the *Gurkhan* from east and west. Kuchlug was, in fact, defeated, but the sultan dealt the Kara-Khitan army a crushing defeat and Kuchlug exploited this situation to make the *Gurkhan* his prisoner and to take possession of that part of Turkestan which he had ruled. The Buddhist neophyte Kuchlug attracted the hatred of the Islamic population. He forbade public religious services, and the Imam of Khotan, who refused to abjure Islam, was held in chains, naked, hungry and thirsty for several days before being crucified on the gates of the Madrasa.[105]

Kuchlug's activities in Kara-Khitai did not escape the attention of Genghis Khan, who decided to mount a campaign against him. Personal desire for vengeance – Kuchlug had killed the son of Arslan-khan of the Karluk, who had been married to a daughter of Jochi[106] – was not Genghis' sole motivation. Kuchlug had gathered Naiman tribesmen around him to form an army, was a potential threat to the security of the Mongol empire and had to be defeated. In 1218 a Mongol corps of 20,000 men under the command of Jebe appeared before Kashgar, where Kuchlug was at that time. Jebe proclaimed Genghis Khan's precept that every religion should be respected and that each should follow the religion of his forefathers. The local population, persecuted for their religion and brought to despair by the high taxes exacted from them, saw the Mongols as liberators from the hated rule of the Buddhist Kuchlug. Rebellion broke out. Kuchlug was forced to flee but was captured and killed.[107]

Juvaini and Rashid ad-Din both depict the campaign against Kuchlug as a consequence of the massacre of the Mongol caravan at Otrar – but that massacre did not take place until 1219. An-Nasawi maintains that the decision to mount an expedition against Kuchlug was taken earlier and that Genghis Khan despatched his son Jochi against Kuchlug as soon as he learned that the latter had taken control of the areas of Kashgar and Balaghasun. According to Tu Ji, the order for the expedition was given as early as 1216.[108]

War with Sultan Muhammad of Khwarazm

The expedition against Kuchlug brought the Mongols into contact with the troops of the Sultan of Khwarazm but Genghis was at that time anxious to avoid conflict with the ruler of the strongest military power in Asia. Jochi, who was in supreme command of the Mongol forces, therefore sent a message to Sultan Muhammad, stressing that he had not come with hostile intentions and that he was prepared to hand over to the sultan the plunder which the army had taken. Jochi added that his father had instructed him to engage in no hostile activities against the sultan's troops and to make no proclamations which might offend the sultan.[109]

The sultan harboured less peaceful intentions towards Genghis Khan, whose victories in China had caused a stir in Inner Asia. According to Juzjani, when the sultan heard of these victories he sent ambassadors to Genghis Khan to discover whether the rumours were true and to gather details of the Mongol military strength. The envoys were received in friendly fashion by Genghis Khan at his military camp in China. Interested in opening trade relations with Inner Asia, Genghis requested the envoys to inform the sultan that he regarded the sultan as the ruler of the West, just as Genghis was ruler of the East; that he hoped for peace between them and that the merchants of one country would be free to visit and trade in the other. The sultan, however, regarded Genghis Khan as a rival. Rashid maintains that as early as 1205 Muhammad had decided to attack China; Juzjani remarks that it was the sultan's intention to conquer the Chin empire.[110]

Muhammad's response to Jochi's message was: 'Even if Genghis Khan has instructed you not to wage war against me, Allah, the All-Powerful, has ordered me to fight you and has promised me good fortune in the struggle. There is for me no difference between yourself, the *Gurkhan* and Kuchlug-khan; you are all idolaters. Let there then be war in which swords are broken and spears are shattered.' The ensuing battle lasted all day. During the night the Mongols retreated but, in the face of an enemy twice their strength, they had shown themselves to be serious opponents.[111]

Unlike the sultan, however, the major merchants of Inner Asia and the feudal leaders linked with them had a strong interest in trading with the Mongols. As soon as the news of the fall of Zhongdu was received three Bokharan merchants provisioned a caravan and set out for Genghis Khan's main camp. Their goods were purchased at generous prices and when they prepared to return home Genghis Khan instructed the princes, princesses and dignitaries to provide personnel who would take goods back to the Khwarazm-shah. At the same time three envoys were sent with a message for the sultan, in which Genghis Khan informed him of the capitulation of North China and offered the commencement of trading relations 'on which the welfare of the world depends'.[112]

The wording of Genghis Khan's message is handed down in differing versions in our sources. Juzjani's version runs: 'I am master of the lands of the rising sun while you rule those of the setting sun. Let us conclude a firm treaty of friendship and peace. Merchants and their caravans should come and go in both directions, carrying the valuable products and ordinary goods from my land to yours, just as they do from your land to mine.'

Rashid ad-Din offers: 'Now that the frontier lands between us have been purged of the enemy and completely conquered and subjugated and neighbourly relations established between us, reason and magnanimity demand that we move along the road of peaceful accord. We should undertake to assist and support each other in times of need and to ensure the security of the caravan routes from disastrous incidents in order that merchants, on whose flourishing trade the welfare of the world depends, may move freely hither and thither . . .' Nasawi provides the following: '. . . you well know that . . . my land is so rich in treasures that it is unnecessary to seek them elsewhere. If you will ease the way for merchants from both sides it will be for the good of all and to our mutual advantage.'[113]

Genghis Khan's peaceful intentions were regarded with suspicion and his offer as deception. The twentieth-century Russian historian Petrushevski assumes that, as early as the campaign in China, Genghis Khan had already planned the conquest of Inner and West Asia, even of Eastern Europe(!); but the extrapolation of such a predetermined plan from later events is not really convincing. Genghis Khan's actions were determined by the prevailing political and military alignments. The Mongol campaign against Kuchlug was not directed against the Khwarazm-shah – Kuchlug had to be destroyed in order to prevent a Naiman revolt; and the immediate cause of the raid by Jebe and Subodei into southern Russia was the assistance against the Mongols which Sultan Muhammad received from the Kipchaks. A clash would probably have taken place between Genghis and Muhammad at a later date but, at the time hostilities began, Genghis was clearly provoked by the sultan.[114] I do not believe that Genghis Khan was at this point planning war against the sultan. His report of the subjugation of North China was not in accord with the facts. The Jurchid were fighting back bitterly and had retaken a large number of cities; a force of some 60,000 men[115] under Mukali was locked in a long struggle in North China and a second contingent had to remain in the Mongol homeland to guard against any uprisings by the recently conquered tribes.

Genghis Khan's message to Sultan Muhammad offers no evidence of any demand that the latter submit to Genghis – although, according to an-Nasawi's biography of Jalal ad-Din, Muhammad's son, the message is said to have included the phrase: 'You are the best loved of my sons.' In the diplomatic language of those days such a phrase did express a claim of suzerainty but, significantly, the ominous phrase is not reported by either Juvaini or Juzjani. Buniyatov reports that Sultan Muhammad was outraged by Genghis' presumption. He summoned one of Genghis' envoys, a Khwarazmian, appealed to his patriotism and demanded to know whether Genghis had indeed conquered North China. The envoy's confirmation of this fact led Sultan Muhammad to accept Genghis Khan's peace offer but, as later events indicate, he was determined on war and sought only to gain a breathing space during which he strengthened the defences of Samarkand and took measures to concentrate his troops before provoking hostilities.[116]

In the same year, 1218, a Mongol trading caravan arrived in Otrar. The governor of the city, Inal-khan (a cousin of the sultan's mother, Terken-khatun),[117] reported to the sultan that the merchants sent by Genghis Khan were involved in espionage and were attempting to spread panic among the population. This report would be accurate, but the accusation could be made against most foreign caravans. It was generally known that merchants acted as spies and brought back from their distant travels valuable information about the situation in a country, the disposition of troops, the morale of the population and the party factions at court. It was also not unusual for such merchants to be involved in propaganda. Those sent by Genghis Khan would have spread stories about the power of the Mongol leader and the invincibility of his armies; they would have described the fearful fate which awaited those who resisted him, but also sung the praises of his generosity and his tolerance in religious matters.[118]

Juzjani attributes Inal's action to greed for the treasures brought by the caravan; this view is supported by an-Nasawi, who describes Inal-khan's report as a slander. Juvaini and Rashid ad-Din both attribute the action to the fact that Inal was insulted by the presumption and arrogance shown towards him by an Indian member of the caravan. Neither of these motives would, however, have emboldened Inal-khan to such a serious breach of generally accepted international custom had he not had orders from the sultan, or at least his tacit agreement. The Islamic chroniclers are unanimous in ascribing blame for the blood-bath to Muhammad. Juvaini and Rashid maintain that the sultan ordered the massacre of the merchants, Juzjani and an-Nasawi that the governor sought the sultan's permission.[119]

In the face of this outrageous provocation Genghis decided that war was inevitable, but he made one last attempt to prevent its immediate outbreak, sending envoys to the sultan with a demand that the governor be handed over to him. 'You have, by signing our accord, pledged youself to protect the merchants and not to harm them; but you have acted faithlessly and broken your word. Disloyalty is disgraceful, especially disgraceful in the case of a sultan of Islam. If, however, you maintain that Inal-khan's deed was not carried out at your behest, then hand Inal-khan over to me so that we may punish him for his crime, thus reassuring the masses and preventing the spilling of blood. Otherwise, it is war . . .'[120]

Sultan Muhammad had, as early as the encounter with Jebe, shown his determination to fight. He had no intention of allowing the Mongols to penetrate into his sphere of influence and he regarded the rise of Genghis Khan to the leadership of the nomad peoples of Central Asia as a potential danger to the security of his realm. He also feared that if he handed over Inal-khan such an act would alienate his mother and the Turkic feudal leaders loyal to her. He ordered Genghis' envoys to be killed. 'How much Muslim blood was shed because of this murder!' laments Nasawi.

The killing of an envoy has been a *casus belli* among all peoples at all times. Genghis was outraged by the action of the sultan: 'The Khwarazm-shah is no king, he is a bandit!' he exclaimed. 'If he were a king he would not have killed my merchants and my envoys who went to Otrar. Kings do not kill envoys!' Juvaini reports that when Genghis learned of the massacre he climbed to the top of a hill, bared his head, raised his face to Heaven and prayed to Heaven for three days: 'I was not the instigator of these tribulations. Grant me the strength to exact vengeance!'[121] Genghis Khan made his typically careful preparations for the now inevitable war.

Genghis' opponent – the Khwarazm-shah as he was traditionally known outside his empire, although he had taken the title, Sultan, Son of the Sultan[122] – was from a Turkic but Iranized family and was recognized as one of the most powerful rulers in Asia. His empire stretched from the Aral Sea in the North to the Persian Gulf in the South, from the Pamirs in the East to the

Zagros Mountains in the West, encompassing the greatest part of Inner Asia, Afghanistan and the whole of Iran. It had only recently become a political unit and was heterogeneous, the nomadic Turks and the sedentary Iranians hostile to each other. 'We are Ghurs, you are Turks and we can never live together', the emirs of the Ghurs told the Khwarazm-shah's governor.[123]

There were also marked differences among the ruling class. Muhammad was a Turkmen, his mother a Turk. Juzjani says she was the daughter of the Kipchak khan, Akran; an-Nasawi maintains that she belonged to the Baya'ut clan of the Yämäk. Juvaini comments that she was a cruel and violent woman, responsible for the downfall of the dynasty; Nasawi speaks of her sense of justice and her impartiality. Both sources, however, stress the authority of the Queen Mother over Sultan Muhammad. Terken-khatun had her own court, her own officials and controlled apanages and fiefs. Juvaini comments that her power extended over the sultan, his finances and his senior officers and officials, while Nasawi explains that if contradictory orders were issued by her and by the sultan, action was always taken on the most recently dated instruction.[124] Terken-khatun, who supported her kinsmen and the nomadic Kipchaks, nursed such a bitter hatred against Jalal ad-Din and his mother that she refused to flee when captured by the Mongols. 'How could I lower myself to be dependent upon the mercy of Ai Chichen [the mother of Jalal ad-Din] . . . even imprisonment by Genghis Khan and my present humiliation and shame are better than that', she exclaimed.[125]

The centralized policies which the sultan attempted to introduce had also caused discontent among his feudal lords, many of whom had been deposed, imprisoned or killed. There were twenty-two feudal lords in prison in Urgench at the beginning of the war with the Mongols; Badr ad-Din al-'Amid, who submitted to Genghis Khan after the fall of Otrar, declared: 'The Khan should know that the sultan is, in my eyes, the most hated creature of Allah, because he has destroyed many of my relatives. If I were in a position to take vengeance on him I would do so, even if it cost me my life.'[126] The mass of the people suffered most under Muhammad's rule, the violence and the lawlessness of the tax farmers driving the heavily taxed peasants and citizens to desperate acts of resistance. In addition, Sultan Muhammad had, through his quarrel with the Caliph of Baghdad – the Caliph, it is alleged, even sent an envoy to Genghis Khan urging him to attack Muhammad – offended the religious sensibilities of the Faithful and had estranged a section of their religious leaders. Genghis Khan was fully informed by his Islamic advisors of the situation in Khwarazm. He was well aware that Muhammad could not proclaim the Holy War which would have united his people.[127]

Before taking the field Genghis Khan summoned a Khuriltai at which he proclaimed new laws and promulgated orders for the prosecution of the war. At the instigation of his favourite wife, Yisui, according to the *Secret History*, Genghis also decided the question of the succession in the event of his death.[128]

The nomination of a successor presented Genghis Khan with a tricky dilemma. The Mongols had no dynastic tradition. According to accepted nomad custom the *ulus* belonged to the tribe and this concept enabled an uncle or brother of a deceased khan to lay claim to the succession as senior member of the clan. However, the establishment of the patriarchal family system strengthened the tendency to nominate a son as heir to the throne.[129] The eldest son received the right to claim the succession, but the youngest son who, according to family law, was heir to his father's *ordo*, wives and servants (*nutuk*) was in a privileged position to advance a justifiable claim to succeed his father as leader. Thus, after the death of Ögödei, Da'aritai-otchigin attempted to secure the succession and Arig-böke, the younger son of Tolui, was elected Kha'an by the Mongols after the death of his brother, Möngke. Juvaini maintains: 'according to the laws and customs of the Mongols the position of the father was transferred to the youngest son of his senior wife . . . but it was Genghis Khan's order that he should be succeeded by Ögödei'. This statement is challenged by Ayalon, who ascribes it to the court historian's desire to strengthen the legitimacy of the Il-khan dynasty and argues that the Mongols did not adhere to the principle of ultimogeniture.[130]

Antagonism between the systems of primo- and ultimogeniture found clear expression within the Golden Horde and disputes over succession had serious consequences in all four Mongol khanates;[131] even during the Yuan dynasty a brother or nephew was considered to have greater rights of succession than a son.[132] In China itself, under the influence of the Chinese system, the trend towards primogeniture gradually became established and on the occasion of one Yuan succession struggle a Minister at Court commented: 'As Shizu's [Khubilai's] example teaches, younger sons have no claim to the succession.'[133] The principle of primogeniture never, however, became fully effective among the Mongols because the instability of the tribal groupings meant that a weak son, or one still a minor, could not be elected khan. When all was said and done the wish of the father and, in practice, the influence of the mother would be no less decisive. Thus Ambakai was elected khan by the wish of Kabul-khan, although the latter had seven sons of his own; Guyuk, Möngke and Temur owed their election to their mothers.[134]

Genghis had struggled to achieve his supreme position on behalf of his family and was determined to hand it on to his descendants. Jochi, his first-born, was to succeed him. But Jochi suffered from the suspicion of illegitimacy and scarcely had Genghis called on Jochi to speak when Chaghatai burst out: 'When you say, "Speak Jochi", do you mean to declare him your successor? How could we allow ourselves to be ruled by that Merkit bastard?' This resulted in a hand-to-hand struggle between the two brothers and Genghis Khan sat silent while they grappled with each other, until Kököchös the Ba'arin was able to quieten the fighting cocks.[135] Chaghatai then put forward a compromise. Turning to Genghis Khan he said: 'Ögödei is a peaceful man. We want to elect Ögödei.' Genghis did not conceal his displeasure. 'Is Jochi not the eldest of my sons?' he demanded. 'You shall talk of him in such terms no more'; and he called on Jochi to give his opinion on Chaghatai's proposal.

Genghis Khan could scarcely have found it easy to appoint Ögödei as his successor, fearing that after his death it would lead to war between the brothers; fratricidal war was indeed only prevented after the death of Ögödei by the premature demise of Guyuk. Ögödei is described as a good-tempered, conciliatory and generous person, but he lacked his father's strength of will. He was also addicted to drink and pleasure and was often taken to task by his father on these counts. Juvaini and Rashid both relate the following anecdote which indicates that, when in his cups, Ögödei could be violent and callous.

There were, it is said, rumours that the girls of one clan were to be forced into marriage, whereupon these girls were all immediately betrothed or married to their own kinsmen. When Ögödei

14 Ögödei Kha'an.

heard of this he ordered that all girls over the age of seven should
be brought together and that wives of less than one year should
be taken from their husbands. Of the 4,000 girls thus assembled
the daughters of the emirs were singled out and those present
were ordered to consummate marriage with them on the spot, an

act which caused the death of two girls. (Rashid simply states that they fled.) Of the remainder, those who appeared worthy were selected for the harem; others were distributed among the keepers of the leopards and wild animals (Rashid: beaters and falconers) or among the palace servants, while some were sent to the brothel or the diplomatic rest-house to serve travellers. The remainder could be carried off by those present, Mongol and Muslim alike. According to Rashid ad-Din, the fathers, brothers, husbands and relatives of these young girls watched this happen without having the courage or the opportunity to oppose it.[136]

Rashid ad-Din mentions that Genghis vacillated between Ögödei and Tolui in the matter of nominating a successor.[137] Tolui was the youngest of his sons, constantly in Genghis' company, and he had shown his military prowess during the campaign in China. He seems, however, to have been a cruel person who, during the western campaign, is reported to have sat on a throne and watched the massacre of prisoners. Tolui may also not have offered the same guarantee of preserving the old Mongol traditions which Genghis could expect from Ögödei – Tolui's wife, the clever and energetic Kerait princess, Sorkaktani, herself a Nestorian Christian but a friend of all religions, even contributed to the support of Islam.[138]

Kirakos of Gandzak reports that, just before his death, Genghis characterized his sons as follows: 'Chaghatai is warlike and loves the army, but he is arrogant; . . . Tolui is also a victorious warrior, but he is mean; . . . Ögödei, however, has from childhood been gifted and generous.'[139] Il-khan Ghazan, referring to Genghis' detestation of meanness, exclaimed: 'It would be splendid if one were always in a position [to make gifts of money]. Of what use is a ruler who can do this one day but not another?'[140] The nomads laid a not surprising emphasis on generosity as an important characteristic of a ruler – a personal quality to which Genghis Khan owed his rise to supremacy in no small degree. In this respect Ögödei completely fulfilled his father's expectations. After his election as Kha'an, Ögödei distributed all the valuables held in the imperial treasury. Guyuk Kha'an later attempted to exceed even his father's reputation for generosity.[141]

The question of the succession having been decided in favour of Ögödei, Genghis strengthened his army with auxiliary troops from the Han and Khitan subject peoples of China and with contingents placed at his disposal by the *idikut* of the Uighurs, the ruler of the Karluk and the king of Almalik.[142] The Mongolian-Turkic forces then set out on the western campaign. Summer 1219 was spent on the Irtysch, where Genghis arranged large-scale battues which served as army manoeuvres and provided provisions for the army. In autumn of that year he approached the Otrar area.

With the same skill he had shown in the campaign against the Jurchid, Genghis sought to exploit to his advantage rivalries among the upper ranks of the Khwarazmians, to fan the flames of mistrust and dissension among them, and to paralyse the will to resistance among the population through proclamations and propaganda. Before the Mongols attacked a city Genghis' 'Order to the emirs, the leading citizens and the multitude of ordinary people' was proclaimed. In this the Conqueror announced that God had granted him all the Earth from sunrise to sunset. 'He who therefore submits to Us will receive mercy for himself, women, children and possessions; but he who does not submit will, together with women, children and relatives, be destroyed.' When Jebe, for example, invested the city of Nishapur he called on the Khwarazmian emirs to capitulate, and as a guaranty that the promise would be honoured he sent them a seal (*al-tamgha*) and a copy of Genghis' proclamation.[143]

Buniyatov explains how Genghis dispatched the chamberlain Danishmand – who was also sent to demand the capitulation of Zarnuk – to Terken-khatun, the mother of the sultan, with the following message. 'You know how dishonourably your son has dealt with your rights. I am now, with the consent of several of his emirs, taking the field against him, but I shall not attack your possessions. If you accept this offer, send someone to me who will reassure you [that you can rely upon my word] and we will then cede to you Khwarazm, Khorasan and the parts of those [territories] which lie on this side of the Amu-darya,' Buniyatov also reports that, in order to increase the Khwarazm-shah's suspicions of his mother's Turkish troops Genghis, at the suggestion of the defector Badr ad-Din al-'Amid – whose father, uncle and several cousins had been executed, probably as members of the religious faction opposed to the sultan – circulated false letters in which Terken-khatun's emirs appeared to offer their services to Genghis Khan and expressed their readiness to carry out his orders. These letters were fed to the Khwarazm-shah by a member of Genghis' retinue masquerading as a defector.[144]

These machinations did not fail to have the desired effect. Muhammad's tactics, castigated by his son Jalal ad-Din as those of a cowardly wretch,[145] were dictated by mistrust of his feudal lords and his military commanders. He feared to entrust his forces to a single commander lest, if victorious, such a commander might turn against him. The numerically superior Khwarazmian forces were thus never committed to a pitched battle; the troops were spread out between the cities and were defeated one by one. Muhammad put dynastic before national interests. He himself did not take part in the battles, fleeing as soon as the Mongols approached. In these conditions resistance was sporadic and, as in Sistan, it was often the beleaguered citizens who offered the stiffest resistance.[146]

Genghis' army may have been numerically inferior but its discipline was draconian and it was commanded by leaders who were unquestioningly loyal to him. In February 1220 Otrar, whose governor could expect no mercy from the Mongols, fell after a bitter five-month siege. Qaracha, sent by the sultan with 50,000 men to defend Otrar, slipped out of the city at night but was captured by the Mongols and, on the orders of Genghis' sons, who commanded the siege, was executed as a traitor to his ruler. Inal-khan barricaded himself with 20,000 troops in the inner citadel; the battle lasted for another month until most of the defenders had been killed and Inal, short of weapons, was forced to shower the attacking Mongols with roof tiles.[147] He was finally captured and executed, but it is likely that Nasawi's story of his agonizing death – Genghis is said to have ordered molten silver to be poured into his ears and eyes – is a fabrication. Genghis and Tolui did not wait for the fall of the city but moved on with the main Mongol army across the Kizil Kum desert towards Bokhara, leaving Chaghatai and Ögödei in command of the besieging forces at Otrar.[148]

The city of Bokhara had been the scene of social struggle when, under the leadership of a craftsman, Sanjar, the population had rebelled against the feudal-clerical government which was supported by the civic patricians. Sultan Muhammad had then come to the assistance of the aristocratic party and annexed the city to the Khwarazmian empire in 1207.[149] On the approach of the Mongols the main garrison of 12–20,000 men evacuated the city.[150] 500 Turkish troops remained behind, barricaded into the citadel. The following day (in February or March 1220) the population surrendered.[151] They were driven out of the city and the men were forced into *hashar* service, compelled to accompany the Mongol army and play the role of cannon-fodder at future sieges. Bokhara was plundered and, during this episode, fire broke out and destroyed the city. Juvaini maintains that the city was set alight on the orders of Genghis Khan. The city, however, consisted of closely packed wooden houses and it would have been difficult to avoid fire during the sacking. Barthold comments that the fire cannot be attributed to an order by Genghis but must have broken out accidentally. One can also give little credence to Juvaini's story of the desecration of the mosques and the holy books of Islam. Such a deed would have been a direct contradiction of Genghis' order to respect all religions, and Genghis was too astute a statesman to arouse the religious fanaticism of the Muslims.[152]

The treatment of the population of Bokhara can be taken as a model. If, however, a town put up stiff resistance and caused the Mongols heavy losses, then after the capture of the town the male inhabitants were massacred, except for craftsmen who, like the women, were distributed among the victors and dragged away to slavery. This was, for example, the Mongol practice at Urgench, whose population had put up a bitter struggle. On the other hand, as Rashid comments, towns which capitulated were left undamaged; Juzjani maintains that, on the orders of Genghis Khan, no towns in Khorasan were damaged except in the Herat area.[153]

The fall of Bokhara had a psychological effect which brought into the open the tensions within the Khwarazmian empire. Sultan Muhammad's strategic plan of spreading his troops among the cities – a tactic strongly criticized by Jalal ad-Din – proved to be a disastrous mistake since, thanks to the Chinese and Muslim siege experts in Genghis Khan's armies, cities no longer proved an insuperable obstacle for the Mongolian cavalry, which was now also supplemented by infantry raised from the occupied territories.

Genghis Khan moved on from Bokhara to Samarkand. This rich and flourishing trading centre which, but for the opposition of his mother, Muhammad had intended to make his residence, was strongly fortified. A complete army of Turks and Tadzhiks had

15   *The Mongols' captives led away.*

been allocated to its defence – Juvaini puts the garrison at
110,000 men, 60,000 élite Turkish troops and 50,000
Tajiks – and it was generally assumed that the city could hold out
for years against any attack.[154] Yet the influential merchant
princes and the opposition clerics had common interests with
Genghis and were unwilling to fight him. After a sortie, attempted by the Turkish troops[155] with the use of elephants, had
been dealt with by the standard Mongol tactic of coaxing them
into an ambush, a delegation of senior clerics came to Genghis
Khan and offered to surrender the city to him. They and 50,000
of their followers were guaranteed their lives and protection – if
this figure is even approximately accurate it indicates that a large
number of citizens declared themselves to be mosque functionaries
in order to avail themselves of the protection of the clergy. The
inhabitants were driven out of the city, 300 craftsmen were
distributed among the princes, princesses and military commanders, the remainder were allowed to return to the city and a fine of
200,000 dinars was imposed on them. Five days later the
remaining 30,000 Kangli-Turks of the garrison surrendered and
were massacred.[156]

According to Juzjani the fall of Samarkand took place on 19
March 1220, after a ten-day siege. Juvaini places the event in
May/June, but this would suggest that Genghis had taken two
months for his march from Bokhara and, as Boyle comments, this
date is contradicted by Juvaini's statement that Genghis spent

the spring in the neighbourhood of Samarkand. Nor can it be reconciled with Juvaini's assertion that Sultan Muhammad set off for Iraq on 12 March.

The fall of Samarkand decided the outcome of the war. Pursued by Jebe and Subodei, Sultan Muhammad fled from one area to another, and wherever he went he called on the populace to gather their valuables and flee, since opposition to the Mongols was pointless.[157] Terken-khatun, after receiving the message from Genghis Khan, ordered the execution of all the feudal lords, their sons and officials held hostage at her court – twenty-two persons in all.[158] She then fled to one of the most remote fortresses in Mazandaran where, four months later, a shortage of water supplies compelled her to surrender to the Mongols. The sultan's children were killed, the ladies of the harem were distributed among the victors and Terken-khatun was taken into the *ordo* of Genghis Khan, then moved to Mongolia, where she lived for many years in humiliating conditions.[159] The sultan himself fled from his pursuers to die of pneumonia in January 1221 on a small island in the south-eastern reaches of the Caspian Sea.[160]

The war did not end with the death of the Khwarazm-shah. Before his death he altered his previous instructions and nominated Jalal ad-Din as his successor. Jalal was a bold, energetic but cruel person. After the flight of Terken-khatun a struggle for power broke out among the feudal lords. The Turkish feudal leaders were opposed to Jalal ad-Din, who left Khwarazm, withdrawing through Khorasan to Afghanistan in order to organize resistance there against the Mongols. At Parwan he was able to defeat a unit of the Mongol army commanded by Shigi-khutukhu, the first Mongol defeat of the whole campaign. Genghis was distressed by his adopted son's defeat, but did not allow his feelings to show, 'Khutukhu has always been accustomed to win battles and has never come face to face with the cruel blows of fate. Now that he has experienced these, he will be more careful, his experience will be greater and he will have a better idea what war is about.'[161]

Genghis set out in pursuit of Jalal ad-Din, leaving command of the Mongol forces in Khwarazm to his sons. Juvaini suggests that only Chaghatai and Ögödei were present but Rashid names all three elder sons, and the evidence, including the quarrel between the three sons during the siege of Urgench and the story about withholding Genghis' share of the spoils, indicates that Jochi did take part in the campaign.[162] Forced marches brought Genghis to the Indus as Jalal was preparing to cross it. Encircled by Mongol troops, Jalal was forced to fight. His army was destroyed but Jalal was able to save himself by forcing his horse into the water and reaching the far bank. The Mongols wanted to pursue him but Genghis held them back, expressing his astonishment at the daring of his opponent thus: 'A father should only have sons like this!'[163] Jalal ad-Din did not give up the struggle. He continued fighting for years until he was finally murdered by a Kurd in 1231.

The Mongols had conquered the greater part of the Khwarazm-shah's empire but had not fully subjugated it. Nevertheless when he received news of a Tangut rebellion Genghis Khan decided to return home. Initially he intended to return via India and sent messengers to Sultan Il-Tutmish in Delhi seeking free passage. But the natural obstacles, the high mountains covered with eternal snows and thick impenetrable forests, the climatic conditions, ignorance of the routes – according to Juvaini Genghis found his way barred and turned back – and disease within the ranks of his army, caused Genghis to hesitate. Again according to Juvaini, Genghis constantly used a sheep's shoulder-blade to consult the oracle, but received no favourable replies.[164] There were also unfavourable omens. Chinese sources report that a unicorn appeared and, in human speech, warned the Mongol vanguard: 'Your ruler must turn back home immediately.' This encounter with a beast (rhinoceros?) completely unknown to the Mongols must have demoralized the vanguard and increased the army's unwillingness to advance; the realization of the foolhardiness of the adventure was, however, decisive. Genghis turned back towards Peshawar.[165]

The world conqueror and the Taoist monk

In spring 1222 Genghis was encamped in the southern Hindu Kush, where he also spent the summer, and it was there that he held his meetings with the Taoist sage, allegedly 300 years old, and called Changchun ('Eternal spring') of whose existence Genghis had previously learned.[166] Genghis was now no longer young, and his health had suffered from the exertions of the western campaign; the words of his wife, Yisui, before he set out on the campaign had reminded him that he was mortal. His work was not complete, he feared death and remembered the aged Taoist, who appeared to possess the secret of longevity. Genghis despatched Liu Zhonglu and Ja'far with a letter to the sage, commanding his presence. The patriarch was not 300 years old, but he was born in 1148 and, already over 70 when he received Genghis' message, shrank from the exertions of the long trip. Genghis, however, insisted and the patriarch set out. After a long and exhausting journey Changchun reached Samarkand on 3 December 1221, where he received a letter bidding him travel on to Genghis' camp in the Hindu Kush.[167] Their first meeting took place in spring 1222, when, to Genghis' initial query about the elixir of life, Changchun replied that, although there were medicines to protect life, there was none which could prolong it.[168] Genghis did not allow himself to show his disappointment. He treated the patriarch with the greatest respect and kindness and they met on several occasions.

The two men were from totally different worlds – the energetic Genghis who sought life's fulfilment in warfare and conquest; the recluse, Changchun, whose ideal was passivity. Despite the contrast Changchun understood how to gain Genghis' trust and friendship. Genghis listened patiently to the monk's teachings on how to rule the people, the reproaches regarding Mongol morality and customs, the appeals for sexual moderation and the exhortations to give up hunting; and he attached such importance to Changchun's words that he had them written down. He believed in the monk's magical ability and declared to the assembled princes and dignitaries: 'The Han honour the Holy Eternal One just as you honour Heaven. I am more than ever convinced that he is indeed a Man of Heaven.'[169]

Genghis was reluctant to permit the old man to return to China but Changchun insisted. On his departure Changchun was given a charter which ensured him and his pupils of protection and freedom from taxes.[170] Genghis did not forget the Taoist monk. He dispatched messengers to follow him, bearing letters enquiring after his health and whether he had sufficient provisions and post horses – and reminding Changchun to pray constantly for Genghis' long life. Following Changchun's return to China in 1223 Genghis entrusted him with the administration of all monks throughout the empire – a further expression of favour by

16   *Genghis Khan's camp.*

Genghis towards Changchun which was to be aggressively exploited by the Taoists against the Buddhists.[171]

The death of Jochi

Genghis met with his sons Chaghatai and Ögödei in spring 1223, but Jochi remained in Khorasan. There had been a quarrel between Jochi and his brothers during the siege of Urgench. That city belonged to the territory which Genghis had allocated as a fief to Jochi and the latter attempted to protect the city from destruction, promising the population that if they surrendered without fighting it would not be destroyed; as evidence of his good intentions he allowed no plundering by his troops.[172] Juzjani asserts that Jochi turned not only against his brothers but also against Genghis Khan's conduct of the war and alleges that Jochi even intended to kill his father. 'Genghis Khan is mad to have massacred so many people and laid waste so many lands', Jochi is supposed to have exclaimed. 'I would be doing a service if I killed my father when he is hunting, made an alliance with Sultan Muhammad, brought this land to life and gave assistance and support to the Muslims.'[173] When Genghis was informed by Chaghatai of these plans he gave orders that Jochi should be secretly poisoned.

The words attributed to Jochi must be completely fictitious since Sultan Muhammad was no longer alive in 1223; but the disagreement between Jochi and Genghis Khan is undoubtedly historically true. Rashid ad-Din's version of the disagreement is that, after his return home. Genghis sent for Jochi. When the latter refused to obey Genghis sent Chaghatai and Ögödei against him but, before it came to actual hostilities, news was received of Jochi's death.[174] It is accepted fact that Jochi showed a tendency towards independence but it is unlikely that, at age forty, he died a natural death and Genghis cannot escape suspicion of having been the instigator of that death. Genghis had every reason to fear that his own death would lead to armed conflict between Jochi and Chaghatai. If Genghis was indeed responsible for Jochi's death, he was not motivated by personal feelings but by political considerations, concern for the future unity of the empire.

The return to Mongolia

Before beginning the next stage of the march homewards Genghis Khan made arrangements for the administration of the conquered lands. He received a report on the significance and state of the towns from Mahmud Yalavach al-Khwarazmi, one of the ambassadors originally sent by Genghis to the Khwarazm-shah.[175] Yalavach was to play a very important role in the administration of the empire under Genghis and his successors. Appointed *basqaq* of Ghazna by Genghis, while his son Mas'ud was at the same time appointed to administer other cities, father and son were later, because they were the Muslims with the best understanding of the management of cities, appointed by Ögödei to administer the eastern and western areas of the empire respectively. Guyuk later appointed Yalavach to administer the Khitans, Transoxania, Turkestan and other areas previously administered by his son, and Möngke adopted the taxation system which Yalavach introduced in Transoxania.[176]

Darughachi,[177] personal respresentatives of the Khan, provided with a Seal of Office and full plenipotentiary powers in their area, were installed in the cities. They were responsible for collecting taxes, levying troops from among the local populace, organizing the courier service, conducting the census and dispatching tribute to the court.[178] Equally important was their responsibility for the supervision and control of local feudal lords and officials.

Attempts have been made to equate, on etymological grounds, *darughachi* with *basqaq*,[179] but this does not appear to accord with the fact that, in the official nomenclature of the Golden Horde and in Iran, *darughachi* and *basqaq* are listed separately, the *basqaq* being subordinated to the *darughachi*.[180] This subordinate ranking of the *basqaq* is explained, not on the basis of official functions, but rather because the *darughachi* were Mongols – or persons regarded as equivalent to Mongols – while the *basqaq* were local officials. Genghis himself held a very charitable view of the concept 'Mongol'. When Ila Liuge, widow of the Khitan leader, begged him to release the son of the dead Khitan and accept the son of a minor wife into his service, Genghis replied: 'But Xiedu has now become a Mongol. He accompanied me on the western campaign and has rendered great services.' The Yuan Kha'ans were less tolerant in this respect and in the fourteenth century instructions were issued that non-Mongols who filled such posts using adopted Mongol names were to be stripped of their appointments.[181]

The first *darughachi* were probably installed in 1211 when the *Idikut* of the Uighurs and the King of Almalik recognized Genghis Khan's suzerainty. When the Taoist Changchun arrived in Almalik at the end of September 1221 he was greeted by the King of the Basurman (Muslims) and the *darughachi* of that city, and then at Samarkand by the governor (*darughachi*), Ila Ahai. In

China the Khitan Shimo Yesen was appointed *darughachi* of the Liaoyang capital in 1215 and in the same year Ja'far received the title of imperial *darughachi* for the area north of the Huanghe and south of the Iron Gate.[182]

In the days of Genghis Khan the role and functions of individual officials were not exactly defined and military commanders who held administrative appointments often overstepped their authority.[183] Chinese sources always described the *darughachi* according to the actual functions they performed, using the traditional local official titles: *xingsheng* ('Provincial Administrator'), *liushou* ('Town Commandant'), *shang-guan* ('Chief Administrator)' or *Chenshou* '(Garrison Commander'); and while Ila Chuzai and Chingai are reported to have given themselves the title 'chancellor' (*zhongshu xianggong*) the Mongols described them as 'secretaries' (*bichechi*).[184] Spuler compares the senior city officials (*darughas*) with the permanent commandants (*basqaqs*) in Russian cities, but the powers of a *darughachi* in Genghis' day did, now and then, far exceed those of any town mayor. The *darughachi*, who represented the ruler, supervised the local officials, and Ja'far was, as we have just seen, appointed *darughachi* for the whole of the occupied area of North China.[185] During the Yuan dynasty the *darughachi* were civil servants and their succession was regulated by the rules (*chengyin*) applicable to the civil service.[186] In the P'ags-pa inscriptions the city *darughachi* (*balaghas-un darughas*) are placed after the officers and soldiers (*tserig-un noyad tserig kharan*).[187] As chief administrators of provincial districts they were, however, listed at the head of the military or civil authorities. The *darughachi* alone, as personal representatives of the ruler, possessed the authority to take decisions, while the routine work of administration was delegated to the Inner Asiatic or Chinese officials attached to them and whom they supervised. In the apanages the *darughachi* were, in the first instance, responsible for the collection of the taxes for the imperial treasury.[188]

In 1224, having completed these arrangements for the administration of his new empire, Genghis moved eastwards to spend summer on the Irtysch. The garrisons which he left behind in the conquered territories cannot have been large but the high loss of life among the populace and the fear of the pitiless Mongols had broken his opponents' resistance. In spring 1225 he set off, back to the homeland in Mongolia,[189] where he issued instructions and laws designed to preserve his work and ensure that it was continued by his descendants. Carpini reports that one instruction was: 'Anyone who . . . on his own authority seeks to seize the position of emperor, shall be executed without mercy or pity.' A second instruction set his descendants the task: 'They shall conquer the whole world and shall live in peace with no people which has not freely submitted to them.'[190]

Genghis Khan's last campaign

Genghis Khan had one last task to complete. Not only had the Tanguts earlier refused him auxiliary troops for his western campaign, they had also taken advantage of his absence to rebel. The overthrow of the Tanguts would also assist in bringing to a successful conclusion the struggle with the Jurchid, who, after Mukali's death in 1223, had retaken some of the territory occupied by the Mongols.

In summer 1226, despite his advanced age, Genghis Khan accompanied by his favourite wife, Yisui, placed himself at the head of the army which attacked the Tangut empire. The Tanguts offered stiff resistance but were defeated in a decisive battle and the Mongol forces approached the Tangut capital Ningxia. But Genghis was ill and he felt that his hour of death was approaching. Concerned for the succession he summoned his sons Ögödei and Tolui – Jochi was already dead and Chaghatai did not take part in this campaign – and spoke to them as follows: 'My sickness is too serious to cure and one of you will have to defend the throne and the power of the state and expand this structure which has been given such firm foundations . . . Because if all my sons should wish to be Khan and ruler, refusing to serve each other, will it not be as in the fable of the single-headed and the many-headed snakes.'[191] When Genghis had delivered this exhortation the sons had to undertake in writing that they would recognize Ögödei and his successors as Khan.[192]

The princes and the leaders met and Tolun-cherbi suggested breaking off the campaign. Genghis decided to send a message to the Tangut ruler but the communication was answered in insulting terms by the Tangut commander, Asa-gambu (probably identical with Weiming linggong). When his words were delivered, Genghis Khan – 'his body on fire with fever' – exclaimed: 'Since he makes such great speeches, how could we withdraw? Even if it kills me I shall go and take him at his word. May Eternal Heaven be my witness!'[193] Asa-gambu was defeated. The Tangut king surrendered but was killed and fearful revenge was meted out on the Tangut people. Genghis Khan's last campaign ended in a blood-bath.[194]

The death and burial of Genghis Khan

The cause of Genghis Khan's death was obviously known only to a few persons in his immediate entourage and the reports which our sources offer about this are conspicuously vague and conflicting. The court historian, Rashid ad-Din, and the *Yuanshi* speak in very general terms of an illness which, according to Juvaini, was incurable and was aggravated by the unhealthy climate; Abu'l Faraj states that the illness was malaria. According to the *Secret History*, however, Genghis died from internal injuries which he received in winter 1226 during a wild horse *battue*. The author of the *Shenwu* offers no indication of the cause of death.[195] The ignorance of the Mongols about the actual cause of Genghis Khan's death is illustrated by the statement of Marco Polo that Genghis died of an arrow wound in the knee, received during the siege of a city. Genghis was wounded by an arrow at the siege of Xijing during the Chin campaign of 1212 and, as Pelliot remarks, is unlikely to have died of ·a wound received fifteen years earlier.[196]

Legends soon grew up about the death of the World Conqueror. Plano Carpini reports that Genghis was struck by lightning.[197] Juzjani relates that the king of the Tanguts prophesied that, if the blood ran white as milk from his wounds, Genghis would die three days later; when this prophecy about the blood came to pass Genghis took the matter to heart, his strength waned and three days after the execution of the Tangut king his heart failed, 'and Genghis took the road to Hell'. Shastina in the *Shara Tudzhi* also links Genghis' death with a Tangut prophecy, relating that the Tangut king told Genghis: 'If you kill me your body will suffer; if you do not kill me your dependants will suffer.'[198] Later Mongol accounts suggest that Genghis was the victim of an act of revenge by the beautiful Kurbelzhin, wife of the Tangut ruler, who is said to have inflicted a wound on Genghis' reproductive organ during sexual intercourse.[199] One must be content to establish that, like many other aspects of the World Conqueror's life, the circumstances of his death remain unresolved. It is possible, however, to say with certainty that Genghis Khan died in August 1227; only in specifying the actual day of his death do our sources disagree.[200]

Dreadful vengeance was exacted by the Mongols for the death of Genghis Khan; in accordance with his orders, not only the Tangut ruler but the total population of the capital was massacred. The body of the World Conqueror was then placed on a cart and the trip home began. Genghis had ordered that his death was to remain secret and so all living beings encountered by the funeral cortège were massacred.[201]

Later accounts relate that the journey was interrupted near the Muna Mountains in the Ordos. The cart became bogged down in mud and could not be moved; this was taken as a sign that Genghis Khan wished to be buried at this location. Burial of the ruler in the Mongolian homeland was of the greatest importance to the Mongols in order that Genghis' spirit would continue to protect his people and his clan, and one of his faithful followers besought Genghis' spirit not to desert his people, queens and children; only then did the ruler relent, permit the continuation of the journey, and the cart could be moved.[202]

This anecdote is likely to have a historical basis. We must consider that the Mongols of those days had no knowledge of embalming – the art was known to the Scythians and to the Khitans but, even in the days of the empire, the Mongols did not embalm their rulers.[203] Thus, given the heat of August and the obviously slow progress of the funeral cortège, one is inclined to accept the view, expressed by Schmidt in *The History of the Eastern Mongols,* that the World Conqueror's body was not brought back to his homeland and that only relics are entombed in Mongolia.[204] During the seventeenth century Genghis Khan's burial place was certainly regarded as being in the Ordos region – although bLo-bzan and the anonymous author of the *Altan tobchi* reject such rumours, maintaining that only Genghis' shirt, tent and felt

17   Lamentation at the bier of Genghis Khan.

boots were buried in the Ordos.[205] There is no obvious reason why this should have been done, and a passage in Sagang-sechen does hint that Genghis Khan's coffin was empty when it reached Mongolia. He writes that when the funeral cortège arrived in the Mongolian homeland the Mongols were unable to remove 'the golden body' from the coffin.[206]

Officially, the internment of Genghis Khan took place in the Mongolian homeland, probably on Burkhan-kaldun.[207] The area was declared a prohibited zone (*koruk*), the location was rendered unrecognizable and an Urianghai guard was allocated to protect it.[208] When Ögödei ascended the Mongol throne, forty 'moon-faced virgins of sunny disposition and unblemished character' were selected from the families of the nobles and emirs, dressed in choice garments, bedecked with jewels and rich ornaments and, together with specially selected horses, sacrificed to the spirit of Genghis Khan.[209] Khubilai Kha'an, who later introduced the official ancestral cult according to the Chinese model, had eight burial chambers constructed for the dead Genghis Khan and his wives.[210] From the sixteenth century the cult of Genghis Khan was transferred to the Ordos and the eight white tents (*naiman tsagan ger*) were moved to that area.[211]

4

Personality and Achievements

The man

Genghis was an imposing figure. The Chinese, Zhao Hong, writes: 'The ruler of the Tatars [*sic*], Temuchin, is of tall and majestic stature, his brow is broad and his beard is long. His courage and strength are extraordinary.' Genghis' eyes bespoke a lively spirit. 'Your son has flashing eyes and a lively face', Dai-sechen said to Yisugei when he saw the eight-year-old Temuchin for the first time. Despite the strains of the wars which he fought throughout his whole life, Genghis Khan kept his robust health even in old age. Juzjani comments that, according to the evidence of witnesses who saw him during the fighting in Khorasan, Genghis Khan was distinguished by his height, powerful build, strong constitution, his lack of grey hair and his cat's eyes. The picture of Genghis Khan offered by Mostaert leaves the impression of a calm and peaceful person – a stark contrast to Ögödei with his violent and alcohol-ridden features.[1]

The personal appeal which Temuchin exercised over people, young people in particular, is reflected in innumerable anecdotes. Bo'orchu became a friend of Temuchin the first time they met and later, when Temuchin sent for him, Bo'orchu quit his rich home without taking leave of his father. Dai-sechen's son lent his support in obtaining his father's agreement for Temuchin to marry Börte. Despite the doubts and objections of their father, the children of Sorkan-shira gave the escapee Temuchin shelter and hid him in a cart of wool, thus saving him from the Tayichi'ut troops searching for him. The Khitan Ila Ahai, Chin envoy to the

18   *Genghis Khan.*

court of the Wang-khan, was to impressed by Temuchin at their first meeting that he spontaneously entered Temuchin's service and even fought with him against the Wang-khan.[2]

Apart from his personal powers of attraction Temuchin possessed those qualities which the nomads valued most highly in their leaders. The magnanimity and generosity of Genghis Khan were widely recognized; it was said of him: 'He dresses his people in his own clothes and allows them to ride his own horses.' Genghis never forgot a service rendered to him. Sorkan-shira and his children assisted the young Temuchin to escape from Tayichi'ut captivity; Temuchin, when appointed Khan, turned to Sorkan-shira at the Great Assembly and declared: 'I remember that kind service; in the dark of the night, in the light of day, my heart always remembers it.'[3]

Korchi had prophesied Temuchin's accession to power. When the prophecy was fulfilled Genghis proclaimed: 'You once made a prophecy. Now that it is fulfilled I grant you this boon. Seek out the most beautiful women and maidens from among the subjugated tribes and select thirty for yourself.' Genghis made a further decree: 'I give him command of a regiment to serve him as frontier troops against the forest peoples, in order that he may select those pasturelands he desires as far as the Irtysch River . . .'[4] The horse-herders Badai and Kishlik were also given command of regiments and were created *Darkhan*. Bo'orchu and Mukali were granted equal shares of the Juyin tribe of Kara-Khitai: 'Select their most handsome young men and let them carry your falcons', said Genghis, 'Select their most beautiful maidens and have them sew the garments of your women.'[5]

In 1227 Tolun-cherbi recommended breaking off the campaign against the Tanguts on account of Genghis Khan's illness. As Genghis realized that his hour of death was approaching, he recognized the correctness of that proposal and thought how he could reward Tolun. 'Tolun shall take this mobile palace of the King of the Tanguts, together with all its vessels, goblets and bowls', was his last testament.[6]

Genghis was also considerate towards the children of those who fell in battle. Kuildar died as a hero during the Battle of Kalakalzhit-elet and at the Khuriltai of 1206 Genghis declared: 'Our friend Kuildar was one of the first to swear that he would lay down his life in battle. Because of this service his descendants, down to the last generation, shall be entitled to the "orphan's grant".' Turning to To'oril of the Narin he announced: 'Your father, Chagkhan-ko'a, who always fought with the greatest devotion in front of me, was killed by Jamuka during the battle of Dalan Balzhut. In gratitude for that father, To'oril shall now receive the "orphan's grant".'[7]

Genghis' comrades-in-arms were now to taste the fruits of their faithful service. Rashid records a *bilik* in which Genghis informs his bodyguard: 'It is my intention that your wives and daughters shall be dressed from head to foot in gold embroidered dresses, ride quiet geldings and have clean and pleasant tasting water to drink; your herds shall have good pastures and the highways shall be cleared of rubble and rubbish.' The members of the bodyguard deserved such good fortune; as Genghis said: 'You my grizzled nightguards, who stood guard around my tents in the cloudy night, permitting me to slumber in peace and quiet, you have raised me to this throne.'[8] Genghis was unstinting in his recognition of the role played by his comrades-in-arms in his rise to power. 'Bo'orchu and Mukali have brought me to this position by encouraging me when I was right and dissuading me when I was wrong. You two', announced Genghis at the Khuriltai in 1206, 'are to me as the shafts of a cart, the arms of a body.'[9]

Favours were distributed without attention to social origin or race. Shepherds and stable lads were appointed to command regiments. The achievements of Ja'far were acknowledged after the fall of Zhongdu with the words: 'It is largely thanks to Zhabaer's [Ja'far's] services that I have achieved this.'[10] Genghis also cared for the ordinary tribesmen and their families. In a letter to the Taoist Changchun, he wrote: 'I care for my soldiers as if they were my brothers'; and, indeed, officers were not allowed to beat members of the bodyguard, soldiers were not required to undertake tasks beyond their physical abilities and the ordinary soldiers had the same food as their officers. Genghis was also supportive of tribes and followers who fell on hard times and a tax was raised from the army to provide such persons with cattle, felt and sheep's milk cheese. In so doing Genghis was not motivated by humanitarian considerations. He was fulfilling his tribal duty, a duty which was also accepted by his successors. Ögödei introduced an annual cattle tax to support the tribal poor and needy, and Marco Polo recounts the measures introduced by Khubilai to support people who fell on hard times.[11]

It was not easy to gain Genghis Khan's trust. When Ila Ahai entered Temuchin's service he had to bring his brother Tuka with him as a hostage; Naya'a was distrusted because he took three days longer than expected to escort the princess Kulan to Genghis; Jelme fell under suspicion because he undressed in order to penetrate an enemy camp to bring *kumis* to the wounded Temuchin; army commanders were required to enrol a son or brother as hostage in the bodyguard. When, however, Genghis was once convinced of a person's loyalty he gave them his total confidence. During the campaign in China, Mukali proved himself a successful general and a clever statesman and was appointed Viceroy of China with the rank *guo-wang* (king).[12] Genghis decreed that this title was to be held in perpetuity by Mukali's male descendants and also gave Mukali the right to raise a nine-pointed standard – white with, unusually, the moon represented on it in black – in front of his residence. 'When Mukali plants his standard and gives an order', Genghis instructed his army commanders, 'it is as if I were personally present.'[13]

The life-style of the World Conqueror remained as simple as it had been on the steppe. Genghis frowned upon luxury. 'Heaven grew weary of the excessive pride and luxury in China . . . I am from the barbaric North . . . I wear the same clothing and eat the same food as the cowherds and horse-herders. We make the same sacrifices and we share our riches. I look upon the nation as a new-born child and I care for my soldiers as if they were my brothers . . .'. Genghis explains in a letter to the Taoist sage. Changchun.[14] Genghis also disapproved of the pompous forms of address customary in Asia. 'Names and honorifics are not to be especially stressed in speech', he ordered. 'The Khan's name is to be spoken in the same way as that of anyone else.'[15] His letters to Changchun offer eloquent testimony to the simplicity of Genghis' dealings with his acquaintances. In one letter he writes: 'Have you been well provided with post-horses *en route*? Have you received *en route* adequate supplies of food and drink? Do you feel well in body and spirit? Here, I think of you constantly, Holy Eternal One. I have not forgotten you. Do not forget me!' Another letter is couched in similar terms: 'Since you left me, Holy Eternal One, not a day has passed that I have not thought of you. Holy Eternal One, you must not forget me either.'[16]

There was no court ceremonial in the World Conqueror's camp. The relationship between the leader and his comrades-in-arms was frank and informal; Genghis permitted them to criticize him and followed their exhortations when he found these to be well founded. He spared the life of his uncle Da'aritai after Bo'orchu, Mukali and Shigi-Khutukhu had argued so long with him that 'smoke issued from his nose'.[17] Again, on the recommendation of these same companions, Genghis moderated his rage against his sons Jochi, Chaghatai and Ögödei when they attempted to withhold his share of the spoils from the town of Urgench, and he agreed with the objections raised by Shigi-khutukhu when the latter felt disadvantaged during the distribution of rewards.[18]

Thanks to these characteristics Genghis Khan was able to gather around him men on whose devotion, loyalty and willingness to make sacrifices he could rely absolutely. Numerous anecdotes bear witness to the close bonds which linked the ruler and his companions. We have seen how Jelme cared for the wounded Genghis Khan after the battle of Köyitän and, risking his own life, penetrated into the enemy camp to fetch a drink to still his leader's thirst. When snow fell after the defeat by the Kerait ruler and Genghis had to spend a night in the open without a tent, Bo'orchu laid his fur cloak as a covering on the ground and watched over Genghis all night without moving a step from his side – in Mukali's biography in the *Yuanshi* he is also said to have participated in this act. In the *Secret History* we learn that, at the battle of Dalan–nemurges against the Tartars, Bo'orchu held his own felt blanket over Genghis, day and night, in order to protect him from the streaming rain. 'That was an example of his heroism' was Genghis Khan's praise of Bo'orchu's service at the Khuriltai in 1206.[19]

The devotion of his companions certainly saved Genghis from death on several occasions. During the campaign against the Naimans he was accompanied by only seven riders. They were hungry and Gu'un-u'a, a Jalair follower, caught a young two-year-old camel and was lighting a fire to roast the meat when, suddenly, a group of enemy riders appeared and Genghis' horse fell, hit by an arrow. Six of Genghis' followers were struck with fear but Gu'un hastened to Genghis' side, gave him his own horse and strode off on foot to die fighting the enemy.[20] The same devotion was later shown by Gu'un's son Mukali. Riding with an escort of thirty through a wooded ravine, Genghis feared that he might fall into a trap. 'There could be bandits here. What should we do?' he demanded of Mukali. 'I will protect you with my body', replied the latter. Suddenly enemies did emerge from the wood and arrows rained down upon the group. Mukali spanned his bow, shot three arrows – and three foes fell dead. 'Who are you?', demanded the enemy leader. 'I am Mukali', proudly answered the warrior. He then loosened his saddle from his horse and, using it to shield Genghis, brought the latter to safety.[21]

Genghis was just as merciless and cruel towards his enemies as he was generous and liberal with his friends and comrades-in-arms. The idea of vengeance was the basis for the nomads' sense of justice; the duty to avenge was handed down from generation to generation. Genghis acknowledged this duty; his life was ordered by the idea of vengeance and he never forgot any insult to himself or to the clan. Buri-bökö had to die because he injured Belgutei during a feast. The Merkit tribe was exterminated because they once attacked Genghis' camp and abducted Börte. When Genghis sent Subodei into the field against the Merkits he confessed: 'I send you on this campaign because, in my childhood, I was caused such fear by the Uduyit of the Three Merkits who thrice encircled [me on] Mount Burkhan-kaldun. I have sworn another oath now against this most hated tribe; let them be sought out at the ends of the earth or the depths of the ocean.' Genghis added: 'Should Heaven grant you the strength and power to capture Tokto'a's sons, what does it avail us to send them here to me. Execute them on the spot!'[22]

Genghis took fearful revenge on the Tartars. A family council decreed: 'In days gone by the Tartars killed our ancestors and forefathers. We will sacrifice them in revenge and retribution for our ancestors and forefathers, by massacring all except the youngest. They will be massacred down to the very last male and the remainder will be shared out as slaves among us all.' Similarly because Tarkutai-kiriltuk, a minor chief of the Tayichi'ut, had held the youthful Genghis prisoner, the male members of the Tayichi'ut tribe, sons and grandsons included, were massacred after Genghis' victory over the Tayichi'ut.[23]

Vengeance was a moral duty, approved by Heaven, and Genghis was convinced of his right to exact vengeance. Before his campaign against the Jurchid he called on Heaven to assist him in the impending battles and he justified his intention with the words: 'O Eternal Heaven! You know that Altan Khan is responsible for this turmoil. He it was who, without justification, executed Ambakai and Ökin-barkak, who had been captured and handed over to the Jurchid by the Tatars. These were the elder ancestors of my father and grandfather and I seek to avenge their death.'[24] When Sultan Muhammad of Khwarazm massacred the Mongol caravan and had the Mongol envoys executed a desire for vengeance overrode all other considerations. Genghis abandoned the theatre of war in China and took the field against the sultan.[25]

This desire for vengeance remained with Genghis Khan until his death. The Tangut ruler had provided no auxiliary troops for Genghis' campaign against Sultan Muhammad and the scorn later shown by his minister Asu-gambu also provoked Genghis. Although suffering from a terminal illness, Genghis led the 1227 Tangut campaign to the very end. 'Eternal Heaven, be my witness. Even if it kills me I will go and take Asu-gambu at his word [to fight him]', he cried. After the victory over the Tanguts and the killing of the Tangut ruler, Genghis commanded: 'At my [funeral?] feasts you shall tell how the whole people has perished and you shall tell of its slaughter and destruction.'[26]

Insults against the Mongol nation and the imperial family were as pitilessly avenged as personal slights. The arrogant words of the queen of the Naimans about the Mongols were not forgotten. When an Onggirat prince voluntarily submitted to Genghis Khan, the latter decided to reward him with one of his daughters in marriage. The daughter did not, however, appeal to the prince: 'Your daughter looks like a frog and a tortoise. How can I accept her?' commented the Onggirat, rejecting the gift – an impudent answer for which he paid with his life.[27] Chivalrous treatment of defeated enemies was alien to Genghis' mentality. He mocked Gurbesu of the Naimans, humiliated Terken-khatun and had all the children of the shah of Khwarazm killed, even the youngest, the favourite son of the sultana. This act by Genghis was totally different from the treatment of the imperial Sung family by his grandson Khubilai Kha'an. The Sung empress was received at

Khubilai's court with honour and was provided with the respect and luxury which 'as a great lady' she merited.[28]

Life on the steppe made a warrior of every youngster and Genghis believed that a man's fulfilment was to be found in the intoxication of battle. On one occasion he asked Bo'orchu and other comrades what they thought was man's highest bliss. They answered that it lay in falconry, when one rode out in spring on a sturdy gelding, the hunting falcon on the wrist and loosed it against the prey. Genghis answered: 'You are mistaken. Man's greatest good fortune is to chase and defeat his enemy, seize his total possessions, leave his married women weeping and wailing, ride his gelding, use the bodies of his women as a nightshirt and support, gazing upon and kissing their rosy breasts, sucking their lips which are as sweet as the berries of their breasts.'[29]

We must, however, seek in vain in the life of Genghis Khan for any heroic deed such as that of Napoleon on the Pont d'Arcole. The author of the *Secret History* is pleased to depict Genghis as a timorous person. He mentions Temuchin's youthful fear of dogs – a quite understandable fear when we consider that in Mongolia dogs attack even adults; when surprised by his mother while questioning Kasar, Genghis trembles before her and says; 'When I have caused my mother to be wrathful I tremble before her, and I am ashamed of myself.' When the Merkits attack his camp he leaves his newly wed wife, Börte, to her fate and confesses; 'I have been sore afraid'; and he deserts his family when they are defending themselves against the Tayichi'ut raiders. Even his comrades-in-arms do not appear convinced of his heroism, and when Bala-kalzha queries the basis of Genghis' reputation as *ba'atur*, Genghis responds with stories of actions which scarcely appear credible and which, doubtless, actually bore little resemblance to his account of them.[30]

Even if no heroic tales of battle have been handed down regarding Genghis, he did, when circumstances required it, expose himself to danger on several occasions. Thus he showed his spirit by going off alone after the raiders who had stolen the family's horses; he would ride through enemy country accompanied by only a small escort; he took part in the battles in his earlier years; after his defeat at Kalakalzhit-elet he risked being taken prisoner by his enemies when he remained on the field of battle until his missing companions joined him. At the battle of Köyitän he was wounded by an arrow in the neck and again at the siege of Xijing in China he was stuck by a stray arrow.[31] It is not, however, the role of a general to fight in the foremost ranks and it was not in Genghis' character to expose himself heedlessly to danger. He did, however, in confronting Mönglik and his six sons alone in his tent after the execution of the shaman Teb-tengri, show that he was capable of keeping a cool head.[32]

Genghis Khan was from a nation of hunters and he shared his people's love of the hunt. 'As soon as the children are two or three years old', reports Carpini, 'they begin to ride . . . and then a small bow, suitable in size to their age, is given to them and they are taught to shoot.' The first hunting trophy was celebrated by anointing a finger with the fat of the trophy. As a child Genghis had shot birds and caught fish to contribute to the nourishment of his family. Vigorous by nature, Genghis sought to work off his excess energies by hunting, for which he retained his love and in which he participated until his death. On the western campaign he once fell from his horse during a hunt and was attacked by a boar. The Taoist sage Changchun learned of this and reproached Genghis, claiming that this was a bad omen and that he should give up hunting. Genghis replied: 'We Mongols go hunting while we are still children. This is a habit which I cannot renounce.' When out hunting during his final campaign against the Tanguts Genghis was thrown from his horse and, according to the *Secret History*, this fall was the cause of his death.[33]

In war as in the hunt, booty was the nomad's aim. The economic infrastructure of the animal-breeders was finely balanced and if their own herds were decimated they could only survive by indulging in plundering raids. Distribution of the booty was regulated by custom and Genghis became jealous when his rights in such matters were infringed. Thus, over a petty matter in his youth – it was a question of a bird or a fish – he killed his half-brother Bekhter in cold blood because the latter had withheld Temuchin's share. He made enemies of his relatives Altan, Kuchar and Da'aritai, who had elected him Khan, by taking from them the booty which they had appropriated during the Tartar campaign. When his sons Jochi, Chaghatai and Ögödei withheld his portion of the spoils from the siege of Urgench, Genghis did, on the recommendation of his close comrades, agree not to inflict a punishment – but the *Secret History* tells us: '. . . he chided them thoroughly, quoting from the speeches of the ancients and sayings from the past. He scolded them . . . until they were not able to wipe the sweat from their brow.'[34]

Material possessions held little appeal for Genghis; although he never permitted his rights to be infringed he was generous in his distribution of gold, pearls and clothes to his followers. His disinterest in commercial matters is shown by his reaction when he intended to give his sister Temulun in marriage to Botu of the Ikires and the Ikires tribal elders came to finalize the marriage contract. When Genghis asked how many animals Botu possessed the elders answered: 'He owns thirty horses, half of which we will bring as the bride price.' Genghis was incensed by this. He exclaimed: 'If one is concluding a marriage and discusses value, then one is acting like a merchant. The ancients had a saying that unity of purpose is a fortune in affliction. If you, the people of the Ikires, follow Botu and serve me faithfully that will suffice.'[35]

No matter how highly Genghis rated the services of his comrades-in-arms, the support of higher powers was decisive in his advancement. Genghis shared the Mongol belief that the supernatural spirits which populated the world influenced a man's fate. The spirit of Burkhan-kaldun had protected him on the occasion of the Merkit raid. 'My life has, like that of a louse, been preserved by the Burkhan-kaldun', he exclaims. The influence of such spirits was, however, restricted to their locality, while the Eternal Blue Heaven reigned over the whole earth. Genghis turned to Heaven on the eve of decisive battles and it is noteworthy that he never sought to win Heaven's favours by means of sacrifices, relying solely on the justice of his cause. On the eve of one campaign he ascended a mountain where he communed with Heaven, declaring that he was not responsible for the impending war and justifying his intentions. 'If You consider my cause to be just then send me help and strength.'[36] Genghis Khan's descendants maintaned this custom: Hulegu climbed a hill and prayed to Heaven before his battle with the Caliph of Baghdad; Juvaini reports that, before the battle with the Hungarians, Batu spent a day and a night on a hill, speaking to no one, but praying and lamenting. The belief that Heaven was the protector of the nomad peoples was widespread among the Mongols and the Turks. In the letters of later Mongol rulers Genghis Khan was spoken of as the Son of God; but although

19   *Shaman devil mask.*

belief in the heavenly origin of rulers was fairly widespread, it seems likely that it was a late Mongol theory, probably borrowed from the Chinese concept of the Son of Heaven.[37]

The intermediaries between man and the supernatural forces were the shamans, whose gifts of observation and intuition won them the reputation of possessing supernatural powers, of riding on a white steed to Heaven, communing there with the spirits and returning to communicate their will. Because of the authority which they possessed among the people the shamans exerted a decisive influence on the personal life of the Mongol. They also influenced political events. The oracle was consulted, for example, before every campaign; and Marco Polo relates that before the decisive battle with Wang-khan (whom Marco calls Prester John) Genghis sought additional predictions concerning the outcome of the battle from Christian and Muslim astrologers. Genghis shared the Mongol belief in the supernatural powers of the shamans and, as Juvaini remarks, was in the habit of being guided by everything said by the shaman Teb-tengri.[38]

In the magical world of the Mongols, soothsayers played as important a role as the shamans. Genghis was no less superstitious than his contemporaries. He separated from his wife Ibaka because of a bad dream; he caused the Taoist Changchun to come to him in Samarkand from distant China in the hope that the latter might provide the elixir of longevity; he surrounded himself with men such as Ila Ahai and Ila Chuzai, who were versed in the art of reading the future from the shoulder-blade of a sheep.[39]

Genghis met Ila Chuzai in China, was attracted by the Khitan's tall stature and long beard and gave him the Mongol nickname *urtu sakel* – 'long beard'.[40] In April 1218 Ila Chuzai was ordered to join Genghis and accompanied him on the western campaign. Chuzai's knowledge and skill in prophecy won him Genghis' trust, but one must not exaggerate his political role under Genghis. The Mongol historiography does not mention him at all and he served under persons such as the Kerait Chingai, the Muslims Yalavach and Ja'far, the Uighur Tata-tonga and the Khitan Ila Ahai. But Ila Chuzai did win Genghis' trust by prophesying a change in the Chin government, a prophecy which was substantiated the following year by the death of the Chin emperor – and, as Song Zihen remarks, Genghis thereafter required Ila Chuzai to foretell the outcome of every campaign.[41]

Typically, however, Genghis kept personal control of all prophecies. He himself practised the art of prophecy and would compare his interpretation of the oracle's utterances with the interpretation provided by Ila Chuzai. Before he decided to retreat in India, for example, he constantly consulted the oracle using a sheep's shoulder-blade. Juzjani also maintains that Genghis was instructed in the secrets of magic. He would on occasions fall into a trance, when the words he uttered were written down and then used by him to guide his future actions – an anecdote quoted by Juzjani as proof that Genghis was 'in league with devils, who were his friends'.[42]

Genghis Khan well understood how to harmonize the rational and irrational; utterances by the oracles either coincided with his own assessment of the situation or were deployed as propaganda to his own advantage; and, although superstitious, Genghis Khan quickly overcame his awe of the shamans when it was a question of the survival of his supremacy. When the influence among the Mongols of the shaman Teb-tengri threatened Genghis' primacy, Genghis quickly enticed the son of Yisugei's faithful servant into a trap and had him killed.

Genghis Khan's dominant trait of character was his desire for power; all other considerations and feelings were subjugated to this desire. If anyone stood in his way, or if he regarded someone as a potential rival, he showed no pity, paying no attention to services which he had received, nor to blood ties. Corpses paved his road to power. Sacha-beki and Taichu, Altan and Kuchar, who had elected him Khan, were executed; he caused his *anda* Jamuka, perhaps even his son Jochi, to be killed – as he had himself in his youth killed his half-brother Bekhter – and his brother Kasar escaped death only because of the intervention of Mother Hö'elun. In the struggle against his *anda* and leader, Wang-khan, Genghis availed himself of means which were scarcely loyal. He who valued loyalty above all things forgot that it was Wang-khan's support which had brought him to power.[43]

Naturally, Genghis was able to advance justifications for these actions. Sacha and Taichu had betrayed the national cause by refusing him assistance in the struggle against the Tartars; Altan and Kuchar had declared their support for Wang-khan when it was a question of re-establishing Mongol supremacy over the Land of the Three Rivers; Jamuka had fought on the side of the

Naimans; Wang-khan had attacked Genghis. But were such justifications the true bases for Genghis' actions? Did he not rather kill Sacha and Taichu, Altan and Kuchar, even his *anda* Jamuka, because he saw in them rivals who might dispute his claim to supremacy? And was the break with Wang-khan not brought about by Genghis' claim to the Kerait throne, a matter about which Wang-khan was, to the very last, disposed to come to an agreement?

Genghis believed that his actions were justified by his pre-destination for greater things. The idea of heavenly predestination occurs early. After the battle with the Merkits he expressed this thought in the words: 'Heaven and Earth increased my strength. Foreordained for this by Mighty Heaven I was brought here by Mother Earth'; and again, after the victory over the Keraits: 'With the assistance of Eternal Heaven I have been able to overcome the Kerait nation and have attained this high position'.[44] During the Khwarazmian campaign Genghis announced: 'Inform the emirs, the leading citizens and the mass of ordinary people that Heaven has granted me all the Earth, from sunrise to sunset'. This claim was repeated by Hulegu, who informed the Caliph of Baghdad: 'Eternal Heaven chose Genghis Khan and his descendants and made us a gift of the whole Earth, from east to west.'[45]

Genghis derived his claim to world supremacy from his belief that he had been invested with a heavenly mission. The leaders of non-Mongol tribes and peoples who refused to acknowledge this supremacy were treated as enemies and rebels; recognition of the supremacy of the Mongols became the corner-stone of Mongol international policy. As Guyuk Kha'an wrote in his letter to Pope Innocent IV: 'This command is sent to the Great Pope . . . Your request to submit and to be subservient to Us, sent to Us through Your ambassadors, has been examined. If You wish to act according to Your own words then You, Great Pope, together with all the Kings, must come here in person and do homage to Us.'[46] And Carpini reports: 'The Mongols do not make peace with anyone who has not submitted to them, because of the instruction of Genghis Khan that they should seek to bring all peoples under their yoke.'[47] This philosophy of the ruler's mission could not, however, have been translated into action had it not been in accord with the nomadic drive for expansion, of which Genghis is the most prolific exponent rather than the originator.

The Mongol idea of a world empire is usually traced back to Chinese influences, a thesis which has again been advanced by Herbert Franke.[48] The idea of a world empire did not, however, require the stimulus of a foreign philosophy; it was founded in the limitless expanses of the steppe, explained by the nomadic economic structure,[49] and the concept is expressed in the titles adopted by the nomadic Khans. Jamuka took the title *Gurkhan* ('universal khan'); Temuchin that of *Chinggis Khan* ('oceanic khan'). When Tayang-khan learned of Temuchin's victory over the Keraits he exclaimed: 'How can there be two rulers on earth! Let us go and fetch that Mongol!'[50] The Mongol concept of a universal empire differed from that of the Chinese. The latter regarded the adoption of Chinese culture by the defeated nations as an essential part of the concept, whereas only economic interests were important to the nomads. Genghis' successful campaigns stimulated the nomadic drive for expansion and the creation of a world empire became the aim and the fulfilment of that drive.

Genghis Khan used terror as a strategic weapon in his military plans and his laws were draconian. In his youth he murdered his half-brother Bekhter in cold blood; he had his relatives and his *anda* Jamuka executed and ordered the complete extermination of such tribes as the Tartars and the Merkits. Are we to assume that Genghis acted from natural cruelty, that he regarded himself as 'The Scourge of God'? I do not believe that this was so. When there was no resistance the population was spared. On the way from Bokhara to Samarkand those townships which capitulated were, according to Juvaini, in no way molested; Juzjani confirms that, with the exception of Herat, towns suffered no damage – and this on Genghis' specific orders. The *Yuanshi* reports that when, during the campaign in Liaoxi many people were murdered by the Mongol troops, Taben, a man from the area of the Yiwulu Mountain in Liaodong who had joined the Mongols, condemned this action in the following terms: 'The basis of the state is its people. If, when a country has been conquered, the populace is then murdered, what advantage does the state have? Moreover, if the innocent are killed this simply stiffens the enemy's will to resistance. This is not in accord with the leader's wish!' It is reported that Genghis rejoiced when he learned of Taben's words.[51]

The warriors of Jalal ad-Din are reported by an-Nasawi to have driven pegs into the ears of Mongol prisoners while Jalal, smiling broadly, looked on. Jalal also handed prisoners over to the mob to be beaten to death on the streets, while in the palace courtyard he himself personally beheaded prisoners. There are no reports of such atrocities perpetrated by Genghis and the order that molten lead should be poured into the mouth of the governor of Otrar cannot be laid at his door.[52] It is just as unbelievable that Genghis should have ordered women's stomachs to be slit open in order to search for pearls which they might have swallowed – an incident related by both Juvaini and Rashid, although not attributed by either to any order by Genghis Khan.

Genghis had a passionate nature which could be unrestrained when it was a matter of vengeance. He was pitiless in those cases in which resistance had been encountered, but his actions were usually not dictated by emotion and he seldom allowed himself to be provoked into impulsive actions. Juzjani records the following characteristic anecdote.

Tolui brought with him to Genghis from Khorasan an Imam who had by some miracle survived falling from the fortified walls of a town. Genghis liked the man and had him teach him about Islam and about earlier Muslim kings. In the course of one such conversation Genghis asked the imam how great a reputation he, Genghis, would leave behind. Before the Imam answered he extracted a promise from Genghis that his life would be spared. He then said: 'The reputation of a ruler survives as long as the people live; but how can that reputation endure if the servants of the Khan torture and massacre the population. Who will survive to recount the tale?' Genghis was enraged by the answer; his bow and arrows fell from his hands to the floor and he turned his back on the speaker. Soon thereafter, however, he pulled himself together, turned to the Imam and said: 'I thought that you were a clever and cautious person, but it is clear from your words that your understanding and your powers of comprehension are limited. There are many kings in this world. Wherever the hoofs of Muhammad's horse bear him, I will continue to slaughter and destroy, and peoples in other parts of the world and the rulers of other lands will recount my deeds.'[53]

Genghis likewise demanded that others should control their feelings. When Mutugen, Chaghatai's favourite son, was killed at

20   *Khubilai Kha'an.*

the siege of Bamiyan, Genghis called his sons to him and, in order to test them, accused them of failing to follow his orders and instructions. Chaghatai, still unaware of his son's death, threw himself on his knees before Genghis and called out: 'If I twist your words I should die!'. Genghis then informed him of the death of Mutugen, forbidding him to weep or lament. Difficult although it was, Chaghatai stifled his grief until, on some pretext, he was able to withdraw onto the steppe where he broke down in tears.[54]

Despite his self-control, Genghis was of a passionate nature, in loving as well as in hating. He had four adopted sons, brought back from his campaigns – Guchu of the Merkit, Kökochu of the Besut (a sub-tribe of the Tayichi'ut), Shigi-khutukhu of the Tartars and Boroghul of the Jurkin[55] – and the strength of his affection for these adopted sons is highlighted by the following anecdote, related by Rashid ad-Din.

When Shigi-khutukhu, whom Temuchin had picked up in the plundered Tartar camp, was fifteen, he left camp one day, despite the cold and the heavy snows, to hunt a herd of gazelles. In the evening Genghis noticed his absence and enquired where he was. When Genghis learned that he had gone from the camp he was furious: 'The boy will perish in such cold and snow!' he exclaimed and, normally so controlled, struck out with a stick at the camp commandant who had given the boy permission to leave camp.[56]

Genghis' affection for a Tangut boy was to save the lives of the inhabitants of the town of Ganzhou. Genghis had, on an earlier occasion, come across the boy while hunting, taken a liking to the lad and brought him home with him. The boy's father was governor of the town of Ganzhou during the Tangut campaign. Tsagan (the name by which the boy was known among the Mongols), who took part in that Mongol campaign, sent his father a message in an arrow, calling on him to surrender the town. The governor was ready to comply but was killed by a group of officers. After the town had been stormed Genghis, as was his custom when a town offered fierce resistance, ordered the massacre of the populace. In tears Tsagan begged the leader to spare the inhabitants, pointing out that a group of thirty-six officers, rather than the populace as a whole, were responsible for the resistance. The normally pitiless Genghis did, in fact, allow himself to be moved and the inhabitants were spared.[57]

Genghis showed particular affection for and kindness to his grandchildren. When he returned home from the western campaign he was met by Tolui's sons, the ten-year-old Khubilai and the eight-year-old Hulegu. They proudly showed him their first hunting trophies, a hare and a wild goat, and Genghis personally carried out the old Mongol custom of anointing their finger.[58] We can also assess how deeply Genghis was wounded by the death of his grandson Mutugen at the siege of Bamiyan by the extent of the vengeance which he extracted for that death. He ordered the extermination of all living things in the town, human or animal; no prisoners or loot were to be taken, the town was to be laid waste and never rebuilt, so that no living creature would ever inhabit it again.[59] Yet the following story, reported by Li Zhichang, indicates that Genghis was not without human feelings, even towards members of a foreign and hostile people: one day during the western campaign he saw a Muslim leading an ox which was turning the wheel used to raise water from a well 100 feet deep; touched by pity he ordered that the man should be freed from taxes and corvée labour.[60]

We know little about Genghis' emotional life. Genghis had a healthy disposition, doubtless found pleasure in sex, and he brought a new wife home from every campaign. Carpini reports that the most beautiful maidens of the empire were selected and presented to Genghis each year; some he retained, others he presented to his sons and comrades-in-arms. Rashid maintains that Genghis had a harem of 500 wives and concubines, and the *Yuanshi* lists the names of twenty-three wives and sixteen concubines.[61] A favourite wife accompanied him on every campaign – Kulan on the western campaign, for example, and Yisui on the final campaign against the Tanguts. Genghis retained his sexual appetite into old age and during the western campaign a convoy of maidens is said to have been dispatched to him from far-off China. Juzjani asserts that during the western campaign 12,000 virgins, selected for Genghis from among the prisoners, followed the army on foot.[62] Two divisions of virgins, about the same number as the whole of Jebe's expeditionary force, marched behind the army into enemy territory! This is clearly a gross exaggeration!

The princesses who were presented to Genghis in homage and as a sign of submission symbolized for him a sense of achievement and strengthened his feeling of power. Genghis never allowed himself, however, to be seduced into sexual excesses, and he exhibited to a ripe old age an extraordinary capacity to withstand the travails of warfare and hunting. He does not appear ever to have had a passion or a deep love for any woman. In his youth he abandoned Börte to her fate, thinking only of his own safety when his camp was raided by the Merkits; in old age Kulan and Yisui enjoyed his especial affection. He subjected Naya'a to a rigorous interrogation because the young Mongol officer had delayed three days in bringing the Tartar princess, Kulan, to him, and his anger abated only when he had evidence that the maiden had not been molested. But it was doubtless offended vanity that his rights might have been transgressed which motivated Genghis' attitude, rather than any feeling of jealousy with regard to a girl whom he did not even know.[63]

The following anecdote from the *Secret History* does, however, indicate that the World Conqueror was not immune against jealousy. During a feast Genghis noted that Yisui appeared uneasy; he became suspicious and ordered that those present in the camp should assemble according to their tribes. A good-looking young man was left standing alone; it was Yisui's betrothed. Genghis cried out: 'What spying mission has brought him here? We have already taken the measure of such as he. We can make short work of him. Take him from my sight.' The *Secret History* reports that the unfortunate man was immediately beheaded.[64] It is typical of Genghis' sense of justice that, as in the cases of the executions of the Jurkin princes Sacha and Taichu, and of his relatives Altan and Kuchar, the decision should not be attributed to personal motives. Genghis always found a justification for such acts of vengeance; in this particular case his wife's betrothed was executed as a Tartar spy.

The Mongols attributed no great importance to the virginity of their women. Genghis did not hold it against Börte that, during her captivity with the Merkits, she was given as wife to Chilger-bökö, the brother of Chiledu. Although he bestowed a greater degree of favour on younger and more beautiful wives, he showed Börte the respect due to her as his senior wife, her sons enjoyed a special position above all others, the empire was divided among them alone and at decisive moments in his life Genghis took advice from Börte. It seems probable that Börte was well versed in magic, a gift which, as is evidenced by the numerous witchcraft trials during the empire period, the Mongols ascribed to their women.[65]

Genghis sought to be just and fair towards his sons. He suppressed his personal feelings and intended to make Jochi his heir, despite the suspicion of illegitimacy. He judged his sons according to their abilities and Rashid ad-Din relates that Genghis pronounced the following assessment of them: 'Whoever wishes to learn the *Yasa*, rules, laws and *bilik* should turn to Chaghatai; whoever is inclined towards magnanimity and generosity and seeks the good things and the riches of life should attach himself to Ögödei; but whoever dreams of great deeds and renown, deeds of military valour, the conquest of empires and the subjugation of the world, should enter the service of Tolui.' And, interestingly, in accordance with these judgements Genghis, according to Juvaini, entrusted his sons with the following spheres of activity: *Tusi* (Jochi) was entrusted with hunting, Chaghatai with the administration of the *Yasa*, Ögödei with the administration of the empire and Tolui with command of the army and the organization of military equipment.[66]

Genghis held Ögödei in high regard because of the latter's powers of conciliation. When Jochi and Chaghatai quarrelled during the siege of Urgench, Genghis entrusted supreme command to Ögödei, whose placatory nature enabled him to settle the quarrel between his brothers and bring the siege to a satisfactory conclusion. After the battle with the Keraits, Ögödei, Bo'orchu and Boroghul were missing at roll-call; Genghis remained in position to await the missing warriors. Finally Bo'orchu appeared and then, some time later, Boroghul turned up with the wounded Ögödei on the horse in front of him. When Genghis saw the wound – Ögödei had been struck in the neck vein by an arrow – 'he shed tears and his heart was sore', reports the *Secret History*.[67]

Genghis shared the nomad attitude towards the way of life of civilized nations, finding their life and activities strange and threatening. Yet the illiterate Genghis was not uneducated and he expanded his understanding of the world from contact with the many representatives of foreign cultures in his entourage. From the Muslims Yalavach and Mas'ud he learned of the importance of cities; the Khitans Ila Ahai and Ila Chuzai would have acquainted him with the principles of the Confucian ethic and he learned about Taoist contemplation in his discussions with Changchun.

History usually depicts Genghis Khan as the destroyer of flourishing civilizations; yet he was not opposed to culture, in as far as the foreign cultural elements could be useful to the nomads. He grasped the importance of writing and, after the defeat of the Naimans, had the Mongol princes instructed in the Uighur script. He valued highly those who had the gift of languages and writing and when he learned of a young Uighur. Mengsusi (Mungsuz), who at age fifteen was experienced in the literature of his people, he had the boy brought to him and prophesied: 'This boy has fire in his eyes. The day will come when he will be of great value.' Genghis expressed his pleasure at the humanistic teaching of the Uighur Yelian Temur; he valued the medical expertise of the Iranians and had an eye infection treated by a Persian doctor; craftsmen were spared and scribes attained high positions. But everything else which was of no value to the Mongols was destroyed without pity; corpses, ruins and devastation, the destruction of irreplaceable cultural treasures accompanied his campaigns.[68]

In such circumstances we would expect that historians who experienced or were witnesses of the aftermath of these campaigns would have handed down to us a picture of Genghis Khan as the Scourge of God, a cruel conqueror and a pitiless despot. But this is not the case. The southern Chinese Zhao Hong was an eyewitness of the bloody trail of the Mongol campaign in North China; in his personal travelogue he, nevertheless, describes Genghis Khan in the following terms: 'This man is brave and decisive, he is self-controlled and lenient towards the population, he reveres Heaven and Earth, prizes loyalty and justice'.[69]

One certainly can not accuse Plano Carpini of partiality towards the Mongols. He wrote his *History of the Mongols* in 1247 in order to awaken Europe to the danger of an attack by this feared and hated nation, and his hatred led him to the thesis that the Mongols had learned theft, robbery and plundering from Genghis Khan. But even he has to admit: 'During his travels through foreign countries he [Genghis] constantly sought to attract as many people as possible to himself and make them his allies. And above all he understood how to win over his own countrymen, so that they willingly followed him as leader in every reprehensible deed.'[70]

The Muslim Rashid ad-Din praises the liberality by which Genghis won the hearts of people and remarks that Genghis was distinguished among all these nations by his magnanimity.[71] It is true that Rashid was court historian to the Il-khans, but his assertion is no mere sentimental paean of praise; Genghis' magnanimity can be documented many times over.

The Venetian Marco Polo reports: 'He [Genghis] was a man of great steadfastness and sense, also a heroic figure; I tell you that when he was elected King he ruled with such moderation and justice that he was loved and revered by all, almost as a god rather than a ruler.' Marco Polo served the Mongol Yuan dynasty and was pro-Mongol, yet he must, in the circles in which he lived and worked, have had contact with Persians and other Inner Asians. He does not, however, speak of devastation or massacres in Iran and Khorasan, but maintains, on the contrary: 'When he [Genghis] captured an empire, town or village by force of arms, he did not cause anyone to be killed, robbed or harmed, nor did he deprive them of their property.'[72]

There are certainly other voices, such as that of Ibn al-Athir, which are distinguished by their hate for the conqueror who brought such devastation upon their country. Genghis certainly bore the responsibility for the Mongol prosecution of war, planning terror as a strategic military weapon. Yet most authors do not seem to ascribe the destruction and devastation caused by the Mongols during their campaigns of conquest to any personal cruelty in the nature of Genghis Khan, perhaps because such acts of war were not unusual at that time. Vernadsky points to the blood-bath carried out by the Crusaders in Jerusalem in 1099, in which not even women and children were spared. Attention has already been drawn to the fate of the Mongol soldiers captured by Jalal ad-Din. The Khitan and Jurchid mode of warfare also exceeded in cruelty that of Genghis Khan's armies. When the Khitan armies invaded North China goods and herds were plundered in an area of several hundred *li* in order to provision the troops. Young and healthy were put to the sword, the old and children were thrown into the graves. After the conquest of cities the Jurchid hewed down all mature males; they spitted children on their lances and danced joyously around them.[73]

Genghis' personality combined the power and the passion of a child of nature with the self-discipline which reason demanded of him. In private he was a warm-hearted friend, a father concerned for the well-being of his family and those around him, a simple, likeable person. As ruler he was consumed by unbounded ambition, did not shrink from any means which would achieve his aim and was utterly merciless in suppressing all resistance.

We should not, however, judge the nomads of the thirteenth century by the standards and concepts of the present day. Genghis Khan personified for the Mongols the ideal ruler – strict, but just and generous. The Mongol nation, as Marco Polo attests, followed him blindly and revered him 'almost as a god'.

The conquests

Political as well as material considerations underlay the campaigns of conquest which Genghis Khan undertook after his elevation as Khan. The expectation of rich plunder was the best means of restraining centrifugal aspirations and desire for independence, of creating unity among the tribes and ensuring their obedience. Economic considerations were, however, more compelling. The struggle for power on the steppe – and perhaps also climatic influences – had seriously decimated the herds of the homeland and these had to be replenished. This was the sole aim of the initial Mongol attack on the Tangut empire and the Mongols withdrew from that country as soon as they had amassed a rich haul of animals. The first campaign in China was also simply a plundering raid. In front of the besieged capital, Zhongdu, Genghis Khan refrained from destroying the enemy; he turned homewards, contenting himself with gifts from the Chin and with the spoils which he had taken during the fighting.

Mongol warfare followed the steppe tradition. Peoples who resisted were exterminated; others were enslaved, the men were forced to serve in the Mongol forces, the cities were plundered and then abandoned. Such war aims did not, however, accord with the views and interest of the Khitan and Chinese feudal lords, nor those of the Muslim merchants in Genghis Khan's retinue, who were interested in the continuing exploitation of the sedentary populace. Genghis Khan was not deaf to their suggestions and, after the fall of Zhongdu in 1215, he advanced territorial claims against the Chin emperor – the surrender of the lands north of the Yellow River. Garrisons were left behind in the towns and governors (*darughachi*) were appointed. The territorial expansion of his empire was not, however, foremost in Genghis Khan's considerations and he did not aspire to become Chin emperor nor sultan of Iran. Genghis was much more concerned with events in the homeland than with conquering foreign lands. Thus he deputed to Mukali supreme command in China and quit that campaign in order to exact vengeance from the Merkits, subdue the forest tribes and pursue Kuchlug, son of the Naiman king; and he broke off the western campaign when he learned of the Tangut rebellion.

There was no preconceived plan behind Genghis Khan's campaigns of conquest. Khitan defectors urged him into war against the Chin; Jebe and Subodei were dispatched against the Kipchak because that tribe had killed Genghis' son-in-law and had supported the Khwarazm-shah in his struggle against the Mongols. A conqueror's delusions of grandeur are, however, fuelled by success. Genghis Khan would become intoxicated by the victories of the Mongol forces and feel strengthened in his belief that he had been selected by the Eternal Heaven and had a claim to rule the whole world. In the light of the poor life-style and the many misfortunes of his youth, his rise to be the most powerful potentate in Asia must have appeared to be a miracle and we cannot be surprised that he ascribed this to supernatural powers.

The historian is also faced with the problem of how it was possible for a small, poor, backward nation of hunters and animal-breeders to conquer the most powerful and civilized states of Asia, states which disposed of inexhaustible reserves of people. The answer has been sought in a military context; attention has been drawn to Genghis' ability as a a commander, to the strategy and tactics of the Mongol armies, the superiority of the Mongol cavalry. One cannot be satisfied with such explanations. In his battles on the steppe Genghis Khan suffered as many defeats as he gained victories. The tactic of coaxing the enemy from defended positions by means of a pretended withdrawal and then turning to overwhelm him, the flanking movements to encircle him, were no innovation. Nomadic armies had practised such manoeuvres from time immemorial. Discipline in the Jurchid army was no less severe than that of the Mongol army.[74] The Jurchid, as well as the Turkic and Iranian cavalry, were in no way inferior to that of the Mongols. The Mongols were unable to gain victories of any consequence during the first Tangut campaign; the war against the Jurchid lasted a decade, despite the Jurchid being compelled to fight on two fronts; the victories in Iran were not achieved by the cavalry. The superiority of the Mongols must be ascribed to other factors.

The Mongol army was organized on principles which differed from those of the enemy armies. Appointment to command was based solely on ability and results, not on birth or position in the tribal hierarchy. One of Genghis' *bilik* states: 'He who is able to command ten men in battle formation will be able to command a thousand or ten thousand in battle formation, and he deserves such a command.' Officers who were not able to meet the demands of their appointment were removed and their commands entrusted to subordinates.[75] The possibility of unrestricted promotion – every soldier carried a marshal's baton in his knapsack – gave rise to lively competition among the warriors. The military commanders owed their promotion to Genghis Khan and he could rely on their unconditional loyalty and military efficiency.

This process of selection provided the Mongol army with élite cadres. One does not find such men as Mukali, Jebe or Subodei in the enemy camps, where rivalry and a desire for independence were rife among the military commanders. The Chin emperor and Sultan Muhammad believed their commanders capable of treachery and rebellion, and military plans were dictated by dynastic interests rather than by strategic requirements. The most able general cannot, however, win victories unless supported by troops who are prepared for battle. The Mongol soldier went to war well equipped, physically and militarily. He was accustomed to suffer exhaustion, privation and hardships patiently and he had, by participating in *battues* mastered the tactics which would be employed against the enemy.

Genghis Khan did not demand of his men anything which was beyond their physical ability. He declared in one *bilik*: 'There is no greater warrior than Yisubei and no man who possesses his ability! But because he does not suffer from the hardships of a campaign, shrugs off hunger and thirst, he assumes that all others, *nökböd* and soldiers alike, who accompany him are equally able to bear those hardships, whereas they cannot. For this reason he is not suitable to command an army.'[76] Ill-treatment of soldiers by officers was not tolerated. In the service regulations promulgated for his bodyguard Genghis decreed: 'You unit commanders shall not, simply because you have been appointed to command, rebuke [without permission from me] my bodyguards, who are equal to you. If you strike, kick or beat them, then you shall receive beating for beating and blow for blow!'[77]

Juvaini highlights the principle of equality which pervaded the Mongol army: 'They all give of their best', comments the Persian historian, 'irrespective of rank and without consideration for a person's riches or influence.' The soldiers had the right to the same food as their superiors. 'No emir dare satisfy his hunger before his men; on the contrary all food is equitably shared', comments al-'Umari; and, in his letter to Changchun, Genghis explained how he cared for his soldiers as if they were his brothers. The fighting spirit of the Mongol army was strengthened by the nomadic feeling of superiority towards town-dwellers and farmer peasants, and above all by the belief in the invincibility of Genghis Khan. The *Yasa* was regarded as a talisman which guaranteed victory on the battlefield, and we have already noted Marco Polo's comment on the degree of reverence in which Genghis was held by the Mongols.[78]

Nevertheless, the outcome of the struggle against the most powerful states of Asia would doubtless have been different if the decision had depended solely on the battlefield. The preconditions for the military victory were achieved by Genghis Khan's diplomatic and political skills; his exposure and subsequent exploitation of the internal weaknesses of the enemy determined in advance the outcome of the wars. Genghis showed great skill in exploiting to his advantage the national, social and religious rifts in the enemy camps.

In the war against the Chin Genghis appeared as the ally of the Khitans, appealing to their national pride and the mutual hatred of the Jurchid; as he said to Ila Chuzai: 'The Liao and the Chin are hereditary enemies and I have exacted vengeance on your behalf.'[79] The expectation of rapid preferment and the generous treatment of defectors caused many Chinese to enter Mongol service; the rivalry and the desire for independence among the Jurchid commanders and governors was skilfully exploited by the Mongols.

During the Khwarazmian campaign the Mongols fanned the flames of the racial and religious enmities among the heterogeneous population which had only recently been incorporated into a single political unit. Genghis was able to rely on the support of the Muslim merchants, for whom the common interest in international trade and the security of the trade routes in the event of a Mongol victory raised expectations of exceptionally high profits. Merchants and opposition clerics joined in exhorting the populace to offer no resistance to the Mongols. Thus Danishmand-hajib proclaimed before the walls of Zarnuk: 'I, Danishmand-hajib, a Muslim born of Muslim parents, come as an envoy of Genghis Khan to rescue you from the brink of extermination. Genghis Khan has come here with a large army and if you intend to show resistance he will in an instant turn your fortress into a desert and the steppe into the bloody River Jaihun. If you take my advice and submit to him your souls and possessions will remain unharmed.' Similarly, Badr ad-Din al-'Amid informed Genghis Khan of the disagreement between the sultan and his mother and persuaded Genghis to inflame the sultan's suspicions by means of forged letters.[80]

Psychological warfare is no modern innovation; Genghis Khan used it on a large scale. As early as the struggle for the steppe he had spread the claim that Heaven had destined him as ruler; members of Mongol trading caravans spread stories intended to cause panic among the local populace; forged letters were fed to Sultan Muhammad which strengthened his mistrust of his Turkic units; freedom of religion was proclaimed; those who offered no resistance were promised that life and property would be spared;[81] terrible destruction was threatened in the event of resistance; bloody examples were designed to spread fear and reduce the populace's will to resist.

Genghis Khan's policies bore fruit and the strength of the Mongol army increased in the course of his campaigns. In China numerous Khitan troops and Chinese units joined the Mongols, contributing significantly to the Mongol victory. Uighur and Karluk auxiliary troops, as well as Khitan units, took part in the western campaign; Chinese siege technicians, joined by Muslim engineers, were of incalculable service to the Mongols during the siege of Khwarazmian cities.

The Mongol victory should not to be looked upon as a miracle. The rich civilized states fell to the dynamism of poor herdsmen who were accustomed to misery and poverty. In China, where only the ruling Jurchid circles had adopted the foreign Chinese culture, while the mass of the people had retained their traditional mode of life and their military skills, the Mongols faced the stiffest resistance and it took over a decade of fighting to break the power of the Jurchid. Faced with the Mongol onslaught, the Khwarazmian empire, however, disintegrated into its constituent parts. Centrifugal forces gained the upper hand and, because of the enmity between Sultan Muhammad and the Caliph of Baghdad, and in the face of the religious tolerance proclaimed by Genghis Khan, a united front under the banner of a Holy War failed to materialize.

5

The Structure of the Mongol World Empire

The administration of the empire

Nomad empires were loose associations of tribes, which banded together, either in the face of impending danger or in order to carry out some warlike enterprise. Because of the traditional way of life of the nomads, in which mobility was in constant opposition to established structures, such associations were not very stable; the tribes maintained their independence and the alliances disintegrated as quickly as they formed. By the time of Genghis Khan the tribe was, however, no longer the strong force which it had once been and Genghis put an end to this unstable and constantly changing nomadic political system.

In accordance with the system on which the army was organized, the whole Mongol nation was divided into units of families, ten, one hundred and one thousand families – a system which the khans of the Golden Horde extended to the population of Russia.[1] Once allocated to such a unit, a person was not allowed to quit it on pain of death. Carpini describes the system very clearly, commenting: 'The Tartar emperor exercises amazing power over all his subjects. No one dares to settle in any part of his empire unless specifically directed to that area by the emperor himself. He personally designates the residence of the chiefs (*duces*), who designate the residence of the chiliarchs, who in turn control the residence of the leaders of "hundreds" and the latter that of the leaders of "tens". 'This system permitted the centralized control of the state. Juvaini comments: 'One of the greatest innovations was the appointment of these leaders of units of tens,

hundreds and thousands which made possible the exact imple-
mentation of plans and the speediest transmission of orders'.[2]

This method of organizing the population in decimal units was
a break with the traditional tribal system. The leaders of the units
were appointed by the ruler, the appointment was heritable[3]
but the appointees could be summarily dismissed. The populace
subordinated to them belonged to the military unit but they owed
the commander neither taxes nor corvée labour and could, if
necessary, be transferred to another commander.[4] Strict military
discipline limited aspirations towards independence. The companions (*nökböd*) were incorporated into the bodyguard and committed to regular military service. The bodyguard (*keshig*) was
expanded to 10,000 men, an élite corps which not only protected
the ruler but was also an instrument of power which could be
employed on any task at any time.[5]

Genghis Khan was not, however, able to divorce himself
completely from the traditions of the steppe. He regarded the
conquered peoples as belonging to himself and to his family,
dividing them among the members of his clan and his meritorious
military commanders. He transferred authority over parts of the
empire to his sons,[6] but on condition that they should extend their
rule over neighbouring peoples. The expansion of the empire
required this measure, which in no way signified the division of
the empire into autonomous splinter states. The *ulus* of Genghis'
sons were subject to central imperial control and were required to
provide contingents of troops for undertakings decided on by
the ruler, such as Hulegu's campaign in Iran; they also had to
contribute a portion of their booty to the ruler of the empire.
Yarghuchi were appointed by the central government; these were
in charge of administration and justice, monitored the actions of
the princes and informed Genghis Khan of all that happened
in the *ulus*.[7] The rights of holders of apanages were similarly
restricted. Those households allocated to them in China had to
render a silk tax; but the tax was collected by the *darughachi*,
officials of the central government, and 70 per cent of the tax was
retained for the central treasury.[8]

The frontiers of the individual *ulus* were not clearly demarcated;
even during Genghis' lifetime this led to quarrels between his sons
and to aspirations towards independence. These differences became obvious at the siege of Urgench when, because this area was

designated as his fief, Jochi sought to protect the town and the populace of Khorasan from destruction; Juzjani even asserts that Jochi intended to ally himself with the Muslims and found an independent state. Despite the measures introduced by Genghis Khan the feudal system did hold dangers for the cohesion of the empire. While Genghis was alive it was possible to keep the centrifugal forces within limits. After his death those forces constantly received fresh stimulation and this eventually led to the break up of the empire into four independent khanates.

The Mongols were convinced of the superiority of the nomad culture. They were accustomed to a free life, subject to no form of regular taxation. On special occasions – as, for example, when Temuchin wished to provide for his poverty-stricken ally, Wang-khan[9] – a tax (*kubchir*) was levied. Such special taxes, also raised for the support of poor and needy clansmen, or on the occasion of a tribal chief's wedding or journey, were not, however, permitted to endanger the growth of the herd. In contrast to the sons of the soil, who were defenceless against the exactions of their masters, the nomad could, thanks to his mobility, evade such taxes by fleeing; a positive consensus was thus essential if taxes were to be raised among the nomads. As we have already seen, tradition required the tribal chiefs to support tribal members who fell into poverty and for this purpose a tax was imposed on the army. Rashid ad-Din comments: 'Earlier, while their [Mongol] customs and rules were still valid, an annual *qubchur* of horses, sheep, cows, felt, milk products etc. was levied on the army for the benefit of impoverished hordes and followers.'[10]

The main duty imposed on the Mongols was military service; defeated enemies, if not massacred, were incorporated into the victorious formations as serfs who owed their masters military and other service. Town-dwellers and farmers were of no use, neither in the Mongol army nor to the Mongol economy and, doubtless, many an old warrior expressed the view that they should kill such useless persons and turn the agricultural land into pastures. During the reign of Ögödei a representative of the 'Old Mongol' party did, in fact, submit a request that the total populace of Northern China should be massacred and the occupied lands be turned into pastures. Ila Chuzai rebutted this proposal, pointing out that by imposing taxes the government's requirements in silver, materials and rice could be met. 'How can it be suggested that the Northern Chinese are of no value?' he objected.[11]

Such nomadic demands must have struck a chord with Genghis Khan. He shared the conviction of his people about the superiority of their nomad culture – and his order that the Mongols should never forsake their way of life or their customs was still respected into the fourteenth century.[12] It never crossed his mind that the conquerors might possibly live together or work together with the defeated nations, let alone that the nomad culture would merge with the cultures of the town-dweller and farmer, an aim which his grandson Khubilai attempted to realize in China.[13] Wherever the attitude of the population was hostile, thousands upon thousands were massacred and large areas of the conquered country were transformed into pastures or hunting grounds. Genghis Khan realized, however, that the nomads were dependent on supplies from the agricultural lands and that he had to take into account the views of the Khitan and Chinese feudal lords,
as well as those of the Muslim merchants in his retinue, whose income was derived from the work of the populace. Town-dwellers and farmers were allowed to survive, but were subject to an unrestrained policy of exploitation.

Plundering the defeated enemy had always been the main nomadic aim of war. Military law was paramount in the occupied territories and requisitioning took place as the ruler saw fit to order. Collection of tribute for the court was the responsibility of officials known as *darughachi* and *basqaq*, between whose respective roles it is not possible to differentiate exactly since their functions appear to have varied according to location and period. It is even difficult to assess accurately their subordination, but Berezin assumes that in the Golden Horde the *darughachi* belonged to the *ulus* administration, while the *basqaq* was despatched from the imperial court to occupied territories in order to conduct the population census, collect taxes and carry out certain other general administrative duties.[14]

The military nature of the *basqaq* appointment is stressed by several authors who describe the *basqaqs* as military commandants, or as dispatched by the emperor to provide military protection to the *darughachi* while the latter collected taxes.[15] A Juvaini text, also used by Rashid al-Din, states that, after the capture of Bokhara, Genghis Khan appointed a Turk and a

Mongol to protect (*basqaqi*) the notables from molestation by the Mongol military. Juvaini uses the phrase in a similar sense when he writes elsewhere that Tukel, as *basqaq*, was entrusted with protecting the province.[16]

Spuler differentiates between the duties of *basqaqs* according to the country in which they were appointed. He writes: 'In Russia the Tatars had, in addition to their city prefects (*darughas*), their regular commandants (*basqaqs*) in the individual Russian cities'. In Iran on the other hand, according to the same author. 'the *basqaqs* were there to supervise and support the ruler in carrying out his financial responsibilities'.[17] The Armenian historian Babayan maintains that in Transcaucasia Baichu commanded the army while Arghun, as *basqaq*, was responsible for civil and financial administration; and it is Doerfer's opinion that the emir commanded the Turkic-Mongol troops while the *basqaq*, who held the position of intermediary to the local population, was thus also the tax-collector.[18]

The chroniclers' use of language often determines their definition of an appointment. Thus, Juvaini asserts that Jochi appointed Chin Timur as *basqaq* in Khorasan, while Rashid ad-Din maintains that Chin Timur held the appointment of *shahna* and that the district *basqaqs* were subordinated to him. Juvaini also uses the term *basqaq* in the sense of *darugha* (supervisor) when he writes that the Mongol Mengu-bulad was appointed to be the *basqaq* in charge of craftsmen in Tabriz.[19]

The actual rank of the *basqaq* varied just as much as did the nature of his appointment. When Korguz took over the administration of Khorasan, Arghun was, as *basqaq*, subordinate to him – yet there are examples of *basqaqs* who had viceregal powers. Plano Carpini writes: 'In those lands in which the local princes have been permitted to return home, *bascacos* [*bastacos* must be corrected to *bascacos*] are appointed as viceroys (*prefecti*) and the princes must, like all others, obey their every order, otherwise they will be treated as rebels and the relevant city or district will be devastated and the inhabitants killed.[20]

In general the term *basqaq* was applied to those executive officials who were acquainted with the conditions in the western areas of the empire; mainly entrusted with financial administration, in particular the collection of taxes, they had for this purpose troops at their disposal. Some authors assume that the office of *basqaq* existed before the Mongol invasion and it is suggested that the term originated in the Kara-khitan empire. The term is found in western sources; in the *Yuanshi* there is only one mention of a *basiha* (*basqaq*) named Hesimali (Ismail) in Kesan (Kasan, a city in Fergana). The expression was unknown in China. It is found neither in the Yuan archives, nor in the *Secret History* or later Mongol histories.[21]

In addition to the *darughachi* and the indigenous *basqaq*, plenipotentiaries extraordinary of the Great Khan were frequently despatched to raise special taxes, a practice which continued into the reign of Ögödei. The Chinese Xu Ting complained: 'The *Dada* [Tatar] ruler sends, whenever it pleases him,[22] officials from the steppe to the lands of the Han to set *chaifa* taxes. In Yenjing [I myself], Ting, have seen [in this role] the Minister Hu . . .' – whom Wang Guowei correctly identifies as Shigi-khutukhu, who supervised the population census of Northern China in 1235.[23] 'The extortion of goods has become worse [than before]; matters are now so bad that the guilds of beggars and teachers must deliver silver as a *chaifa* tax.'

In the bilingual texts *chaifa* represents the Mongol term *alban kubchiri*[24] and thus includes corvée as well as a tax on property;[25] in other Chinese transcriptions of the fourteenth century, however, the term is applied only to corvée labour (*alba*). The expression *chaifa* is used to denote taxes imposed upon the Mongols as well as the defeated population in China. Xu Ting includes, in the *chaifa* exacted from inhabitants of the steppes, not only the collection of animals and animal products, but also the recruitment of servants. In Northern China the *chaifa* tax consisted of each adult having to deliver a silk tax, calculated in silver, and also to provide fodder, provisions and equipment for official messengers and the army as it marched through. The term did not include trading or land taxes; thus in the patent granted to Changchun the land tax (*fushui*) is specifically listed as well as the *chaifa*.[26]

The populace was particularly oppressed by the excessive demands of the official messengers (*elchi*), who rode hither and thither through the occupied territories, requisitioned horses and provisions for themselves and their escorts, spent the night in private dwellings and mistreated the inhabitants. The burden which the courier service imposed on the populace can be gleaned from a description by Rashid ad-Din which, although it refers to the situation in Iran before Ghazan's reforms, was probably also applicable in some degree to the period of Genghis Khan.

Rashid asserts that the official messengers commandeered horses, not only from the herds of the Mongols on their pasturelands but also from caravans and travellers who had come from China, Hindustan and other near and far-off lands, even from emirs, *basqaqs* and others who were on their way to court. The situation was so serious that robbers disguised themselves as emissaries (*elchi*), robbed travellers of their horses, plundered their baggage and confiscated their letters of protection and their travel authorisations. Couriers were not satisfied with commandeering only horses and supplies; they quarrelled and took everything on which they could lay their hands. In the dwellings where the couriers took quarters they damaged and wore out carpets, bedding and household utensils, used the doors as firewood, destroyed the gardens; and what they stole was sold on the streets. Even when dispatched on relatively unimportant missions they took an escort of 200–300 men and those of higher rank might even take 500–1,000. Rashid's description, which sought to stress the reforms introduced by Ghazan, may not be free from exaggeration, but in China too the extortions practised by emissaries (*elchi*) gave rise to constant complaints. It is clear from official documents of the Yuan dynasty that messengers and emissaries quartered themselves in private dwellings and in temples, annoyed the inhabitants, demanded unnecessary quantities of supplies, beat those in charge of post stations and interfered in local justice.[27]

Reports of the situation in later times allow us to form a picture of the caprice with which taxes were imposed and of the methods used to collect them. Rashid reports that, prior to Ghazan's reforms, the *kubchir* was exacted twenty or thirty times a year in Iran. Those who could not pay were ill–treated, tortured and thrown into chains and their children were taken from them; those who fled and were captured were killed. A contemporary Russian song ran: 'If a man had no money, they took his child. If he had no child, they took his wife. If he had no wife, he himself was taken.' In a poem dedicated to Juvaini, the Persian poet Pur-i Baha Jami laments: 'Young and old groaned under the *qubchur*'. These quoted texts mirror the conditions in later times; we may,

21   *Paitze*. Tablet of authority issued by Mongol Kha'ans.

however, assume that oppression and despotism were no less widespread during the years immediately following the Mongol occupation.[28]

Driven to despair, the populace fled. The 'Fallow Fields' period began in China and the same situation was prevalent in Iran. The military campaigns resulted in a drop in the numbers of taxpayers. The flight from the land assumed threatening proportions and it became obvious that a regular system of taxation must be introduced if the provisioning of the army and the income of the state treasury were not to be endangered.[29] Tribute was adapted to the economic structure of the conquered nations. The measures introduced by Yalavach in Transoxania – later adopted as a model by Möngke Kha'an – set a fixed tax, appropriate to the property owned and the ability of the taxpayer to pay. The *kubchir* was calculated on a monetary basis and was imposed only once a year; payment of the tax secured freedom from any other imperial tax obligation during the year.[30]

In addition to their tribute to the central court, the inhabitants of the occupied territories did, of course, still have to pay the customary local taxes, the land tax (Mongolian: *chang*) due by the farmers and the trading tax (Mongolian: *tamgha*) due by the merchants. It is clear from the patent granted to Changchun that a land tax already existed at the time of Genghis Khan.[31] There is, however, no reference in that patent to a trading tax and, although the Yuan emperors were later to cite the authority of Genghis Khan for their tax regime it seems unlikely, given the Mongol interest in encouraging trade, that there was any general trading tax in his days. It is possible that it was introduced during the reign of Ögödei Kha'an[32] and during the reign of Khubilai Kha'an it was set at one-thirtieth of the value of the transaction. In the Il-khan empire the *tamgha* tax – which Rashid ad-Din was to abrogate in Isfahan[33] – was imposed not only on goods such as wood, soap, fruit and fabrics sold in the bazaar, but also on all manufacturing and trading establishments, including the brothels, in the towns.[34]

These steps towards a regular system of taxation would, however, scarcely have put an end to the despotism and extortion practised by the Mongol rulers or by local feudal lords and officials. The Chinese chronicles comment: 'Initially the Yuan had no well-ordered system of taxation.'[35]

The administration of countries with a sedentary population caused the Mongols great problems. The Mongols had no cadres suitable for this task; they were not linguists, nor were they accustomed to a money economy. They were thus forced to rely upon the services of multilingual, literate members of the defeated nations. Men like the Muslim Yalavach and his son Mas'ud, the Khitans Ila Chuzai and Ila Ahai, the Kerait Chingai and the Uighur Tata-tonga, who under Genghis were largely responsible for the administration and the taxation policies in the occupied territories, made considerable contributions to healing the wounds of war, introducing reconstruction and creating a more orderly way of life for the conquered nations. The apparatus of administration was taken over by the subject nations. 'The Dada follow the system of the Chin bandits', comments Zhao Hong, who came across not only Khitans, the brothers Ila Ahai and Ila Tuka, but also Jurchid and Chinese acting as ministers at the court of the viceroy, Mukali. Local administration remained in the hands of indigenous officials.[36]

The Mongols were not only inexperienced in administration; they were also a small and diminishing minority in the occupied territories and, in order to ensure their continuing rule, required the support of certain sections of the local population. Genghis Khan was aware of the influence of religion on the mass of the population; by granting tax exemptions and proclaiming religious tolerance he was able to gain the support of a substantial number of clergy of all confessions, who prayed for the victory of the Mongols and for the welfare of their ruler.[37]

The interests of the major merchants and their allied feudal lords coincided with those of the Mongols. Muslim merchants had rendered Genghis priceless services during the wars and the outlook for profitable international trade had never been so promising as under his rule. The security of the trade routes, and the personal protection available, permitted the transport of the costliest goods with minimum risk; generous payments made possible unbelievable profits. Most Uighur and Persian merchants were happy to enter Mongol service as tax officials and financial advisors,[38] while Genghis' policy towards the feudal lords was to exploit to his own advantage the rivalries and enmity between them and to bind them individually to himself by confirming their privileges.

The centralized control of the empire and the multinational composition of its population made it necessary to establish a secretariat, which would present the ruler's commands in writing, translate these into the different national languages and issue official documents regarding tax exemption, safe-conduct etc. As early as his victory over the Naimans, Genghis had taken the Naiman chancellor, Tata-tonga, into his service as Keeper of the Seal, ordering that henceforth all imperial decrees were to be authenticated by a seal. The discussions which Genghis had with Changchun in 1222 were recorded in Turkish, Chinese, Persian and Mongol. Literate linguists – mainly Uighurs – appointed as secretaries (*bichechi*) exercised great influence on the general administration of the empire because they were responsible, not only for recording and translating edicts and instructions, but also for preparing guidance for the collection of taxes. They kept the accounts of income and expenditure and, as Rashid points out, thanks to their positions of trust – which included custody of the Great Seal (*ulugh tamgha*) – they completely controlled the financial system and quite often misused their position to enrich themselves. Rashid quotes the example of the *Hakim* who, by bribery, obtained receipts for double supplies.[39]

The expansion of the empire required an extension of the courier service and the introduction of compulsory support duties on this postal network (*ulagha*). Those inducted, who were responsible for the supply of horses, provisions and fodder, were accorded the same status as those inducted for military service. The new courier service was probably based on the Turkic system, of which mention is made as early as the seventh century. The Chinese postal system was only introduced during the reign of Ögödei, who claimed for himself the distinction of having introduced post stations to speed up the courier service and thus the carriage of urgent official documents.[40]

Apart from measures designed to ensure Mongol rule, the conquerors did not interfere in the internal affairs or the social life of the conquered nations – as long as these did not lead to open conflict with Mongol customs. Thus, Genghis forbade ritual slaughter of animals, because he regarded the Muslim refusal to eat the dishes offered to them as disrespect for Mongol customs; but in China, in accordance with Chinese legal practice, marriages

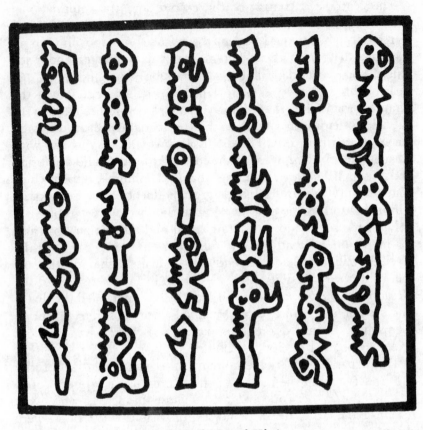

22   *Seal of Mongol Kha'an.*

under Levirate law were forbidden for the Han and Bohai. Not until the reign of Khubilai Kha'an was an attempt made to impose this nomad custom on the defeated nations.[41]

The principles established by Genghis Khan for the administration of the empire were adopted by his successors and were adapted in each of the individual khanates to the socio-political structure and the traditions of the conquered peoples. This system enabled primitive livestock-breeders to maintain for 150 years their rule over peoples who were hundreds of times more numerous and who belonged to the oldest civilizations of Asia.

Genghis Khan's legislation

In his organization of the empire Genghis Khan created the model of a state which was a direct contrast to the traditional nomadic tribal league. As a legislator he also pursued the aim of creating new norms, in order to adapt the nomadic way of life to the requirements of a world empire, and in order to secure for ever the rule of his descendants. One *bilik*, transmitted by Rashid ad-Din, states: 'If in the future of 500, 1,000 or 10,000 years, successors who will be born and ascend the throne preserve and do not alter the custom (*yosun*) and the law (*yasa*) of Genghis Khan, which must be applied to [all important events of] the people, Heaven will support their rule and they will always have happiness and joy [in life].' Genghis issued a stern warning against deviating from the path which he had ordained: 'If the great, the military leaders and the emirs of the many descendants of the ruler who will be born in the future, should not adhere strictly to the law, then the power of the state will be shattered and come to an end; no matter how they then seek Genghis Khan, they shall not find him.'[42]

Anarchy and lawlessness was prevalent among the Mongol tribes at the time of Genghis' birth. Soon after his defeat of the Kerait ruler he proclaimed his intention of ending this situation and introducing order on the steppe. He convoked a great assembly at which he announced 'good and strict laws [*yasaha*]'. These laws were to apply to all tribes and, according to al-'Umari: 'He despatched his messengers to the separate and non-allied tribes informing them of his position and his justice, his laws and his generosity.'[43]

The Uighur script, adopted from the Naimans, was to be the instrument which ensured that these laws were accurately transmitted without suffering any alterations. From then on the orders, instructions and commands of Genghis Khan were written on scrolls and bound in volumes. Juvaini refers to the work as the 'Great Book of the Yasas' (*Yasa nama-i buzurg*) and Chinese sources as 'The Great Yasa' (*da zhasa*).[44] The scrolls were preserved in secret archives and were known only to the senior family members of the ruling house. Maqrizi is thus mistaken when, citing the evidence of a source who claimed to have seen a copy of the *Yasa* in the library of a madrasa in Baghdad, he asserts that, when the 'Book of the Yasa' was completed, it was carved on tablets of iron. The *yasa* which that source claimed to have seen would probably have been the *yasa* of an Il-khan, perhaps that of Ghazan.[45]

The *Yasa* of Genghis Khan does not represent a legal code drawn up at one particular point in time and it is not a systematic work. It is a collection of orders and decrees which Genghis Khan issued, as circumstances required, over a period of time; this collection would have been edited into its final form when, on the occasion of his coronation, Ögödei Kha'an introduced the ceremony of the presentation of Genghis Khan's *Yasa*.[46]

The work has not survived and the preserved fragments do not transmit verbatim the wording of Genghis Khan. Some fragments may be completely fictitious as, for example, when Armenian chroniclers attribute to the *Yasa* Christian beliefs, such as the commands to love our neighbours as ourselves, to do no evil and to forgive those who trespass against us. Other fragments – such as those regulations which authorize tax exemptions for the descendants of Ali, fakirs, lawyers, muezzin, those who wash corpses etc. – may refer to the *yasas* of later Mongol rulers. One can scarcely attribute to Genghis Khan an understanding of the Islamic world. The Il-khans, however, were well acquainted with it and it was at the siege of Baghdad that Hulegu issued the edict to protect those learned in Islamic law, the sheikhs, the descendants of Ali and the *erke'un* (Christians).[47]

There are wide differences of opinion concerning the content and the character of the work. Most authors support the view that in the *Yasa* Genghis Khan codified Mongol common law. Vernadsky is, however, correct to raise the objection that, while there was no necessity to codify and record the common law, there was a need to commit to paper the new laws which Genghis Khan introduced because of the development of the nomad state into a world empire.[48] Apart from a few religious taboos, the transmitted fragments of the *Yasa* introduce new measures into the Mongol legal system and do not concern themselves with common law. The *Yasa* does not mention compensation, one of the fundamental institutions of the nomadic legal system from time immemorial; no new laws are promulgated for murder or for the abduction of women. The *Yasa* concerns itself with private law, family law and the law of inheritance, the law of property and the law of contract, only in those cases in which new measures were being introduced. Such a measure was, for example, the law on lost property, which was introduced in the interest of travellers, especially merchants, and served to protect trade. (The attribution to the *Yasa* of the regulation making a third bankruptcy a criminal offence seems likely to be mistaken.) In the words of al-'Umari: 'Everything in the *Yasa* which is ascribed to him [Genghis Khan] arose solely from his reasoning, his empathy and his ability to give of his best'; or as Juvaini comments: 'Genghis Khan laid down those laws which he concluded were necessary.'[49]

In accordance with the basic principle of preserving supreme power for Genghis Khan and his descendants, the *Yasa* contains directives for the mobilization of the army, the prosecution of military operations and relations with foreign nations. As Juzjani remarks, mobilization of the army or destruction of towns and countries were carried out as laid down in the 'Great Book of the Yasa'. Likewise, Plano Carpini reports that when Genghis Khan returned home from the western campaign he proclaimed that the Mongols should subjugate the whole world and should have no relations with nations which had not submitted to them.[50]

The 'Great Book of the Yasa' was only for the use of the Kha'an, ruler of the empire. The administrative division of the Mongol empire into three *ulus* (the Golden Horde, the Il-khanate and the Chaghatai *Ulus*) required, however, the introduction of separate regulations for these provinces; Abu'l Mahasin maintains that individual *yasas* were promulgated for the three khanates. There is also a reference in the *Yuanshi* to a five-part legal code, promulgated by Genghis Khan at the instigation of the Chinese Guo Baoyu, and intended for use in northern China. This legal code, which Guo Baoyu presented to the ruler in the interest of the Chinese population, includes the following regulations: when the army takes the field it is not allowed to massacre the civil population without cause; only the most serious crimes will be punished by death; other 'general' offences will be punished with beatings, according to the nature of the offence; every adult of Mongol and Inner Asian (*semu ren*) families listed in the military register is liable to conscription; among the Northern Chinese (*Hanren*) only one in three adults will be conscripted from those families who own four acres (*qing*) of cultivated land; the age limits for military service are from fifteen to sixty; households which are directed to the postal service will be given parity of treatment with the families of soldiers; a civilian tradesman may own only one acre of land; Buddhists and Taoists, who are of no value to the state and who bring harm to the people, are banned.[51]

Parallel with these legal codes the legal process was also recorded in writing. The decisions reached by Shigi-khutukhu in civil and criminal cases were, after submission to and approval by Genghis Khan, set down in writing and bound in volumes. Law sprang from the sovereign will of the ruler and the precepts (*bilik*) enunciated by Genghis Khan had the same legal validity as his orders (*yarlik*) or his laws (*yasa*). We may safely assume that there were collections of the *bilik* and it was from these that Rashid ad-Din quotes Genghis' maxims. Some writers such as Vassiliev and Zamtsarano regard the *Yasa* as a collection of such maxims, but I believe that the *yasa* and the *bilik* were recorded in two separate collections. The *Yasa* was only available to the Genghisides, whereas the collection of *bilik* was available to wider circles. Rashid, for example, transmits the contents of the *bilik*, but has nothing to report about the *Yasa*.[52]

The Mongol empire was born of war and the army was the instrument of power on which Genghis Khan's supremacy was founded; a considerable part of Genghis' legislation is thus dedicated to military organization. Draconian punishments were introduced in order to strengthen the discipline among the warriors and their commanders; collective responsibility was made a guiding principle. Before the battle with the Tartars Genghis Khan declared: 'If during the attack or retreat a soldier's baggage, bow or saddle falls to the ground and the warrior behind him rides on without dismounting to help, that warrior will be executed.' Carpini reports: 'If two, or three or more members of a troop flee, they are punished with death. If a whole troop flees but the squadron does not, all members of the troop are executed. In short, all who flee are killed, except in the case of a general withdrawal. Equally, if two or more members of a troop make a spirited advance and are not supported by the other members of the troop, the latter are killed; and if one or more members of a troop are captured and are not rescued by their fellow troopers the latter will be executed.' Al-'Umari quotes the words of 'a reliable source' who told him: 'If, when one of their regiments joins battle, 999 men are killed and one man escapes, he will be executed because he did not remain with his regiment; the only exception is if he returns victorious.'[53]

Everyone, irrespective of rank and position, was subject to the same discipline. Juvaini comments: 'Their [the commanders'] obedience and loyalty is so strong that, if the commander of a division makes a mistake, no matter how great a distance – even from sundown to sunrise – separates him from the Khan, the latter will send a single rider to administer the appropriate punishment: if his head is forfeit, the messenger will behead him, if gold is demanded the messenger will take it from him.'[54] The army was based on the principle of success. Incompetent officers were removed from command and replaced by one of their subordinates; and, as we have already seen, the soldiers were protected against ill-treatment by their officers.

Genghis Khan brought to the task of establishing peace and order throughout the empire the same merciless severity with which he enforced discipline in the army. Robbery and plundering, a facet of nomad life and the cause of continual campaigns of revenge and feuds between tribes and clans, hindered international trade, in which the herdsmen had a vital interest. Genghis Khan employed draconian punishments in order to root out this basic evil. The Chinese Peng Daya reports: 'Whoever is guilty of robbery is executed and his family and goods are given to the victim's family.' Plano Carpini confirms: 'If anyone in the lands under their control is caught robbing or stealing he is killed without mercy'; and Kirakos of Gandzak comments: 'They [the Mongols] have such a hatred of theft that it is punished by the most terrible death.'[55] Supervisors were appointed on the trade routes; if animals or goods were found the finder was required to bring these to the supervisor or be accused of theft. If the owner turned up he was able to obtain his lost property from the supervisor without any difficulty.[56]

Peace and order within the state depended on peace within the family. Adultery could lead to feuds and was thus liable to the death penalty. 'Whoever commits adultery will be executed, whether or not they have previous convictions' is one of the *Yasa*'s articles. Plano Carpini confirms: 'One of their laws or customs is to kill both the man and woman who are caught in adultery; and it is the same for unmarried girls: whoring results in the killing of the man as well as the woman.'[57]

Adultery with women from a foreign tribe was, however, tolerated because this did not endanger the harmony of the clan. 'They take as many wives as they wish', comments Kirakos, 'but they show no mercy to those who commit adultery with their wives, although they themselves consort with women of other tribes wherever they can.' In order not to commit a criminal offence, they will first of all kill the husband, comments Juvaini. He writes: 'If a woman who is captured by a Mongol has a husband no one will enter into a relationship with her. If an Unbeliever [i.e. a Mongol] desires a married woman he will kill the husband and then have relations with the woman.'[58]

Genghis Khan's concern for peace and order even led him to act against alcoholism. Genghis himself was no teetotaller and did not scorn drinking. When the Onggut chief Alakush sent him six bottles of wine, Genghis was delighted with the gift, drank three beakers of it and then stopped. '[If one drinks] a little of this it enlivens the mind', he commented, 'but [if one drinks] too much it befuddles the mind.' Genghis was aware of the consequences of alcoholism. The commoners (*qarachu*) drank away their horses, their herds and all their belongings and became beggars. One of Genghis' *bilik* pointed out that alcoholic drink intoxicated the good and the bad to the same extent, without respect for position and character; it numbed the senses and the limbs; hands lost their ability to grasp properly, limbs their ability to move, the mind the ability to think sensibly. Genghis, a student of human nature, was, however, realistic in formulating his command for moderation: 'If there is then no means to prevent drunkenness, a man may become drunk thrice a month; if he oversteps this limit he makes himself guilty of a punishable offence. If he is drunk only twice a month, that is better – if only once, that is more praiseworthy. What could be better than that he should not drink at all? But where shall we find a man who never drinks? If, however, such a man is found, he deserves every respect.'[59]

The success of an undertaking often depended upon honest reports from military scouts and intelligence agents. One article in the *Yasa* declared: 'Deliberate lying will be punished by execution.' The Mongols were in general honest, as is illustrated by Juzjani's anecdote about two soldiers who, caught sleeping when on night guard, admitted their guilt at their trial and were executed. A Persian eyewitness was astonished by their confession, since it would have been impossible to prove the charge. This was answered by a Mongol officer: 'You Tadzhiks would have lied. A Mongol prefers to tell the truth rather than lie, even if a thousand lives might be at risk.' The *Secret History* reports that Jamuka, on the occasion when Wang-khan [and Temuchin] were late at the agreed rendezvous, demanded: 'Do the Mongols regard a "Yes" as an oath or not?' Genghis Khan's proscription of lying was, according to Rashid, also used against those who brought false charges; in the case against Korguz, Ögödei quoted a section of Genghis Khan's *Yasa* which condemned slanderous plaintiffs to the death penalty.[60]

The state of order which was to prevail throughout the empire was also to be evident in the running of the ordinary household. 'He who is able to manage his house is able to control a domain [*mulk*]', is the gist of one *bilik*; another commands: 'When a husband goes hunting or to war, his wife must maintain the household, so that the messenger or guest who dismounts there finds all in order and the wife is able to provide him with good food and everything else he may require.'[61]

Religious taboos were sacred to Genghis Khan and he gave them legal status. Thus one article of the *Yasa* decrees death for anyone who urinated in ashes or water. Plano Carpini reports that it was also forbidden to urinate inside a dwelling. Anyone who did this intentionally was punished by death; a person who did so inadvertently was subject to a heavy fine, paid to his accuser, so that the inhabitants, their dwelling and all their goods could be purified. For fear of thunderstorms it was forbidden to bathe in water or even wash hands in running water during spring and summer; similarly, clothes were not allowed to be washed but had to be worn until they were worn out.[62] The Taoist Changchun was aware of these prohibitions and said in a conversation with Genghis Khan: 'I understand that in summer the Mongols may not bathe in rivers, may not wash their clothes, may not make felt and may not collect mushrooms.'[63] The edict on cleanliness of the water was, it is suggested by Alinge, a mere matter of hygiene. But the idea of hygiene was unknown to Genghis Khan, who forbade anything to be designated unclean, and there was scarcely danger of pollution of running water. Fear of offending the spirits of fire and water, thus giving rise to thunderstorms, would lie at the root of the prohibition.[64]

Maqrizi attributes to the *Yasa* yet other rules which al-'Umari lists as traditions and customs (*adab*) and which scarcely required the sanction of law. The conditions of nomad life, for example, made hospitality a duty and al-'Umari comments that the law of the steppe stipulated: 'Anyone who calls on people who are then eating shall, without asking permission, sit down and eat with them.' Hospitality was, however, also misused to dispose of enemies, as Genghis Khan's father, Yisugei, learned to his cost. Custom therefore required that food was not accepted from another unless that person first ate of that food, 'not even if the host were an emir and the guest a prisoner'. Kirakos of Gandzak confirms that when someone offered the Mongols food and drink, they would not partake of it until the giver himself ate and drank of it – this from fear of poisoning.[65]

Genghis Khan interfered in the normal life of the nomads only in cases which endangered public order. It is, however, surprising that his legislation did not grapple with the problem of abduction, which had in the past certainly been the cause of continual feuds and campaigns of revenge. Perhaps, following the campaigns of conquest and the subsequent satisfaction of the Mongol demand for women, abduction of women no longer presented the law-giver with a problem. Even more striking, however, is the absence of a legal ruling on the crime of murder. Muslim writers do report that a section of the *Yasa* provided that the killing of a Muslim was to be compensated by a fine of forty gold bezants, that of a Chinese by a fine of an ass. But, since the life of a Muslim and a Chinese would have been equally unimportant in the eyes of Genghis Khan and the fixing of a punishment in gold coinage was a concept foreign to the law-giver, it is certainly inaccurate to attribute such a regulation to the *Yasa*. Under nomadic common law the crime of murder was expiated by compensation to the family of the victim. If the victim was, however, a member of another tribe or clan, the nomad sense of justice demanded that revenge was exacted on the clan or tribe responsible for the crime; indeed, Genghis Khan had launched wars in the name of this basic principle. Genghis Khan the legislator now resisted prohibiting the blood feud, which had itself served as a justification for his actions, and had even been their driving force.[66]

Genghis Khan's legislation did not seek to embrace every aspect of Mongol jurisprudence. Family and inheritance law, property law and the law of debt continued to be generally subject to common law tradition – as Alinge stresses, the law governing claims to straying animals was, because of the regularity of the occurrences, essential for the preservation of internal peace.[67] The legislator did not interfere in existing legal relationships unless these extended beyond the circle of the family or clan, or of the national, religious or occupational unit; but he did claim the right to pass judgement if public order and general peace were endangered.[68] Such legal processes were subject to the decisions of the supreme judge, Shigi-khutukhu, who was responsible for justice at imperial level. The execution of the sentence was, however, left to those in whose favour judgement had been delivered; it was in line with this principle that Genghis Khan handed Iturgen over to his brother Kasar in order that the latter might execute judgement on him. This principle outlasted the division of the empire: Ögödei returned Korguz to the Chaghatai *ulus*, where he had made defamatory statements, and Chaghatai's widow, Kara Oghul, had him executed in an agonizing fashion.[69]

The principle of equality before the law was unknown in Asia; there was among the Mongols a very strong consciousness of rank[70] and a special legal procedure applied to members of the 'golden family'. According to Rashid ad-Din, one of Genghis Khan's *bilik* stated: 'If a member of our family infringes a law [*yasa*] once he shall be admonished; if he transgresses a second time he shall be punished according to the *bilik*; if he is guilty a third time he shall be sent off to the distant area Balzhin-kulzhur – by the time he has gone there and back he will have seen reason. If he does not better his ways he shall be chained and thrown into prison. If, on his release, he has seen reason, then well and good; if not, his relations shall come from near and far and, after consultation, shall decide what is to be done with him.' Special regulations governed the punishment of a *darkhan*, for whom nine sentences were remitted, and also the execution of nobles, which was carried out without shedding their blood. In Chinese legal codes eight groups of persons were, by tradition, subject to special courts (*ba-yi*). 'Physical punishment is not applicable to dignitaries', was a basic tenet of Confucianism.[71]

Genghis Khan retained for himself the right to punish members of his bodyguard. 'If they transgress against the *Yasa* report this to me', he ordered. 'If they have deserved death they will be beheaded, if they have deserved a beating we will lay them out and beat them.' Genghis was an autocrat and the ruler's will was the highest law. Juzjani writes: 'Genghis Khan bound the people of all tribes by oaths and vows to obey him in all things. If he ordered a son to kill his father, he would have to obey.' Plano Carpini comments: 'The Tartar emperor exercises admirable power over all his subjects . . . If at any time, anywhere, he gives them an order, whether it is war, life or death, they obey without demur. Even if he covets an unmarried daughter or sister, she will be handed over without protest.'[72]

Infringement of the *Yasa* was punishable by death and, indeed, the formula used by the Yuan emperors, 'punish according to the *zhasa* of Genghis Khan' meant 'execute'. According to Juzjani's incomplete list, the *Yasa* prescribed the death penalty for the following offences: adultery and moral offences, theft, lying and embezzlement, taking a bite of food from someone else's mouth, entering running water, polluting running water with water in which one had washed. Lesser offences were punished with three, five or ten strokes forcefully administered with a rod. Beatings were also used as a disciplinary measure, inflicted for minor infringements of military regulations.[73] Caprice on the part of the ruler did, however, have certain limitations: trials, as well as political proceedings, were held in public and the ruler had to take account of general feeling expressed by his followers. When Genghis Khan sought to execute his uncle Da'aritai, Bo'orchu, Mukali and Shigi-khutukhu objected and Genghis had to yield. The same companions also, as we have seen, played a similar role when Genghis' sons attempted to withhold his share of the booty after the siege of Urgench.[74]

Genghis Khan's law was designed for the Mongols. It addressed the legal relations of a nomadic people, not the complicated legal relations of a sedentary people. As in the administration of the empire, justice was based on a dual system; the Mongols and the nomads were subject to Mongol law, the private legal matters of the subjugated sedentary races were regulated by their local traditional legal principles.

Genghis Khan's religious policies

Throughout his lifetime Genghis Khan preserved his shamanistic belief in a world of spirits and demons which exercised an influence on man's fate, but he learned of the existence of other gods through contact with Nestorians and Buddhists. Hostility towards strange religions was foreign to shamanism and reason bade Genghis beware of calling down the wrath of these gods. Genghis was tolerant. As a statesman he knew the danger to internal peace represented by wars of religion, and as a conqueror he recognized that the proclamation of religious freedom was a powerful weapon in his struggle against peoples of other religions. Genghis thus ordered that all religions should be respected and that none should be given precedence over the others – or, as al-'Umari formulates the command, that no religion should have the right of fanatical proselytization against another.[75] The success of this policy was obvious in the struggle against the Muslims. In Khotan the Mongols were welcomed as liberators; the religious freedom proclaimed by Genghis Khan prevented a Holy War during the struggle with the Khwarazm-shah. In Georgia there was a strong rumour that the Mongols were Christian, and a procession led by a priest welcomed the Mongol military with the traditional offering of bread and salt.[76]

Genghis Khan came into contact with the representatives of several religions – Christians, Buddhists, Taoists and Muslims – but appears to have had little interest in their dogma and teaching. He bade Changchun visit him, not to be lectured on Taoism but to receive the elixir of longevity; Buddhism and Christianity remained for him alien teachings. The report which appears in later Mongolian and Tibetan accounts of an embassy sent by Genghis Khan to the chief lama of Saskya contains anachronisms which indicate it to be a later fabrication.[77]

Genghis was not, however, indifferent to the dogmas of strange religions when the tenets of such religions conflicted with Mongol customs. He thus passed laws regarding the slaughter of animals when the Muslims refused to eat meat which had been slaughtered according to Mongol custom; and like his successors he certainly did not tolerate that a foreigner might, on grounds of his religion, refuse to marry an in-law, or perform ablutions in running water in accordance with Islamic rites.[78]

Shamans and priests played a role as intermediaries between men and their gods and spirits. The shaman Teb-tengri exercised a strong influence on Genghis Khan, who also believed in the magical powers of the Taoist, Changchun – 'He is indeed a man of Heaven', he exclaimed.[79] In his letters Genghis always exhorted Changchun to pray for his longevity; he expected other clergy to do likewise and the tax exemptions granted to religious communities were linked to the condition of prayers for the ruler's long life. Reasons of state also required that Genghis won over the leaders of foreign religions. Having used the shamans for his purposes during the struggle for supremacy of the steppe, he recognized the influence which clerics exercised over the local population and this influence was to be utilized for the pacification of the conquered lands. As Genghis wrote to Changchun: 'Have you won over the common people to my side?.'[80]

Genghis awarded tax exemptions and immunity patents to members of foreign religions, raising these persons to the status of *darkhan*, but it is doubtful whether these privileges were of such a general character as later Kha'an's ascribed to them. We know of only those patents which Genghis Khan issued in favour of the Buddhist Haiyun and the Taoist Changchun. An Armenian manuscript of 1248 reports: 'In those churches which remained untouched they [the Mongols] left the servants of the church in peace to practise services according to the tenets of their religion; they unscrupulously demanded [from them], however, extortionate contributions of men and cattle, except in the case of small churches and similar buildings and the people who served these.'[81]

Genghis Khan's religious policies were dictated by statesmanlike considerations and, as we shall see, they bore fruit. When, however, religion posed a danger for internal peace, Genghis Khan attacked without mercy. He had Teb-tengri executed, despite the services which the shaman and his father, Mönglik, had rendered; and Juvaini asserts that the *Yasa* of Genghis Khan contained the order to root out the Isma'ilis, without sparing even the child in the cradle.[82]

The legacy of Genghis Khan

At a time when the fragmented Mongol nation, weakened by feuds and tribal wars, lived in constant insecurity and anarchy, the aims pursued by Genghis Khan – the unification of the Mongol tribes and the establishment of stable conditions in the land – corresponded to the needs and the aspirations of the Mongol people. His strength of will, never broken by reverses or defeats, his unfaltering energy, his realistic assessment of prevailing political alignments and his exploitation of whatever opportunities these afforded him, enabled him to achieve his goals. The Mongol nation was united, peace and order ruled in the empire, trade flourished and the campaigns of conquest brought rich booty to the homeland.

Juvaini contrasts the living conditions of the Mongols before the rise of Genghis Khan with the economic upsurge after his conquests. He writes that in the early days the Mongols dressed in the skins of dogs and mice and ate the flesh of those animals. The new world became a paradise for this people. Their pockets and purses were stuffed with treasures, their everyday clothing was adorned with jewels and embroidered with gold; they had more than enough to eat and a surplus of beverages, which flowed for them as did the Oxus River. Plano Carpini also states: 'They [the Mongols] are very rich in animals, namely camels, cattle, sheep and goats; and we believe that the numbers of their horses and mares are not to be found anywhere else in the world . . . The Emperor, army commanders and other nobles have a surplus of gold, silver, silk and pearls.' Carpini further comments that the clothes and the head-dresses (*bogdak*) of the rich wives were of purple material and brocade, often decorated with costly jewels.[83] Rubruck mentions that even the women's trousers were made of fur and that the rich lined the body of their dresses with silk and the arms with cotton. Vincent de Beauvais writes that men and women of the nobility dressed in brocade or purple cloth, but that all women usually wore buckram dresses. Peng Daya comments that, in contrast to the olden times, they wore clothes of cotton, silk or gold-worked brocade. Rubruck remarks that these fabrics were imported from China, Persia and other countries, while the furs came from Russia, Greater Bulgaria, Hungary and Circassia. By the end of the thirteenth century fabrics were being imported from Egypt and, through Venetian traders, even from Europe.[84]

Trade also flourished. The skilled workers deported from China and Iran had brought to Mongolia craft skills and technical knowledge hitherto unknown to the Mongols. During his trip to the West Changchun came across a colony of Chinese craftsmen in Uliasutai. Ögödei had a magnificent palace erected in Karakorum which astonished travellers. Guyuk's throne and his imperial seal were crafted by the Russian goldsmith Cosmas. The Parisian goldsmith Guillaume Bouchier designed for Ögödei's palace a golden tree underneath which were four golden lions from whose jaws flowed wine, fermented mares' milk, mead and arrack. Karakorum had become a world centre, the rendezvous for a colourful mixture of peoples, each living according to its own customs and habits. Contact with different races and religions expanded the world view of the Mongols and raised their cultural expectations.[85]

The economic upsurge had, however, been dearly purchased. The Mongols had paid a high cost in blood; many warriors fell or died of disease during the campaigns of conquest. Now a large proportion of the Mongol military had to serve as garrisons in foreign lands and live there under conditions which were strange to them, especially when Khubilai Kha'an and the Il-khan Ghazan later attempted to settle sections of these garrisons in self-supporting farming colonies. The treasures which flowed into

23   *Karakorum and Erdene Dzuu Monastery.*

the Mongolian homeland were, in the main, of advantage to the upper classes, although the ordinary soldiers did of course share in the booty, bringing back from the campaigns weapons, horses, women and military slaves – who looked after the soldiers' weapons and horses.[86] The pretensions of the nobles increased, however, with their wealth; the exploitation of the common people reached levels unknown in bygone days.

The previous style of life of the nobles had scarcely differed from that of the common people. We have already noted Genghis Khan's protestations to Changchun that he wore the same rags and ate the same food as the cattle and horse herders; Kirakos of Gandzak confirms that masters and servants were served the same food.[87] However, although Rashid describes the princesses of the Il-khan empire, for example, as living in very modest circumstances, contact with civilized nations did accustom some of the Mongol upper class to a life of luxury. Carpini reports that golden fittings adorned the bridles, breastplates, saddles and tail harness of the horses of the senior commanders who came to Guyuk's election; when receiving the Egyptian ambassador, Berke wore a magnificent costume which astounded even Sultan Baibars; the splendour at the court of Khubilai Kha'an evoked the admiration of Marco Polo, who recounts that Khubilai presented each of his 12,000-strong bodyguard with a golden belt and with thirteen robes of different colours, adorned with jewels and costly pearls, for each of the thirteen annual festivals, also that 40,000 persons attended a banquet given by Khubilai.[88] On the occasion of the week-long festivities for Möngke's accession to the throne, 2,000 carts loaded with wine and fermented mares' milk, 300 horses and oxen and 3,000 sheep arrived each day to feed the guests; according to Juvaini, even the normal catering for the court and people of Karakorum required the arrival every day from all parts of the empire of 500 carts loaded with food and drink; Rubruck reports that for the 300 men in his court camp Batu required the daily delivery of the milk of 3,000 mares.[89] When Changchun reached the camp of Temuge, the younger brother of Genghis Khan, a wedding was being celebrated; Li Zhichang recounts that there were several thousand tents and carts and that the fermented mares' milk must have been brought in from a radius of 500 *li*. On Changchun's departure Temuge presented him with several hundred oxen and horses.[90]

24 'The Silver Tree' at Karakorum.

The court consisted not only of the court officials and the harem, but also of the many foreigners employed in the Mongol retinue and the 10,000 men of the bodyguard. The common people had to provide horses – and mares' milk – for the whole court; Ögödei instituted a regular animal tax for this purpose. The duty to provide horses and supplies for the courier service, used by an ever-increasing number of people on duty or trading trips, was becoming increasingly onerous. Those assigned to the postal service were often unable to meet the demands made of them and either fled or sold their women and children. Under Khubilai, the grandson of Genghis Khan, Mongolia itself was impoverished and, after the transfer of the capital from Karakorum to China, it sank politically and economically, to the level of an unimportant province.[91]

The position of the Mongols in the conquered lands also deteriorated. After the end of the campaigns there were no more deliveries of booty and the Mongols had to become used to a money economy. Many fell into debt; evidence of the sale of children offers eloquent testimony to their plight. In the fourteenth century the government in China was constrained to create a special authority which would purchase the freedom of Mongol slaves, but after a year this action had to be discontinued because the numbers of children thus released had already risen to 10,000.[92] The situation was similar in Iran and in his private correspondence Rashid ad-Din speaks of Mongols being sold in the slave markets. Ghazan, lamenting the fact that the descendants of some of Genghis Khan's most meritorious emirs were either sold as slaves to the Tadzhiks or reduced to a life of destitution, gave orders that young Mongols should be bought free and taken into state service; placed in special units under the command of Pulad-chingsang, their numbers are said to have reached 10,000.[93] The Mamluks imported their slaves mainly from the Kipchak region and many Muslim traders were to be found there, purchasing and transporting children abroad. There is also evidence in the repeated prohibitions of the Yuan emperors of a similar significant overseas trade in Mongol slaves from China.[94]

The introduction of the system of 'thousands' led to a reorganization of the social structure, the leaders of the new units usurping the power and the authority of the tribal nobility. The dashing companions (*nökböd*) who had elected their own leader were now incorporated into the bodyguard (*keshig*). It was from their ranks that the civil administrators of the empire were selected and, accustomed to life at court, they gradually lost their warlike virtues; nomadic freedom of movement gave way to a rigid organization in which, under threat of the death penalty, no one dared abandon his allotted position.

The accumulation of wealth in the hands of the upper classes led to an increasing change in the individual strata of Mongol society. The *qarachu* became the *albatu*, liable to taxation and corvée service. New standards were introduced in assessing individual strata of society; those foreigners who were literate and linguists enjoyed a greater influence on the overall administration of the empire than did the Mongol warriors. Knowledge of the Uighur script, comments the Persian historian somewhat ironically, became the particular indicator of knowledge and ability. The careers of Korguz and Arghun confirm these remarks. Juvaini writes that Korguz's father was a man of the people; but Korguz learned Uighur, began his career teaching Mongol children and then became the governor of Khorasan. Arghun's father was an Oirat, who sold his son for a haunch of beef. Later, when Arghun had learned the Uighur language, he was employed as a secretary (*bichechi*). When Korguz was entrusted with the administration of Khorasan and Iraq Arghun was attached to him as *basqaq*. He succeeded Korguz after the latter's execution and became one of the most able administrators in the Mongol empire. The 'academics' – doctors, astronomers and clergy – achieved a diminution in the influence of the shamans.[95] Genghis Khan had an eye complaint healed by a Muslim doctor; doctors were appointed to the highest posts, receiving honorary titles and titles of nobility[96] and Marco Polo highlights the role of the Buddhist priests at the court of Khubilai Kha'an. Chinese literati also lost their influence on the government of the country; the literary examinations – the traditional Chinese system for the selection of officials – were scrapped; clerks and scribes were promoted to official positions on the basis of technical competence.

The evidence of chroniclers and travellers enables us to identify the striking changes wrought on Mongol morality by Genghis Khan's legislation. Juvaini comments that Genghis Khan rooted out the scandalous customs of the Mongols such as adultery and theft. 'War, strife, bodily harm or murder do not exist, robbers or thieves on a grand scale are not to be found among them', remarks Plano Carpini, 'and for this reason their houses and the carts in which they store their wealth have neither locks nor bolts.' Juzjani writes that no one except the owner would dare pick up even a whip lying on the ground. Ibn Battuta, describing how during his travels in Iraq two horses went astray during the night, reports that although the travellers left the country soon afterwards the horses were brought to them on their journey twenty days later. He also comments that although there were many pack animals in the Kipchak area, these could be left unattended because of the severity of the Turkic laws against theft.[97]

It is true that later, as a result of feuds and struggles in some parts of the empire, the evil of robbery did increase considerably. Such robbers included Mongols, Tadzhiks, Kurds and Syrian Arabs – even overseers (*totqu'al*) and customs officials participated in plundering travellers – while the local population sometimes supported the bandits, many of whom had only taken to the woods and banded together because of poverty.[98] The situation was similar in China, to which Taichar and Ila Chuzai were dispatched from Mongolia in order to reinstate order, and where many of the bandits were the sons of distinguished families, even relatives of the governor, the Khitan Shimo Xiandebu.[99] Yet, in Iran for example, conditions under Mongol rule were considered a lesser evil than the anarchy and chaos which followed the death of the last Mongol Il-khan, Abu Sa'id.[100]

The evidence of European travellers is that peace and order existed within families. Carpini remarks: 'Their women are chaste and one hears of no immorality among them . . . Despite the numbers [of the Mongols] there is no strife between them.' Marco Polo admired the marital fidelity of the Mongols: 'On no account will they lay hand on the wife of another man', he writes, 'because they regard that as a most evil and disgusting deed. The fidelity shown by the men towards their wives is remarkable, and the wives are very virtuous.'[101]

The severity of the laws and the authority of Genghis Khan guaranteed security in public and private life. Thanks to the safety of the trade routes and the generosity of purchasers, international trade increased as never before. Such trade, however, benefited only the upper classes; it brought the common people an additional burden of providing accommodation for the travelling merchants. It also did the state economy irreparable harm. The wealth which the merchants acquired, often in exchange for luxury goods, was exported from the country when the merchants left for home. The Mongols, unaccustomed to a money economy, became economically dependent on such merchants, who loaned them money at usurious rates.

Genghis Khan's religious policies could not prevent religious strife within the nation but they contributed in no small degree to securing and underpinning Mongol rule in the conquered lands, where religious leaders supported the Mongols in pacifying the subjugated peoples. The Armenian Catholicus Konstantin in his 'Pastoral Message' of 1251, called upon the Armenian people to obey the conqueror; he gave his blessing to the Khan and his riders, 'who have shown their good will towards us', and called upon the people to pray for the well-being of the Khan 'who has today been installed as our Tsar'. The princes of the churches sought to interpret as universally valid those individual privileges which they received from Genghis Khan. During his visit to the court of Möngke Kha'an, King Het'um I of Armenia, for example, presented a petition to the Kha'an requesting that 'in all the lands occupied by the Tatars and those which they might later occupy, all Christian churches and their clerics, including monks, should be exempted from all socage and even from taxation'. Genghis Khan's successors interpreted such privileges in liberal or more restricted fashion, depending upon the policies of the actual ruler; in every case, however, their edicts invoked the commands of Genghis Khan's *Yasa*.[102]

In addition to the customs and traditional concepts of the nomads there were substantive obstacles to the conclusion that the empire must be centrally governed in order to ensure its cohesion; these included the expansion of the empire, its heterogeneous population with their differing economic and social structures. Genghis Khan did not implement the system of 'thousands' with full rigour. The ruler and the members of his family received areas of land (*qubi*) which belonged to them personally (as *inju*). On the overthrowal of the Chin empire by Ögödei almost half the registered population were divided among the ruling family, meritorious commanders also receiving apanages over which they had complete control. Apanage holders received not only the labour of the people but also an annual income in silver, paper money and silk. Under the strong government of Khubilai the rights of these feudal lords were restricted; the collection of the taxes was brought under the control of the central government, with 70 per cent of the income going directly to the state treasury; criminal justice was transferred to the central administrators; the troops were allocated to the local communities. The holders of the apanages, who were now treated as government officials, resisted such limitations on their independence; in the Il-Khan empire the struggle with apanage holders assumed at times the character of a civil war.[103]

The administrative division of the empire into *ulus*, which were allocated to Genghis Khan's sons, increased the centrifugal forces within the empire. According to Mongol custom, Jochi received the most distant lands, beyond the Irtysch; Chaghatai received parts of Turkestan; Ögödei received the region on the Ili and the youngest son, Tolui, the homeland with the parental domains. The frontiers of the *ulus* were not fixed – they were to be extended by conquest – and disagreements over those frontiers were to lead to the fateful struggle between the Il-khans and the Khans of the Golden Horde. As long as Genghis Khan was alive the unity of the empire was not endangered – aspirations towards independence are levelled at Jochi, but any open move against Genghis Khan was pointless. The struggle for the succession broke out, however, after Ögödei's death. Firstly the rulers of the Golden Horde and then, in the reign of Ghazan, the Il-khans became converted to Islam. Estrangement between the members of the Mongol ruling family quickly increased and the economic, ideological and political contradictions between the different *ulus* led to the dissolution of the empire into virtually independent states.

The later fratricidal war between Khubilai and Arigh-böke divided the Mongols into two camps. Al-'Umari characterizes the relations between Khubilai Kha'an and the rulers of the khanates as being akin to the supremacy exercised by the Caliph. 'In the event of some important event, such as war or the execution of a senior emir, the ruler of the khanate would inform the Kha'an – without, however, requiring to obtain the latter's agreement. It is', comments the writer, 'merely a question of preserving a custom.'[104] Because of his strong personality Khubilai was, however, able to exert an influence on the Il-khanate. He imposed the succession of the Buddhist Arghun to the throne of the Il-khans, and Abaka and Arghun ascended the throne only after being invested by Khubilai. 'Khubilai is the elder brother; how could one ascend the throne without his permission?' remarked Abaka. In the Il-khan empire the administrative organization, legislation and the creation of the bodyguard copied the models introduced by Khubilai in China; under the rule of Geikhatu an attempt was made to introduce paper money in Iran, as Khubilai had done in China – an attempt which failed because of a boycott by Muslim merchants. Even in the Chaghatai *ulus* the designations given to the authorities mirrored the organization of the central and provincial administration in China. The Golden Horde, however, because of its distant location and the earlier conversion of its rulers to Islam, loosened its bonds with the empire before the defection of the other khanates.[105]

Struggles also broke out within the individual khanates. The religious tolerance enforced by Genghis Khan was unable, even during his lifetime, to prevent the Chinese Taoists using the patent granted by Genghis to Changchun as a means to persecute the Buddhists.[106] After Genghis Khan's death religious wars flared up throughout the whole empire. Guyuk supported the Christian faith and under the influence of his Nestorian ministers, Kadak and Chingai, the Muslims were subjected to discrimination and persecution and, according to Juvaini, no Muslim could raise his voice to denounce this state of affairs. A similar situation existed in the *Ulus* Chaghatai, where, according to Juzjani, the word Muslim could not be uttered in the ruler's presence except in an insulting context.[107]

Chaghatai adhered strictly to Mongol customs. In accordance with the decree of Genghis Khan, Muslims were not allowed to slaughter animals according to the rites of the *Shari'a*; nor were they permitted to pray in public or to cleanse themselves in running water.[108] In China, after the conversion of Khubilai to Buddhism, the Buddhists occupied Taoist temples and burned Taoist books.[109] Berke, Khan of the Golden Horde, proclaimed that religious ties were stronger than those of blood. Before taking the field against the Il-khan Hulegu he proclaimed: 'Hulegu has destroyed Islamic cities, he has dethroned the Muslim ruling houses . . . he has, without consulting his relatives, destroyed the

Caliph. If the Eternal God will assist me, I will bring him to account for the blood of the innocent.'[110]

When the rulers of the Golden Horde allied themselves with the Mamluk sultans against the Il-khans, the threat to the empire from Islam caused Khubilai to initiate an anti-Muslim campaign which led to the exodus of Muslims from China. In the realm of the Il-khans Christians were persecuted. In 1295, after his conversion to Islam, Ghazan ordered the destruction of Buddhist temples, idols, churches and synagogues in Tabriz and other Islamic cities; those churches remaining in Tabriz were destroyed by the ordinary people in 1298. Following Hulegu's withdrawal from Baghdad the Christians were massacred and the Buddhists were faced with the alternative of converting to Islam or leaving the Il-khanate. In Samarkand the Christians sought protection against the Muslims from a senior Mongol commander. When that Mongol commander imposed the death sentence on a Christian youth who had converted to Islam the Muslims sent a petition to Berke of the Golden Horde, who, according to Juzjani, dispatched a commando of Turks with orders to destroy the members of this Christian sect 'and they were despatched to Hell.'[111] The non-observance of Genghis Khan's decree of religious tolerance contributed in considerable measure to the divisions among the Mongols and, in the long run, to the fall of the Mongol empire.

Genghis Khan's campaigns of conquest in Inner Asia had damaging consequences for the flourishing culture of Islam. Many cities were destroyed, libraries with irreplaceable treasures were burned, irrigation systems were destroyed, many craftsmen were taken off into slavery and the peasant farmers fled. It is true that under the Il-Khans Hulegu, Abaka and Ghazan, strenuous efforts were made to rebuild the cities, to lighten the burden on the peasant farmers, to prevent the extortions of the tax-collectors and to restore order in the land. Indeed, Juvaini, speaking of Bokhara and Samarkand, says that in his day (i.e. 1259/60) earlier levels of prosperity and well-being had in many cases been re-established and in other cases almost achieved; and, describing these cities, al-'Umari writes: 'despite its hard fate . . . and all the misfortunes which befell it, Samarkand still remains a feast for the eyes.'[112] Yet internal feuding and the struggle between the Golden Horde and the Il-Khans brought about the final decline of the flourishing culture in this region. Ghazan complained: 'I have inherited no wealth from my forefathers . . . I rule a ruined country.' The economic structure of the country also changed after the Mongol conquest. Turkic nomadic tribes from Eastern Turkestan and from Kazhakstan colonized the area in the wake of the Mongols. They transformed agricultural land into animal grazing grounds; livestock breeding largely supplanted agriculture.[113]

In China the immediate consequences of the Mongol conquest were devastating. As a result of the desolation caused by the years of war, the enslavement of a large part of the population and the extortion practised by Mongol feudal lords, who transformed the fields of the Chinese peasants into grazing and hunting grounds, the flight from the land was so great that this became known in Chinese history as the 'Fallow Period'. The installation of foreign, mainly Inner Asiatic tax-farmers led to an unbearable exploitation of the population and awakened a feeling of xenophobia among the Chinese people. The Cathayans, according to Marco Polo, hated the government of the Great Khan because it had installed Tartars and many Saracens as governors over them and they felt themselves to be serfs.[114]

It was, however, not the first time that Northern China had been conquered by foreign peoples. It had been under nomad rule since the tenth century – and Genghis Khan's viceroy, Mukali, was not one of the radical supporters of nomad culture who demanded the eradication of the rural population and the transformation of agricultural land into pastures. Khubilai too, whose conquest of Southern China restored the unity of the Chinese nation, and who has gone down in history as one of the greatest emperors of China, was open-minded towards foreign cultures. Moreover, after the Mongol conquest of Southern China the Chinese were, because of the economic dependence of Northern China on the bread-basket of Southern China, able to regain important political positions and strengthen their influence on the government.

Individual cultures were undoubtedly enriched by the exchange of knowledge and the intellectual wealth brought by foreigners who served the Mongols. The Chinese became acquainted with Iranian medical and astronomical sciences, which were highly regarded in Asia. In 1267 a Persian presented to Khubilai's court an 'eternal calendar' and the drawings for seven astronomical instruments. Under Khubilai a department was established for the study of Western calendrical sciences, also an administration of Western medicine under the leadership of a Western Christian, Aixies (Isa). Medical, Mongolian and Muslim schools were founded in the provinces, interpreters were trained, translated literature was sponsored, geographic knowledge was extended. Under the influence of the Mongols the colloquial language also penetrated Chinese literature and the theatre, displacing the classical style and its fossilized conventions.

In Iran in turn, contact with the Chinese aroused interest in Far Eastern arts and sciences, and the expression of this interest was found in the translation of Chinese works, mainly on medical subjects. Contacts in the field of art, especially in the field of book illumination, have left behind ineradicable traces. The influence of Chinese art is even discernible in Europe in the Italian artists of the fourteenth century.[115]

There are differing assessments of the historic role of Genghis Khan and the quarrel about his personality has, from time to time, become polemical. Thus a central point in the quarrel between Chinese and Soviet historians in the 1960s has been the

25   *1962 memorial celebrating the eighth centenary of Genghis Khan's birth.*

question whether, from a historical point of view, the conquests of Genghis Khan should be assessed as progressive. Chinese historians have responded positively to this question, pointing out that the creation of the Mongol world empire demolished barriers, thus facilitating cultural and material exchanges between East and West. Soviet historians, on the other hand, stress the consequences of the conquests: human losses, the destruction of flourishing cultures, the decline in the material and cultural development of the conquered peoples.[116] It is, in my opinion, pointless to argue whether Genghis Khan's influence was progressive or negative. Genghis Khan did not awaken the forces which brought about the destruction of the old tribal order. He did not unleash the expansionist forces of the nomads, nor did he discover the idea of a universal empire, which found its expression in his campaigns of conquest. He was, however, the most distinguished exponent of such forces; it was he who accelerated their evolution and development and who brought them to fulfilment.

The conquests of Genghis Khan were neither the first nor the last attempt by the nomads of Central Asia to impose their rule over civilized nations. The underlying concept of the universal empire was, however, new and this concept was to maintain the ruling position of the conquerors for years after the death of Genghis Khan – although eventually to shatter on the superiority of the economic structure of the peasant farmer over the restricted possibilities of expanding the animal–breeding economy. After the conclusion of hostilities in the campaigns of conquest there was no more war booty and the conquerors slipped into economic dependence on the conquered but civilized peoples.

This process of decay was accelerated, not only by the expansion of the empire and by the subsequent national and religious contrasts, but also by changes taking place in the ethnic composition of the Mongol nation itself. Some Mongols remained behind in the occupied territories. In Iran, in the Golden Horde and in the *Ulus* Chaghatai they mixed with the local population and became assimilated into the Turkish culture. In China assimilation into the Chinese culture was accelerated during the Ming dynasty by the edict forbidding the Mongols to marry among themselves. Foreign ethnic elements also penetrated Mongolia. Although individual groups, such as the Sarta'ul, formed closed units, the many women brought home from the campaigns resulted in a dilution of Mongol racial purity – and, as we have already noted, Yuwen Mouzhao, writing of conditions at the time of the Liao dynasty, when relatively few women from foreign tribes had been abducted by the Mongols, commented that the children born of the marriages of Mongols to Khitan and Han women were utterly unlike the Mongols. The process of disintegration was accelerated by quarrelsomeness and rivalry between the members of the Mongol ruling family, also by a Mongol longing for the accustomed way of life in the homeland – except perhaps in the Golden Horde, where the Mongols found conditions which suited their way of life and where their rule lasted for hundreds of years.[117]

The achievements of Genghis Khan have disappeared, but their memory remains alive among the Mongolian people. The national consciousness of sharing a common destiny, never completely extinguished among the people despite the struggles which broke out on the steppe after the demise of the empire, has been revived in modern times. From the days of Genghis Khan onwards, Mongolia became Mongolian. The Mongols were, however, no longer the nation of the era of Genghis Khan.

Notes

XTS	*Xin Tangshu*
XXSS	Wu Guangcheng, *Xixia shushi*
XYJ	Li Zhichang, *Xiyou ji*
XYS	Ke Shaomin, *Xin Yuanshi*
XYSKZ	Ke Shaomin, *Xin Yuanshi kaozheng*
YCBS	*Yuanchao bishi*
YDZ	*Yuan dianzhang*
YS	*Yuanshi*
YSLB	Shao Yuanping, *Yuanshi leibian*
YSYWZL	Hong Jun, *Yuanshi yiwen zhenglu*
YWL	Su Tianjue, *Yuan wenlei*
ZAS	*Zentralasiatische Studien*
ZDMG	*Zeitschrift der deutschen morgenländischen Gesellschaft*
ZGL	Tao Zongyi, *Zhuogeng lu*

Preface

1 For the tradition of the text see especially Hung, 'The Transmission of the Book known as The Secret History of the Mongols'.

2 The passages contained in the *Altan tobči* have been published by Louis Ligeti under the title *Histoire secrète des Mongols: Texte en écriture ouigoure incorporé dans la chronique Altan tobči de Blo-bzan Bstan'Jirn* (Budapest, 1974).

3 For the relationship of these texts see Pelliot and Hambis, *Campagnes*, XV.

4 Hung, 'Transmission'; Ledyard, 'The Mongol Campaigns', pp. 1–22; Waley, 'Notes'; Grousset, *L'empire mongol*, p. 303, n. 1.

5 Doerfer, 'Zur Datierung', pp. 86–111; de Rachewiltz, 'Some Remarks', pp. 185–206; Ratchnevsky, 'Šigi-qutuqu' pp. 118–19.

6 See Ratchnevsky, 'Šigi-qutuqu', pp. 114ff.

7 See p. 150.

8 For Pulad's contribution to Rashid's *History of the Mongols* see Togan, 'The Composition', p. 67.

9 *Collected Chronicles*, vol. III, p. 207.

10 Cf, Tikhvinski's introductory article to the anthology *Tataro-Mongoly v Azii i Evrope* (Moscow, 1970).

Chapter 1 The Origins and Boyhood Years of Genghis Khan (Temuchin)

1 See Viktorova, 'K voprosu o naimanskoi teorii', p. 149. The Mongol name first appears in *LS*: Wittfogel and Feng, Liao, p. 96.

For the various transcriptions of the name, see Pelliot, *Campagnes*, pp. 215f.

2 Ratchnevsky, 'Zu einigen Problemen', p. 131, n. 1.

3 Tao Zongyi (*ZGL*, 1, 16b) classes the Naimans as Inner Asiatic (*semu ren*). There are numerous references to the names and titles of the Naiman rulers and nobles. See Pelliot, *Campagnes*, p. 298; Murayama, 'Sind die Naiman Türken oder Mongolen?', p. 197; Poucha, *Geheime Geschichte*, pp. 59–60.

4 Ratchnevsky, 'Zu einigen Problemen', p. 132, n. 4.

5 In the *SH* the name Black Khitans is transliterated by the dental -*d* (the two -*t* as against six -*d* noted in de Rachewiltz's *Index* must be ascribed to a textual distortion; see Pelliot, *Notes on Marco Polo*, vol. I, p. 227), while the name of the Khitans remaining in China has *t* (cf, Pelliot, *Campagnes*, p. 252). Chinese transliteration offers *Kidan* in both cases. [Except in exact quotations Ratchnevsky prefers to use the form -*t*.] On the question of the earliest mention of the Khitans see Wittfogel and Feng, *Liao*, pp. 1–2.

6 See Pelliot, *La Haute Asie*, p. 28. Potapov (*Ocherki*, p. 101) assumed that the Naimans were Mongol-speaking; but Howorth (*History of the Mongols*, vol. I, pp. 693–4) had already sought to establish the Turkic-speaking nature of the Naimans, and the [Mongol] theory is further undermined by the quoted researches of Murayama and Viktorova.

7 *Collected Chronicles*, vol. I/1, p. 137.

8 Wyngaert, *Itinera*, p. 115; Rockhill, *The Journey*, p. 117.

9 Pelliot, *Campagnes*, p. 305; *SH* §143.

10 *Zhuogeng lu*, 1, 15a; *Collected Chronicles*, vol. I/1, p. 127 and vol. I/2, p. 108.

11 *Mengwuer shiji*, 20, 1b.

12 *Collected Chronicles*, vol. I/1, p. 127 and vol. I/2, p. 108.

13 Turkic: *toquz* (*dokuz*) ('nine'); Turkic: *sarigh*, Mongol: *shar* ('yellow'). For the personality see Pelliot, *Campagnes*, p. 241ff.; also *Collected Chronicles*, vol. I/1, p. 111ff.

14 *Collected Chronicles*, vol. I/1, p. 137.

15 Pelliot, *Campagnes*, p. 208.

16 Grousset, *L'empire mongol*, p. 125, n.

17 Budge, *The Chronography*, vol. I, p. 352; d'Ohsson, *Histoire des Mongols*, vol. I, pp. 48–9, n.; Pelliot, *Campagnes*, p. 208. On this question see also Yule, *Cathay*, vol. III, p. 23; Rockhill, *The Journey*, p. 110, n. 2.

18 *Collected Chronicles*, vol. I/1, p. 130.

19 *Collected Chronicles*, vol. I/1, p. 130.

20 Cf. p. 12.

21   *Collected Chronicles*, vol. I/1, p. 127.
22   Raverty, *Ṭabakāt-i-nāṣirī*, vol. II, p. 936.
23   For the name and the origin of the Tartars see Wang Guowei, 'Dada kao', *Guantang jilin*, XIV, 6b-12a; Pelliot, *Campagnes*, pp. 2–9; Risch, *Johann de Plano Carpini*, pp. 278–87. Cf. also Wittfogel and Feng, *Liao*, pp. 101–2; Cleaves, 'The Mongolian Names', p. 424; Doerfer, *Türkische Elemente*, vol. I, pp. 433–4; Poucha, *Die Geheime Geschichte*, pp. 57–8; R, Stein 'Leao-che', p. 56. On the question of the ethnic relationship to the Mongols see note 43 below.

Editorial Note   Except in titles or quotations the commonly accepted English form Tartar has been selected in preference to the strictly correct *Tatar*. Although Slavonic and Germanic languages use the original form, English – and the Romance languages in general – commonly use the form with -r, derived from medieval Latin, *Tartarus*, which refers to the mythological Greek *Tartaros*. This medieval corruption, attributed by some to the visit of the Hungarian monk, Brother Julian to Greater Hungary, became widely used following the thirteenth-century report on the Mongols by Plano Carpini, *Ystoria Mongalorum, quos nos Tartaros appelamus* (*Sinica Franciscana*, vol. I, pp. 27–130.)

24   *Collected Chronicles*, vol. I/1, p. 101.
25   *SH*, §§133, 135; *Collected Chronicles*, vol. I/1, p. 93.
26   *Collected Chronicles*, vol. I/1, p. 102.
27   The Merkits are mentioned by the end of the eleventh century in *LS*. For the various transliterations of the name see Pelliot, *Campagnes*, p. 227.
28   *SH*, §109; Marco Polo, *La description du monde*, p. 98.
29   Tao Zongyi, *ZGL*, 1, 15b; *Collected Chronicles*, vol. I/1, p. 114; Rockhill, *The Journey*, p. 111, n. 2; Wyngaert, *Iterina*, p. 207.
30   *LS*, 26, 2b.
31   Pelliot, *Campagnes*, p. 227.
32   *Collected Chronicles*, vol. I/1, p. 157.
33   Vladimirtsov, *Le régime social*, p. 61; Vladimirtsov, *Genghis-khan*, p. 9.
34   *Collected Chronicles*, vol. I/1, p. 123f. and vol. I/2, p. 47.
35   Vladimirtsov, *Le régime social*, p. 41; *Collected Chronicles*, vol. I/2, p. 47.
36   *SH*, §39.
37   The etymology of the word *Mangqol* (Monghol) is uncertain. There are erroneous derivations from the adjective *möng*, to which several meanings are attributed: Rashid ad-Din, *Collected Chronicles*, vol. I/1, p. 154 – 'weak' or 'innocent'; Schmidt, *Geschichte der*

Ostmongolen, p. 380 – 'bold', 'daring', 'fearless'; Kowalewski, *Dictionnaire*, vol. III, p. 2029 – 'rich' or 'impetuous'. One must reject the derivation from *monggoo* (*Asia Polyglotta*, p. 260) used by Erdmann, *Temudschin*, p. 513, n. 2 – 'stupid', 'fatuous' – since, in the sense of 'stupid' or 'fatuous', the *SH* uses the word *mungqaq* (§17, *Bodunchar-mungqaq*), a word which has survived in modern Mongolian. There is, for phonetic reasons, no question of accepting the derivation (Wang Guowei, 'Menggu kao', *GTJIL*, 15, 2b) from the tribal name *Wajiezi* (Karlgren: *niwat-kiat*), with the approximate phonetic value *mäkäs*. Banzarov's hypothesis ('O proiskhozhdenii imeni *Mongol*', p. 169f.) that *Mong-qol* reflects the name of a river raises the problem that a River Mong is unknown, also that the related Mona mountain must be rejected for phonetic and geographic reasons. Derivation from a geographic name would not, however, be unjustified. The nomads did adopt the names of mountains and rivers in their homeland as tribal and clan names. A parallel to *Mang-qol*, 'the River Mang', is offered by the name of the historical line of the *Mangqut*, which could be ascribed as the plural form of 'the Mang Cliff' (*Mang-qun*).

Account has been taken of the derivation from *Mengwu*, a Shiwei tribe of the Tang period. Pelliot, ('L'édition collective', p. 126, n. 2) suggests that in the Middle Ages *Mengwu* had the phonetic form *mung-nguet* (Karlgren, *Grammata serica; mung-ngwet*) and represented the standard transliteration of *Monghol*. The transliteration indicates a *-t* ending, whereas the *-l* ending is standard in Mongol language texts, even in the singular.

Tu Ji's assumed derivation (1, 3b) from the name *Mang-qoljin-qo'a*, the ancestress of the Borjigid (*SH*, §3), offers no additional explanation of the etymology of the name *Mangqol*. For the rendering of the Mongol names in the Chinese texts see note 38 below.

In Turkic the name is rendered as *Moghul*, in Persian as *Mughal* [correctly: *Mughul*] (Cleaves, 'The Mongolian Names', p. 424).

38   Peng Daya deduces that the name *Menggu* comes from that of a similar sounding mountain. The Mongols are supposed to have given this name to their empire – it would mean silver in Mongol – because the Jurchid had named their dynasty 'The Golden' (*HDSL*, I, 1a). Tu Ji (I, 1b) adopts this interpretation, pointing out that the Khitans and the Koreans (*Xinlo*) both named their dynasties after metals; but Wang Guowei criticizes this on the grounds that the Chin dynasty had not then been founded. Munkujev ('Kratkie svedeniya', p. 145, n.) points to the folk-etymological character of the derivation from the Mongol *münggü(n)* ('silver') and comments that a Menggu mountain is unknown. Quite apart from *Menggu*, one finds the

following variations in Chinese texts: *Meiguxi, Moge-Shi[weil]*, *Maoge-Shi[wei]*, *Mangguzi, Mengguzi, Mengguosi, Menggusi* etc. (Wang Guowei, 'Menggu-kao', *GTJL*, XV, 2b). The fluctuation in the rendition of the vowels is a natural phenomenon but it is striking that nasalization is not indicated in some variants.

The word *Menggu*, because of its similar sound, suggested itself as a possible equivalent of the Monggol *mangghus* ('man-eating demons'); the Chinese could also have associated *Manqol* with the Chinese *manglu* ('demons').

39   Li Xinchuan, *Yaolu*, 96, 1594, *Zaji*, 19, 590; Yuwen Muozhao, *DJGZ, 22, 2b*; Hong Jun, *YSYWZL*, shang, 1/2; Ke Shaomin, *XYSKZ*, 1, 1b; Tu Ji, *MWSJ*, 1, 1a; Pelliot, 'L'édition collective', 126, n. 2.

40   Vladimirtsov, *Genghis-khan*, p. 11.

41   *DJGZ*, 22, 2b, and 12, 2b.

42   Professor Herbert Franke (*Oriental Art*, vol. II/1 (1949), pp. 41–2) offers a different interpretation of the phrase *yen huo*.

Editorial Note   Reviewing vol. IV of Professor Otto Franke's *Geschichte des Chinesischen Reiches*, Professor Herbert Franke comments as follows on Otto Franke's translation – which Ratchnevsky appears to use – of the quoted passage from the *Da-Jin guozhi*. 'This is a gross anachronistic blunder. During the 12th century tobacco was certainly not yet known by Mongol tribes. . . . *yen huo* is an expression, probably of Taoist origin, meaning "cooked food". The text must therefore be translated: "As they live on uncooked food, their sight is very good".'

43   *XYSKZ*, 1, 1b. On this question see Ratchnevsky, 'Les Che-wei étaient-ils des Mongols?', p. 230.

44   Wyngaert, *Itinera*, p. 205, *MDBL*, 4b.

45   *Yaolu*, 133, 2139 and *Yaolu*, year 1127, 40, 774.

46   *LS*, 22, 7a.

47   *Zaji*, 19, 590. See also *DJGZ*, 22, 2b.

48   *Qidan guozhi*, 22 Boyle, vol. I, p. 21, *Collected Chronicles*, vol. I/2, p. 8.

49   *Collected Chronicles*, vol. I/2, p. 18.

50   *Collected Chronicles*, vol. I/1, p. 92ff. Grousset (*L'empire mongol*, p. 27) also assumes that the Jalair could be of Turkic ancestry. The descendants of the Jalair captured during the raid became vassals (*ötögus bo'ol*) of Genghis Khan's clan; Mukali was one of these.

51   Cf. the lengendary account of the battle with the Jalair (*YS*, 1, 2a f.)

52   *YS*, 12a; *LS*, 25, 3a, notes for the year 1089 that Mogusi the

Zubu (*Zubu* was the term for Tartar under the Khitans and Jurchid; see Wang Guowei, 'Dada kao', *GTZL*, 14, 7b ff.) ruled all the tribes, Mogusi rebelled against the Liao in 1082 (*GTZL*, 70, 23a) and the rebellion was not crushed until 1095 (*GTZL*, 25, 7b and 26, 1b).

53 *SH*, §52. For Kabul-khan see *Collected Chronicles*, vol. I/2, pp. 35f.

54 Cf. Toyama, 'Da-Jin diaofa lu', *TSKK* (1936), vol. II/2, pp. 421–43, quoted by Vorobiev (*Zhurzheny i Gosudartsvo Zhin*, p. 329).

55 *Collected Chronicles*, vol. I/2, p. 35. The Meng-ku rebelled in winter of the fifth year *shaoxing* (1135–6) according to Li Xinchuan: *Yaolu*, 96, 1594; (in *Zaji*, 19, 590: 'the beginning of the Period *shaoxing*' (1131–62), *MDBL*, 3b, notes similarly that during the Period *tianhui* fighting broke out between the Mongols and the Jurchid. According to *DJGZ*, 22, 2b, the first rebellion of the Meng-ku took place in the period *tiaquan* (1139–40).

56 *Yaolu*, 133, 2143. Yuwen Mouzhao mentions the campaign on one occasion under the year 1138 (*DJGZ*, 10, 1a), and on a second under the year 1146 (*DJGZ*, 12, 2a).

57 *Yaolu*, 148, 2388 and 155, 2514. Cf. *DJGZ*, 12, 3a.

58 *DJGZ*, 22, 3a.

59 'Menggu kao', 6b.

60 *Yaolu*, 148, 2388 and 155, 2143.

61 *Beile* (in *DJGZ*, *bojilie*) is a Tungusic title. Cf. Pelliot, 'Notes sur le Turkestan', *TP* (1930), pp. 24–5. *Olun beile* (*bojilie*) is probably a hydrid combination of the Mongol *oro(n)* ('throne') and the Tungusic *beile*, The Mengwu had belonged to the Shiwei confederation in which Tungusic elements were probably dominant. (Cf. Ratchnevsky, 'Les Che-wei', p. 251).

62 *Yaolu*, 156, 2529; also *DJGZ*, 12, 3a.

63 According to *SH*, §52, after the death of Kabul-khan, and in accordance with the latter's wishes, Ambakai ruled all the Mongols, although Kabul-khan had seven sons. Rashid ad-Din (*Collected Chronicles*, vol. I/2, pp. 41–2) reports, however, that Kabul-khan's son, Kutula, was made khan and that Ambakai was ruler of the Tayichi'ut. The relationship of the Tayichi'ut to the Mongol league is not clear. In connection with the election of Kutula as khan, *SH*, §57 uses the expression *qamuq Mangqol Tayici'ut*. Haenisch, de Rachewiltz and Damdinsuren take this expression to mean 'the whole Mongol league **and** the Tayichi'ut', while Kozin and Pelliot translate it as 'all the Mongol-Tayichi'ut'. Munkujev ('Zametki', p. 354), treating the question at greater length in a note, allies himself with the latter interpretation. In favour of this interpretation is the fact that in

the *SH* the expression *Mangqol* is used as a collective name, often in conjunction with *qamug* or *irgen* (cf. Rachewiltz, *Index*), not as a reference to a single tribe. But it is not apparent why the Tayichi'ut are listed separately if they belonged to the Mongol league. The text in *SH*, §57 offers no conclusive answer to this. The word Tayichi'ut is omitted in a following sentence, in which it is said that, after the *qamuq Mangqol Tayici'ut* have elevated Kutula to the khanship, the *Mangqol* held festivities with dancing. According to Rashid (see above), Ambakai was the rule of the Tayichi'ut and not the successor of Kabul-khan. Evidence regarding the origins of the Tayichi'ut is contradictory. Rashid ad-Din (*Collected Chronicles*, vol. I/1, p. 180) points out that some Mongol chronicles name Nachin, Kaidu's uncle, as the father of the tribe, yet according to the *Altan debter* the Tayichi'ut are descended from Čaracqa-lingqum (*Čaracqa-lingqu* of the *SH*), the son of Kaidu-khan. According to *SH*, §47, Čaracqa-lingqu's sons, Senggum-bilge and Ambakai, adopted Tayichi'ut tribal names. The Tayichi'ut were very numerous and lived amicably with the Kiyats, comments Rashid (*Collected Chronicles*, vol. I/1, p. 181). On the relationship between the Tayichi'ut and the Kiyats, see also Tamura, *Chūgoku seifū ōchō no kenkyū*, pp. 373, 378 n. 9. In *SWQZL*, 1b, the Tayichi'ut are described as *Agni*, and they are said to belong to the forest people (*Collected Chronicles*, vol. I/1, p. 113; cf, *SWQZL*, 2a). The enmity between the Tayichi'ut and the Kiyats arose after the death of Yisugei, when the Tayichi'ut deserted the camp of his widow.

64 *Collected Chronicles*, vol. I/2, p. 13; *SH*, §47, See Pelliot, *Campagnes*, pp. 132–3.
65 *Collected Chronicles*, vol. I/1 p. 104 and vol. I/2, p. 41.
66 *SH*, §53, *Collected Chronicles*, vol. I/2, p. 42.
67 Conflicting accounts from *Collected Chronicles*, vol. I/1, p. 105, vol. I/2, p. 42, and *SH*, §53.
68 *Collected Chronicles*, vol. I/2, pp. 41–2.
69 *Collected Chronicles*, vol. I/2, p. 43.
70 *SH*, §58.
71 In 1161 the Chin emperor sent yet another letter to the ruler of the Meng-ku. This is reproduced in 'San-chao beimeng huibian' (O. Franke, *Geschichte*, vol. V, pp. 132–3).
72 Boyle, vol. I, pp. 21–2. See also Rashid ad-Din, *Collected Chronicles*, vol. I/2, p. 7.
73 Wyngaert, *Itinera*, pp. 47–8. Cf. Rubruc, *Itineranium*, p. 176: 'They eat all dead animals'; Kirakos (trans. Khanlaryan), p. 161: 'They eat all unclean animals without distinction, even mice and reptiles.' See also Risch, *Johann de Plano Carpini*, p. 98, n. 5.

74 *SH*, §254.

75 Rashid ad-Din (*Collected Chronicles*, vol. I/1, p. 176) reports that traditional marriages existed between the Baya'ut and the Genghisides.

76 For this institution see Vladimirtsov, *Le régime social*, pp. 80ff. Cf. also Munkujev, 'Zametki', pp. 360–2; Federov-Davydov, *Obshchestvenny stroi*, pp. 36–8. On the false reading of *unagan bo'ol* see Pelliot, *Campagnes*, p. 85. One must reject 'Slave of the Ancestral Spirits' (Rygdalon, 'O mongol'skom termine *ongu-bogol*'), which is based on this false interpretation.

77 They make the accusation: 'These sons of great ladies attack and kill us (*SWQZL*, 11a). Cf. *YS*, 1, 4b; *Collected Chronicles*, vol. I/2, p. 90.

78 *Collected Chronicles*, vol. I/2, p. 259.

79 It is characteristic that *nökhör* has been adopted as a loan word with the basic meaning of 'servant', as in Persian *nawkar*, in Dari (Pashto?) *nukar*, or Ottoman *nüker* (Nemeth, 'Wanderungen', pp. 11, 20). On the status of the *nökhöd* see Vladimirtsov, *Le régime social*, pp. 110ff. The status of the *bo'ol* was lower than that of the *ötögus bo'ol*. Rashid ad-Din (*Collected Chronicles*, vol. I/1, p. 159) reports that because Udachi was a simple serf (*ötele bo'ol*), his family gave no girls [to any other clans] and took no wives [from any other clans]. Because the Baya'ut Sorkan was clever and bright he, however, became a respected person and was therefore regarded as an *ötögu bo'ol* [for *öngu* read *ötögu*], comments Rashid (*Collected Chronicles*, vol. I/1, p. 177). The relationship between the *bo'ol* and his master was dependent on individual factors and Genghis, for example, paid no attention to the social status of a person, but rather to his abilities.

80 *Bosaqa-un bo'ol*. *SH*, §137.

81 *SH*, §15.

82 *Collected Chronicles*, vol. I/2, p. 259; Boyle, vol. I, p. 21.

83 In the Chinese transliteration in *YCBS* the name appears as *Yesügei*; in the Uighur script, however, it has the initial syllable *yi*, as is also the case in the Chronicles *bLo, bzans, Saghan-sechen, Lomis*, in the *Altan tobci anonymous*, in the *Shara tudzhi* and others, as well as in the Tibetan records (see *Hor chos byun*, Huth, p. 24). The name is obviously derived from *yisü* ('nine'), and in the Chinese transliteration of *yisü* the same vowel changes can be noted: in the Interpreter's Dictionary, *Hua-Yi yiyü* ('nine') is given as *yesu* (Lewicki, *La langue mongole*, p. 170). On this question, see Pelliot, *Campagnes*, pp. 1–2; *Hambis*, 'A propos de la "Pierre de Genghis-khan" ' (*Mélanges*, vol.

II, p. 156); Rachewiltz, 'Some remarks on the Stele of Yisüngge',
Tractata Altaica, p. 500, n. 24).

84 According to Rashid ad-Din (*Collected Chronicles*, vol. I/1, pp.
79, 153), the Borjigid clan was a branch of the Kiyat, to which the
Jurchid, Changsi'ut and the Kiyat-Sayar also belonged (cf. Pelliot,
Campagnes, p. 118). For the meaning of the world *borjigin* see
Campagnes, pp. 118–21, in which Pelliot dissociates himself from the
traditional Rashid etymology, according to which *borjikin* means
'dark blue eyed'. Pelliot points to the possible derivation from *borjin*
[no'osun] ('[wild duck] *borjin*'). This etymology is also adopted by
Poucha (*Geheime Geschichte*, p. 76). Doerfer (*Mongolische Elemente*,
p. 224) also interprets the name as 'the wild duck people [hunters?],
or the Clan with the Wild Duck totem?'. But, as Doerfer comments,
Rashid's etymology could still have a historical basis, (See note 88
below.)
85 *SH*, §21; *Collected Chronicles*, vol. I/2, p. 14.
86 *SH*, §18.
87 The tribal name *Baya'ut* was widespread among the Turkic
peoples and is verified among the Kangli and Kipchaks (Pelliot,
Campagnes, p. 87). According to Nasawi, Terken-khatun, the wife
[*Editorial Note*: mother!] of the shah of Khwarazm belonged to the
Bayawut, a sub-tribe of of the Yämäk, See *Campagnes*, p. 88;
Buniyatov, p. 24; *SH*, §15.
88 *Collected Chronicles*, vol. II, p. 193, n. 51; *TS*, 217, *xia*, 10b. Cf.
Eberhard, *kultur und Siedlung*, p. 221. The light colour of the
Kirghiz hair and eyes is also stressed in reports by Islamic and modern
travellers (Ligeti, 'Mots de civilisation', p. 151). Zhao Hong (*MDBL*,
26) notes that Genghis differed from the other Tartars, who were
small, by his tall stature, his broad brow and long beard, Genghis was
amazed when he first saw his grandson Khubilai: 'All our children are
red-haired, but this boy has black hair; clearly he takes his old uncles',
he exclaimed (*Collected Chronicles*, vol. II, p. 153). According to
Marco Polo (*La description du monde*, p. 110), Khubilai did have
black eyes but his complexion was fair, 'tinged with red, like a rose'.
The ancestress of the Borjigid, Alan-ko'a, was, according to the *Secret
History* (§8) the daughter of a Kori-Tumat noble, but Rashid ad-Din
(*Collected Chronicles*, vol. I/1, p. 152) maintains that she was from
the Korola tribe.
89 Yisugei was the third son of Bartan-bagatur and the grandson of
Kabul-khan (*SH*, §50; *Collected Chronicles*, vol. I/2, pp. 43, 49 and
vol. I/1, p. 155; *YS*, 1, 3a). The Tayichi'ut were descended from
Čaracqa-lingqum, the son of Kaidu (*Collected Chronicles*, vol. I/1,

p. 180). Cf. *SH*, §47, in which Ambakai, the grandson of Čaracqa-lingqum, is falsely stated to be the son. For this see Pelliot, *Campagnes*, p. 132; *Collected Chronicles*, vol. I/2, p. 27 and the Chinese paraphrase of the *Secret History* (Pankratov, p. 44), according to which Ambakai adopted the tribal name Tayichi'ut.

90 *Collected Chronicles*, vol. I/2, p. 47; Pelliot, *Campagnes*, p. 14.
91 *Collected Chronicles*, vol. I/2, pp. 43; *YS*, 1b; *XXSS*, 39, 9b; *Collected Chronicles*, vol. I/2, p. 50; Raverty, vol. II, p. 935; *MDBL*, 2b.

Editorial Note The Mongol army was organized on a simple and effective decimal basis and its commanders were designated Leaders of Ten, One Hundred, One Thousand and Ten Thousand, even though (see note 166 below) the larger units were seldom at full strength. Since the Mongol army was, at least initially, basically a cavalry force, I have normally translated the Mongol military designations in terms of cavalry units and refer to the leaders as commanders of such units, rather than as 'Leaders of Ten', 'Leaders of One Hundred' etc.

Mongol Term	Size of Unit	English Terminology
Arvan	10 men	Troop
Zuun	100 men	Squadron
Myangan	1,000 men	Regiment
Tumen	10,000 men	Division

A typical Mongol army under a corps commander (usually a Genghiside prince or a senior general) would normally consist of two or three divisions. It should be noted that the actual strength of a *tumen* was usually about 6,000 men.

92 *SH*, §177.
93 *Collected Chronicles*, vol. I/2, pp. 43, 50.
94 *SH*, §177.
95 *Collected Chronicles*, vol. I/2, p. 51; *SH*, §§54–7, 100, 112; *Altan tobči*, ed. Cleaves, pp. 28, 156, and p. 20; According to Sagang-sechen (Schmidt, p. 63), Bekhter and Belgutei had different mothers, Goa-abaghai and Daghachi; and Shastina (*Shara tudzhi*, p. 129) reports that three women, Manghulun, Börte and Qoghuchin, were abducted by the Merkits. Little credibility, however, attaches to the theories of these latter authors since by their day the tradition from the Genghis epoch had been largely lost. On this question see also Hong Jun, *YSYWZL*, 1, 16.

Editorial Note   In *SH*, §99 Ko'agchin is specifically described as Hö'elun's servant: *Oëlun ekhin gert zartslagdakh Ko'agchin emgen borch uguulruun* ('Old Woman Ko'agchin, a servant in Hö'elun's tent, rose and said').

In *SH*, §103 Cleaves has Temuchin describe Ko'agchin as 'Mother Koagchin'. In Sh. Gaadamba's 1975 version of the *Secret History*, however, Ko'agchin is described by Temuchin as '*sorgog* = vigilant' and '*unench* = loyal, devoted', adjectives perhaps more approppriate to a servant.

96   For various accounts of Temuchin's birth see *SH*, §59; *Collected Chronicles*, vol. I/2, p. 75; *YS*, 1, 3b; *SWQZL*, 1, 1b; *Altan tobči*, vol. II, p. 1; Shastina, *Shara tudzhi*, p. 165.

The reputed location of Temuchin's birth, on the right bank of the Onon River, upstream from the island Yeke Aral and close to the confluence of the Balzhi River, is still known by its old name. See Haltod, *Mongolische Ortsnamen*, no. 3963; Hong Jun, *YSYWZL*, I, 1a, 17; Perlee, p. 9; Tu Ji, 1, 17; Erdmann, p. 572; Pelliot, *Notes*, vol. I, p. 282 and *Campagnes*, p. 10–11; Rachewiltz, *The Secret History*, §59, n.; also further bibliographical material cited by these authors.

97   Khanlaryan, p. 173; also Boyle, 'Kirakos of Ganzak', p. 20; *SH*, §21; *LS*, 1, 1a. Poucha (*Geheime Geschichte*, p. 45 and 'Zum Stammbaum', p. 448) points to the connection with the *Astracult* and its appearance in Mongol folklore. In addition to Poucha's reference to the Tibetan tradition, note should also be taken of the Mongol, Persian and Arab texts quoted in Lech, p. 179.

98   See Lattimore, 'The Temüjin Theme', pp. 317–18; *Altan tobči*, p. 26; Shastina, p. 66.

Rubruc, ed. Wyngaert, p. 307; Ibn Battuta, *Voyages*, vol. III, p. 22; Buniyatov, *An-Nasawi*, p. 47, and the Greek historian Pachymeres (d'Ohsson, vol. I, p. 36), all regard the name as indicative of a family of smiths; according to Juzjani (Raverty, vol. II, p. 935) Temuchin was actually the son of a blacksmith. See also Pelliot, *Notes*, vol. I, pp. 289–91. Munkujev (*Men-Da bei-lu*, p. 96) notes that the Selenga Buriats regard a bare mountain, on the left bank of the Shilka River to the north of Selenginsk, as the location where Genghis, one foot on each bank, wrought iron. Rockhill (*The Journey*, p. 249, n.) saw several hills which take their name from such stories. Cf. Timkovsky, quoted by d'Ohsson, vol. I, p. 36.

99   *Collected Chronicles*, vol. I/2, p. 74; Pelliot, *Notes*, vol. I, 286–7, 308; *MDBL*, 3a; *YS* 1, 32b; *SWQZL*, 79a; *ZGL*, 1, 11a and 3, 6b. Cf. *XYSKZ*, 2, 1b; *Lidai fozu tongzai*, 32, 37a.

100   Wang Guowei, 'Dada kao': *GTJL*, 14, 26b; Tu Ji, *Mengwuer*

shiji, 2, 1a. Dating of Yisugei's battle with the Tartars as 1162 (second year *dading*) by Wang Guowei or 1154/5 (twenty-sixth year *Shaoxing of the Sung*) by Tu Ji is irrelevant, since both authors base these dates on their assumed birth year of Temuchin.

101   1186 can be accepted with some certainty as Ögödei's year of birth (Pelliot, *Notes*, vol. I, p. 287); Chaghatai was probably born in 1185 and there is doubt as to Temuchin being the father of Jochi (See p. 35 below). From a Rashid ad-Din text (Šigi Qutuqu, p. 92), we can also deduce that in 1182–3 Temuchin had not yet reached puberty.

102   *Altan tobči*, ed. Cleaves, p. 28; *SH*, §99.

Editorial Note   Ratchnevsky uses the date 1164. It must be assumed from his argument that this is a misprint for 1155 and this has been substituted.

103   Zhao Hong, *MDBL*, 3a; *Jinshi*, 1, 4a; Franke, 'Chinese Texts', p. 442, n. 38.

104   Rashid ad-Din (*Collected Chronicles*, vol. I/2, p. 51) comments that Yisugei had no daughter by Hö'elun. On the differing list of Temuchin's siblings provided by Zhao Hong, cf. the comments in Munkujev, *Men-Da bei-lu*, p. 138, n. 146f. For the official histories see *Collected Chronicles*, vol. I/2, p. 51; *YS*, 107, 3a. For the ages of Temuchin and his siblings see *Altan tobči*, ed. Cleaves, p. 28; for the ages of the half-brothers see note 120 below.

105   *SH*, §116. See U-Köhalmi, 'Der Pfeil', p. 129 for information on these arrows.

106   Pelliot, *Campagnes*, p. 232; *QDGZ*, 1, 2a; *SH*, §117; *LS*, 1, 2a; Doerfer, *Mongolische Elemente*, pp. 149–52; Vladimirtsov, *Le régime social*, p. 76. Wang Guowei (*GTJL*, 16, 25b–26a) has expressed the suspicion that the Mongols took the word *anda* from the Khitan tongue; but the word, as well as the custom, would appear to have been widespread among the Altaic peoples and is derived from the Mongol word *andaghar* (Turkic; *and* = oath). See Pelliot, *Campagnes*, p. 232; also Wittfogel and Feng, *Liao*, 239.

107   Cf. Ratchnevsky, 'La condition de la femme mongole', p. 511.

108   *SH*, §64; *Collected Chronicles*, vol. I/1, pp. 104, 160. Pelliot, ('Les formes avec et sans *q/k* initiaux', p. 77, n. 1) has expressed the view that the Khitans used the form 'Onggirat' and that 'Qonggirat' was the Jurchid form of the tribal name. For the various forms of the name see Pelliot, *Campagnes*, pp. 403ff.

109   Pelliot, *Campagnes*, p. 409; *SH*, §66.

110   *Collected Chronicles*, vol. I/1, p. 162; *YS*, 118, 1a. According to the *YS* text Dai-sechen's son was named Antong.

111   *Collected Chronicles*, vol. I/2, pp. 18–19; Juvaini, trans. Boyle, vol. II, p. 394. Cf. Vladimirtsov, *Le Régime social*, p. 59. For the custom in Temuchin's times see *Secret History*, §§120, 155 etc.

Editorial Note   For biblical evidence of the custom see *Genesis*, 29, 30.

112   Cf. Krader, *Social Organisation*, pp. 39, 89; also Noboru Niida, *Chūgoku hōseishi*, p. 253. For the evidence of Carpini and Rubruck see Ratchnevsky, 'La condition', p. 512.

113   *SH*, §67. This duty of steppe hospitality was strengthened by Genghis Khan in the *Yasa* (Lech, p. 97; Sylvestre de Sacy, p. 162). The Oirat-Mongol Legal Code of 1640 imposed a fine of one sheep on those who refused *kumis* to a thirsty person (Golstunski, *Mongolo-Oiratskie Zakony*, text p. 16, trans. p. 52).

114   *SH*, §70. It was not unusual for a woman to lead warriors into battle. Qi-fei, the sister-in-law of Jingzong, the Liao emperor (968–83), led the Khitan troops sent against the *Dada* (Tartar) and brought the latter under Khitan rule (*QDGZ*, 19). When panic broke out at court on the occasion of Zongyuan's rebellion the wife of the emperor, Daozong (1055–1101), rode out at the head of the army against the rebels and suppressed the rebellion.

115   *SH*, §73. Cf. *Collected Chronicles*, vol. I/2, p. 85; *SWQZL*, 3a: *YS*, 1, 4a.

116   Rashid ad-Din (*Collected Chronicles*, vol. II p. 112) remarks that, because of this refusal of remarriage, Sorkaktani is accorded precedence over Hö'elun, who, according to Rashid, was given in marriage by Genghis Khan to Mönglik.

117   *Collected Chronicles*, vol. I/2, pp. 47–8.

118   *SH*, §74.

119   *SH*, §§77–8.

120   *MDBL*, 6a; Pelliot, *Campagnes*, p. 186; *MWSJ*, 22, 9a; YS, 3, 2b; *Collected Chronicles*, vol. II, p. 146. Wang Guowei bases himself on the description of the Tayichi'ut attack (*SH*, §79) and the rustling of the horses (*SH*, §90). His arguments are not sound. Belgutei is named in both texts before Kasar. Kasar offers to pursue the horse-thieves because he is a better archer than Belgutei. The fact that Belgutei is named in other sections of the *Secret History* after Kasar is a reference to rank rather than to age, the order of rank of the sons among the Mongols being determined by the rank of the mother. Cf. Ratchnevsky, 'La condition', p. 516; also *SH*, §99, in which Belgutei is listed after Temuchin's youngest brother, Temuge-otchigin.

121   *YS*, 117, 1b. Belgutei's short biographical entry in *YS*, 117,

1a–b is expanded by Tu Ji (*MWSJ*, 22, 9a–11a). Cf. also Pelliot, *Campagnes*, pp. 185–7; Munkujev, *Men-Da bei-lu*, p. 138, n. 147.

122 　*SH*, §81. Criminals were treated in this way even during the Empire. When Sharif ad-Din was arrested by Körguz a wooden collar was placed around his neck and he was entrusted to a succession of gaolers. (Boyle, vol. II, 536).

123 　*SH*, §§79–81, 149.

124 　*Collected Chronicles*, vol. I/2, pp. 84, 248; vol. I/1, pp. 115, 86. See *SH*, §80 for Temuchin's capture by the Tayichi'ut.

125 　*SH*, §§152, 150; *Collected Chronicles*, vol. I/1, pp. 190f. Jaqa-gambu in the *SH*, *Jā-gambō* in Rashid ad-Din, is the Tangut title *Ja-gambo (Tibetan: rgya-gambu)*, which Rashid defines as 'the great emir of a province' (*Collected Chronicles*, vol. I/2, p. 109 and vol. I/1, pp. 130–1). Rashid gives his personal name as *Karaidai* ('the Kerait'). See Pelliot, *Campagnes*, pp. 226–7, regarding the title.

126 　*MDBL*, 3a. Cf. *SWQZL*, 12a, also the note on this subject in Pelliot, *Campagnes*, p. 157. For Temuchin's captivity among the Jurchid see pp. 50.

127 　*SH*, §84–7.

128 　According to Rashid's *History of the Tribes*, the Suldu were subject to the Baya'ut (*Collected Chronicles*, vol. I/1, p. 176) and the son of Sorkan-shira belonged to the personal retinue of Tudas, a Tayichi'ut princeling (*Collected Chronicles*, vol. I/2, p. 90), the Baya'ut being themseleves *ötögus bo'ol* of the Tayichi'ut (*Collected Chronicles*, vol. I/1, p. 177).

129 　*Collected Chronicles*, vol. I/1, p. 173. Tolui was not born until the end of the 1180s: see Hung, 'The Transmission', p. 482; Ratchnevsky, 'Šigi Qutuqu', p. 94; and according to *SH*, §146, Sorkan-shira joined Temuchin only after the battle of Köyitän.

130 　See p. 21, also note 110 above.

131 　*SH*, §§88–9; cf. *Collected Chronicles*, vol. I/1, pp. 173–4. Rashid ad-Din's chronology of Temuchin's youth is, however, unreliable. See *Collected Chronicles*, vol. I/2, p. 76, which gives Temuchin's age as thirteen years on the death of Yisugei.

132 　*SH*, §24; *Collected Chronicles*, vol. I/2, p. 43.

133 　*SH*, §§90–2; *YS*, 119, 19a.

134 　In this *SH* text Bo'orchu explains to Temuchin that he is Nayan's only son, but in *SH*, §120 there is mention of a younger brother. Bo'oruchu has a Biography in *YS*, 119, 19a–20a. Cf. Tu Ji, 28, 1a–4b; *Collected Chronicles*, vol. I/1, pp. 169–71 and the detailed comments by Pelliot, *Campagnes*, pp. 342–60. For the differing transcriptions of the name see Pelliot, *Campagnes*, p. 343; Hambis,

Le chapitre CVIII, pp. 146–7. The form *Boghurči* in many texts results from metathesis.

135 For these *bilik* see: *Collected Chronicles*, vol. I/2, p. 264; vol. I/2, p. 265 and vol. I/1, p. 169.

136 *SH*, §205.

137 *SH*, §94.

138 *SH*, §95.

139 *La description du monde*, p. 132.

140 *Collected Chronicles*, vol. I/1, p. 127.

141 *SH*, §152.

142 *Collected Chronicles*, vol. I/1, p. 130.

143 *XXSS*, 37, 16b. On the fratricide see: *SH*, §150; *SWQZL*, 18a; *Collected Chronicles*, vol. I/1, p. 130. For contradictions in the texts, see Pelliot, *Campagnes*, pp. 233ff.

144 For the use of *Je* as an emphatic particle see 'Šigi-qutuqu', p. 89, n. 7.

145 *Emusgel* (*emusgek* is a false reading) is the present brought by the bride to her parents-in-law. In the same paragraph the gift is said to be *šitkul*. For this expression see Mostaert, *Sur quelques passages*, p. [32], n. 29, *bawulǰu* in the sentence '*gergei bawulǰu emusgel čima-da abčiraba*' seems to be corrupt. True, *gergei ba'ulgha* is actually verified (see Kowalewski, *Dictionnaire*, vol. II, p. 1062, also bLobzans, *Altan tobči*, ed. Cleaves, p. 48), but in the Chinese interlinear version *bawulǰu* is translated as *bu zhu* (Pankratov, p. 105), which offers no satisfactory meaning. In the Summary the text is: 'Now I have brought with me the present which my wife brought to her parents-in-law . . .'

146 *SH*, §96.

147 See p. 78.

148 *Lech*, p. 93.

149 *SH*, §97. Tu Ji (*MWSJ*, 29, 1a–2a) offers a biography of Jelme. Cf. also Ke Shaomin, *XYS*, 123, 6869.

150 *SH*, §§99, 102.

151 *SH*, §103. Cult ceremonies in honour of Burkhan-kaldun were continued until recent times. See Banzarov, 'Chernaya vera', p. 70.

152 According to the *SH* the name can be read as either *Joči* or *Jöči*, and it is found twice combined with *-da* and twice with *-de* (Street, *The Language*, p. 4). Pelliot decided on the palatalized form, which is rejected by Poppe (*HJAS* (1950), p. 265), also by Doerfer (*Mongolische Elemente*, p. 299). The Turkic form Tuši (*Toši?*) is found in Juvaini and the Arabic-language sources. For the meaning 'guest' see Pelliot, *Notes sur l'histoire de la Horde d'Or*, pp. 10–28. The few

sparse biographical notes in *YS*, 117, 2a–b and in *Collected Chronicles*, vol. II, pp. 64–5, have been expanded by Tu Ji (34, 1a–4b) and Hong Jun (1, 4, 133–142).

153   *Collected Chronicles*, vol. I/1, pp. 97–8. Cf. vol. I/1, p. 115 and vol. II, p. 65.

154   *SH*, §104.

155   In *SH* the tribal name is given as *Jadaran* and is derived from *Jat* ('foreign'). The eponymous ancestor is given as *Jajiradai* as well as *Jadaradai* (§40). Pelliot (*Campagnes*, p. 28) considers the etymology to be completely fictitious. Rashid ad-Din (*Collected Chronicles*, vol. II/1, p. 90) intersperses the tribal name *Jajirat* with *Juriat*.

156   *SH*, §201. In *SH*, §§128–9 Taičar is listed as Jamuka's younger brother, but in §201 Jamuka has no brother; other sources describe Taičar as a relative, or as belonging to Jamuka's tribe. See p. 44.

The Chinese interlinear version glosses *domoqči* as *hao chang hua* ('to love long speeches'). 'Gossip' is the usual translation, but Rintchen defines the phrase as 'a woman who persistently talks her husband into doing what she wishes' (Gumilev, *Poiski*, p. 259).

157   *Collected Chronicles*, vol. I/1, pp. 190–1. Cf. Jamuka's biography in Tu Ji, 20, 1b–3b.

158   *SH*, §§104, 106, 108.

159   *SH*, §110, *asara-* has the Chinese gloss *shouji*, a technical term which, in the case of Levirate marriages, has the meaning: 'to take over the wife of a dead father or brother by way of inheritance'. Cf. Ratchnevsky, *Code*, vol. II, p. 130, n. 3. It is clear from the facts that Chilger took Börte as his wife.

160   Pelliot, *Campagnes*, p. 266; *SH*, §254.

161   *SH*, §§117–8.

162   *SH*, §§118–9.

163   Barthold, 'Chingis Khan', p. 617, also 'Obrazovanie imperii Chingis Khana', pp. 258–9); Vladimirtsov, *Gengis Khan*, p. 30 and *Régime social*, pp. 107–8. The thesis of the 'democratic' Jamuka arises from a false interpretation of the word *uyidangqa* in Börte's remark; *Jamuqa anda uyidangqa ke'ekden büle'e* ('It is said of friend Jamuka that he easily becomes tired of the olden days'). The Chinese gloss for *uyidangqa is hao yenjiu* (Pankratov, p. 150). The fact that 'old' is not used in the sense of 'old order' or 'old convention' is clear from the following sentence; *edö'e bidan-aca uyituq čaq bolba* ('Now the time has come that he is tired of us').

164   *SH*, §90. On the occasion of the Merkit attack Ko'agchin says that she had been involved in the sheep-shearing (*SH*, §100).

165   *SH*, §113.

166   *SH*, §106. Although the words 'Unit of 10,000' [Division]

cannot be taken literally – even during the Empire a 'Unit of 1,000' [Regiment] consisted of no more than 500–600 men – the numbers involved must have been considerable.

167 *SH*, §§118, 127.

168 The text offers *Zhaolie*. For the transcription of the name see Pelliot, *Campagnes*, p. 142.

169 *SWQZL*, 10b. Cf. the description of the incident in Rashid, *Collected Chronicles*, vol. I/1, pp. 89–9.

170 *YS*, 1, 4b. *Zhong* ('crowd' or 'mass') describes in this context the vassal subjects, the descendants of the subjugated tribes, in contrast to the tribal members. Those responsible for compiling the *YS* give Temuchin a retrospective title, *taishi*, which he never held.

171 *SWQZL*, 11b–12a. Cf. *Collected Chronicles*, vol. I/2, p. 90.

172 According to the text: 'Önggur, the son of Mönggetu-kiyan came to Temuchin, and others with their čangši'ut and their Baya'ut.' The text appears to be corrupt (Pelliot, *Campagnes*, pp. 79ff.). Önggur was the leader of the Baya'ut (*Collected Chronicles*, vol. I/2, p. 87). Rashid (*Collected Chronicles*, p. 49) does not include the sons of Bartan-bagatur in the genealogical table. According to the genealogy, Čangši'ut was the eldest son and the successor of Möngädu-qiyan. He was a cousin of Temuchin since Möngädu-qiyan was the eldest son of Bartan-bagatur and Yisugei was the third son (*Collected Chronicles*, vol. I/2, pp. 46, 48). It would thus be family rather than social considerations which influenced them to join Temuchin. The Baya'ut belonged to the *ötögus bo'ol* and there were traditional marriage alliances between them and the Genghisides (*Collected Chronicles*, vol. I/1, pp. 176–7).

173 *SH*, §§120, 122. The various references to Bo'orchu's brother are confusing. The *SH* names him in §120 as *Ögölen-čerbi*, in §124 as *Ögölei-čerbi*, yet in §94 states that Bo'orchu had no brothers.

174 Relations between the tribes themselves and with their subject and vassal tribes merit separate investigation.

175 *SH*, §121. Korchi was not satisfied with Temuchin's promise that, if the prophecy was fulfilled, he would be given command of a regiment, demanding that as an additional reward he should be given thirty beautiful women and that he should have the right to select them. Temuchin granted this additional request; after the victory over the Tumats, Korchi received his thirty Tumat maidens, See *SH*, §241.

176 *SH*, §206. As Kutula rode out to fight the Merkits on one occasion he stopped by a tree on the Qorqonar River. He dismounted there and prayed to the Old God for assistance, undertaking that, in the event of success, he would decorate the tree and make it a place

of pilgrimage. Kutula won his victory, returned to the spot, decorated the tree and then danced with his warriors beneath it. Thus runs the story which Rashid ad-Din heard from Pulad-čingsang [Bolad-chengxiang] (*Collected Chronicles*, vol. III, p. 192).

At this spot on the Qorqonar River Kutula was made ruler of the whole Manqol-Tagichi'ut [see note 63 above] and afterwards there was dancing around the tree until they 'sank up to their thighs and the dust rose to their knees' (*SH*, §57). Cf. *Collected Chronicles*, vol. II, p. 145.

177 Boyle, vol. I, p. 39. Cf. *Collected Chronicles*, vol. I/1, p. 167.
178 *SH*, §113.

Chapter 2   Rise to Supremacy on the Steppe

1 Cf. Vladimirtsov, *Le régime social*, p. 101.
2 *SH*, §122.
3 *SH*, §49. Cf. *Collected Chronicles*, vol. I/2, pp. 33, 49, *SH* §179 mistakenly ascribes the Jurkin ancestry to Yisugei's father, Bartan-bagatur. The Jurkin were descended from Yisugei's [*sič*] elder brother, Ökin-barkak.

Editorial Note Ratchnevsky's statement that Ökin-barkak was Yisugei's elder brother is clearly a misprint. Ökin-barkak was, as correctly noted earlier by Ratchnevsky, the eldest son of Kabul-khan and thus Bartan-bagatur's elder brother and Yisugei's uncle. Yisugei's elder brothers were Nekun-taishi and Möngadu-kiyan. Ökin-barkak's son, Sorkatu-jurki, is designated by Ratchnevsky on p. 55 as the founder of the Jurkin. Buri-bökö, the Jurkin wrestler, was the son of Khutukhtu-munggur, another son of Kabul-khan. (See *SH*, §§47–50; also Dynastic Tables, p. 279.)

4 Vladimirtsov, *Gengis Khan*, p. 33.
5 Pelliot's translation '. . . et te donnerons pour ton ordo [leurs] filles et [leurs] dames. . .' does not reproduce the full text of the *Secret History*.
6 The expression *qari irgen* or *qari ulus* refers to foreign peoples or states. Cf. in later Mongolian literature, *dörben qari ulus*, which corresponds to the Chinese phrase *Si-Yi* ('the four Barbarian [Nations]'). See Bawden, *Altan tobči*, p. 131, n.
7 For the terms *utu*, *utura-* ('furthest point of hunt', 'to be at the furthest point of the hunt') see Pelliot, *Campagnes*, p. 144.
8 *qari siri*: Pelliot reads *silli* = 'noble' instead of *siri*, and suggests that *qari* may represent *qara*, as in bLo-bzans, *Altan tobči*. In the

Chinese interlinear version the expression *qari siri* is rendered as *jia-huo* (Pankratov, pp. 161, 162) and connected with *jia-zai* = 'movable family goods' (see *Code* II, 148 for this expression). Haenisch translates the expression as 'belongings and goods', Damdinsuren as *yum* = 'belongings'. Shastina uses 'house and servants' (*Altan tobči*, p. 99).

9 *SH*, §123. For the meaning of the word *Genghis* (*chinggis*) see pp. 89–90.

10 *SH*, §125.

11 For Toghrul's and Jamuka's replies see *SH*, §§126, 127.

12 *SH*, §128.

13 *SH*, §201; *YS*, 1, 4a; *SWQZL*, 4a; *Collected Chronicles*, vol. I/2, p. 85.

14 *SH*, §129. According to *SWQZL*, 4a–5a, Jamuka's coalition consisted of the Tayichi'ut, the Ikires, the Uru'ud, the Noyakin, the Barulas and the Ba'arin. *YS* speaks only of 'several Tayichi'ut tribes'.

15 *küriyen* (*güre'en* in *SH*), *yi* = wing in *SWQZL*. For this term see Pelliot in *TP*, pp. 130, 290; Doerfer, *Türkische Elemente*, p. 477.

The list of the thirteen camps is given in Rashid ad-Din, *Collected Chronicles*, vol. I/2 pp. 87–8, and in *SWQZL*, 6b–9b, although these two sources differ on some details. Both sources mention the presence in Jamuka's camp of Altan, Da'aritai and Kuchar, but the leaders of the Jurkin, Sacha-beki and Taichu are not named in *SWQZL*. Pelliot (*Campagnes*, pp. 49–139), offers a very detailed examination of the tribal names on the list. Cf. Tu Ji, 10b–12a.

Editorial Note For a more recent analysis of *küriyen* see Fujiko Isono, 'Küriyen Reconsidered', *Journal of the Anglo-Mongolian Society*, vol. 12 (1989).

16 *SH*, §129. For the name and location of *Dalan Balzhut-Baljus*, which lies in the valley of the Kerulen near the Senggum tributary, see Pelliot, *Campagnes*, 37–49; Tu Ji, 1, 12a. Rashid's transcription *Talan Baljus* (see Poppe, 'On Some Geographical Names', p. 41) from the Mongolian *tala* ('plain') is erroneous (Pelliot, *Campagnes*, p. 37).

17 The Korolas of Rashid's text might be the Barulas of the *SWQZL*. Cf. Pelliot, *Campagnes*, pp. 59–60. They were related to the Ikires and the Onggirat, but were constantly at war with these tribes (*Collected Chronicles*, vol. I/1, p. 165).

18 Cf. *SWQZL*, 10a; *YS*, 1, 4a.

19 Ratchnevsky, *Code*, vol. I, p. 9. Grousset (*L'empire mongol*, p. 81) draws attention to such an execution during the days of the Warring

Empires, and Hulsewé (*Remnants of Han Law*, pp. 122–3), to such incidents during the creation of the Han dynasty.

20 U.-Köhalmi, 'Sibirische Parallelen', pp. 255–7.
21 Lech, p. 101.
22 *SWQZL*, 10a.
23 *SH*, §129. Cf. Pelliot, *Campagnes*, p. 136.
24 Grousset, *L'empire mongol*, pp. 81–2; Pelliot, *Campagnes*, pp. 135. See also pp. 50–1.
25 *SH*, §201.
26 *SH*, §130.
27 According to *SH*, §131 and *Collected Chronicles*, vol. I/2, p. 92, the man belonged to the Katagin tribe.
28 *SH*, §§50, 140. For the name Buri (Böri) ('strong man') see Pelliot, *Campagnes*, pp. 189f., where Pelliot mistakenly [*sic*] describes Buri as Jurkin. Concerning wrestling matches among the Siberian peoples, see U.-Köhalmi, 'Sibirische Parallelen', pp. 258ff. For the Mongol revenge on Buri, see pp. 55–6.

Editorial Note   The leaders of the Jurkin were Sacha-beki and Taichu, Buri was their uncle who left his own family to join the Jurkin (*SH*, §140).

29 *SH*, §132. This episode is also reported in *Collected Chronicles*, vol. I/2, pp. 91ff.; *SWQZL*, 14a–15a; *YS*, 1, 5a.
30 *Collected Chronicles*, vol I/2, p. 87.

Editorial Note   Cleaves' translation of Belgutei's words in *SH*, §131 reads: 'The wound is not yet [grievous]. I fear lest, because of me, there be for the brethren displeasure on one side and the other. I am not disabled. I am somewhat better. At the moment when the elder brethren and the younger brethren are hardly become accustomed to one another, let the elder brother abstain [from doing something which could make an end to the agreement]. Wait a moment!'

31 *Collected Chronicles*, vol. I/2, p. 92.
32 For the Merkit campaign, see p. 36. For the dating of the Tartar campaign, see Pelliot, *Campagnes*, pp. 195–9.
33 *Collected Chronicles*, vol. I/2, p. 248.
34 See pp. 50, 106.
35 Rashid describes Jagambu as Toghrul's younger brother but Pelliot (*Campagnes*, p. 247ff.) offers weighty arguments in favour of both the *Gurkhan* and Jagambu being Toghrul's uncles. Tu Ji (20, 6b) gives the date of Jagambu's flight as 1186.
36 The Chinese interlinear version of the *SH* glosses jaukut as *jinren* i.e. people of the Chin or Jurchid. Rashid ad-Din (*Collected Chroni-*

cles, vol I, p. 146) uses the term to embrace the peoples of China –
the Tanguts, the Jurchid and the Koreans (*Solongha*).

37   *Collected Chronicles*, vol. I/2, p. 128. *SWQZL*, 40a offers the
same version. The parallel text in *YS* (11a) which reads 'Your
younger brother *Zhaganbo* was in the land of the Chin and so I sent
messengers to him in haste to require his return' appears to have been
revised. The 'threatening words and gestures', which would presup-
pose Temuchin's presence in China, are replaced by messengers who
deliver his demands.

38   *Collected Chronicles*, vol. I/2, pp. 94, 249. See pp. 54–5. The *YS*
(1, 6a) does not mention the battle with Jagambu but does report
that, after Temuchin's victory over the Jurkin, Jagambu came and
submitted to Temuchin. It is Hong Jun's opinion (*YSYWZL*, I, 1a,
25) that the report of Temuchin's battle with Jagambu does not
represent historical fact.

39   *MDBL*, 3a.

40   See Pelliot, *Campagnes*, pp. 233ff.; *Collected Chronicles*, vol. I/2,
p. 109. See also note 35 above.

41   *SH*, §177. The Turkic title *inanch* ('trustworthy'), was widespread
among the Uighurs (Hamilton, *Les Ouighours*, p. 152). In *SH* the
name of the Naiman ruler is presented in the Mongol form *Inancha*;
in Chinese sources it is given as *Yinanchl*. Temuchin fought both his
sons, Tayang and Buiruk. (See pp. 57–8.) In *History of the Tribes*
(*Collected Chronicles*, vol. I/1, p. 131) Rashid confuses events and
reports that the *Gurkhan* rather than Erke-kara deposes Toghrul and
takes his place.

42   Although the *SH* relates that Temuchin sent messengers to
Wang-khan, Rashid's version of messengers sent by Wang-khan to
Temuchin is more logical.

The marsh area *Güse'ür* or *Küse'ür* is identified by Pelliot as lying
north of the Gobi Desert and south or south-west of the Tula River
(*Campagnes*, p. 254); Ke Shaomin places it south or southwest of the
Kerulen River (*XYSKZ*, 2, 4a), while Perlee (p. 8) offers the exact
co-ordinates 43N 109E.

Editorial Note   These co-ordinates place Güse'ür near Khatanbulag
in the East Gobi Aimag of the MPR. The nearest marshlands to that
spot are probably those near Khanbogd, on the border of the South
and East Gobi Aimags at 43N 108E.

43   *SH*, §§151, 177; *Collected Chronicles* vol. I/2, pp. 110, 249;
SWQZL, 18b–19a; *YS*, 1, 6a; *XXSS*, 38, 3a.

44   *XXSS*, 38, 3a.

45   *Collected Chronicles*, vol. I/2, p. 249. Rashid (vol. I/2, p. 110)

wrongly equates the Year of the Dragon to the 582nd year of the *Hijra* = 1186, rather than the correct reading of the 592nd Year of the *Hijra* = 1196; the earlier Year of the Dragon was 1184. See also Pelliot, *Campagnes*, pp. 196ff.

46   *YS*, 10, 11b. Cf. Pelliot, *Campagnes*, p. 197. *chingsang* is the Mongol transcription of the Chinese title *chengxiang* ('minister').

47   *Collected Chronicles*, vol. I/2, p. 93; *SWQZL*, 15b; *YS*, 1, 5b. The *YS* does not mention the award of the title *cha'ut-quri* to Temuchin, presumably regarding this title as too insignificant for the founder of a dynasty. For the meaning of the hybrid word *cha'ut-quri* see Pelliot, *Campagnes*, pp. 203–7, *Notes*, vol. I, pp. 291–5; Tu Ji, 2, 13a–14a; Wang Guowei, *SWQZL*, 16a; Ke Shaomin, *XYSKZ*, 2, 3b.

Editorial Note   Cleaves, *Secret History of the Mongols*, p. 63, glosses *ch'aut-quri* as the Sung phrase *chao-ta'o*, apparently used by the Chin as 'Pacification Commissioner'. The title *cha'ut-quri* translates as 'Warden of the Marches'.

48   *SH*, §133.
49   Pelliot, *Campagnes*, p. 213.
50   See p. 58.
51   *Collected Chronicles*, vol. I/2, p. 119; Sorkan's prognosis is also repeated in *History of the Tribes* (*Collected Chronicles*, vol. I/1, p. 177). For the rivalry between Temuchin and Kasar, see p. 99. *Alak-udur* is incorrectly designated a Merkit by Rashid. He was the son of the Tartar princeling *Meguzhin-se'ultu*, killed by Temuchin during the attack on the Tartars (Pelliot, *Campagnes*, pp. 429–30).
52   *SH*, §136; *YS*, 1, 5b.
53   *SWQZL*, 19b.
54   *Collected Chronicles*, vol. I/2, p. 93.
55   *Collected Chronicles*, vol. I/2, p. 128.
56   *SH*, §§136, 139.
57   *SH*, §140.
58   *SH*, §§157, 158, 153.
59   *Collected Chronicles*, vol. I/2, pp. 111–12, 118–19.
60   1201 is the first date cited in the *SH* and it can be regarded as reliable. It coincides with that offered by Rashid (*Collected Chronicles*, vol. I/2, p. 119).
61   *Dongqayit* in the *SH*. For the name see Pelliot, *Campagnes*, p. 228.
62   *Collected Chronicles*, vol. I/2, pp. 9, 128.
63   Rashid's Summary (*Collected Chronicles*, vol. I/2, p. 249) offers the correct interpretation of The Year of the Snake and the text (*Collected Chronicles*, vol. I/2, p. 111) must be corrected.
64   *Collected Chronicles*, p. 94.

65 For the name see Pelliot, *Campagnes*, p. 271.
66 *Collected Chronicles*, vol. I/2, p. 111. Cf. *SWQZL*, 20ff.; *YS*, 1, 6a. According to *SH*, §162, Kutu, the son of Tokto'a-beki, was also captured by Wang-khan.
67 Pelliot, *Campagnes*, p. 265.
68 *SH*, §§150, 177.
69 *YS*, 1, 6b.
70 *Collected Chronicles*, vol. I/2, pp. 111, 128.
71 *Collected Chronicles, vol. I/2, p. 139;* Pelliot, *Campagnes*, p. 309.
72 *Collected Chronicles*, vol. I/2, p. 112. The Year of the Dog (1202) in *SH*, §158 is inaccurate, as is the report of the death of Buiruk-khan [near Lake Kizil]. This, according to Rashid ad-Din, only occurred in 1206 (*Collected Chronicles*, vol. I/2, p. 150).
73 *SH*, §160.
74 Senggum must be the Mongol transliteration of the Chinese title *jiangjun* ('military commander') which in Pelliot's opinion is itself derived from *xianggong* ('minister') (*Campagnes*, p. 334). The name of Toghrul's son was Nilka (Ilka). See Pelliot, *Campagnes*, p. 333.
75 *SH*, §163. Cf. *Collected Chronicles*, vol. I/2, pp. 114f.; *SWQZL*, 22b–23b; *YS*, 1, 7a.
76 *Poiski*, p. 264.
77 *SH*, §164.

Editorial Note   It was the custom to bury persons of rank on high ground.
      Senggum was not Toghrul's only son. Dokuz-khatun, the daughter of Toghrul's son Uikut was, after the defeat of the Kerait, given in marriage to Genghis Khan's son Tolui – and then later married to his son, the Il-khan Hulegu. See p. 80.

78 *Collected Chronicles*, vol. I/2, p. 116. *SH* offers *Sa'ar-ke'er*. Pelliot places this location between the Tula and the upper Kerulen rivers (*Campagnes*, p. 27; *Notes*, pp. 320–5). Perlee, however, believes it lay in the area of the upper Selenga River.
79 *Collected Chronicles*, vol. I/2, p. 116. According to *SH*, §149, Tarkutai was still alive after the Battle of Köyitän.
80 *SH*, §162. See below for the account of Jamuka's campaign against Temuchin and Wang-khan.
81 *YS*, 1, 7b.
      The Katagin and Seljiut tribes were sworn enemies of Temuchin. Years earlier, when Temuchin and Jamuka sent a messenger to them with an offer of an alliance, the messenger was abused and sent back besmeared with sheep entrails (*Collected Chronicles*, vol. I/2, p. 117).

The Onggirat were actually on their way to join Kasar who, possibly misinterpreting their intentions, attacked and robbed them (*YS*, 1, 8a; *SWQZL*, 27b–28a). Thereupon they allied themselves with Jamuka (*Collected Chronicles*, vol. I/2, p. 119).

82   According to Rashid, a stallion, an ox and a dog were sacrificed and during the sacrifice the following words were spoken; 'O Lord of Heaven and Earth, hear the oath we swear! If we break our word and endanger this alliance may we suffer the same [fate] as these animals.' (*Collected Chronicles*, vol. I/2, p. 117). Pelliot doubts the accuracy of Rashid's version (*Campagnes*, p. 411, n. 7).

   SH, §141 speaks of the sacrifice of a stallion and a mare, while *SWQZL*, 26b and *YS*, 1, 7b both refer only to a white stallion. Cf., however, the oath taken by the allies after the election of Jamuka (*YS*, 1, 8a).

83   *Collected Chronicles*, vol. I/2, p. 117; *SWQZL*, 25a–26a; *YS*, 1, 7b.

84   Pelliot, *Campagnes*, pp. 418–19.

85   *Collected Chronicles*, vol. I/2, p. 118.

86   Pelliot, *Campagnes*, pp. 418–19.

87   The Chinese gloss of *gur* is *pu* = general/common/popular. Rashid gives this title the meaning 'Master of Sultans and Kings' (*Collected Chronicles*, vol. I/1, p. 120). Juzjani translates the title as *han-i-hanen* (Raverty, vol. II, p. 911). For the title see also Pelliot, *Campagnes*, pp. 248–9; *Notes*, vol. I, pp. 225–6. In the *SH* one finds, inexplicably, *gürqa* and *qa* (see Rachewiltz, 'The Secret History', §141, n.).

88   *SH*, §141. Cf. *Collected Chronicles*, vol. I/2, p. 120; *SWQZL*, 28b; *YS*, 1, 8a.

89   See Hong Jun, 1, 1a, 35; Tu Ji, 2, 21a; Wang Guowei, *SWQZL*, 3, 2b. Perlee's identification as the modern *Khuiten Suu* between the Onon and Kerulen rivers must be erroneous. The modern Mongolian *khuiten* ('cold'), and many locations bear the name 'cold water'. See Haltod, *Mongolische Ortsnamen*, nos. 6897–908.

90   The *jada* or *yadah* stone is a bezoar stone (Pelliot, *Notes sur l'histoire de la Horde d'Or*, p. 8). Juvaini reports that during Genghis Khan's campaign in China a Kangli used the *jada* stone to conjure up rain (Boyle, vol. I, p. 193; cf. d'Ohsson, *Histoire des Mongols*, vol. II, p. 614). Such practices are also mentioned by an-Nasawi (Buniyatov, p. 287). Marco Polo recounts that Khubilai Kha'an had sorcerers in his retinue 'who prevented a single drop of rain falling on the palace' (*La description du monde*, p. 96). See also Yule, *Ser Marco Polo*, vol. I, p. 310; Rockhill, The Journey, p. 254, n.; Doerfer, *Mongolische Elemente*, p. 286, which offer further references.

91 *SH*, §143. Cf. *Collected Chronicles*, vol. I/2, p. 122; *SWQZL*, 32b; *YS*, 1, 9a.
92 *Collected Chronicles*, vol. I/2, p. 122.
93 *SH*, §§142, 148. *SH*, §142 indicates that Auchu was a Mongol, §148 that he was a Tayichi'ut. Rashid (*Collected Chronicles*, vol. I/2, p. 121) believes him to belong to the Katagin tribe. Pelliot dedicates a long note to Auchu in *Campagnes*, pp. 158–62. Sources other than the *SH* place the campaign against the Tayichi'ut before Jamuka's election as *Gurkhan*.
94 *SH*, §§145, 202, 221. We learn now for the first time that Jelme's initial service was to save Temuchin's life during the attack by the Merkit. Cf. Jelme's biography in Tu Ji. *MWSJ*, 29, 1a–3a.
95 *SH*, §146.
96 *SH*, §147.
97 *Collected Chronicles*, vol. I/1, p. 194. Cf. *SWQZL* 12a. See Jebe's biography in Hong Jun, vol. II, pp. 18, 237–43; Tu Ji, 29, 4a–18a. For the name see Pelliot, *Campagnes*, pp. 155f.
98 *SH*, §§200, 188, 185.
99 *SH*, §§149, 200. Cf. *Collected Chronicles*, vol. I/1, pp. 187–8, also the note dedicated to Naya'a by Pelliot (*Campagnes*, pp. 162–3).
100 *Collected Chronicles*, vol. I/2, p. 116, also vol. I/1, p. 174.
101 In 'The Life of Genghis Khan' (*Collected Chronicles*, vol. I/2, p. 120) Rashid offers an erroneous interpretation of the Year of the Dog. In his summary (vol. I/2, p. 251), however, he specifies 1202 for the campaign against the Tartars. This date is confirmed in *YS*, 1, 8b and in *SWQZL*, 30a.
102 This is in the area of the Khalkha River. Tu Ji (2, 18b) points to the River Nemergen, which rises north of Soyoerji Mountain and flows into the Khalkha. Rashid (*Collected Chronicles*, vol. I/2, p. 119) writes about the Battle of Dalan-nemurges in the context of an earlier campaign by Temuchin against Alak-udur, whom Rashid incorrectly designates as 'an emir of the Merkit'. The references appear to relate to the same campaign.
103 *SH*, §153. Cf. *YS*, 1, 9a.
104 *SH*, §153.

Editorial Note This Khubilai is, of course, not the grandson of Genghis Khan, the future Khubilai Kha'an, who was not born until 1215. Khubilai-noyan was a younger brother of Jelme and one of Genghis Khan's 'four Dogs of War' (Jelme, Khubilai, Jebe and Subodei). See Thomas J. Barfield, *The Perilous Frontier* (Oxford, 1989), p. 193, n. 5; René Grousset, *The Empire of the Steppes*, trans. Naomi Walford (Rutgers University Press, 1970), p. 214.

105   *Collected Chronicles*, vol. I/2, p. 121.
106   *SH*, §§154, 107.
107   *Collected Chronicles*, vol. I/2, p. 122. In the *History of the Tribes* (*Collected Chronicles*, vol. I/1, p. 132), based on the translation by Smirnova, the name is given as Genghis Khan. Berezin (*Collected Chronicles*, vol. I, p. 101) offers the correct reading.
108   *SH*, §165.

Editorial Note   Even today the *khoimor* or place of honour is a well designated area of the Mongol *ger*. It is situated in the north area of the *ger*, facing the door (the *ger* should always be erected facing south), and is just in front of what would in the past have been the shamanist or Buddhist altar. By the door of the *ger* are the cooking and washing areas. Senggum is thus indicating that Kerait girls who marry Mongols are treated as servants rather than as honoured wives.

109   *SH*, §166.
110   For the expression *čaqa'an-a sača'asu qaranda*, see Mostaert, *Sur quelques passages*, p. 176.
111   *SH*, §§167, 181.
121   *La description du monde*, p. 77.
113   *SH*, §168. Cf. *Collected Chronicles*, vol. I/2, pp. 123–4; also *SWQZL*, 35a and *YS*, 1, 9b/10a, both of which accuse Wang-khan of participating in this plot.
114   *SH*, §§202, 219.
115   *Collected Chronicles*, vol. I/1, p. 133.
116   *SH*, § 170. *Collected Chronicles*, vol. I/2, p. 126. Poppe, 'On Some Geographical Names', p. 41. See also Hong Jun, *YSYWZL*, I, 1a, 38.
117   *SH*, §171; *SWQZL*, 37a; *YS*, 1, 10a.
118   *Collected Chronicles*, vol. I/2, p. 126.
119   *SH*, §208.
120   *SH*, §174.
121   *YS* (1, 12b) reports: 'Altan, Kuchar, Jamuka and others plotted to murder Wang-khan. They were, however, unable to carry out their plan and so fled to the Naimans.'
122   *SH*, §170.
123   *Collected Chronicles*, vol. I/2, p. 126.
124   *SH*, §§172–3. According to Rashid (*Collected Chronicles*, vol. I/2, p. 126), Temuchin withdrew directly to the Baljuna.
125   *SH*, §175; *Collected Chronicles* vol. I/2, p. 126; cf. *SWQZL*, 37b.
126   d'Ohsson, *Histoire des Mongols*, vol. I, p. 45; *YSYWZL* I, 1a, 39; Pelliot *Campagnes*, p. 46; Poppe, 'On Some Geographical Names',

p. 40; Perlee, p. 6; de Rachewiltz, 'The Secret History', *PFEH*, vol. 16, p. 58. For the name Baljuna/*Baljuni* see Pelliot, *Campagnes*, p. 42.

127   *SH*, §176; *Collected Chronicles*, vol. I/2, p. 126; *SWQZL*, 37a–38b. According to *YS*, 1, 11b Temuchin subdued the Nirkin, a clan of the Onggirat.

128   *Collected Chronicles*, vol. I/1, p. 165, and vol. I/2, p. 132. For details of the Nunjin clan see Pelliot, *Campagnes*, pp. 71ff.

129   *SH*, §182. See p. 106 for further details of Ila Ahai.

130   Al-'Umari, Lech, p. 94; *YS*, 120, 10a.

131   *YS*, 120, 6b.

132   Pelliot, 'Une ville musulmane', *JA* (1927), p. 265, n. 2. *SH*, §§182–3, 203; cf. Lech, pp. 184–5, n. 26. *Collected Chronicles*, vol. I/2, p. 126 and the biographies in the *YS*, especially in *YS*, 1, 12a.

133   Cleaves, 'The Historicity of the Baljuna Covenant', pp. 357–421, especially p. 391 for the dating of the covenant. *YS*, 120, 6b. *Collected Chronicles*, vol. I/2, p. 126. See p. 71 for estimates of Temuchin's troops at that time.

134   *SH*, §175. *SWQZL*, 47b. *YS*, 1, 12a. It is surprising that Jurchedei's biography in *YS*, 120, 8a ff. does not mention his participation in the Baljuna Covenant.

135   Cf. pp. 61–2.

136   *SH*, §177.

137   Rashid attributes to Temuchin a motive which most certainly did not underlie this particular deed. See p. 55.

138   *Collected Chronicles*, vol. I/2, pp. 127–9. This is the basis for *SWQZL*, 38a–43a and for *YS*, 1, 10b–11b.

139   *SH*, §178, *Collected Chronicles*, vol. I/2, p. 131.

140   *YS*, 1, 11b, 12a.

141   *SH*, §179.

142   *Collected Chronicles*, vol. I/2, p. 130; cf. vol. II, pp. 139–40.

143   *YS*, 1, 11b.

144   *SH*, §179. The *Secret History* is the only one of our sources which records this message from Temuchin to Jamuka. *Collected Chronicles*, vol. I/2, p. 130 and *SWQZL*, 45a include these words in a message sent from the Narin to Toghrul.

145   *SH*, §181. Again, only the *Secret History* gives the contents of the message.

146   *SH*, §181. *Collected Chronicles*, vol. I/2, p. 131.

147   *Collected Chronicles*, vol. I/1, p. 135, and vol. I/2, p. 132. *SWQZL*, 50a. *YS*, 1, 12b.

148   *Collected Chronicles*, vol. I/2, p. 132.

149   *SH* §183.

150 *SH*, §183.
151 *SH*, §184. Cf. *Collected Chronicles*, vol. I/2, p. 133.
152 For name and location of Checher, see Pelliot, *Campagnes*, pp. 123ff.
153 *SH*, §185. Cf. *Collected Chronicles*, vol. I/2, p. 133; *SWQZL*, 51b; *YS*, 1, 12b. Marco Polo learned of the battle between Genghis Khan and Wang-khan (whom he calls Prester John) and transmits a legend which, before the battle, prophesied Genghis Khan's victory (*La description du monde*, pp. 79–80).
154 *SH*, §188; *Collected Chronicles*, vol. I/2, p. 134; *SWQZL*, 51b; *YS*, 1, 13a. Cf. Raverty, vol. II, p. 944 n.
155 *Collected Chronicles*, vol. I/2, p. 133. For the legend of Prester John see the works listed by Lech (p. 181, np 20). Cf. also de Rachewiltz, *Prester John and Europe's Discovery of East Asia*.
156 *SH*, §§185–6.
157 *SH*, §20. Cf. *Collected Chronicles*, vol. I/1, p. 186.
158 *Collected Chronicles*, vol. I/1, p. 131. See also Ratchnevsky 'La condition de la femme mongole', pp. 517–18, 522.
159 *SH*, §186. *Collected Chronicles*, vol. I, p. 101.
160 *SH*, §187. Cf. *SH*, §219.
161 Boyle, vol. I, pp. 37–8, *MDBL*, 12b. See also Munkujev, *Meng-Da beilu*, p. 41.
162 *SH*, §219.
163 Defrémery and Sanguinetti, *Voyages*, vol. II, p. 410.
164 *SH*, §202.
165 Doerfer, *Türkische Elemente*, vol. II, p. 461.
166 *ZGL*, 1, 22b.
167 Demiéville, 'La situation religieuse', p. 202. Waley, *Travels of an Alchemist*, p. 8. Cf. the translation by de Rachewiltz, 'Personnel and Personalities', p. 133, n. 1).

Editorial Note Haiyun was Ch'an Buddhist and he and his master, Chung-kuan, came to the attention of Mukali, Genghis' viceroy in China. When Genghis received Mukali's report, he responded with instructions that 'the old Reverend One and the young Reverend One . . . are not to be treated with disrespect by any one and are to rank as *Darkhan*'. (Waley, pp. 6, 7, 8.) There appears to be no evidence that the Taoist Changchun was actually created a *Darkhan*, although, by a decree of Genghis in the third month of the year 1223, he and his pupils were exempted from taxation and socage.

168 Etani Toshiyuki, pp. 185–202.
169 Vladimirtsov, *Le régime social*, pp. 217f., 229ff.; Vladimirtsov, *IAN* (1926), p. 235.

170   Shastina, *Russko-mongolskie otnosheniya*, p. 95.

The institution was generally widespread among nomadic tribes. The title *Darkhan* is attested to under the Khitans (Wittfogel and Feng, *Liao*, p. 433). According to Pelliot ('Neuf Notes', p. 250) the Tu-chueh probably adopted the title from the Mongol-speaking Juan-juan or Avars. The title *Tarkhan* is verified by Meander in the sixth century (d'Ohsson, *Histoire des Mongols*, vol. I, p. 45, n. Cf. C. Mueller, *Fragments Historicum Graecorum*, vol. IV, p. 227, quoted by Rockhill, *The Journey*, p. 164, n.).

Tarkhan were cited on the Kul-tegin inscription (Doerfer, *Türkische Elemente*, vol. I, p. 362) and among the Uighurs in the seventh century (Hamilton, *Les Ouighours à l'époque des Cinqs dynasties*, p. 155). The following privileges were listed as appertaining to the title: the right to enter the ruler's tent without being summoned and the Ninefold Pardon down to the ninth generation (Eberhard, *Conquerors and Rulers*, p. 98, n. 7).

The etymology of the word is unknown. It is said that the word originally meant 'smith' (Eberhard, *Conquerors and Rulers*, p. 98, n. 7) and that meaning has been retained in Mongolian usage (Cheremissov, *Buryatsko-russkii slovar'*, p. 189). The name of the mountain Darkhan is interpreted by the Mongols as the Mountain of the Smith (i.e. Genghis Khan) (d'Ohsson, vol. I, p. 37 n.). Kowalewski (*Dictionnaire*, vol. III, p. 1676) offers the meanings 'artist' or 'craftsman' and provides the compounds *temur darkhan* ('blacksmith') and *altan darkhan* ('goldsmith'). The word is, however, also used with the meaning 'tax free', and the modern root word *Darkh* means 'privilege'. The Ordos distinguished between major and minor *Darkhan*, who were exempt from taxation, socage and requisitioning (Mostaert, *Dictionnaire Ordos*, vol. I, p. 122). For the word in Turkic, see Frye, 'Tarχun-Türχün', pp. 105–29. For the institution among the Mongols, see Etani Toshiyuki, pp. 185–202; Han Rulin, *Studia Serica*, vol. I/1 (1940), pp. 155–84. For additional bibliographies see Doerfer, *Türkische Elemente*, vol. II, pp. 460–74; Lech, pp. 186–7; Schurmann, 'Tributary Practices', pp. 322–5. See also the Decree published by Cleaves in *HJAS* (1953).

171   Lech, p. 94.

Editorial Note   Although the Oirats appear to have submitted to Temuchin at this time, one of their major leaders, Kuduka-beki, remained opposed to Temuchin.

172   Boyle, vol. I, p. 39. Cf. *Collected Chronicles*, vol. I/2, p. 135.
173   *SH*, §189. *Collected Chronicles*, vol. I/2, p. 72, also vol. I/1, p. 138. Pelliot, *Campagnes*, pp. 308–9.

174 *SH*, §189. See Mostaert, *Sur quelques passages*, p. 110, for the hendiadys *ghar köl* ('hands and feet') used for 'hands'.

175 Hong Jun, *YSYWZL*, 1, 1a, 27. Cf. Pelliot, *Campagnes*, p. 364; Doerfer, *Mongolische Elemente*, p. 248.

176 Tao Zongyi (*ZGL*, 1, 16b) lists them as *semu ren*, i.e. as non-Mongols. Rashid (*Collected Chronicles*, vol. I/1, p. 140) also notes that they are a separate people and only resemble the Mongols. Cf. Murayma, 'Sind Die Naiman Türken oder Mongolen?', p. 196. See also chap. 1, note 3.

177 *Collected Chronicles*, vol. I/1, pp. 131, 139. Friendly relations continued between Alakush and Temuchin even after the latter's attacks on the Chin.

178 *Duru-yin gu'un* (*duri-yin gu'un* in *SH*, §225) is translated as *baishen* in the Chinese gloss. The Chinese expression indicates 'private citizens who are not in government service'. In military terminology *baishen* describes the ordinary soldiers in contrast to the officers, (des Rotours, *Traité des fonctionnaires*, vol. II, p. 840. n. 2). Kozin's translation 'freemen' is incorrect (cf. Mostaert, *Sur quelques passages*, p. 252. This destroys the basis for the assumption made by Natsagdorj ('Nekotorie voprosy', p. 56) that the phrase refers to the prosperous section of the population.

179 *SH*, §§191, 193.

180 *Collected Chronicles*, vol. I/2, p. 147.

181 This stratagem was used successfully by the Mongols in Hungary in 1241 (Martin, *The Rise*, p. 40). Shigi Khutukhu sought to utilize it in the campaign against Jalal ad-Din and it is mentioned by Carpini (Wyngaert, p. 59). It was also used in more modern times. Consten (*Weideplätze*, pp. 207–10) relates that, one dark night in 1912 during the siege of the Chinese in the town of Kobdo, the Mongol rebels set dummies on the backs of old useless camels and drove these towards the ramparts. To the delight of the Mongols the Chinese squandered their costly and scarce ammunition in an attempt to repulse this sham attack.

182 For the expression see de Rachewiltz, 'Secret History', *PFEH* (1978), p. 71.

183 *gurdun-u tukhul*. The comparison with the wheel is an indication of height of growth (Haenisch: 'wheel-high'; Damdinsuren: 'small' [rather than breadth]; Ligeti; 'fat'; Rachewiltz: 'round = fat'). Cf. the phrase *chi'un-tur ulizhu kidu-* ('to measure from the wheel pin of the wagon').

Editorial Note Cleaves, *The Secret History of the Mongols*, p. 123, n. 41, offers the plausible explanation that the phrase refers to the fact that small calves were tied to the wagon wheel to prevent them following the mother and sucking her milk.

184   *SH*, §194, Cf. *Collected Chronicles*, vol. I/2, p. 147; *SWQZL*, 55a; *YS*, 1, 13b–14a.

185   *SH*, §§195, 201.

186   *Collected Chronicles*, vol. I/2, p. 123; *SH*, §166.

187   *SH*, §196 records that Tayang-khan was captured.

188   *SH*, §196. *Collected Chronicles*, vol. I/2, p. 148, *SWQZL*, 56a, and *YS*, 1, 14a name only the Dörbets, the Tartars, the Katagin and the Seljiut. The Onggirat had already joined Temuchin (see p. 71) and the Tartars had been destroyed (*SH*, §154). This comment in the *Secret History* can, therefore, apply only to tribal sub-clans or groups.

189   *SH* §197; *Collected Chronicles*, vol. I/2, p. 149; *SWQZL*, 56b; *YS*, 1, 14a.

190   *Collected Chronicles*, vol. I/1, p. 116.

191   *SH*, §196. *SH*, §200 speaks of five companions. Rashid (*Collected Chronicles*, vol. I/1, p. 191) reports that there were sixty followers, of whom thirty were executed by Temuchin for surrendering Jamuka. For the location of Tanglu-ula see Pelliot, *Campagnes*, p. 209.

192   *SH*, §§200–1.

193   *SH*, §§170, 195. Because of the role which the *Secret History* ascribes to Jamuka, Gumilev (*Poiski*, pp. 274ff.) allows himself to be misled into the theory that Jamuka was active in the enemy camp as Temuchin's agent and informer.

194   *SH*, §201. Blood was, according to the belief of the old Mongols, the seat of the spirit and execution without spilling blood would thus retain the spirit as clan guardian. See U.-Köhalmi, 'Sibirische Parallelen', pp. 260f. In contrast, death by boiling in vessels was designed to destroy the spirit.

195   Cf. *Collected Chronicles*, vol. I/1, p. 191, and I/2, p. 227. *YS* and *SWQZL* do not mention Jamuka's execution. For the name Eljigidei see Hambis, *Le chapitre CVII*, p. 29, n. 1. According to Pelliot (*Campagnes*, p. 221), Eljigidei was a nephew of Temuchin.

196   *Collected Chronicles*, vol. I/2, p. 89, and vol. I/1, p. 191. *SH*, §200.

Chapter 3   Genghis Khan, Ruler of the Mongol Empire

1   Cf. *SH*, §245. As Rumyantsev notes in his commentary on Banzarov's *Chernaya vera*, the personal spirit (*sulde*) of a great man

could become the protective spirit of a nation or army and the Mongols therefore designated Genghis Khan's standard *sulde* (*Sobranine sochinenii*, pp. 274–5, n. 120). Doerfer (*Türkische Elemente*, vol. I, p. 619) draws attention to the difference between 'standard' (*tugh*) and 'flag' (*orongga*) and Hong Jun (*YSYWZL*, 53) also comments that *tugh* is not a 'banner' (*li*). Ke Shaomin (*XYSKZ*, 3, la) does, however, draw attention to the use at the parallel position in *Menggu yuanliu* of the word *wuerluge* (*orongga*) as equivalent to *tugh*.

2   *SH*, §202; *Collected Chronicles*, vol. I/2, p. 150; *SWQZL*, 57a; *YS*, 1, 14b.

3   Rashid ad-Din interprets the word as the plural of *ching* ('firm' or 'strong') (*Collected Chronicles*, vol. I/1, p. 167; vol. I/2, p. 150).

In §230 of the *Secret History* the meaning 'righteous' or 'loyal' is used; in the Juyongguan Inscription of 1445, 'firm' (Lewicki, *Inscriptions*, p. 54; Poppe, *The Mongolian Monuments*, p. 63).

The plural form *chinggis* derived from *ching* is not possible in Mongolian (Schmidt, *Die Geschichte der Ostmongolen*, p. 379; Pelliot, *Notes*, vol. I, p. 297), but Khara-Davan (*Čingis chan*, p. 32) points out that the word *chinggis* was used by the Oirats and the Kalmucks to mean 'strong', also that Doerfer (*Mongolische Elemente*, pp. 313f) draws attention to the Yakut form *chingis* (*chigis*) ('hard' or 'cruel'). These two authors suggest that the word became taboo after the death of Genghis Khan. That would be unusual since the World Conqueror's own name, Temuchin, did not become taboo.

Banzarov's derivation ('O proiskhozhdenii slova *Chingis*', pp. 175–7) from the title *jabgu* of the Xiongnu rulers is erroneous – according to Karlgrenz, *Grammata serica*, nos. 633d, 784k the medieval pronunciation was *iap-guo* and the archaic pronunciation was *diap-g'wag*.

Zhao Hong's explanation that the title is derived from the Chinese *tianzi* ('Son of Heaven') is eccentric; and Haenisch's hypothesis ('Mongolische Miszellen', pp. 65–6) that the Mongolian *ching* is a rendering of the Chinese *zheng*, as in the phrase *Zheng zhu* ('legitimate ruler') is unlikely to receive much support.

The tales in later Mongolian chronicles, which suggest that *chingis* is the onomatopoeic representation of a bird cry, belong to the realm of fables.

4   von Ramstedt, 'Mogholica', p. 25; Pelliot, 'Les Mongols et la Papauté', vol. 23, p. 23.

5   Pelliot, 'Les Mongols et la Papauté', vol. 23, p. 45. The *Secret History* (§280) describes Ögödei as *dalai-yin qahan* and Ibn Battuta calls the World Conqueror *Tängiz-khan*.

6   Lewicki, *Les inscriptions mongoles*, p. 53, paras. 11, 13.
7   Pelliot, *Notes*, vol. I, p. 301; *Collected Chronicles*, vol. I/1, p. 76.
8   *Collected Chronicles*, vol. I/1, p. 167; Minovi and Minorsky, 'Naṣir al-Dīn Ṭūsī on Finance', p. 767. The abstract meaning of *Dalai* ('great' or 'limitless') has been kept in the west Mongolian languages, Oirat and Kalmuck (Khara-Davan, *Čingis chan*, pp. 33–5) and also in Ordos with the meaning *'beaucoup'*, *'en grande quantité'*, *'en grand nombre'* (Mostaert, *Dictionnaire Ordos*, p. 115).
    For further literature on the meaning and derivation of the name, see Pelliot, *Notes*, vol. I, p. 296–303; Doerfer, *Mongolische Elemente*, pp. 312–15; Erdmann, *Temudschin*, pp. 599–609. Cf. also Munkujev, *Men-Da bei-lu*, pp. 109–11; Cleaves, 'The Sino-Mongolian Inscription of 1362', p. 98 n. 26; Rumyantsev, n. 36 in Banzarov, *Sobranie sochinenii*, pp. 315–17; Vernadsky, *The Mongols and Russia*, p. 28; Poucha, *Die Geheime Geschichte*, p. 54.

Editorial Note   The most recent discussion of this vexed question is: Igor de Rachewiltz, 'The Title Činggis Chan/Chaγan Re-examined', in *Gedanke und Wirkung: Festschrift zum 90. Geburtstag von Nicholaus Poppe*, ed. W Heissig and K. Sagaster (Wiesbaden, 1989), pp. 281–98.

9   *SH*, §205. The sentence which follows contains an anachronism since Mukali was only granted the title *guo-wang* ('viceroy') in 1218.
10   *SH*, §§203–23.
11   *YS*, 98, 2a.
12   Vernadsky, *O Sostave*, p. 54; *YDZ*, 826b, See Ratchnevsky, *Code*, vol. I, p. xliii ff, for the system of military succession.
13   *QDGZ*, 23; p. 189.
14   The names of the regimental commanders are listed in *SH*, §202. Cf. the list prepared by Rashid (*Collected Chronicles*, vol. I/2, p. 267–74) on the basis of the *Altan debter*.
15   *SH*, §219.
16   Vladimirtsov, *Gengis-khan*, pp. 59, 60. *SH*, §§192, 219.
17   See: *SH*, §§202, 207, 213, 218, 221–3. Cf. Ratchnevsky, 'Šigi-qutuqu', pp. 99ff. and *Collected Chronicles*, vol. I/1, p. 176.
18   Boyle, vol. I, p. 32.
19   *Collected Chronicles*, vol. I/2, p. 260.
20   See p. 191; Lech, p. 98; *SH*, §223.
21   See p. 84; *SH*, §228, *Kötöchin* is glossed as *jiaren* ('members of the household') and *bandang* ('servants').
22   Boyle, vol. I, p. 29. See also al-'Umari (Lech, p. 97).
23   *YS*, 124, 6a. Tu Ji, *MWSJ*, 45, 1a–b. See also p. 191.

24   *SH*, §§242, 203. The word *guchu* ('strength') has, by mistake, been omitted from Pelliot's text.

Editorial Note   Neither is the modern Mongolian word *khuch* ('strength') included in Gaadamba's 1975 version of the *Secret History*.

25   *SH*, §203. For *Köke debter* see Pelliot, *Notes sur le Turkestan*, p. 39.
26   *YS*, 117, 1b; the Chinese translation is *duanshi guan*. For the institution *yarghuchi* see Tamura, *Chūgoku seifū ōchō no kenkyū*, pp. 444–63. Cf. also *Code*, vol. I, p. 52, n. 1, and *SH*, §203.
27   Tamura, *Chingis-kan no yasa*, p. 392. See also pp. 187ff.

Editorial Note 1   For a more sceptical discussion of the *Yasa*, see D.O. Morgan, 'The Great *Yāsā* of Chingiz Khan and Mongol Law in the Ilkhānate', *BSOAS*, vol. 49/1 (1986), pp. 163–76, summarized in Morgan, *The Mongols* (Oxford, 1986), pp. 96–9.

Editorial Note 2   See also '(Old) Mongolian Script' in *Information Mongolia* (London, 1990), p. 60, for a suggestion that the Mongolian script was developed much earlier than the thirteenth century, being adopted by the Mongols and the Uighurs simultaneously from the Sogdians.

28   See pp. 2, 155–6; Wyngaert, pp. 44, 303; *SH*, §§216, 272; Radloff, *Aus Siberien*, vol. II, pp. 52–5; Wittfogel and Feng, p. 267; Buniyatov, p. 287; Marco Polo, *La description du monde*, p. 96; Khanlaryan, p. 173.
29   *Collected Chronicles*, vol. I/1, p. 167.
30   Pelliot, *Sur la légende d'Uyuz-khan*; Boyle, vol. I, p. 39; *Collected Chronicles*, vol. I/1, p. 167.
31   *SH*, §244.
32   See p. 54.
33   Pelliot, *Campagnes*, p. 172. Cf. Grousset, *L'empire mongol*, pp. 146–7.
34   Shastina, *Obraz Chingis-khana*, pp. 440–1, *Altan tobči*, p. 206; Schmidt, *Geschichte*, p. 72. For the relationship between Temuchin and his brother Jochi-Kasar, see Natsagdorj, *Chingis Kasar khoer zhorchie*.
35   *Collected Chronicles*, vol. I/2, p. 51, vol. I/1, pp. 106, 165; *SH*, §244. On the occasion of the distribution of the subject tribes Jochi-kasar's sons were also disadvantaged, receiving only 1,000 persons (*Collected Chronicles*, vol. I/2, p. 277).
36   *SH*, §245. The multi-linguistic nature of these adherents indicates

the heterogeneous composition of Genghis Khan's nation. It included Kirghiz and Khitans as well as Keraits, Naimans and Oirats.

37   *SH*, §245. See pp. 48, 56–7, also U.-Köhalmi, 'Sibirische Parallelen', p. 258.

38   *SH*, §§245–6.

Editorial Note   Professor Thomas J, Barfield (*The Perilous Frontier*, Oxford, 1989, p. 194) stresses the secular aspect of this struggle, highlighting the ambitions of Mönglik's sons after the death of Mother Hö'elun, and suggesting that Teb-tengri sought to inherit some of the tribes held jointly by Mother Hö'elun and Otchigin.

39   *SH*, §216. For *beki* see Pelliot, 'Notes sur le *Turkestan*', pp. 49ff.; Doerfer, *Mongolische Elemente*, pp. 235f. The title *beki* was usually borne by the eldest sons of the tribal chieftains. See Vladimirtsov, *Le régime social*, pp. 60–2.

40   *Collected Chronicles*, vol. I/2, p. 150; *SWQZL*, 57a; *YS*, 1, 14b.

41   *Collected Chronicles*, vol. I/2, p. 151, vol. I/2, p. 150; *SWQZL* 57b–58a; *YS*, 1, 15a. Rashid states that the Kirghiz lords sent a counter-mission to Genghis with a declaration of their submission. Cf. also Barthold, 'Kirgisi', pp. 505f.

42   *SH*, §§197–8; *SWQZL*, 58b, 59b; *YS*, 1, 15a; *Collected Chronicles*, vol. I/2, p. 152. *SH* places the campaign against Tokto'a and Kuchlug in the year 1205, but I adhere to Rashid's chronology.

Editorial Note   We have, of course, just learned that Buiruk-khan was defeated and killed at least a year earlier. The apparent *non-sequitur* doubtless arises because this section is based on the *Secret History*, whose chronology on these events is, apparently, two years behind that of Rashid. The story, as related, indicates that, after the defeat of Buiruk-khan, Tokto'a and Kuchlug withdrew from the Black Irtysch, beyond Lake Zaisan to the Irtysch River.

43   According to *SWQZL*, 59a, the *idikut* had the Kara-Khitan governor killed.

44   *SH*, §238. Cf. the text of the message in *Collected Chronicles*, vol. I/2, p. 152; *SWQZL*, 59a.

45   *Collected Chronicles*, vol. I/2, p. 163. Cf. vol. I/2, p. 153; *SWQZL*, 58b–59a. According to Juvaini (Boyle, vol. I, p. 45) the *idikut* only recognized Genghis' suzerainty after the successful first Mongol campaign against the Chin; *YS*, 1, 15a, however, asserts that the Uighur leader came and submitted as early as 1209.

46   *SH*, §235; *Collected Chronicles*, vol. I/2, pp. 153, 163; *SWQZL*,

61a; *YS*, 1, 16a. The *Secret History* reports this submission as taking place immediately after the Assembly of 1206.

47   S.G. Jenkin, 'A Note on Climatic Cycles'.

48   *YS*, 150, 9b. *Collected Chronicles*, vol. I/2, pp. 149–50. Rashid comments that this first incursion into Xi-Xia took place in the Year of the Ox (1205) – not in 1202 as given by the translator. The year 1205 is confirmed in both *SWQZL* and YS. *SH*, §198 does not mention the first Tangut campaign but designates 1205 as the year of the pursuit of Kuchlug and Tokto'a. See note 42 above.

According to *XXSS*, 39, 10a the Mongol troops were commanded by Qiegulitu and Ila Ahai, *Collected Chronicles*, vol. I/2, p. 149 and *YS*, 14, 14b specify that Genghis commanded the campaign; but this is unlikely since, at that time, Genghis was occupied with the elimination of his enemies in Mongolia. Cf. Martin, 'The Mongol Wars', p. 199; *SWQZL*, 57a.

49   Kychanov, 'Mongolo-tangutskie voiny', pp. 47f. Cf. Martin, 'The Mongol Wars', p. 198.

50   Martin, 'The Mongol Wars', p. 198. For the role of the deserters see the section on the campaign in China (p. 106ff.).

51   *linggong* is the Chinese title, rendered as *lingqu* in the *Secret History* (§47; *Charaqai-lingqu*).

52   *DJGZ*, 21, 4b.

53   Martin, 'The Mongol Wars', p. 201.

54   *SH*, §250; *Collected Chronicles*, vol. I/2, p. 153; *SWQZL*, 60b; *YS*, 1, 15a–b. For the first Tangut campaign see Martin, 'The Mongol Wars', pp. 195–202; Kychanov, 'Mongolo-tangutskie voiny', pp. 47–51.

55   Martin, 'Chingis Khan's First Invasion', p. 184. The Chin had, of course, always to reckon with the possibility of a renewal of hostilities.

56   *YS*, 1, 14b, 16a. The titles listed in the *YS* text, *xing zhongshu*, *taishi* and *taifu*, are, of course, anachronisms since they did not exist in Genghis' day. Ahai accompanied Genghis on the western campaign and died soon afterwards at the age of 73. Khubilai Kha'an conferred on him the posthumous title 'Loyal Military Duke' (*YS*, 150, 9a–10a). See p. 72 for an earlier reference to Ila Ahai.

Editorial Note   Ratchnevsky presumably means that these were Chinese titles and not conferred by Genghis. For the title *taishi*, for example, see p. 2 concerning Yeliu-taishi, Khitan ruler of Kara-Khitai. Tuka may have acted as a hostage for Ila's good faith, but he is unlikely to have been, initially at least, a member of other than a very embryonic bodyguard. Temuchin's bodyguard of eighty Nightguards and seventy Dayguards was formally constituted, as one of his military reforms, during the preparations for the Naiman campaign in 1204, i.e. after the Baljuna and after the defeat of Wang-khan. See p. 84.

57 *YS*, 150, 9a.
58 *YS*, 1, 14b, *YSXB*, 12.
59 *DJGZ*, 21 4b; *XXSS*, 40, 1a. Cf. de Rachewiltz, 'Personnel and Personalities', p. 98.
60 *YS*, 1, 14b–15a.
61 See pp. 110–11.
62 *YS*, 149, 20a.
63 Martin, 'Chingis Khan's First Invasion', pp. 190, 201.
64 *YS* 1, 15b. Cf. the text in Li Xinchuan, *Zaji*, 19, 585. It may have been an oversight in the revision of the *Yuanshi* text which alerts us for the first time to Genghis' duty of tribute to the Chin emperor.

Editorial Note But see p. 12 for the statement that, after the defeat of the *Menggu* by the Tartars near Lake Buir, the *Menggu* paid tribute to the Chin emperor.

65 *Collected Chronicles*, vol. I/2, p. 163. Cf. *SWQZL*, 61b.
66 *Collected Chronicles*, vol. I/2, p. 263. See p. 12.
67 Raverty, vol. II, p. 954.
68 According to *YS*, 1, 16a, Genghis Khan set out on the campaign in January or February – but the Wusha fortifications were only captured by Jebe in August. Tu Ji (3, 9b), who comments that the march could not have begun so early in the year, sets the departure of the Mongol army in May/June, and this is probably accurate. *SWQZL*, 61b states that Genghis only took the oath in autumn, a date which cannot be reconciled with later events. See also Wang Guowei, 'Jinjie hao kao', *GTJL*, 15, 14a ff. Cf. Zhao Hong, *MDBL*, 14a; *Collected Chronicles*, vol. I/1, p. 140; Mullie, 'Les anciennes villes', pp. 203ff. A *li* is approximately one-third of a mile.

Editorial Note For a discussion of the frequently dubious assertions regarding the concept of 'the Great Wall of China', see Arthur Waldron, *The Great Wall of China; from History to Myth* (Cambridge, 1990). See Also Morgan, *The Mongols*, p. 66, for a reference to an earlier article by Waldron, 'The problem of the Great Wall of China', *HJAS*, vol. 43/2 (1983), pp. 654, 656.

69 *Collected Chronicles*, vol. I/1, p. 141.
70 *YS*, 149, 5b–6b. Cf. Tu Ji, 51, 1a–b. Liu Bailin was joined by Jiagu Changge in submitting to Genghis Khan. Liu Bailin died in 1221 at the age of 72. Xuande fu is the modern Xuanhua fu.

71 Shimo Ming'an has a biography in *YS*, 149, 5b–6b. See also *Collected Chronicles*, vol. I/2, p. 167; *SWQZL*, 63a.

72 *YS*, 16a; *SH*, §247. Rashid ad-Din (*Collected Chronicles*, vol. I/2,, p. 165) does not mention the forcing of the pass. He reports that Jebe was sent to attack the eastern capital, Dongjing, and captured that city through a feigned withdrawal.

73 Raverty, vol. II, p. 954. *YS*, 120, 6a–7b. The Chinese transcription of the name is Zhabaer-hohze (Ja'far Khwaja). Later in 1222 Ja'far was involved as a contact to Changchun. Ja'far is said to have died aged 118, when he was posthumously awarded the highest honours.

74 *YS*, 1, 16b–17a; 143, 2a; *SWQZL*, 67b; *Collected Chronicles*, vol. I/2, p. 172.

75 There are some discrepancies in the dates provided by our sources. *YS*, 1, 17a records for July/August 1213 that the Chin commander (*liushou*) of Xijing, Hushahu, deserted the town; according to *JS*, 13, 5a, Hushahu had already left Xijing in the eleventh month (December 1211/January 1212; Tu Ji (*MWSJ*, 3, 12b) places the taking of the pass in the ninth month (October/November) 1213; *DJGZ*, 23, 3b–4a reports that the pass of Jijing was abandoned by Hushahu in the eighth month (August/September 1213).

The circumstances of the emperor's deposal are dealt with in great detail in Hushahu's biography (*JS*, 132, 19b ff.) and in the official annals (*JS*, 13, 6b, ff.). Cf. *DJGZ*, 23, 4a, f. and O. Franke, *Geschichte*, vol. IV, pp. 261–20 The *Yuanshi* remarks laconically 'In the eighth month [August/September 1213] Hushahu of the Chin killed his ruler Yunji,' Rashid and *SWQZL* make no mention of this *coup d'état*.

Editorial Note Ratchnevsky indexed only one Hushahu. This regicide cannot, however, be the Hushahu who was defeated seventy-four years earlier by the Menggu at Hailing in 1139. See p. 9.

76 *YS*, 1, 16b, 17a; *JS*, 14, 3b. The name of Otchigin, Genghis' youngest brother, is rendered in Chinese as *Wochen-nayen*.

77 Wyngaert, pp. 56, 47–8.

78 Matthew Paris, vol. IV, p. 386, quoted by Rockhill, *The Journey*, p. 64, n.

79 *Collected Chronicles*, vol. II, n. 110.

80 *QDGZ*, 10, 9b–10a; Wittfogel and Feng, p. 425, n. 164.

81 Beazley, n. 40; Risch, *Johann de Plano Carpini*, p. 97, n. 3.

82 Cf. des Rotours, 'Quelques notes sur l'anthropophagie', pp. 386–427. See also p. 82 for the situation during the siege of Zhongdu in 1215.

83 YS, 1, 17b, 18a; JS, 14, 3b; *Collected Chronicles*, vol. I/2, p. 171; SWQZL, 67a.

84 YS, 1, 18a; SH, §249. Our other sources mention only the gift of the princess.

85 O. Franke, *Geschichte*, vol. IV, p. 272.

86 Tu Ji, 49, 8b. Dongjing in the text must be corrected to Beijing. See also note 72 above.

Editorial Note   The Zhongdu of this chapter is, of course, as can be established from the accounts of its various vicissitudes at the time of the Mongol incursions into China, the then capital Yenching, close to the site of the **modern** Beijing (Capital of the People's Republic of China). The introduction of a second 'Beijing' – for the 'Northern Capital' (Pei-ching) – in the original *Činggis-Khan* is, at this point, confusing and has, in the interests of clarity, been omitted from this text.

In his translation of *The Secret History of the Mongols* Cleaves refers to this town as *Buiging*. Gaadamba, in his 1975 edition of the *Secret History*, uses *Beigin* in this context, while glossing Zhongdu as *Beizhin*. Cleaves, commenting in a note (*Secret History*, p. 189, n. 35) that this city is Pei-ching or 'northern capital' (in Manchuria), glossed as Ta-ning, the name by which it was known under the Yuan and the Ming, refers his readers to Lucien Gibert, *Dictionnaire historique et géographique de la Mandchourie* (Hongkong, 1934), pp. 737, 831–2. Ta-ning (also known as Ta-ning-ching) was, according to Herrman, the former Ta-ting, the Central Residence of the Liao. See Albert Herrmann, *An Historical Atlas of China* (Edinburgh, 1966), pp. 34–5.

Many accounts of the Mongol campaigns in Northern China in the years 1211–15 refer to Mukali's attack on the northern-capital. Some identify this city as Mukden (which has been known as Shen-yang by the Yuan, Kai-yuan by the Ming and Sheng ching or Shun t'ien fu by the Ching), or Liao-yang, slightly south of Mukden, one of the Chin secondary capitals and the former eastern residence of the Liao.

The Liaodong province is clearly a reference to the present Liaotung Peninsula, which under the Yuan dynasty was known as Liao-yang. (Herrmann, *Historical Atlas*, p. 41.)

87 See Shimo Yesen's biography, Tu Ji, 49, 8b–10b.

88 YS, 1, 18b; *Collected Chronicles*, vol. I/2, p. 174; SWQZL, 68b. Fuxing was his original name, Chenghui his later adopted name. See his biography in JS, 101, 1a–5a.

89 SH, §252; Ratchnevsky, 'Šigi-qutuqu', pp. 98–103.

90 Raverty, vol. II, p. 965.

91   In the chapter of the *Yuanshi* dealing with apanages (*YS*, 95, 34a) only the last entries define fiefs by territory.
92   *YS*, 1, 18b.
93   *YS*, 147, 8b–12a. Cf. Tu Ji, 36, 1a–2b; Giles, *Biographical Dictionary*, no. 1730.
94   *YS*, 1, 19a. For the campaign in Northern China see *YS*, 1, 15b–18b; *Collected Chronicles*, vol. I/2, pp. 163–77; *SWQZL* 62–72; *SH*, §§247–53. Cf. also the account in Martin, 'Chingis Khan's First Invasion'; Melikhov, 'Ustanovlenie vlasti', pp. 67–70; O. Franke, *Geschichte*, vol. IV, pp. 267–74; Grousset, *L'empire mongol*, pp. 215ff.; Vladimirtsov, *Gengis Khan*, pp. 78–83.
95   *Collected Chronicles*, vol. I/2, p. 178; *YS*, 1, 19b. *SWQZL* 72b, notes the appointment in 1218. Attention has already been drawn to the anachronism in *SH*, §206.
96   See Pelliot, *Campagnes*, p. 285 for variations of the name.
97   *Collected Chronicles*, vol. I/2, pp. 177–8, 255, and *SWQZL*, 72b give the year as 1217. *SH*, §236 reports the expedition immediately after the *Khuriltai* of 1206, clearly an anachronism.
98   See Chap. 1, n. 175.
99   *Collected Chronicles*, vol. I/2, pp. 178, 255–6, *SWQZL*, 72b, and *YS*, 1, 19b all give the date as 1217. Again the *Secret History* (§241) stands alone, quotting the Year of the Hare (1207).
100   *SH*, §138; *Collected Chronicles*, vol. I/1, p. 171. For the name see Pelliot, *Campagnes*, pp. 372ff.
101   *SH*, §241; *Collected Chronicles*, vol. I/2, p. 178.
102   *Collected Chronicles*, vol. I/1, pp. 151, 256; vol. I/2, p. 151, give the date of this campaign by Jochi as 1218. Cf. Barthold, *Sochineniya*, II/1 (1963), p. 506; *SWQZL*, 74a. *YS* does not mention the campaign; *SH* quotes 1207.
103   *SH*, §239. The epithet *öljeitu* ('fortunate') applied to a forest tribe appears strange in the light of the antagonism between the herders and the forest tribes.

Editorial Note   Cleaves glosses this as: 'fortunate, because they now belong to the Mongols' (*The Secret History*, p. 174, n. 25).
The roles attributed in this section to Kuduka-beki of the Oirats are somewhat confusing: in 1217 he is involved on behalf of the Mongols in the Tumat campaign, yet in 1218 he is the first to 'submit' to Jochi.
The chronology of these various campaigns is also confusing and although Ratchnevsky accepts the Rashid dates of 1217–18 in preference to the contention in the *Secret History* that the campaigns were in 1207, a case can certainly be made for the latter. Not only

does it seem strange that Korchi should have delayed ten years before claiming his thirty beautiful Tumat maidens but, more significantly perhaps, an earlier date for at least one of the campaigns is more in keeping with what we are told about Jochi. Born in 1184, he would have been twenty-three years of age in 1207, probably the age at which he would have been entrusted with his initial campaign, on which Genghis Khan congratulates him (see pp. 117–18). It is unlikely that Jochi's initial 'blooding' on the battlefield would have been postponed until the age of thirty-three; and, indeed, we know that Jochi was already in joint command of the right wing of the Mongol army at the initial siege of Zhongdu in 1214 (see p. 112).

104   *SH*, §239.
105   Boyle, vol. I, pp. 61–6, 70–4; *Collected Chronicles*, vol. I/2, pp. 179–83.
106   Boyle, vol. I, p 75.
107   Boyle, vol. I, pp. 67–8; *Collected Chronicles*, vol. I/1, p. 83.
108   Boyle, vol. II, p. 368; *Collected Chronicles*, vol. I/2, p. 189; Buniyatov, p. 52; *MWSJ*, 29, 5a.
109   Buniyatov, p. 51. Juvaini reports in the same vein; 'We have no authority to fight you. We have come with another purpose – to recover booty which has escaped our net.' (Boyle, vol. II, p. 371.) Cf. *Collected Chronicles*, vol. I/2, p. 190.
110   Raverty, vol. II, pp. 96, 963–6; *Collected Chronicles*, vol. I/2, p. 157.
111   Buniyatov, p. 53; Boyle, vol. I, p. 69; vol. II, p. 372.
112   Boyle, vol. I, p. 79.
113   Raverty, vol. II, p. 966; *Collected Chronicles*, vol. I/2, p. 188; Buniyatov, p. 78.
114   Petrushevski, 'Pokhod', p. 110.
115   Barthold, 'Turkestan', p. 472.
116   Buniyatov, p. 78.

Editorial Note   This envoy was probably Yalavach. See p. 137.

117   *Inal* is a Turkic title. See Pelliot, *Campagnes*, p. 102, Doerfer, *Türkische Elemente*, vol. III, pp. 196–9.
118   Cf. Vernadsky, *The Mongols and Russia*, p. 117.
119   Raverty, vol. II, p. 967; Boyle, vol. I, p. 79; *Collected Chronicles*, vol. I/2, p. 188.
120   Buniyatov, pp. 79–80.
121   Raverty, vol. II, p. 1041; Boyle, vol. I, p. 80; vol. II, p. 367; *Collected Chronicles*, vol. I/2, p. 189.

122   Barthold, 'Khorezmshah', pp. 535–7. For the Chinese rendering
      of the name *hwārazm*, see Pelliot, *TP* (1938), pp. 16–152.
123   Petrushevski, 'Pokhod', p. 127, n. 16; Falina, *Perepiska*, p. 305.
124   Raverty, vol. I, p. 240; Buniyatov, p. 87. See the notes on
      Terken-khatun by Juvaini (Boyle, vol. II, pp. 465–86) and an-
      Nasawi (Buniyatov, p. 87). The title occurs among the Khitans
      (Wittfogel and Feng, p. 431) and among the Turkic races in the form
      Turkan (Barthold, 'Turkestan', p. 400, n.). For the title see Pelliot,
      Campagnes, pp. 89–91, also Doerfer's criticism of that view in
      Türkische Elemente, vol. II, no. 889.

Editorial Note   As in chap. 1, note 87, there is some confusion about
      Terken-khatun's relationship to Sultan Muhammad, although she is
      generally accepted to have been Muhammad's mother.

125   Buniyatov, p. 85.
126   Buniyatov, p. 82, Petrushevski, 'Pokhod', p. 103.
127   Buniyatov, p. 147. For the authenticity of the Caliph's message
      to Genghis, see Barthold, 'Turkestan', p. 467; Petrushevski, 'Pokhod
      mongolskikh voisk', p. 111.
128   Boyle, vol. I, p. 81; *Collected Chronicles*, vol. I/2, p. 197; *SH*,
      §254.
129   For the system of succession among the nomads, and especially
      among the Khitans, see Wittfogel and Feng, pp. 398–400.
130   Boyle, vol. II, p. 549. Cf. Ayalon, 'The Great Yāsa', pp. 151ff.
      See also *Collected Chronicles*, vol. I/2. p. 130.
131   Fedorov-Davydov, *Obshchestvenny stroi zolotoi Ordy*, p. 73, Cf.
      Jackson, 'The Dissolution of the Mongol Empire', p. 193.
132   Ratchnevsky, *Code*, I, p. xlvi.
133   Francoise Aubin, 'Le Statut de l'enfant', p. 533.
134   *SH*, §52; Ratchnevsky, 'La condition de la femme mongole',
      p. 517.
135   *SH*, §254.
136   Boyle, vol. I, p. 231; *Collected Chronicles*, vol. II, p. 63.
137   *Collected Chronicles*, vol. II, p. 8.
138   Ratchnevsky, 'La condition de la femme mongole', pp. 517–8.
139   Khanlaryan, p. 153.
140   *Collected Chronicles*, vol. III, pp. 215, 217.
141   *Collected Chronicles*, vol. II, p. 35. Cf. the many anecdotes
      regarding Ögödei's generosity (Boyle, vol. I, pp. 218ff.; *Collected
      Chronicles*, vol. II, pp. 51ff); also *Collected Chronicles*, vol. II, p. 121,
      regarding Guyuk's attempts to surpass Ögödei's generosity.
142   Boyle, vol. I, p. 82.
143   Boyle, vol. I, p. 145.

144　Buniyatov, pp. 82–3. See also Barthold, 'Turkestan', pp. 474–5.

145　Boyle, vol. II, p. 379. Nasawi (Buniyatov, pp. 80–91) is equally critical of the sultan's tactics. Ibn al-Athir (Spuler, *Geschichte der Mongolen*, p. 40) suggests that the cause of the victorious advance was because 'the Khwarazm-shah Muhammad, when he conquered Iran, killed and destroyed all the leaders'.

146　See Petrushevski, 'Pokhod', p. 114. Cf. Raverty, vol. II, p. 1048.

147　Boyle, vol. I, p. 82; *Collected Chronicles*, vol. I/2, p. 199.

148　Buniyatov, p. 81; Boyle, vol. I, p. 80; *Collected Chronicles*, vol. I/2, pp. 303, 198; Barthold, 'Turkestan', p. 476.

149　Tolstov, *Po sledam*, p. 287; Barthold, 'Turkestan', p. 424.

150　Juzjani offers 12,000; Juvanini – 20,000; Nasawai – 30,000.

151　According to Ibn al-Athir the Mongols entered the city on 10 February 1220, while Juzjani specifies the 16th. Juvaini and Rashid place the siege in March and the *Yuanshi* (1, 20a) states that Bokhara fell in April 1220. *SWQZL*, 75a gives the fall of Bokhara and Samarkand as 1221, but the *SWQZL* chronology from 1220 to 1223 is one year in error. See Pelliot 'L'édition collective', p. 160.

Editorial Note　It is interesting to compare this statement with that of Waley (*Travels of an Alchemist*, p. 87, n. 2), who alleges that for the period 1220–24 the chronology of the *Shenwu*, *Yuanshi* and the *Collected Chronicles* are in error, placing all events a year late.

152　For the siege and fall of Bokhara see especially Boyle, vol. I, pp. 97–109; *Collected Chronicles*, vol. I/2, pp. 205–6; also the summary by Barthold, 'Turkestan', pp. 476–8.

153　Boyle, vol. I, p. 100; *Collected Chronicles*, vol. I/2, pp. 217, 207; Raverty, vol. II, p. 990.

154　Boyle, vol. I, pp. 116, 117; vol. II, p. 375; *Collected Chronicles*, vol. I/2, p. 206.

155　Little credence can be given to Ibn al-Athir's assertion (Barthold, 'Turkestan', p. 480), that this attempted sortie was made only by the inhabitants and that the Turkish troops did not participate in it.

156　Boyle, vol. I, pp. 121–2; *Collected Chronicles*, vol. I/2, p. 208; Raverty, vol. II, p. 980.

157　Boyle, vol. II, p. 375.

158　Buniyatov, p. 83.

159　Boyle, vol. II, pp. 465–8; Buniyatov, pp. 85–6.

160　Buniyatov, p. 92; *Collected Chronicles*, vol. I/2, p. 213; Boyle, vol. II, pp. 385ff.

161　Buniyatov, p. 100; *Collected Chronicles*, vol. I/2, p. 222.

162   *Collected Chronicles*, vol. I/2, p. 214; Boyle, vol. I, p. 134.

163   Boyle, vol. I, pp. 134–5; *Collected Chronicles*, vol. I/2, pp. 223–4. The battle on the Indus took place in August/September 1221, according to Juvaini; Nasawi (Buniyatov, p. 128) places it on 25 November 1221 – which was a Thursday, not a Wednesday as stated in the Juvaini text. Nasawi recounts that, before fleeing, Jalal killed his mother and the members of his harem in order to spare them the shame of capture. For Jalal's death see Buniyatov, pp. 295–6.

164   Raverty, vol. II, pp. 1045, 1047; Boyle, vol. I, p. 138.

165   *YS*, 1, 22a mentions the appearance of the unicorn in 1224 – which is, as we have already noted for the *YS* chronology of this period, a year too late. For the anecdote see de Rachewiltz, 'Yeh-lü Ch'u-ts'ai', pp. 194–5. Tao Zongyi offers a slight variant of the anecdote (*ZGL*, 5, 1a–b). For an interpretation see H. Franke, *The Legitimation*, pp. 40–2.

166   The Patriarch's secular name was Qui Chuji. Changchun has a biography in *YS*, 202, 9a–11a and in *ZGL*, 10, 2b–6b. Cf. Waley, *The Travels of an Alchemist*, pp. 16ff.

167   The text of the letter is transmitted in *ZGL*, 10, 3a f. and reproduced by Wang Guowei in *XYJ*, *shang*, 3a. *XYJ* mentions only Liu Zhonglu as bearer of the letter but Ja'far is named in Changchun's biography in *YS*, 202, 9a.

168   *XYJ*, *shang*, 45.

169   *XYJ*, *shang*, 46a; *xia*, 6b.

170   The text of the decree is transmitted in *XYJ*, *fulu*, 16b and reproduced by Cai Meibiae (*Yuandai baihua baizi lu*, 1); it has been translated by Chavannes ('Inscriptions', p. 369). Ila Chuzai, expected that this chapter would also apply to Buddhist monks, and the Taoist publication of it led to a rupture of the friendly relations between himself and Changchun. Chuzai devotes a large section of his notes on the western trip (de Rachewiltz, 'The Hsi-Yu lu', pp. 25–37) to justifying his conduct towards Changchun, whom he had initially sponsored with Genghis Khan.

171   *fulu*, 1b–2a; Cai Meibiae; p. 2; Chavannes, 'Inscriptions', p. 369. See also p. 208.

172   *Collected Chronicles*, vol. I/2, p. 216; Buniyatov, p. 137.

173   Raverty, vol. II, p. 1001.

174   *Collected Chronicles*, vol. II, p. 79. Later sources set Jochi's death six months before that of Genghis Khan, i.e. in February 1227, while Genghis was on campaign against the Tanguts (Barthold, 'Turkestan', p. 525), whereas Rashid maintains that Genghis was in Mongolia when he learned of Jochi's machinations. On the question

of Jochi's death see Lech, pp. 216–17 and the references which he there lists regarding later Mongol tradition.

175   Buniyatov, pp. 77–8; *Collected Chronicles*, vol. I/2, p. 188.

176   *SH*, §263.; Boyle, vol. I, p. 257. Cf. Spuler, *Die Mongolen in Iran*, pp. 40–2; In Turkish, *Yalavach* = 'Envoy' (Gabain, *Alttürkische Grammatik*, p. 351; *Drevnetyurkskii slovar'*, p. 228); the Mongol equivalent is *iruvachi* (Ligeti, *Les mots solons*, p. 240). See p. 183 for Yalavach's taxation system.

Editorial Note   Both the Gaadamba 1975 Mongol language version and Cleaves' 1982 translation of §263 of the *Secret History* agree that Genghis Khan brought Yalavach back to govern 'the Khitan city of Zhundu'. (The Gaadamba text reads 'etseg Khoromshi Yalavachyg avchirch, Khyatadin Zhundu (Beizhin) Khotig zakhirulav'). There is no mention in this section of the *Secret History* of Yalavach's appointment as *basqaq* of Ghazna.

177   In *YSLB*, 1, 9a *dalahuachi* (*darughachi*) is glossed as 'an official who is entrusted with a seal' (*Code*, vol. I, p. 32 n. 3). The Mongol word *daru-* (Turkic: *bas-*), from which the term is derived, means 'to stamp' or 'to oppress', but is also used by Kowalewski in the sense 'to impress a seal'. The term *darughachi* has been interpreted as 'oppressor', but Vasary ('The Golden Horde Term', p. 188) has raised the valid objection that it is unlikely that a civil servant would be officially so described. The same author ('The Origin', p. 202) also questions the interpretation of the word as 'an official who applies a seal', but this suggestion that the seal was held and used by an official other than the *darughachi* is scarcely convincing. Control of the seal was the symbol of the appointment, distinguishing the official as the direct representative of the Khan.

178   Palladius, *Starinnoe mongol'skoe skazanie*, p. 255, n. 646, quoted in Ratchnevsky, *Code*, vol. I, p. 32, n. 3. Cf. also Barthold, 'Turkestan', pp. 468–9; Berezin, *Ocherk*, pp. 452–3.

179   Pelliot, 'Les Mongols et la Papauté', p. 116; Pelliot, *Notes sur l'histoire de la Horde d'Or*, p. 72, n. 1; Doerfer, *Mongolische Elemente*, p. 309; Doerfer, *Türkische Elemente*, vol. I, p. 241; Ratchnevsky, *Code*, vol. I, p. 32, n. 3

180   Berezin, *Ocherk*, pp. 449–50; Falina, *Perepiska*, p. 198. Dr Peter Zieme of the Berlin Academy of Science informs me that the composite term *darughachi-basqaq* is certainly found in a Uighur text from Turfan. See pp. 178–9 for role of *basqaq*. Abu'l Ghazi compares the *darughachi* with the local *hakim* who served the Mongols (Lech, p. 210, n. 74).

181   *YS*, 149; 4a; Ratchnevsky, *Code*, vol. I, p. 32, n. 3.

182   Xiyu ji, shang, 30a; cf. Bretschneider, Mediaeval Researches, vol. I, p. 70; YS, 120, 9a; 150, 2a; Waley, Travels of an Alchemist, p. 92.
183   Cf. Berezin, Ocherk, p. 45.
184   de Rachewiltz, 'Personnel and Personalities', p. 133, n. 3, p. 134. n. 1; Code, vol. II, p. 57, n., cf. Cleaves, 'Daruga and Gerege', p. 244; HDSL, 2a.
185   Spuler, Goldene Horde, pp. 316, 338.
186   YDZ, 8, 18a–b; TZDG 6, 10a ff.
187   Poppe, Monuments, pp. 46fgf.
188   YDZ, 9, 9a–13a; cf. Vladimirtsov, Le régime social, p. 129. For the institution of darughachi, see also Yanai Watari, 'Gendai sekai no sankai', pp. 306–23; Yagchid, 'On the daruɣachi of the Yuanshi', pp. 293–441. Cf. Doerfer, Mongolische Elemente, pp. 319ff.; Fedorov-Davydov, Obshchestvenny stroi, p. 30.

Editorial Note   The continuing use of **dogha/darogha** as an administrative title in Chinese Turkestan was noted by Sir Aurel Stein at the beginning of this century. (Ruins of Desert Cathay. London, 1912, vol. I, p. 137.)

Editorial Note   A very full account of the early history of the darughachi and of their important role during the Yuan dynasty can be found in E. Endicott-West, Mongolian Rule in China (Cambridge, Mass, 1989); see especially pp. 16–103.

189   All sources except SH, §264 give spring 1225 as the date of arrival back in Mongolia; de Rachewiltz ('The Hsi-yu lu', p. 63, n. 138) points out that 'autumn' in the SH is probably attributable to a copyist's error.
190   Wyngaert, p. 64. See also Collected Chronicles, vol. I/2, p. 230.
191   The snake with the thousand heads was crushed by the cart because the thousand heads all wanted to escape in different directions; the one-headed snake was saved because the thousand tails followed the single head. See bLo, bzan, Altan tobchi, p. 33, Shastina translation, p. 192. The strength of unity is regularly demonstrated in Mongol literature by the parable of the five arrows, which, when bundled together, cannot be broken by the strongest man – a motif widespread among different peoples of the earth (see Lech, p. 208, n. 70).
192   Boyle, vol. I, p. 182, Cf. Collected Chronicles, vol. I/2, p. 232. Kirakos of Gandzak maintains that it was on this occasion that Ögödei was nominated as Genghis Khan's successor (Khanlaryan, p. 153).
193   SH, §265. Asa-gambu is the Mongolian transcription of a

Tangui title. According to Poucha (*Die Geheime Geschichte*, p. 20), Asa is the rendering of the Tangut tribal name Aza.

194 *Editorial Note* The *Secret History's* account in §268 is: '. . . in the Year of the Pig (1227) Činggis Qahan is ascended to Heaven. After that he was ascended, one gave exceedingly unto Yesui Qadun from the Tang'ud people.' (Cleaves, *The Secret History of the Mongols*, p. 209.)

195 *Collected Chronicles*, vol. I/2, p. 233; *YS*, 1, 23a; Boyle, vol. I, p. 180; *SH*, §265; *SWQZL*, 9a.

196 Pelliot, *Notes*, vol. I, p. 328.

197 Wyngaert, p. 65.

198 Raverty, vol. II, p. 1096, Shastina, p. 133. Cf. *Altan tobči anonymus* (Bawden, §41).

199 Sagang-sechen (Schmidt, *Geschichte*, p. 102); Shastina, *Shara Tudzhi*, p. 133.

200 For the accounts of Genghis's death see the sources listed by Lech, p. 218, n. For the date of Genghis' death see the detailed examination of the question by Pelliot, *Notes*, vol. I, pp. 305–9.

201 *Collected Chronicles*, vol. I/2, p. 233.

202 The speech made on this occasion and ascribed to the Sunit Kulugutei-ba'atur is one of the loveliest monuments of Mongolian medieval literature. The version provided by Sagang-sechen in *Erdeni-yin tobči* is dealt with by Krueger in *Poetical Passages*, that in bLo.bzans, *Altan tobči*, p. 103, has been translated by Shastina (pp. 241–2) and the variation in the anonymous *Altan tobči* by Bawden (pp. 1544–5).

203 The Scythians removed the innards and the brain (Rudenko, *Kul'tura*, pp. 330ff.) When the Khitan emperor Taizong died in 907 during a campaign in China, the Khitans opened his stomach, packed it with several *dou* (1 *dou* = *c.*10 litre) of salt and took the body home on a cart (*QDGZ*, 3). Wen Weijan (*Luting shishi*, 49a), reports that when a member of a rich and noble Khitan family died, the stomach was opened with a knife and the innards removed; the body was washed, packed with sweet-smelling herbs, salt and alum and then sewn up with five-coloured thread. The blood was almost completely removed by means of thin bamboo rods such as were used for writing. The face was covered with a mask of silver and gold and the feet and hands were wrapped in brocade and silk. Cf. Wittfogel and Feng, *Liao*, p. 280, n. See *YS* for the description of the burial of Khubilai ('Über den mongolischen Kult', p. 435).

204 Schmidt, *Geschichte*, pp. 107, 390.

205 Shastina, p. 242; Bawden, §49.

206   Schmidt, *Geschichte*, p. 109.
207   See Pelliot, *Notes*, vol. I, p. 347.
208   *Collected Chronicles*, vol. I/2, pp. 234–5; Pelliot, *Notes*, vol. I, pp. 335ff.
209   Boyle, vol. I, p. 149.
210   Cf. Ratchnevsky, 'Über den mongolischen Kult', pp. 423f.
211   For the cult of Genghis Khan in the Ordos, see Zhamsterano, 'Kult Činggis v Ordose'.

Chapter 4   Personality and Achievements

1   *MDBL*, 2b. *SH*, §62. Raverty, vol. II, 1077. Mostaert, 'A propos de quelques portraits', pp. 141–56.
2   *SH*, §§85, 90, 95. *Collected Chronicles*, vol. I/2, 162. *YS*, 150, 9a.
3   *SWQZL*, 11b–12a. *SH*, §219.
4   *SH*, 207.
5   *SH*, §266–7. This decree cannot have been made during the last Tangut campaign of 1227 since, according to the *Secret History*, Bo'orchu and Mukali were then both dead. Wang Guowei has investigated the expression *Juyin irgen* in a long note (*Yuanchao bishi zhi zhuyin yierjian kao*) in *GTJL* 16, 1b–16b, and his view is that the phrase refers to the *yao* troops of the Jurchid. Cf. Pelliot's remarks in 'L'édition collective', pp. 128–9; and for *jao?* or *jiu* troops see: Wittfogel and Feng, *Liao*, p. 137, n.
6   *SH*, 267.
7   *SH*, §§217–8. Cf. *YS*, 121, 15a.
8   *Collected Chronicles*, vol. I/2, p. 263. *SH*, §230.
9   *YS*, 119, 19b; *SH*, §205.
10   *YS*, 120, 7a.
11   *Collected Chronicles*, vol. III, p. 281; *SH*, §279; *La description du monde*, pp. 145, 147ff.

Editorial Note   See p. 203 concerning a cattle tax imposed by Ögödei to support the Court.

12   Chinese *guo-wang* = Mongolian *go-ong*. According to Rashid ad-Din (*Collected Chronicles*, vol. I/2, 178–9), Genghis learned that the Chinese called Mukali *guo-wang*, regarded this as a good omen and therefore decided to award Mukali the title. *SH*, §206 attributes the reason for the award to Mukali's prophecy to Temuchin by the Qorqonar forest stream. The *SH* dating of the award in 1206 is clearly an anachronism. Rashid offers the exact date of January/February 1218.

13 YS, 119, 4a–b; *MDBL*, 16a. Pelliot believes that this motif was to be found only on Mukali's standard ('Notes sur le Turkestan', p. 32).

14 ZGL, 10, 3a; Cai Meibiao, p. 115. Cf. the translation of the letter in Chavannes, 'Inscriptions', p. 300.

15 Lech, p. 97. Cf. Ab'ul Faraj [Bar Hebraeus]. *Chronicon Syriacum*, p. 411.

16 XYJ, *fulu*, 2a; *xia*, 14b.

17 SH, §242. '*qabar-ača huni quangšitala qaqas keleledeǰu*' Haenisch in his dictionary translates this as: 'Es wurde auf ihn scharf eingeredet, bis man den Rauch aus der Nase holte' (He was talked to sharply until smoke issued from his nose). Mostaert (*Quelques passages*, p. 75), analysing the text of *SH*, 167, comments that the Chinese interlinear version 'to take by force' is a false ideograph for 'choke'. The same is clearly the case in this passage. Damdinsuren translates: 'until smoke issued from his nose' (*Mongolyn nuuch töbchöö*).

Editorial Note Gaadamba in his 1975 version of the *Secret History* uses in §167 the phrase: 'tsagaan idend tsatsakh, khar makhand khakhbahl', which Cleaves translates as 'will choke on the white milk products, will gag on the black meat'. In §242 Gaadamba uses: 'khamraasaa utaa gartal', = 'to cause smoke to come from the nose'.

18 SH, §§260, 203.

19 YS, 119, 1b; *SH*, §205.

20 YS, 119, 1a. Cf. Tu Ji, 27, 1a. The Jalair Gu'un-u'a and his brothers were with the Jurkin when Temuchin defeated the Jurkin princes, Sacha and Taichu. Gu'un-u'a presented his two sons, Mukali and Buka, as personal servants to Temuchin (*SH*, §137). For the transcription of the name see Pelliot, *Campagnes*, p. 138. *gu'un* is the usual transcription in the *Secret History* for kumun ('person'). In modern Mongolian *khun* = man, person.

21 YS, 119, 1b.

22 SH, §§140, 199.

23 SH, §§148, 154.

24 *Collected Chronicles*, vol. I/2, p. 263.

25 *Editorial Note* After the fall of Zhongdu in 1215 Genghis personally withdrew to Mongolia in spring 1216 (see p. 116). He appointed Mukali *guo-wang* (viceroy) in Northern China in 1218 (see p. 149) and launched an army under Jochi and Jebe against Kuchlug in Kara-Khitai in the same year (see p. 119), well before the Otrar incident in 1219 (see p. 122).

26 *SH*, §§265, 267.
27 *Collected Chronicles*, vol. I/1, p. 162.
28 Buniyatov, p. 86; Ratchnevsky, 'Khubilai Khan', p. 762.
29 *Collected Chronicles*, vol. I/2, p. 265.
30 *SH*, §§244, 103, 79. See pp. 29, 31.

Editorial Note   Ratchnevsky is, perhaps, somewhat inconsistent in his assessment of this aspect of Genghis' character. Here he belittles Genghis' stories of his prowess, although earlier (p. 31) he seeks to ascribe any exaggeration to the chronicler, Rashid ad-Din, actually commenting in the text: '. . . and it is difficult to believe that Genghis was capable of such bragging'.

31 pp. 141, 150; *SH*, §§145, 172; *YS*, 1, 16b.
32 See p. 100.
33 Wyngaert, p. 50; *xiyu ji, xia*, 7a; *SH* §265.
34 *SH*, 260.
35 *YS*, 118, 7b.
36 *SH*, 103; *Collected Chronicles*, vol. I/2, p. 263. Cf *Collected Chronicles*, vol. I/2, p. 189; Boyle, vol. I, p. 80, vol. II, p. 367.
37 *Collected Chronicles*, vol. III, 35; Boyle, vol. I, p. 270; Vernadsky, *The Mongols*, pp. 96–7; *Lech*, pp. 194, 178.
38 Boyle, vol. I, pp. 39, 59; Khanlaryan, p. 173; *La description du monde*, p. 79.
39 Ahai and Chuzai belonged to the former Khitan ruling house. According to *WDSJ*, 72, 4b, Abaoji, the founder of the Lioa dynasty, adopted the clan name *Shili* from the area in which the royal clan lived, and translators corrupted this to *Yelu* (cf. *QGZ*, 23, 1a). Since there is no phonetic concordance between the two words, Li Youtang has suggested (*LSJSBM*, 1, 6b) that the character *shi* was misread for *ye*. According to Qian Daxin (*Nianershi kaoyi*, 97, 1b) the members of this royal house dropped the clan name *Yelu* during the Chin period and adopted the name *Ila*, just as the *Shulü* clan changed its name to *Shime*. The reason for this is said to be that the names were not 'nice' (cf. Yao Sui, *Muan ji*, 8, 7b–8a): *yila* was supposed to mean the infantry who marched in front of the cavalry (lit. horses), *shimo* – the slaves (*canghu*). Qian Daxin's explanation is scarcely convincing. *Yila* is undoubtedly the rendering of a Khitan word meaning 'stallion', and the clan name was connected with the Khitan horse cult (de Rachewiltz, 'Some Remarks on the Khitan Clan Names *Ye-lü* ≈ *I-la*', pp. 191ff.); the word is not identical with *yila*, which indicated 'foot-soldiers', auxiliaries in the courier service during the Yuan dynasty, who did not belong to the regular army (*Code*, vol. II, p. 73, n. 2). In the *Jinshi*, members of the Khitan ruling house are

named *Yelü*; *yila* must be the Chinese transliterations of the Khitan word **iru* and its alternative form **ira* (Pelliot, *Notes*, vol. I, p. 221). (*Ye* and *yi* are interchanged at will in Chinese script, as in the name *Yesugei (Yisugei)*.) The reason for the alteration of the name *Yelü* to Ila probably lay in a taboo of the character *lü*, since the members of the *shulü* clan also changed this character. Chuzai himself, in the introduction to *Xiyu ji*, used the surname *Yila* (de Rachewiltz, The *Hsi-yu lu*, p. 18) and is so described in contemporary works (*MDBL*, 11b, *HDSL*, 2a, 7b, 8b) and I have therefore selected the *i* form. On this question, see also: Munkujev, *Kitaiskij istochnik*, p. 91, n. 4; Pelliot, *L'édition collective*, p. 175 n.; Cleaves, 'A Chancellery Practice', p. 502; Wittfogel and Feng, *Liao*, p. 59 n. 1; Mostaert, *Ordosica*, pp. 47–8, and further sources indicated by these authors.

40   *YS*, 146, 1b.

41   *YWL*, 57, 831. Ila Chuzai has a biography in *YS*, 146, 1a–11a. Cf. Tu Ji, 48, 1a–14b. Song Zizhen's epitaph (*YWL*, 57, 830–8) has been translated by Munkujev in *Kitaiskij istochnik*. de Rachewiltz has dealt with the ideological views of the statesman ('Yeh-lü Ch'u-ts'ai', in *Confucian Personalities*, pp. 189–366). Cf. also O. Franke, *Geschichte*, vol. IV, pp. 277ff., vol. V, pp. 149–150; Su Tianjue, *Yuanchao mingchen shilüe*, 5, 1ff.; Giles, *Biographical Dictionary*, no. 2446; Kobayashi, *Genshi*, pp. 193–244. The biography by Abel-Rémusat in *Mélanges Asiatiques*, vol. II, pp. 64ff. has been revised. For further sources see Grousset, *Histoire de l'Extrême-Orient*, vol. II, p. 427 n. 4.

42   *YWL*, 57, 831; *Raverty*, vol. II, p. 1077.

43   *Editorial Note* This criticism of Genghis Khan's behaviour *vis-à-vis* Wang-khan, although doubtless justified, is slightly at variance with Ratchnevsky's defence of Genghis Khan on pages 73, 75, 80. Cf. note 30 above.

44   *SH*, §§113, 187.

45   Boyle, vol. I, p. 145; *Collected Chronicles*, vol. III, p. 36.

46   Pelliot, 'Les Mongols et la Papauté', vol. 23, nos. 1–2 (1922–3), pp. 11–12.

47   Wyngaert, p. 84.

48   Lech, p. 193; Franke, *The Legitimation*, p. 18.

49   Cf. Pritsak, 'Orientierung', pp. 376–83.

50   *SH*, §189.

51   Boyle, vol. I, p. 117; Raverty, vol. II, pp. 990; *YS*, 124, 1a.

52   Buniyatov, pp. 125, 182; Boyle, vol. I, p. 129; *Collected Chronicles*, vol. I/2, p. 218.

Editorial Note On p. 130 of Ratchnevsky's initial account, attributed to the imagination of an-Nasawi (*Buniyatov*, p. 81), states that molten **silver** was poured into the governor's **ears and eyes**.

53 Raverty, vol. II, pp. 1041–2.

Editorial Note Ratchnevsky does not include the rather significant detail that the Imam thought it wise to leave for India as soon as possible!

54 *Collected Chronicles*, vol. I/2, pp. 219–20.
55 *SH*, §138.
56 *Collected Chronicles*, vol. I/1, p. 108.
57 *YS*, 120, 2a.
58 *Collected Chronicles*, vol. I/2, pp. 229–30. For the custom of anointing the finger, see Boyle, 'A Eurasian Hunting Ritual', pp. 12–15. Cf. Ratchnevsky 'Khubilai Khan', pp. 754. This was an important event in the life of the nomad. When the eight-year-old Ghazan brought home his first hunting spoils the ceremony of anointing his finger was celebrated for three days (*Collected Chronicles*, vol. III, p. 141).
59 *Collected Chronicles*, vol. I/2, p. 219.
60 *XYJ*, 39b.
61 Wyngaert, p. 68; cf. Lech, p. 98; *Collected Chronicles*, vol. I/2, p. 68; *YS*, 106, 1b–3a. The names of Genghis' wives mentioned in Persian, Mongol and Chinese sources are listed by Lech (pp. 201–3, n. 49).
62 Raverty, vol. II, pp. 1007.

Editorial Note The convoy of maidens from China (*xiyu ji, shang*, 6b), would probably be that which Changchun apparently objected to joining on his trip to visit Genghis Khan in Samarkand (Waley, *The Travels of an Alchemist*, p. 54).

63 *SH*, §197.
64 *SH*, §156.

Editorial Note SH, §155, recounting how Yisugen-khatun persuaded Genghis Khan to search for her elder sister Yisui, speaks of the latter as having been married. Cf. chap. 5, note 58 (p. 192) for the *Yasa's* ruling on adultery and the Mongol attitude to adultery with married women from foreign tribes.

65 Cf. Ratchnevsky 'La condition de la femme mongole', p. 516. For Börte's role in the break with Jamuka and the struggle with Teb-tengri, see pp. 37, 100.

66   *Collected Chronicles*, vol. II, p. 8; Boyle, vol. I, 40.
67   *SH*, §173.
68   *YS*, 124, 4b, 124, 16b; 129, 8a. For the name *Mungsuz* see: H. Franke, 'A Sino-Uighur Family', p. 36.
69   *MDBL*, 3a.
70   Wyngaert, p. 52.
71   *Collected Chronicles*, vol. I/2, pp. 64–5.
72   *La description du monde*, pp. 76–7.
73   Vernadsky, *The Mongols and Russia*, p. 6; *QDGZ*, 3, 10. See p. 161 concerning the cruelty of Jalal ad-Din.
74   Cf. H. Franke, Chinese Texts in *ZAS* (1975), p. 143.
75   *Collected Chronicles*, vol. I/2, p. 260.
76   *Collected Chronicles*, vol. I/2, pp. 261–2.
77   *SH*, §227.
78   Boyle, vol. I, p. 31; Lech, p. 97; Poliak, 'The Influence of Chingiz Khan's Yāsa', p. 863; *La description du monde*, p. 76.
79   *YWL*, 57, 831.
80   *Collected Chronicles*, vol. I/2. p. 204; Buniyatov, p. 82.
81   See p. 129.

Chapter 5   The Structure of the Mongol World Empire

1   Berezin, *Ocherk*, p. 430; Vernadsky, *The Mongols and Russia*.
2   Wyngaert, p. 66; Lech, p. 98.
3   Although the Yuan emperors maintained the right of hereditary succession to an appointment, they did introduce certain limitations on the rank and age of the successor. *Code*, vol. I, pp. xliii ff.
4   Cf. the prohibition of the Yuan emperors against using soldiers as personal servants (*YDZ*, 34, 46 ff.). There were doubtless abuses in Genghis Khan's days, although these were punishable.
5   For the organization of the bodyguard (*keshig*) under Genghis Khan see: *YS*, 1a–3a. Cf. Chavannes, 'Inscriptions', pp. 429–32; Yanai Watari, 'Genchō kešig kō', *Mōkōshi kenkyū*, pp. 211–63; Qian Daxin, *Shi jia/zhai/houlu*, p. 207. Cf. also Marco Polo's description of the bodyguard (*quesitan*) at the court of Khubilai Kha'an (*La Description du monde*, p. 121), the remarks by Pelliot in *Notes*, vol. II, 815, also those of Yule-Cordier, *Ser Marco Polo*, pp. 379–81. For the word see Pelliot, 'Notes sur le *Turkestan*', pp. 28–31 and Mostaert, *Sur quelques passages*, pp. 244–49. Doerfer, *Mongolische Elemente*, pp. 467–72, indicates additional literature.
6   See p. 207.
7   For the functions of the *yarghuchi* see p. 95. The appointment of

yarghuchi in the *ulus* of Chaghatai and Tolui is noted in *YS*, 120, 3b and 134, 11a respectively.

8   Ratchnevsky, *Code*, vol. II, pp. 92ff.

9   *SH*, §177. Cf. *Collected Chronicles*, vol. I/2, p. 110.

10   *Collected Chronicles*, vol. III, p. 281. Smith, 'Mongol and No-madic Taxation', p. 64, stresses the necessity for a consensus on taxation among the nomads. Cf. also Morgan, 'Cassiodorus and Rashīd al-Dīn'. In the text of al-'Umari (Lech, p. 97), according to which the khan collected the *qalan-*, *qubchur-*, *ulaq*, and *badraqa-* taxes from the soldiers 'who returned to peace and quiet from the slaughter and distress of war'. *qalan-* is glossed by Lech as 'monies: imposed on [cultivated] land' and obviously applies to a later period. Such a land tax could only have been raised from soldiers when the Mongol rulers attempted to accustom their armies of occupation to a settled mode of life and gave them parcels of land (*iqta*) in Iran (see p. 200). The expression, however, appears to have been subject to different interpretations at various times and in different areas. Cf. Alizade, *Istoria Azerbaidzhana*, p. 228; Petrushevski, *Zemledelie*, p. 384; Falina, *Perepiska*, pp. 363–4. For the expression see also Doerfer, *Türkische Elemente*, vol. II, pp. 488–90 and Lech, p. 199.

11   Ratchnevsky, *Code*, vol. I, viii,

12   Barthold, 'Turkestan', p. 529.

13   Cf. 'Khubilai Khan', p. 760.

14   Berezin, *Ocherk*, pp. 452–3.

15   d'Ohsson, *Histoire*, vol. IV, pp. 381, 405; Nassanov, *Mongoly i Rus'*, pp. 11f.

16   Federov-Davydov, *Obshchestvenny stroi*, p. 30 – basing himself on Semenov's essay' 'K voprosu o zolotoordynskom termine *baskak*'; *Collected Chronicles*, vol. I/2, p. 205; Boyle, vol. II, p. 714.

17   Spuler, *Die Goldene Horde*, p. 338; Spuler, *Die Mongolen in Iran*, p. 323.

18   Babayan, *Istoria Armenii*, p. 122; Doerfer, *Türkische Elemente*, 242.

19   See role of *darughachi*, pp. 138–9.; Boyle, vol. II, pp. 506, 511; *Collected Chronicles*, vol. II, p. 33.

20   Wyngaert, p. 86.

21   Semenov, 'K voprosu o zolotoordynskom termine *baskak*'; Vasary, 'The Origin', pp. 201–6; *YS*, 120, 15b.

22   *bushi*: i.e. not at times designated for the collection of regular taxes.

23   *HDSL*, 11b, 13a; Ratchnevsky, ' Šigi-qutuqu', p. 109.

24   See Haenisch, *Steuergerechtsname*, pp. 58ff., also the discussion by Schurmann in *HJAS* (1951), p. 303.

25 *Houa-Yi Yi-Yu* of 1389 (Lewicki, p. 187).
26 XYJ, *fu*, 1b; Cai Meibiae, p. 1. For the expression *chaifa*, see Schurmann, *Mongolian Tributary Practices*, pp. 367–8; Schurmann, *Economic Structure*, p. 103; Ratchnevsky, *Code*, vol. II, p. 76 n. 5.
27 *Collected Chronicles*, vol. III, pp. 251–2, 264–5; YDZ, 7b ff.

Editorial Note Elchi = messenger, courier, envoy, mission; *Elchin said* = Envoy, Ambassador.

28 Berezin, *Ocherk*, pp. 427, 465; Minovi and Minorsky, p. 784.
29 Ratchnevsky, 'Zu einigen Problemen', p. 128; Petrushevski, *Zemledelie*, pp. 38 ff. The figures provided by Petrushevski in 'Iran i Azerbaidzhan', p. 228, are, however, seriously exaggerated.
30 Boyle, vol. II, p. 517.
31 For *dishui*, the land tax in China, see Schurmann, *Economic Structure*, pp. 75ff. For the Iranian *qalan* tax, see note 10 above.
32 Schurmann, *Economic Structure*, pp. 213–4, assumes that the tax was first introduced by Ögödei and quotes Murakami Masatsugu's statement (*Toho gakuho* (1942) pp. 152–8) that the *ortak* merchants were not subject to any trading tax.
33 Falina, *Perepiska*, p. 102.
34 Barthold, 'Persidskaya nadpis', p. 332. Nasir ad-Din uses the term *tamgha* in the context of property tax, whose low level of 1/240th is striking (Minovi and Minorsky, p. 781. For the *tamgha* tax, see also Petrushevski, *Zemledelie*, pp. 386–7.
35 YS, 93, 1b.
36 MDBL, 11a, 14b.
37 See p. 206.
38 Cf. Ratchnevsky, 'Zur Bedeutung des Mongolsturmes', p. 114.
39 YS, 124, 6a; *Xiju ji*, *shang*, 46a; *Collected Chronicles*, vol. III, pp. 275, 298.
   For the role of the *bichechi* in Iran, in China and in the Golden Horde, see Doerfer, *Türkische Elemente*, vol. I, p. 266; de Rachewiltz, 'Personnel and Personalities', pp. 137–8, n.; Vernadsky, *The Mongols and Russia*, p. 212.
40 Turkic: *ulagh*; Mongolian: *ula'a*; Chinese: *zhan*. For the Turkic postal service, see St. Julien, *Memoires*, vol. II, p. 463; Pelliot, 'Deux mots turcs' p. 219. For the organization of the postal service in China, see Olbricht, *Das Postwesen in China*; in Iran, see Spuler, *Die Mongolen in Iran*, pp. 422–5. For the expression *ulagha* see Kotwicz, 'Contributions', pp. 19–30; Pelliot, 'Neuf Notes', pp. 219–21. Additional references are available in Doerfer, *Türkische Elemente*, vol. I, pp. I, pp. 102–7; Lech, p. 200. Cf. the description of the

postal service by Marco Polo (*La description du monde*, p. 141) and by Ibn Battuta (*Voyages*, vol. III, p. 95).

41   Ratchnevsky, 'The Levirate', p. 46.

Editorial Note   But see the story of the Prince of Chernigov as related by Carpini in *Ystoria Mongalorum*. *The Mongol Mission*, ed. Dawson (London, 1955), p. 42.

42   *Collected Chronicles*, vol. I/2, p. 260.
43   *Collected Chronicles*, vol. I/2, p. 135; Lech, 94.
44   Boyle, vol. I, p. 25; *YS*, 2, 1b.
45   *Chrestomathie*, vol. II, p. 160. Ratchnevsky, 'Die Yasa', p. 480f.
46   *YS*, 2, 1b.
47   *Collected Chronicles*, vol. III, p. 42; Ratchnevsky, 'Die Yasa', p. 480f.
48   Berezin, *Ocherk*, p. 405; Riasanovsky, *Mongol'skoe pravo*, p. 10; Riasanovsky, *Fundamental Principles of Mongol Law*, p. 25; Vladimirtsov, *Gengis-Khan*, p. 63; Spuler, *Die Mongolen in Iran*, p. 373; Spuler, *Die Goldene Horde*, p. 362; Vernadsky, 'O sostave', p. 13, etc.
49   Lech, p. 95; Boyle, vol. I, p. 25.
50   Boyle, vol. I, pp. 25, 26; Wyngaert, p. 64.
51   Sylvestre de Sacy, *Chrestomathie*, vol. II, p. 184, n. 39.

Editorial Note   The section of Guo Baoyu's Legal Code, quoted from *YS*, 149, 11b, with respect to Buddhists and Taoists is difficult to reconcile with Genghis Khan's edicts on religious tolerance and, particularly, with the privileges which, as we have seen, he granted to the Taoist Changchun.

52   *SH*, §203; Riasanovsky, *Fundamental Principles*, p. 25; Jamtsarano, *The Mongol Chronicles*, p. 88; *Collected Chronicles*, vol. I/2, pp. 259–65.
53   Lech, pp. 96, 123; Wyngaert, p. 77; Cf. Maqrizi (Sylvestre de Sacy, *Chrestomathie*, vol. II, 161).
54   Boyle, vol. I, p. 31. Cf. the paraphrase by al-'Umari (Lech, p. 96).
55   *HDSL*, 16a; Wyngaert, p. 49; Khanlaryan, p. 172; Boyle, 'Kirakos of Gandzak, p. 201
56   Boyle, vol. I, p. 78. *qarachi*, the so-called *bulaghurchi*. For this expression see Pelliot, *Notes*, vol. I, pp. 112–14 and additional references in Ratchnevsky, *Code*, vol. II, p. 83, n. Cf. the description of the institution by Marco Polo (*La description du monde*, p. 131).
57   Al-'Umari (*Lech*, p. 96), Maqrizi (*Chrestomathie*, vol. II, p. 161), Wyngaert, p. 49.

58 Khanlaryan, p. 172; Boyle, 'Kirakos of Gandzak', p. 202; Raverty, vol. II, pp. 1079.

59 *YS*, 118, 10b; *Collected Chronicles*, vol. I/2, pp. 269, 263.

60 With reference to the intelligence agents, Juzjani cites one of Genghis Khan's *yasas* which imposed the death penalty on an untruthful *aiqaq* (Turkic: 'spy') (Boyle, vol. II, p. 499). Raverty, vol. II, pp. 1080–1; *SH*, §108; *Collected Chronicles*, vol. II, p. 47.

61 *Collected Chronicles*, vol. I/2, pp. 260, 261.

Editorial Note   *Mulkh* actually means 'kingdom' or 'kingship'.

62 Lech, p. 96; de Sacy, *Chrestomathie*, vol. II, pp. 161–2; Boyle, vol. I, p. 204; Wyngaert, p. 40.

63 *XYJ*, *xia*, 66.

64 Alinge, p. 43. Cf. Plano Carpini's and Rubruc's explanations for the prohibition (Wyngaert, pp. 49, 184).

65 Lech, p. 96–7; *Chrestomathie*, vol. II, p. 161; Khanlaryan, p. 172; Boyle, 'Kirakos of Gandzak', p. 201.

66 Ratchnevsky, 'Die Yasa', p. 485; Ratchnevsky, 'Die mongolische Rechtsinstitut der Busse', pp. 177ff.

67 Alinge, *Mongolische Gesetze*, p. 67.

68 In pursuance of his policy of centralization, Khubilai Kha'an restricted the judicial powers of feudal lords and other autonomous administrative authorities. Mixed courts were established in which the representatives of the litigating parties were represented. See Ebisawa Tetsuo, '*Yakudai* no kansuru oboegaki'. Cf. Ratchnversky, *Code*, vol. I, pp. lx f. and the texts cited in the Index.

69 *SH*, §§203, 184; Boyle, vol. II, p. 505. Cf. the action of Ögödei regarding Guyuk, Karghasun and Buri, who had slighted Batu at a feast (*SH*, §§276–7). Rashid ad-Din (*Collected Chronicles*, vol. II, p. 90) asserts that Buri was handed over to Batu, who had him executed; Rubruck also ascribes the execution of Buri to Batu (Wyngaert, p. 224).

70 Belgutei's mother felt that she had been demeaned because, when a prisoner of the Merkit, she was given as wife to a *qarachu* (see p. 15) and Na'uldar refused to fight Ahmad, saying: 'He is of high birth. How could I fight him?' (*Collected Chronicles*, vol. III, p. 84).

71 *Collected Chronicles*, vol. I/2, p. 264; Ratchnevsky, *Code*, vol. I, pp. 17–18.

72 *SH*, §227; Raverty, vol. II, p. 953; Wyngaert, p. 68.

73 Raverty, vol. II, p. 1007. *SH*, §229. See the evidence provided by Doerfer, *Türkische Elemente*, p. 77 for the term *bayasa*(*q*).

74 *SH*, §242. Ögödei accused himself of having secretly killed Dokulku without trial (*SH*, §281).

75 de Sacy, *Chrestomathie*, vol. II, p. 162; Lech, p. 97.

76 They were all massacred (Khanlaryan, p. 138).

77 Ratchnevsky, 'Die mongolischen Großkhane', p. 490.

78 Ratchnevsky, 'The Levirate', pp. 46ff.

79 *Xiyu ji, xia*, 6b.

80 Ratchnevsky, 'Die mongolischen Großkhane, p. 490.

81 Galstyan, *Armyanskie istochniki*, p. 47. 'They depopulated the cloisters and the wonderful churches of the land', bewails Grigor of Akanč (Blake and Frye, 'History of the Nation of the Archers', p. 307).

82 Boyle, vol. II, p. 723.

83 Boyle, vol. I, p. 22; Wyngaert, p. 36. Compare the different descriptions of the *bogdak* in Wyngaert, pp. 34, 182–3; *HDSL*, 6b–7a; *MDBL*, 17b; *Xiyu ji*, 18a–b. Ibn Battuta compares the *bogdak* to a small jewel-encrusted tiara, the upper section of which ends in peacock feathers. (*Voyages*, vol. II, p. 378).

84 Wyngaert, p. 181. Rockhill, *The Journey*, p. 74, n. See also Pelliot, *Notes*, vol. I, pp. 110–12, and Spuler, *Die Goldene Horde*, p. 448.

85 *XYJ, shang*, 22b; Wyngaert, pp. 122, 276.

86 Haenisch, *Die Kulturpolitik*, p. 15.

87 Khanlaryan, p. 172.

88 Wyngaert, p. 117; Spuler, *Die Goldene Horde*, p. 448; *La description du monde*, pp. 122–3.

89 Boyle, vol. II, p. 573; *Collected Chronicles*, vol. II, p. 133; d'Ohsson, vol. II, p. 65; Wyngaert, p. 179.

90 *XYJ*, 16b.

91 *SH*, §280. Ratchnvesky, 'Zu einigen Problemen', p. 129.

92 Ratchnevsky, 'Zu einigen Problemen', p. 130.

93 Falina, *Perepiska*, p. 49; *Collected Chronicles*, vol. III, p. 286.

94 Spuler, *Die Goldene Horde*, pp. 372, 405. Munkujev, 'K voprosu ob ekonomicheskom polozhenii', p. 372.

95 Boyle, vol. II, pp. 523, 505–6.

96 See *Hist.-terminologisches Wörterbuch*, vol. X.

97 Boyle, vol. I, p. 39; Raverty, vol. II, p. xx; *Voyages*, vol. III, p. 84 and vol. II, p. 365.

98 *Collected Chronicles*, vol. III, p. 268.

99 Munkujev, *Kitaiskij istochnik*, p. 72.

100 Morgan, 'Cassiodorus and Rashīd al-Dīn', p. 320.

101 Wyngaert, pp. 46, 50; *La description du monde*, p. 82.

102 Galstyan, *Armyanskie istochniki*, pp. 44–50, 68. Ratchnevsky, 'Die Yasa', p. 484. See pp. 208–9 for later religious strife. Het'um

I's petition was on behalf of 'the white and black clergy', the term 'black' referring to monks.

Editorial Note   In this context the Mongolian term *khar* usually denotes the laity, or at least lay monks.

103   Ratchnevsky, 'Zu einigen Problemen', p. 130; Ratchnevsky, 'Zum Ausdruck *t'ouhsia'*, pp. 175, 179–80.
104   Lech, p. 109.
105   Ratchnversky, 'Die Mohammedanerverfolgungen', p. 164, n. 8; *Collected Chronicles*, vol. III, p. 66; Jahn, 'Das Iranische Papiergeld', pp. 308–340; H. Franke, 'Sino-Western Contacts', p. 68.
106   Chavannes, 'Inscriptions', p. 372; Demiéville, 'La situation religieuse', pp. 200–1.
107   *Collected Chronicles*, vol. II, 121; Boyle, vol. I, p. 259; Raverty, vol. p. II, p. 1146.
108   Raverty, vol. II, p. 1146, Boyle, vol. I, p. 272.
109   Chavannes, 'Inscriptions', pp. 377ff. For the struggle between the Buddhists and the Taoists in China, see Demiéville, 'La situation religieuse', pp. 208ff.
110   Spuler, *Die Goldene Horde*, p. 213; *Collected Chronicles*, vol. III, p. 59.
111   Ratchnevsky, 'Die Mohammedanerverfolgungen', pp. 175, 179; *Collected Chronicles*, vol. III, pp. 165, 179, 217, 316–17; Raverty, vol. II, pp. 1261, 1288–90.
112   Boyle, vol. I, p. 96; Lech, pp. 126–31.
113   *Collected Chronicles*, vol. III, p. 215; Petrushevski, 'Pokhod', p. 100.
114   *La description du monde*, p. 119.
115   O. Franke, *Geschichte*, vol. IV, p. 591; *Hist.-terminologisches Wörterbuch*, vol. IX, p. 1; Jahn, 'Wissenschaftliche Kontakte', pp. 201, 199; Etiemble, *L'Orient philosophique*, pp. 141ff.
116   Cf. Han Rulin, 'Lun Chengjisi-han'; also Tikhvinski, introduction to the anthology, *Tataro-Mongoly v Asii i Evrope* (Mosow, 1970) pp. 3–21.
117   *DJGZ*, 22, 3a.

Glossary

Ail   A group of Mongol tents.
Alba   Corvée, labour tax.
Anda   Blood-brother.
Bagatur/Ba'atur   A military title: 'brave', 'hero'.
Basqaq   Administrator, usually non-Mongol, in occupied territories.
Beki   A chiefly title, indicating a shamanistic role, often held **by the eldest** son of a chief.
Beile   A Tungusic title.
Bilik   Collection of Genghis Khan's verbal edicts.
Bo'ol   Serf, bondsman.
Chaifa   Corvée and property tax (China).
Chang   Land tax (Mongolian).
Darkhan   Mongol title of nobility.
Darughachi/Darugha   Imperial Mongol administrator, usually in occupied territories or apanages; governor.
Eke   Mother, matriarch.
Elchi   Courier, messenger, emissary.
Ger   Mongolian round felt tents (Russian: *yurt*).
Guo-wang   Mongol viceroy in China.
Gurkhan   'Universal' khan.
Idikut   Uighur ruler.
Il-khan   The Mongol Khan of Persia – subordinate to the Kha'an.
Keshig   Imperial Mongol bodyguard.
Khan   Tribal chief.
Kha'an   Great Khan (*kha'agan*). Used here only for the Genghiside emperors.
Khuriltai   Mongol Grand Assembly.
Kubchir   Property tax.

Kumis   Russian term for fermented mares' milk; also used by European travellers (Mongolian: *airakh*).

Mergen   Wise, sage.

Noyan   Mongol feudal noble.

Nökhör   Mongol retainer, companion.

Ordo/Ordu   Camp, horde.

Örtöö   Horse relay service.

Ötögu bo'ol   Ancestral serf, i.e. member of subject tribe.

Ötögus bo'ol   Ancestral subject tribes.

Paitze   Tablet of authority issued by Kha'an.

Sechen   Wise.

Taishi   Minor prince.

Uchin/Ujin   Wife, consort.

Ulus   Nation, state, dynasty.

Wang   Princely title conferred by Chinese emperor.

Yam   Mongolian; strictly, 'ministry', 'department', but used loosely by European writers for Örtöö.

Yarghuchi   *See* **Darughachi**.

Yasa   Genghis Khan's code of laws.

Main Personalities

Ambakai-khan   Mongol chief, captured by the Tartars and executed by the Chin, *c*.1150.

Arghun   Fourth Il-khan. Son of Hulegu.

Arigh-böke   Younger son of Tolui. Disputed succession with his brother, Khubilai Kha'an.

Bartan-bagatur   Father of Yisugei, grandfather of Temuchin.

Batu   Son of Jochi. First Khan of Golden Horde. Led Mongol invasion of Europe in 1241–2.

Bekhter   Half-brother of Temuchin. Killed by Temuchin and Kasar.

Belgutei   Half-brother of Temuchin.

Berke   Son of Jochi. Brother of Batu. Fourth Khan of Golden Horde.

Bodunchar   Early Mongol chief and ancestor of Temuchin.

Bolad [Pulad-chingsang]   Khubilai Kha'an's ambassador to court of Il-Khan Ghazan. Important historical source for Rashid ad-Din's information on Mongols.

Bo'orchu [Boghurchi]   Temuchin's first companion.

Boroghul   A Jurkin foundling. Reared by Hö'elun, killed in Tumat campaign.

Börte   Temuchin's principal wife.

Buiruk-khan   Naiman khan. Son of Inanch-khan.

Buri-bökö   Cousin of Temuchin. Famous Jurkin wrestler.

Chaghatai   Second son of Temuchin.

Changchun   Taoist sage. Visited Genghis Khan in Hindu Kush mountains during Khwarazmian campaign.

Chingai   Kerait defector who became Ögödei Kha'an's chancellor. A Nestorian Christian.

Da'aritai-otchigin   Youngest brother of Yisugei. Uncle of Temuchin and one of his electors as Khan.

Dai-sechen   Onggirat. Father-in-law of Temuchin. Father of Börte.

Dokuz-khatun Kerait Christian princess. Married to Tolui, then later to his son, Il-khan Hulegu.

Genghis Khan First Great Khan of the Mongol Empire. *See also* Temuchin.

Ghazan Seventh Il-khan. Patron of Rashid ad-Din.

Gurbesu Naiman empress. Wife of Inanch-khan.

Guyuk Kha'an Son of Ögödei Kha'an.

Hö'elun-eke Yisugei's principal wife. Mother of Temuchin.

Hulegu First Il-Khan. Son of Tolui. Brother of Möngke Kha'an and Khubilai Kha'an.

Ila Ahai Khitan defector. Double agent, general and senior administrator under Genghis Khan.

Inanch-khan Naiman ruler. Defeated by Temuchin.

Ja'far Khwarazmian merchant. Early supporter, intelligence agent and senior administrator of Genghis Khan.

Jagambu Brother (or uncle?) of Wang-khan.

Jalal ad-Din Son of Muhammad II of Khwarazm.

Jamuka Childhood friend and *anda* of Temuchin. They became bitter enemies in struggle for power.

Jebe-noyan 'The Arrow'. Commanded, with Subodei, the pursuit of Muhammad Shah and the first Mongol incursions into Russia.

Jelme Urianghai tribe. Temuchin's second companion and later divisional commander.

Jochi Temuchin's eldest son – possibly illegitimate and excluded from succession. Sons, Batu and Berke, became Khans of the Golden Horde.

Kabul-khan Temuchin's great-grandfather.

Kadak-ba'atur Kerait commander, pardoned by Genghis Khan because of his loyalty to Wang-khan.

Kasar [Jochi-kasar] Brother of Temuchin.

Khubilai Brother of Jelme. One of Temuchin's 'Dogs of War'.

Khubilai Kha'an Grandson of Genghis Khan, son of Tolui. First Yuan emperor of China.

Ko'agchin Servant, or possibly second wife, of Yisugei. Mother of Bekhter and Belgutei?

Kuchar Mongol prince. Cousin of Genghis Khan.

Kuchlug Naiman prince who fled to Kara-Khitai.

Kuduka-beki Oirat chief.

Kulun Junior wife of Genghis Khan

Kutula Uncle of Yisugei

Möngke Kha'an Grandson of Genghis Khan, son of Tolui and first Kha'an of Toluid dynasty. Brother of Il-khan Hulegu and Khubilai Kha'an.

Mönglik Father of Teb-tengri. Married Yisugei's widow, Hö'elun.

Muhammad II Sultan of Khwarazmian empire.

Mukali Mongol general. Later viceroy of China.

Nekun-taishi Elder brother of Yisugei, father of Kuchar.

Nilka-senggum Son of Toghrul, Wang-khan.

Ögödei Kha'an Third son and successor of Genghis Khan.

Ökin-barkak Eldest son of Kabul-khan. Killed by Chin, together with Ambakai.

Otchigin-noyan Temuchin's younger brother, Temuge.

Sacha-beki Jurkin. Cousin of Genghis Khan.

Shigi-khutukhu Genghis' adopted son. Probable author of *The Secret History of the Mongols*.

Sorkaktani Kerait Christian princess married to Tolui. Mother of Möngke Kha'an, Khubilai Kha'an and Il-khan Hulegu.

Sorkan-shira Herdsman who befriended Temuchin in Tayichi'ut captivity.

Subodei-bagatur Renowned Mongol general.

Suchigu Secondary wife of Yisugei? Mother of Bekhter and Belgutei?

Taichu Jurkin. Brother of Sacha-beki.

Tarkutai-kiriltuk Tayichi'ut chief who held Temuchin captive.

Tata-tonga Uighur scribe. Keeper of Genghis Khan's Great Seal.

Tayang-khan Naiman chief. Son of Inanch-khan.

Teb-tengri Kököchu. Son of Mönglik. Famous Mongol shaman.

Temuchin Eldest son of Yisugei. Elected supreme ruler of Mongols as Genghis Khan in 1206.

Temuge Younger brother of Temuchin.

Temulun Sister of Temuchin.

Terken-khatun Mother of Muhammad Shah of Khwarazm.

Toghrul Kerait ruler. *Anda* of Yisugei and patron of Temuchin – who eventually rebelled against Toghrul and destroyed the Kerait kingdom. *See also* Wang-khan.

Tokto'a-beki Merkit chief.

Tolui Youngest son of Temuchin. Father of Möngke Kha'an, Khubilai Kha'an and Il-khan Hulegu.

Wang-khan Kerait ruler. *See also* Toghrul.

Yalavach Khwarazmian trader. Ambassador and senior administrator under Genghis Khan.

Yisugei Kiyat-Borjigin. Father of Genghis Khan.

Yisugen Junior wife of Genghis Khan.

Yisui Sister of Yisugen; also a junior wife of Genghis Khan.

Dynastic Tables

Ancestors of Genghis Khan

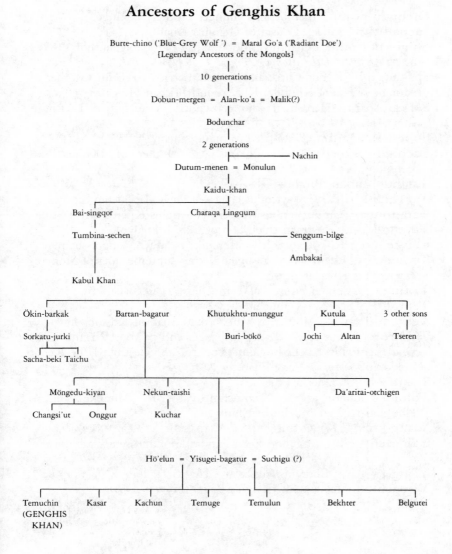

Burte-chino ('Blue-Grey Wolf ') = Maral Go'a ('Radiant Doe')
[Legendary Ancestors of the Mongols]

10 generations

Dobun-mergen = Alan-ko'a = Malik(?)

Bodunchar

2 generations
┌──────────── Nachin
Dutum-menen = Monulun

Kaidu-khan

Bai-singqor   Charaqa Lingqum

Tumbina-sechen   Senggum-bilge

Ambakai

Kabul Khan

Ökin-barkak   Bartan-bagatur   Khutukhtu-munggur   Kutula   3 other sons

Sorkatu-jurki   Buri-bökö   Jochi   Altan   Tseren

Sacha-beki Taichu

Möngedu-kiyan   Nekun-taishi   Da'aritai-otchigen

Changsi'ut   Onggur   Kuchar

Hö'elun = Yisugei-bagatur = Suchigu (?)

Temuchin   Kasar   Kachun   Temuge   Temulun   Bekhter   Belgutei
(GENGHIS
KHAN)

Descendants of Genghis Khan

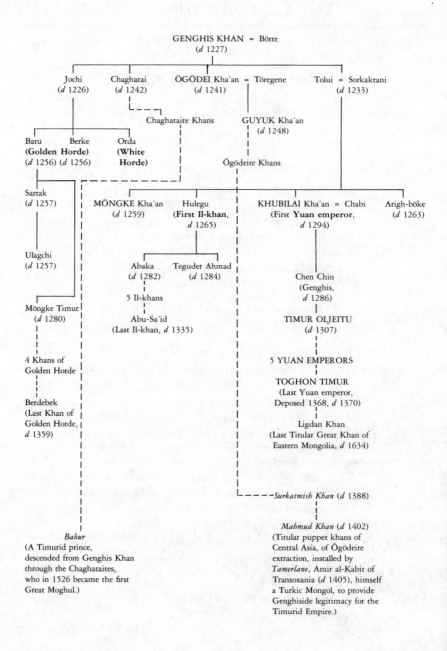

GENGHIS KHAN = Börte
(*d* 1227)

Jochi (*d* 1226)   Chaghatai (*d* 1242)   ÖGÖDEI Kha'an = Töregene (*d* 1241)   Tolui = Sorkaktani (*d* 1233)

Chaghataite Khans   GUYUK Kha'an (*d* 1248)

Batu (Golden Horde) (*d* 1256)   Berke (*d* 1256)   Orda (White Horde)   Ögödeite Khans

Sartak (*d* 1257)   MÖNGKE Kha'an (*d* 1259)   Hulegu (First Il-khan, *d* 1265)   KHUBILAI Kha'an = Chabi (First Yuan emperor, *d* 1294)   Arigh-böke (*d* 1263)

Ulagchi (*d* 1257)   Abaka (*d* 1282)   Teguder Ahmad (*d* 1284)   Chen Chin (Genghis, *d* 1286)

Möngke Timur (*d* 1280)   5 Il-khans   TIMUR OLJEITU (*d* 1307)

Abu-Sa'id (Last Il-khan, *d* 1335)

4 Khans of Golden Horde   5 YUAN EMPERORS

Berdebek (Last Khan of Golden Horde, *d* 1359)   TOGHON TIMUR (Last Yuan emperor, Deposed 1368, *d* 1370)

Ligdan Khan (Last Titular Great Khan of Eastern Mongolia, *d* 1634)

Surkatmish Khan (*d* 1388)

Babur
(A Timurid prince,
descended from Genghis Khan
through the Chaghataites,
who in 1526 became the first
Great Moghul.)

Mahmud Khan (*d* 1402)
(Titular puppet khans of
Central Asia, of Ögödeite
extraction, installed by
Tamerlane, Amir al-Kabir of
Transoxania (*d* 1405), himself
a Turkic Mongol, to provide
Genghiside legitimacy for the
Timurid Empire.)

Chronology

1115   Foundation of Chin dynasty in Northern China.

1125   Kabul-khan attends coronation of Chin emperor, Xi-zong.

1126   Foundation by Yeliu-taishi of the Western Liao Kingdom in Kara-Khitai.

1135/47   Widespread rebellion by Mongol (Meng-ku) tribes against Chin. Humiliating treaty signed by Chin in 1147.

1150s   Mongol leader Ambakai captured by Tartars and handed over to Chin for execution.

1160s   Collapse of the Mongol (Meng-ku) empire early in the decade after decisive defeat by Tartars near Lake Buir.

1165   Approximate date of birth of Temuchin (Genghis Khan) – other dates vary from 1155 to 1167.

1174/5   Temuchin becomes engaged to Börte, daughter of Dai-sechen, a member of a sub-tribe of the Onggirat. Death of Yisugei, Temuchin's father, poisoned by Tartars.

1180   Murder by Temuchin of his half-brother, Bekhter. Temuchin later in Tayichi'ut captivity.

1182/3   Temuchin marries Börte. Obtains patronage of Kerait leader, Toghrul.

1183/4   Abduction of Börte by Merkits. Attack on and defeat of Merkits by combined forces of Toghrul, Jamuka and Temuchin. Börte rescued, but son, Jochi, born on way home, possibly illegitimate.

1185   Temuchin elected Borjigid Khan by his relatives.

1187   Defeat of Temuchin at Battle of Dalan Balzhut – flees. . . . Long gap in Temuchin's life history. May have been in exile in China.

1195   Jurchid campaign against Onggirat leads to Tartar rebellion against Jurchid over booty.

1196   Temuchin attacks and defeats Tartars. Awarded minor Chin title. Killing of Jurkin princes.

1197   Toghrul rescued from exile by Temuchin and restored to throne. Toghrul receives Chin title: *Wang-khan*. Joint attack by Temuchin and Wang-khan on Tokto'a-beki.

1198   Wang-khan attacks Merkits without consulting Temuchin. Retains all booty from campaign.

1199   Joint campaign against Buiruk-khan of Naimans. Wang-khan defects on eve of battle, but is attacked and defeated by Naimans. Temuchin sends troops to Wang-khan's rescue.

1200   Campaign against the Tayichi'ut.

1201   Jamuka is elected Gurkhan and forms coalition against Temuchin. Battle of Köyitän.

1202   Extermination of Tartars by Temuchin at Dalan-nemurges, near Khalkha River. Break with Wang-khan. Battle of Kalakalzhit, defeat of Temuchin and his withdrawal to Baljuna. Swearing of Baljuna Covenant.

1203   War between Temuchin and Keraits. Defeat and death of Wang-khan. Temuchin ascends the Kerait throne.

1204   Campaign against the Naimans.

1205   Betrayal of Jamuka to Temuchin. Jamuka's death. Mongol plundering raid into Xi-Xia, led by Ila Ahai.

1206   Great Mongol *Khuriltai* at which Temuchin is invested with title: *Genghis Khan*. Khitan defectors from Liaodong reach Mongol court.

1207   Defeat of Buiruk-khan; submission of Kirghiz. Attack on Tanguts of Xi-Xia.

1209   Submission of Uighurs to Genghis Khan, who then leads campaign against Xi-Xia.

1210   Stalemate in Xi-Xia campaign. Peace negotiations result in Xi-Xia break with Chin (until 1225). Genghis Khan refuses to pay tribute to Chin emperor. Muhammad II of Khwarazm occupies Transoxania, including cities of Bokhara and Samarkand.

1211   *Khuriltai* on Kerulen River. Opening of hostilities against Chin. Advance into Northern China.

1212   Genghis Khan wounded at Dadong. Withdrawal to Mongolia.

1213   China campaign recommenced.

1214   Siege of Zhongdu (Chin capital – now Peking/Beijing) and peace negotiated. Chin move capital to Nanking (Kaifeng). Rebellion breaks out and Genghis reopens campaign.

1215	Fall of Chin capital, Zhongdu.
1216	Genghis Khan moves back to Mongolia to deal with dissident tribes.
1217	Mukali appointed viceroy (*guo-wang*) of Northern China. Campaign in Mongolia against Keraits and Tumats. Treaty regarding trade relations signed with Muhammad II of Khwarazm. Commencement of Mongol campaign against Kuchlug in Kara-Khitai.
1218	Jochi's clash with and defeat by troops of Khwarazm-shah in Kara-Khitai.
1219	Destruction of Mongol caravan and murder of Mongol ambassadors at Otrar. Commencement of Mongol hostilities against Khwarazm. Fergana Valley campaign.
1220/1	Capture of Bokhara and Samarkand. Pursuit by Subodei and Jebe of Sultan Muhammad to Caspian Sea, where he dies in early 1221. Jalal ad-Din flees to Afghanistan. Battle of Indus. Beginning of Subodei's incursions into Russia.
1222	Taoist Changchun visits Genghis Khan in Hindu Kush Mountains and Samarkand.
1223	Death of Chin and Xi-Xia emperors. Subodei defeats Russians on Kalka River.
1225	Death of Jochi. Genghis Khan's return to Mongolia. Re-establishment of Chin–Xi-Xia treaty relations.
1226/7	Mongol campaign against Xi-Xia.
1227	Death of Genghis Khan.
1227/9	Tolui acts as regent,
1228	*Khuriltai* on Kerulen River. Beginning of the *Secret History*?
1229	Accession of Ögödei Kha'an.
1233	Death of Tolui.
1234	Definitive conquest of Chin empire.

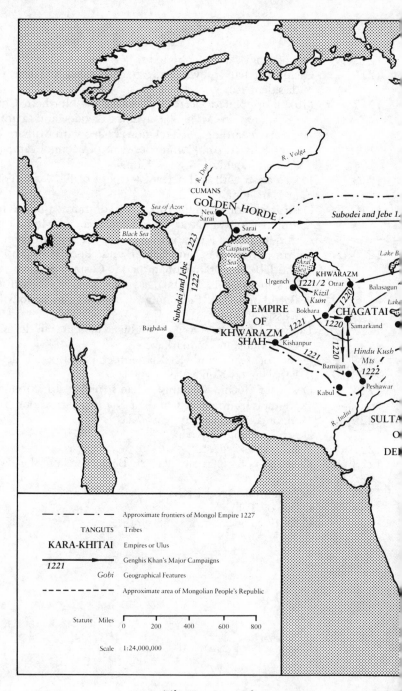

CUMANS

GOLDEN HORDE

Subodei and Jebe 1.

Sea of Azov

New
Sarai

Sarai

R. Don

R. Volga

Black Sea

*Caspian
Sea*

*Aral
Sea*

Lake B

KHWARAZM

Urgench   **1221/2** Otrar

Balasagun

Subodei and Jebe

1223

1222

Baghdad

*Kizil
Kum*

Bokhara

CHAGATAI

Lake

1221

EMPIRE
OF
KHWARAZM
SHAH

Kishanpur

Samarkand

1220

1221

1220

*Hindu Kush
Mts*

Bamijan   **1222**

Peshawar

Kabul

R. Indus

SULTA
O
DE

Approximate frontiers of Mongol Empire 1227

TANGUTS   Tribes

KARA-KHITAI   Empires or Ulus

1221━━━━▶   Genghis Khan's Major Campaigns

Gobi   Geographical Features

- - - - - - - -   Approximate area of Mongolian People's Republic

Statute Miles

0   200   400   600   800

Scale   1:24,000,000

The Empire and Campaigns of Genghis Kh

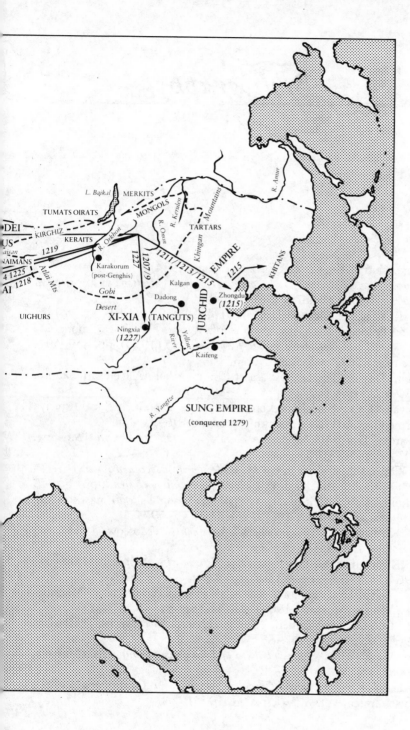

L. Baikal
MERKITS
TUMATS OIRATS
MONGOLS
KIRGHIZ
DEI
US
KERAITS
aisan
1219
NAIMANS
4 1225
AI 1218
Karakorum
(post-Genghis)
Gobi
Desert
UIGHURS
XI-XIA (TANGUTS)
Ningxia
(1227)

R. Orkhon
R. Onon
R. Kerulen
TARTARS
Khingan Mountains
EMPIRE
1215
R. Amur
KHITANS
Kalgan
Dadong
Zhongdu
(1215)
JURCHID
Yellow River
Kaifeng

R. Yangtze

SUNG EMPIRE
(conquered 1279)

1211/1213/1215
1207/9
1227

Bibliography

Alinge, Curt: *Mongolische Gesetze* (Leipzig, 1934).

Alizade, A.A.: *Sozial'no-ekonomicheskaya i politicheskaya istoriya Azerbaidzhana* (Baku, 1956).

Arends, A.K.: 'Rashid ad-Din', *Sbornik Letopisei*, vol III.

Aubin, Francoise: 'Le statut de l'enfant dans la société mongole', *'L'enfant', Recueils de la société Jean Bodin*,35 (1975), pp. 459–591.

–: *See also* Ratchnevsky and Aubin.

Ayalon, David: 'The Great Yāsa of Chingis Khān: A Re-examination', *Studia Islamica* (1971), pp. 151–80.

Babayan, L.O.: Sozial'no-ekonomicheskaya i politicheskaya istoriya Armenii v XIII–XIV vekakh (Moscow, 1969).

Banzarov, Dordzhi: 'Chernaya vera', *Sobranie sochinenii* (Moscow, 1955), pp. 48–100.

——: 'O proiskhozhdenii imeni *Mongol'*, *Sobranie sochinenii*, pp. 167–74

——: 'O proiskhozhdenii slova *Chingis'*, *Sobranie sochinenii*, pp. 175–7.

Barthold, V.V.: 'Turkestan v epokhu mongol'skogo nashestviya'. *Sochineniya* (Moscow, 1963), vol. I pp. 45–597.

——: 'Kirgisy, Istoricheskii ocherk', *Sochineniya* (Moscow, 1963), vol. II/i, pp. 473–543.

——: 'Khorezmshah', *Encyclopaedia of Islam; also Sochineniya* (Moscow, 1964), vol. II/2, pp. 535–7.

——: 'Persidskaya nadpis' na stene Aniiskoi mecheti Manuce', *Sochineniya* (Moscow, 1966). vol. IV, pp. 313–8.

——: 'Obrazovanie imperii Chingis-khana', *Sochineniya* (Moscow, 1968), vol. V, pp. 257–65.

——: 'Chingis-khan', *Encyclopaedia of Islam;* also *Sochineniya* (Moscow, 1968), vol. V, pp. 615–28.

Bawden, C.R.: *The Mongol Chronicle Altan Tobči,* Göttinger Asiatische Forschungen, vol. 5 (Wiesbaden, 1955).

Becquet, Jean and Hambis, Louis (eds.): Jean de Plan Carpin: *Histoire des Mongols* (Paris, 1965). Berezin, I.N. (trans. and ed.): Rashid ad-Din: *Sbornil letopisei; Istoriya Mongolov, Sochinenie Rashid Eddina*. vols. I–II. (St Petersburg, 1858).

——: *Ocherk vnutrennego ustroistva Ulusa Dzhuchieva*.

Blake, R.P. and Frye, R.N.: 'History of the Nation of the Archers (The Mongols) by Grigor of Akanč', *HJAS* (1949), pp. 269–399.

Boyle, John Andrew (trans.): 'Alā' ad-Din 'Atā-Malik Juvainī: *The History of the World Conqueror*, 2 vols. (Manchester, 1958).

——: 'Kirakos of Gandzak on the Mongols', *CAJ* (1963), pp. 199–214.

——: 'A Eurasian Hunting Ritual', *Folklore* (1969), pp. 12–16.

Bretschneider, E.: *Mediaeval Researches from Eastern Asiatic Sources*, 2 vols. (London, 1910).

Budge, E.A.W.: *The Chronography of Gregory Abu'l Faraj, commonly known as Bar Hebraeus*, 2 vols. (London–Oxford, 1932).

Buniyatov, S.M. (trans. and ed.): Sikhab ad-Din: Muhammad an-Nasawi: *Zhizneopisanie sultana Dzhalal ad-Dina Mankburny* (Baku, 1973).

Cai Meibiao: *Yuandai baihua bei jilu*, ed. Xinhua shudian (Beijing, 1951).

Chavannes, Edouard: 'Inscriptions et piéces de chancellerie chinoise de l'époque mongole', *TP* (1904), pp. 357–447.

Cleaves, Francis W.: 'The Sino-Mongolian Inscription of 1362 in Memory of Prince Hindu', *HJAS* (1949), pp. 1–133.

——: 'The Mongolian Names and Terms in the History of the Archers by Grigor of Akanč', *HJAS* (1949), pp. 400–443.

——: 'A Chancellery Practice of the Mongols in the Thirteenth and Fourteenth Centuries', *HJAS* (1951), pp. 493–526.

——: '*Daruγa* and *Gerege*', *HJAS* (1953), pp. 237–59.

——: 'The Historicity of the Baljuna Covenant', *HJAS* (1955), pp. 357–421.

——: *See also* bLo.bzan bsTan.'jin.

——: *See also* Mostaert and Cleaves.

Consten, Hermann: *Weideplätze der Mongolen*, 2 vols. (Berlin, 1920).

Damdinsuren: *Mongolyn nuuc tovčoo* (Ulan Bator, 1957).

Defrémery, C., and Sanguinetti, B.R.: *Voyages d'Ibn Batoutah,* 4 vols (Paris, 1879).

Demiéville, Paul: 'La situation religieuse en Chine au temps de Marco Polo', *Oriente Poliano* (Rome, 1957), pp. 193–236.

Desmaisons, Petr (trans. and ed.): *Šaγara-yi Turk: Histoire des Mongols et des Tatares par Aboul Ghazi Behadour Khan*, vol. II (St Petersburg, 1874).

Doerfer, Gerhard: *Türkische und mongolische Elemente im Neupersischen:* vol. I; *Mongolische Elemente im Neupersischen* (Wiesbaden, 1963); vol. II/1,2; *Türkische Elemente im Neupersischen* (Wiesbaden, 1965,1967); vol. IV, *Türkische Elemente (Schluß) und Register des Gesamtwerkes* (Wiesbaden, 1975).

——: 'Zur Datierung der Geheimen Geschichte der Mongolen', *ZDMG* (1963), pp. 86–111.

Drevnetyurkskii slovar' (Leningrad, 1969).

Eberhard, Wolfram: *Kultur und Siedlung der Randvölker Chinas* (Leiden, 1942).

——: *Conquerors and Rulers: Social Forces in Mediaeval China* (Leiden, 1952).

Ebisawa Tetsuo: '*Yakudai* no kansuru oboegaki', *Genshi keihōshi no kenkyū yakuchū* (Tokyo, 1963), pp. 69–87.

Erdmann, Franz von: *Temudschin der Unerschütterliche* (Leipzig, 1862).

Etani Toshiyuki: 'Ta-la-han ka'o', *Tōyōshi kenkyū* (1963), pp. 61–7, 185–202.

Etiemble, R.: 'L'Orient philosophique au XVIIIe siècle', part I, *Les cours de Sorbonne* (Paris, 1957).

Falina, A.I.: *Ràshid ad-Din: Perepiska* (Moscow, 1971).

Fedorov-Davydov, G.A.: *Obshchestvenny stroi Zolotoi Ordy* (Moscow, 1973).

Feng, Chia-sheng: *See also* Wittfogel and Feng.

Franke, Herbert: *Geld und Wirtschaft in China unter der Mongolen-herrschaft* (Leipzig, 1949).

——: *Oriental Art,* vol. 2 (1949).

——: 'Sino-Western Contacts under the Mongol Empire', *Journal of the Hong Kong Branch of the Royal Asiatic Society,* vol. 6 (1966), pp. 49–72.

——: 'Chinese Texts on the Jurchen: A Translation of the Jurchen Monograph in the *San-cha'o pei-ming hui-pien'*, *ZAS,* vol. 9 (1975), pp. 119–86.

——: 'Chinese Texts on the Jurchen, II: A Translation of Chapter One of the *Chin-shih'*, *ZAS,* vol. 12 (1978), pp. 413–52.

——: 'A Sino-Uighur Family Portrait: Notes on a Wooodcut from Turfan', *The Canada-Mongolia Review,* vol. 4, no. 1 (1978), pp. 33–40.

——: 'From Tribal Chieftain to Universal Emperor and God: The Legitimation of the Yüan Dynasty', *Sitzungsbericht der Bayer. Akad. d. Wiss., Phil.-hist. Klasse* vol. 2 (1978).

Franke, Otto: *Geschichte des chinesischen Reiches,* vol. IV (Berlin, 1948); vol. V [Index] (Berlin, 1952).

Frye, Richard N.: 'Tarχun/Türχün and Central Asian History', *HJAS* (1951), pp. 105–129.

——: *See also* Blake and Frye.

Gabain, A. von: *Alttürkische Grammatik* (Leipzig, 1950).

Galstyan, A.G.: *Armyanskie istochniki o Mongolakh* (Moscow, 1962).

Gibert, L.: *Dictionnaire historique et géographique de la Mandchourie* (Hong Kong, 1934).

Giles, Herbert A.: *A Chinese Biographical Dictionary* (London–Shanghai, 1898).

Golstunskii, K.F.: *Mongol-Oiratskie zakony 1640 goda.* (St. Petersburg, 1880).

Grousset, René: *L'empire mongol* (Paris, 1941).

——: *Le conquérant du monde (Vie de Gengis-khan)* (Paris, 1944).

——: *Histoire de l'Extrême–Orient* (Paris).

Gumilev, L.N.: *Poiski vymyshlennogo tsarstva* (Moscow, 1970).

——: *Tainaya* i *yavnaya* istoriya Mongolov XII–XIII vekov. *Tataro-Mongoly v Asii i Evrope* (Moscow, 1977), pp. 455–74.

Haenisch, Erich: 'Die letzten Feldzüge Cinggis Han's und sein Tod', *AM* (1933), pp. 503–51.

——: *Manghol un niuca tobca'an (Yüan-cha'o-pi-shi)* (Leipzig, 1937).

——: *Wörterbuch zu Manghol un niuca tobca'an (Yüan-cha'o-pi-shi)* (Leipzig, 1939).

——: *Steuergerechtsame der chinesischen Klöster unter der Mongolenherrschaft* (Leipzig, 1940).

——: 'Die Kulturpolitik des mongolischen Weltreiches', *Vorträge und Schriften der Preußischen Akademie der Wissenschaften*, vol. 17. (Berlin, 1943).

——: 'Die Geheime Geschichte der Mongolen (Leipzig, 2nd edn, 1948).

——: 'Mongolische Miszellen', *Collectanea Mongolica: Festschrift für Professor Dr. Rintchen* (Wiesbaden, 1966), pp. 65–9.

Haltod, Magadbürin: *Mongolische Ortsnamen: Verzeichnis der Orientalischen Handschriften in Deutschland*, suppl. vol. 5.1 (Wiesbaden, 1966).

Hambis, Louis: *Le Chapitre CVII du Yuan che* (Leiden, 1945).

——: *Le Chapitre CVIII du Yuan che* (Leiden, 1954).

——: *Marco Polo: La description du monde* (Paris 1955).

——: 'A propos de la "Pierre de Gengis-khan"', *Melanges publiés par l'Institut des Hautes Etudes chinoises*, vol. II (Paris, 1960), pp. 141–57.

——: *See also* Becquet and Hambis.

——: *See also* Pelliot and Hambis.

Hamilton, James R.: *Les Ouighours à l'époque des Cinq dynasties* (Paris, 1955).

Han Rulin: 'Menggu dalahan kao', *Zhongguo wenhua yanjiu suo jikan*, vol. I/1 (1940), pp. 155–84.

——: 'Lun Chenjisi-han', *Lishi yanjiu* (1962), No. 3, pp. 1–10.

Hong Jun: *Yuanshi yiwen zhenghu* [Guoxue jiben congshu], 2 vols.

Howorth, H.H.: *History of the Mongols from the 9th to the 19th Century*, vol. 1 (London, 1876).

Hulsewé, A.F.P.: *Remnants of Han Law* (Leiden, 1955).

Hung, William: 'The Transmission of the Book known as The Secret History of the Mongols', *HJAS* (1951), pp. 433–92.

Jackson, P.: 'The Dissolution of the Mongol Empire', *CAJ* (1978), pp. 186–244.

Jahn, Karl: 'Das iranische Papiergeld', *AO* (1938), pp. 308–40.

——: 'Wissenschaftliche Kontakte zwischen Iran und China in der Mongolenzeit', *Anzeiger der phil.-hist. Klasse der österr.AdW*, vol. 106 (1969), p. 10.

Jenkin, G.: 'A Note on Climatic Cycles and the Rise of Činggis Khan', *CAJ* (1974), pp. 217–26.

Julien, Stanislas: *Mémoires de Hiuan-tsang*.

Karlgrenz: *Grammata Serica*.

Ke Shaomin: *Xin Yuanshi*, ed. Kaiming (1946; reprint Taipei, 1962–9).

——: *Xin Yuanshi kaozheng* (Ke Shaomin xiansheng maizhi di er zhong).

Khanlaryan, L.A.: Kirakos Ganzhaketsi: *Istoriya Armenii: Pamyatniki pis'mennosti vostoka LIII* (Moscow, 1976).

Khara-Davan, E.: *Čingis chan kak polkovodets* (Belgrade, 1941).

Khetagurov, A.A. : *See also* Rashid ad-Din: *Sbornik letopisei*, vol. I/1.

Kobayashi, Takashirō: *Genchō hishi* (Tokyo, 1959).

——: *Genshi* (Tokyo, 1973).

U.-Köhalmi, Käthe: 'Der Pfeil bei der innerasiatischen Reiternomaden und ihren Nachbarn', *AOH* (1956), pp. 109–61.

——: 'Sibirische Parallelen zur Ethnographie der Geheimen Geschichte der Mongolen', *Mongolian Studies*, ed. Louis Ligeti (Budapest, 1970), pp. 249–64.

Kotwicz, Wladislaw: 'Les Mongols promoteurs de la paix universelle au debut du XIII siècle', *RO* (1950), pp. 428–34.

——: 'Contributions aux études altaiques', *RO* (1953), pp. 327–68.

Kowalewski, Josef E.: *Dictionnaire mongol–russe–francais*, 3 vols. (Kazan, 1844–9).

Kozin, S.A.: *Sokrovennoe skazanie*, vol. I (Moscow–Leningrad, 1941).

Krader, Lawrence: *Social Organisation of the Mongol-Turkic Pastoral Nomads* (The Hague, 1963).

Krause, F.E.A.: *Cingis Han: Die Geschichte seines Lebens nach den chinesischen Reichsannalen* (Heidelberg, 1922).

Krueger, John R.: *Poetical Passages in the Erdeni-yin tobci,* Central Asiatic Studies, Monograph Series, vol. VII. (The Hague, 1961).

——: *See also* Poppe: *Mongolian Monuments.*

Kychanov, E.I.: 'Mongolo-tangutskie voiny i gibel' gosudarstva Si-Sia', *Tataro-Mongoly v Asii i Evrope,* 46–61.

Lattimore, Owen: 'The "Temujin" Theme in the Tso Chuan', *Trudy XXV mezhdunarodnogo kongressa vostokovedov,* vol. V (Moscow, 1963), pp. 317–19.

Lech, Klaus: *Das Mongolische Weltreich: al-'Umarī's Darstellung der mongolischen Reiche in seinem Werk Masalik al-abṣār fī mamālik al-amṣār,* Asiatische Forschungen, vol. 22. (Wiesbaden, 1968).

Ledyard, G.: 'The Mongol Invasions of Korea and the Date of *The Secret History*', *CAJ,* vol. 9 (1964), pp. 1–22.

Lewicki, Marian: La langue mongole des transcriptions chinoises du XIV siècle: "Le Houa-Yi Yi-Yü" de 1389 (Wroclaw, 1949).

Liao-Jin-Yuan zhuanji zhonghe yinde, ed. Zhonghua shuju (Beijing, 1959).

Liaoshi, ed Baina ben.

Ligeti, Louis: 'Mots de civilisation de Haute Asie en transcription chinoise', *AOH* (1950), pp. 141–88.

——: 'Les mots solons dans un ouvrage des Ts'ing', *AOH* (1959), pp. 231–72.

——:'Le lexique mongol de Kirakos de Gandzak', *Dissertationes Sodalium instituti Asiae interioris,* vol. 9 (Budapest, 1965), pp. 241–97.

——: *Histoire secrète des Mongols: Texte en écriture ouigoure incorporé dans la chronique Altan-tobci de Blo-bzan Bstan-'Jin* (Budapest, 1974).

Li Xinchuan: *Jianyen yilai chaoye zaji* (Congshu jicheng).

——: *Jianyen yilai xinian yaolu* (Commercial Press).

Li Youtang: *Liaoshi jishi benmo* (1903).

Li Zhichang: *Xiyu ji,* ed. Wang Guowei.

bLo.bzan bsTan.'jin: *Altan tobči,* ed. F.W. Cleaves. Scripta Mongolica, vol. I (Cambridge, Mass., 1952).

Lomi: *Monghol Borǰigid oboγ-un teüke – Mengku shih-hsi-p'u,* ed. Walter Heissig and Charles Bawden, Göttinger Asiatische Forschungen, vol. 9 (Wiesbaden, 1957).

Malov, S.W.: *Pamyatniki drevnetyurkskoi pismennosti Mongolii i Kirgizii* (Moscow–Leningrad, 1959).

Martin, H. Desmond: 'The Mongol Wars with the Hsi Hsia (1205–1227)', *JRAS* (1942), pp. 195–228.

——: 'The Mongol Army', *JRAS* (1942), pp. 46–85.

——: 'Chingis Khan's First Invasion of the Chin Empire', *JRAS* (1943), pp. 182–216.

——: *The Rise of Chingis Khan and his Conquest of North China* (Baltimore, 1950).

Melikhov, G.V.: 'Ustanovlenie vlasti mongol'skikh feodalov v severo vostochnom Kitae', *Tataro-Mongoly v Asii i Evrope* (Moscow, 1970), pp. 62–84.

Meng Si-ming: *Yüandai shihui jieji zhidu*, Yenching Journal of Chinese Studies, monograph series no. 10 (Peiping, 1938).

Minovi, M. and Minorsky, V: 'Naṣīr al-Dīn Ṭūsī on Finance', *BSOAS* (1941), pp. 755–81.

Morgan, D.O.: 'Cassiodorus and Rashīd al-Dīn on Barbarian Rule in Italy and Persia', *BSOAS* (1977), pp. 302–20.

Mostaert, Antoine: 'A propos de quelques portraits d'empereurs mongols', *AM* (1927), pp. 147–56.

——: *Le matérial mongol du Houa I I Iu de Houng-ou* (1389), ed. Igor de Rachewiltz with Anthony Schönbaum, Mélanges Chinois et Bouddhiques, vol. XVIII. (Brussels, 1977).

——: 'Ordosica', *Bulletin of the Catholic University of Peking* (1934).

——: Dictionnaire Ordos, 3 vols. (Peking, 1941–4).

——: Sur quelques passages de l'Histoire secrète des Mongols (Cambridge, Mass., 1953).

Mostaert, Antoine and Cleaves, Francis W.: 'Trois documents mongols des archives secrètes vaticanes', *HJAS* (1952), pp. 419–506.

Müller, C.: *Fragmenta Historicorum graecorum*, vol. IV (Paris, 1868).

Mullie, J.: 'Les anciennes villes de l'empire des Grand Leao au royaume mongol Bārin', *TP* (1922), pp. 105–231.

Munkujev, N.C.: 'O dvukh tendentsiakh v politike pervykh mongol'skikh khanov v Kitae v pervoi polovine XIII v', *Materialy po istorii i filologii Tsentral'noi Azii* (Ulan Ude, 1962), pp. 49–67.

——: *Kitaiski istochnik o pervykh mongol'skikh khanakh* (Moscow, 1965).

——: 'K voprosu ob ekonomicheskom polozhenii Mongolii i Kitaya v XIII–XIV vv', *Kratkie soobshcheniya Instituta narodov Azii*, no. 76 (Moscow, 1965), pp. 136–153.

——: 'Zametki o drevnikh Mongolakh', *Tataro-Mongoly v Azii i Evrope* (Moscow, 1970), pp. 352–81.

——: 'Novie materialy o polozhenii mongol'skikh aratov v XIII–XIV vv', *Tataro-Mongoly v Azii i Evrope* (Moscow, 1970), pp. 382–418.

——: Men-Da bei-lu: Polnoe opisanie Mongolo-Tatar. *Pamyatniki pis'mennosti vostoka* XXVI (Moscow. 1975).

Muruyama Shikhiro: 'Sind die Naiman Turken oder Mongolen?' *CAJ*, vol. 4 (1959), pp. 188–98.

——: 'Einige Eigentümlichkeiten der chinesischen Transkription des *Mongholun niūca tobčaan*', *Trudy XXV – go kongressa vostokovedov*, vol. III (Moscow, 1963), pp. 432–4.

Nasonov, A.N.: *Mongoly i Rus'* (Moscow, 1940).

Natsagdorj, Sh.: *Chingis Qasar khoer zorchil* (Ulan Bator, 1958).

——: 'Nekotorie voprosy feodalisatsii mongol'skogo obshchestva XIII v', *Studia Mongolica*, vol III/4 (Ulan Bator, 1975), pp 51–74.

Németh, J.: 'Wanderungen des mongolischen Wortes nökür–Genosse', *AOH*, vol. 3 (1952), pp. 1–23.

Niida, Noboru: *Chūgoku hōsei shi* (Tokyo, 1969).

Ohsson, C. d': *Histoire des Mongols, depuis Tchinguiz-khan jusqu'à Timour Bey ou Tamerlan, vol. I* (The Hague–Amsterdam, 1834).

Olbricht, Peter: Das Postwesen in China (Wiesbaden, 1954).

Ou-yang Xiu: *Wudai shiji* (Baina ben).

Palladii (Kafarov) P.: 'Starinnoe mongol'skoe skazanie o chingiskhane', *Trudy Chlenov Rossiskoi Dukhovnoi Missii v Pekinge*, vol. IV, (St Petersburg, 1866), pp. 3–258

Pankratov, B.L.: *Juan'-čae bi-ši*, vol. I (Moscow, 1962).

Paris, Matthew: *Chronica majora*. Rolls series. 7 vols. (London, 1872–83).

Pelliot, Paul: 'Chrétiens d'Asie. centrale et d'Extrême Orient', *TP* (1914), pp. 623–44.

——: 'A propos des Comans', *JA* (1920), pp. 125–85.

——: 'Les Mongols et la Papauté', *Revue de l'Orient chrétien,* 3rd series, vol. 23, pp. 3–30; vol. 24, pp. 225–335; vol. 28, pp. 3–84.

——: 'Une ville musulmane dans la Chine du Nord sous les Mongols', *JA* (1927), pp. 261–79.

——: 'L'édition collective des oeuvres de Wang Kouo-wei', *TP* (1928), pp. 113–82.

——: 'Neuf notes sur des questions d'Asie centrale', *TP* (1929), pp. 201–66.

——: 'Deux mots turcs chez Hiuan-tsang', *TP* (1929), pp. 219–21.

——: 'Notes sur le *Turkestan* de M.W. Barthold', *TP* (1930), pp. 12–56.

——: 'Sur *yam* ou *Jam*, relais postal', *TP* (1930), pp. 192–95.

——: 'Sur la légende d'Uγuz-khan en écriture ouigoure', *TP* (1930), pp. 247–368.

——: La Haute Asie (Paris, 1931).

——: 'Les formes à *q-* (*k-*) initiaux', *TP* (1944), pp. 73–101.

——: 'Qubčiri/qubčir et qubči'ur'/qubčur', *TP* (1944), pp. 143–64.

——: Histoire secrète des Mongols (Paris, 1949).

——: Notes sur l'histoire de la Horde d'Or (Paris, 1949).

——: Notes on Marco Polo, 3 vols. (Paris, 1959, 1963, 1973).

Pelliot, Paul and Hambis, Louis: *Histoire des campagnes de Gengis Khan*: Chen-wou ts'in-tcheng lou, vol. I (Leiden, 1951).

Peng Daya and Xu Ting: *Hei-Da shilüe*, ed. Wang Guowei.

Perlee, Kh.: *Nuuc tovčoond gardag gazar usny zarim neriig haij olson n'* (Ulan Bator, 1958).

Petrushevski, I.P.: *Zemledelie i agrarnie otnosheniya v Irane XIII–XIV vekov* (Moscow–Leningrad, 1960).

——: 'Pokhod mongol'skikh voisk v srednuyu Aziyu v 1219–1224 g. i ego posliedstva', *Tataro-Mongoly v Azii i Evrope* (Moscow, 1970), pp. 100–33.

——: 'Iran i Azerbaidzhan pod vlast'yu Khulaguidov (1256–1353)', *Tataro-Mongoly v Azii i Evrope* (Moscow, 1970), pp. 222–54.

Plano Carpini, Johannes de: *Ystoriya Mongalorum quos nos Tartaros apellamus*, Sinica Franciscana, vol. I, pp. 27–130.

Poliak, A.N.: 'The Influence of Chingiz-Khan's Yāsa upon the General Organisation of the Mamluk State', *BSOAS* (1942), pp. 862–76.

Poppe, Nicholas: 'Mongol'skii slovar' Mukaddimat al-Adab', *Trudy Instituta Vostokovedeniya*, vol. 14 (Moscow–Leningrad, 1938).

——: 'On some Geographical Names in the *Jami' al-Tawarīx*', *HJAS* (1956), pp. 33–41.

——: The Mongolian Monuments in hP'ags-pa Script, trans. and ed. John R. Krueger (Wiesbaden, 2nd edn, 1957).

Potapov, L.P.: *Ocherki po istorii Altaitsev* (Moscow–Leningrad, 1953).

Poucha, Pavel: 'Zum Stammbaum des Tschingis Chan', *Asiatica: Festschrift Weller* (Leipzig, 1950), pp. 442–52.

——: Die Geheime Geschichte der Mongolen als Geschichts quelle und Literaturdenkmal (Prague, 1956).

——: 'Über den Inhalt und die Rekonstruktion des ersten Mongolisches Gesetzbuches', *Mongolian Studies*, ed. Louis Ligeti (Budapest, 1970), pp. 377–415.

Pritsak, O.: 'Orientierung und Farbsymbolik: Zu den Farbbezeichnungen in der altaiischen Völkernamen', *Saeculum* (1954), pp. 374–83.

Rachewiltz, Igor de: 'Yeh-lü Ch'u-ts'ai (1189–1243): Buddhist Idealist and Confucian Statesman', *Confucian Personalities*, ed Arthur F. Wright and Denis Twitchett (Stanford, Cal., 1962), pp. 189–367.

——: 'The Hsi-yu lu by Yeh-lü Ch'u-ts'ai', *MS* (1962), pp. 1–128.

——: 'Some Remarks on the Dating of the Secret History of the Mongols', *MS* (1965), pp. 185–206.

——: 'Personnel and Personalities in North China in the Early Mongol Period,' *JESHO*, vol. IX (1966), pp. 88–144.

——: 'The Secret History of the Mongols', *PFEH* vol. 1 (1971), pp. 115–63; vol. 5 (1972), pp. 149–75; vol. 10 (1974), pp. 55–82;

vol. 13 (1976), pp. 41–75; vol. 16 (1977); vol. 18, pp. 43–80.

——: *Index to the Secret History of the Mongols*, Indiana University Publications, Uralic and Altaic Series, vol. 121 (Bloomington, 1972).

——: *Prester John and Europe's Discovery of East Asia* (Canberra, 1972).

——: 'Some Remarks on the Khitan Clan Name Yeh-lü≈-I-la', *PFEH* (1974), pp. 187–204.

——: 'Some Remarks on the Stele of Yisüngge', *Tractata Altaica*, pp. 487–508 (Wiesbaden, 1976).

Radloff, W.: *Aus Sibirien*, 2 vols. (Leipzig, 1893).

Ramstedt, G.I. von: 'Mogholica: Beiträge zur Kenntnis der Moghul-Sprache in Afghanistan', *JSFOu*, vol. XXIII/4 (1906), 60 pp.

——: *Kalmückisches Wörterbuch* (Helsinki, 1935).

Rashid ad-Din: *Sbornik letopisei (Collected Chronicles)*, vol. I, Trans. L.A. Khetagurov (Moscow–Leningrad, 1952); vol. I/2, trans. O.I. Smirnova, vol. II, trans. Yu. P. Verkhovski (Moscow–Leningrad, 1960); vol. III, trans. A.K. Arends (Moscow–Leningrad, 1946).

Ratchnevsky, Paul: 'Die mongolischen Großkhane und die buddhistische Kirche', *Asiatica: Festschrift Weller* (Leipzig, 1954), pp. 489–504.

——: 'Zur Bedeutung des Mongolensturmes in China', *Wiss. Zeitschrift der Humboldt-Universität zu Berlin. Gesellschafts und sprachwiss, series*. IX (1959/60), 1/2, pp. 113–18.

——: 'Die mongolische Reichsinstitution der Buße in der chinesischen Gesetzgebung der Yüanzeit', *Studia Sino-Altaica: Festschrift Erich Haenisch* (Wiesbaden, 1961), pp. 169–80.

——: 'Šigi-qutuqu, ein mongolischer Gefolgsmann im 12,–13. Jahrhundert', *CAJ* (1965), pp. 88–120.

——: 'Les Che-wei étaient-ils des Mongols?', *Mélanges de Sinologie offerts à Monsieur Paul Demiéville*, Bibliothèque des Hautes Etudes chinoises, vol. XX (Paris, 1966) I, pp. 225–51.

——: 'Zum Ausdruck *t'oushia* in der Mongolenzeit', *Collectanea Mongolica: Festschrift Rintchen*, Asiatische Forschungen, vol. 17 (Wiesbaden, 1966), pp. 173–91.

——: 'The Levirate in the Legislation of the Yuan Dynasty', *Asiatic Studies in Honour of Dr Jitsuzō Tamura*, (Kyoto, 1968), pp. 45–62.

——: 'Zu einigen Problemen der Symbiose in China unter den Mongolen', *Das Verhältnis der Bodenbauern und Viehzüchtern in historischer Sicht* (Berlin, 1968), pp. 127–34.

——: 'Über den mongolischen Kult am Hofe der Großkhane in China', *Mongolian Studies*, ed. Louis Ligeti (Budapest, 1970), pp. 417–43.

——: 'Rašīd ad-Din uber die Mohammedanerverfolgungen in China unter Qubilai', [Rashid al-Dīn Commemoration Volume], *CAJ* (1970) pp. 163–80.

——: Un Code des Yuan, Bibliothèque de l'Institut des Haute Etudes chinoises, IV, vol. I (Paris, 1937); vol. II (Paris, 1972).

——: 'Khubilai Khan', *Enzyklopädie: Die Großen der Weltgeschichte*, vol. III (Zurich, 1973) pp. 752–69.

——: 'Die Yasa (Ĵasaq) Činggis-khans und ihre Problematik', *Sprache, Geschichte und Kultur der altaischen Völker, Schriften zur Geschichte und Kultur des Alten Orients*, vol. 5. (Berlin, 1974), pp. 471–87.

——: 'La condition de la femme mongole au 12e/13e siècle', *Tractata Altaica: Festschrift Sinor*, (Wiesbaden, 1976), pp. 509–30.

——:Historisch-terminologisches Wörterbuch der Yüan- Zeit, with J. Dill and D.Heyde (Berlin, 1967).

Ratchnevsky, Paul and Aubin, Francoise: *Un Code des Yuan*, vol. III: *Index* (Paris, 1977).

Raverty, H.G.: *Ṭabakāt-i-nāsirī: A General History of the Muhammadan Dynasties of Asia by the Maulāna, Minhāj-al-Dīn, Abū-'Umarī-'usmān*, vol. II. (London, 1881).

Riasanovsky, V.A.: *Mongol'skoe pravo* (Harbin, 1931).

——:Fundamental Principles of Mongol Law (Tientsin, 1937).

Risch, Friedrich: Johann de Plano Carpini: *Geschichte der Mongolen und Reisebericht*, 1245–1247 (Leipzig, 1930).

Rockhill, W.W.: *The Journey of William of Rubruck* (London, 1900).

Rotours, Robert des: 'Quelques notes sur l'anthropophagie en Chine', *TP* (1963), pp. 386–427.

Rubruck, Guillelmus de: *Itinerarium. Sinica Franciscana*, vol. I. pp. 164–332.

Rudenko, S.L.: *Kultura naseleniya Tsentral'nogo Altaya v skifskoye vremya* (Moscow–Leningrad, 1960).

Rygdylon, E.R.: O mongol'skom termine *ongu-bogol,* Filologiya i istoriya mongol'skikh narodov (Moscow, 1958).

Sacy, Sylvestre de: *Chrestomatie arabe*, vol. II (Paris, 1826).

Sagang Sechen: *Erdeni-yin Tobči,* ed, Francis W. Cleaves with critical introduction by Antoine Mostaert, *Scripta Mongolica*, II, 4 vols. (Cambridge, Mass., 1956).

Schmidt, I.J.: *Erdeni-yin Tobči: Geschichte der Ost-Mongolen und ihres Fürstenhauses, verfaßt von Ssanang Ssetsen* (St Petersburg, 1829).

Schurmann, Herbert: review of E. Haenisch: *Steuergerechtsame der chinesischen Klöster unter der Mongolenherrshaft, HJAS* (1951), pp. 291–306.

——: Economic Structure of the Yüan Dynasty, Harvard-Yenching Institute Studies, vol. XVI. (Cambridge, Mass., 1956).

——: 'Mongolian Tributary Practices of the Thirteenth Century', *HJAS* (1956), pp. 304–89.

Semenov, A.A.: 'K voprosu o zolotoordynskom termine *baskak'*, *IANSSSR, Literatura i yazyk*, no. 2 (1947), pp. 137–47.

Shao Yuanping: *Yuanshi leibian, ed. Qianlong* (1795).

Shastina, N.P.: *Shara tudzhi: Mongol'skaya letopis' XVII veka* (Moscow–Leningrad, 1957).

—: Russko-mongolskie posol'skie otnosheniya XVII veka (Moscow–Leningrad, 1958).

—: 'Obraz Chingis khana v srednevekovoi literature Mongolov', *Tataro-Mongoly v Azii i Evrope* (Moskow, 1970), pp. 435–54.

—: Altan tobči ('Zolotoe skazanie') (Moskow, 1970).

Shenwu qinzheng lu, ed. Wang Guowei.

Sinor, Denis: *Introduction à l'étude de l'Eurasie centrale* (Wiesbaden, 1963).

Smirnova, O.I.: *See also* Rashid ad-Din: *Sbornik letopisei*, vol. II.

Smith, John Masson: 'Mongol and Nomadic Taxation', *HJAS* (1970), pp. 46–85.

Song Zizhen: '*Zhongshu ling Yelü gong shendao bei'*, *Yuanwen lei*, vol. 57, pp. 830–88.

Spuler, Bertold: *Die Goldene Horde* (Leipzig, 1943).

—: *Die Mongolen in Iran* (Berlin, 1955).

—: *Geschichte der Mongolen* (Zurich, 1968).

Stein, R.: 'Leao-tche', *TP* (1940), pp. 1–154.

Street, John Charles: *The Language of the Secret History of the Mongols* (New Haven, Conn., 1957).

Su Tianjue: *Yuanwen lei*, ed. Wanyu wenku.

—: Yuanchao mingchen shilüe, 4 ben.

Tamura, Jitsuzō: Chūgoku seifū ocho no kenkyu, vol. II (Kyoto, 1970).

—: *Chingis-kan no yasa*:

Tao Zongyi: Na cun Zhuogeng lu, 10 ben.

Tikhonov, D.I.: *K voprosu o nekotorykh terminakh*.

Tikhvinskii, S.L.: Tataro–mongol'skie zavoevaniya v Azii i Evrope. *Tataro-mongoly v Azii i Evrope* (Moscow, 1970), pp 3–21.

Togan, A. Zeki Velidi: 'The Composition of the *History of the Mongols* of Rashīd al-Dīn,' *CAJ* (1962), pp. 60–72.

Tolstov, P.: *Po slyedam drevnye-Khorezhmiskoi tsivilizatsii* (Moscow, 1948).

Toyama, Gunji: '*Da-Jin diaofa lu'*, *TSKK*, vol. II/2 (1936) pp. 421–43.

Tu Ji: *Mengwuer shiji (Historical Records of the Mongols)* (Beijing, 1958).

Vásáry, István: 'The Golden Horde Term *daruga* and its Survival in Russia', *AOH* (1976), pp. 187–96.

——: 'The Origin of the Institution of *Basqaqs*', *AOH* (1978), pp. 201–6.

Vernadsky, G.V.: 'The Scope and Content of Chingis Khan's Yasa', *HJAS* (1938), pp. 337–60.

——: 'O sostave velikoi Yasy Chingis khana', *Studies in Russian and Oriental History*, no 1, ed. George Vernadsky (Brussels, 1939).

——: The Mongols and Russia (New Haven–London, 1953).

Viktorova, L.L.: '*K voprosu o naimanskoi teorii proishkozhdeniya mongol'skogo yazyka i literaturnoi pis'mennosti* (XII–XIIIvv.)', *Yazika i narodov vostoka,* Uchenie zapiski LGU, no. 305 (Leningrad, 1961) pp. 137–55.

Vladimirtsov, B. Ya.: *Le régime social des Mongols: Le féodalisme nomade,* trans. M. Carsow. (Paris, 1948).

——: *Gengis-khan,* trans. M. Carsow (Paris, 1948).

Vorobiev, M.V.: *Zhurzheny i gosudarstvo Zhin* (Moscow, 1975).

Waley, Arthur: *The Travels of an Alchemist. The Journey of the Taoist Ch'ang ch'un* (London, 1931).

——: 'Notes on the Yüan-ch'ao pi-shih,' *BSOAS* (1960), 523–9.

Wang Daguan: *Xinzheng lu* .

Wang Guowei: *Haining wang Qing-an xiansheng yishu* (Commercial Press, 1940).

——: 'Dada kao', *op. cit.* Guantang jilin, XIV, 6b–32b.

——: 'Heichzi-Shiwei kao', *op. cit. Guantang* jilin, XIV, 1a–3b.

——: 'Menggu kao', *op. cit. Guantang jilin*, XV, 1a–3b.

——: 'Yuanchao bishi zhi zhuyin yierjian kao', *op. cit. Guantang jilin,* XVI, 1b–16b.

——: 'Jinjie hao kao', *op. cit.* Guantang jilin XV, 13b–26a.

——: 'anda', op, cit., *Guantang* jilin VI, 25b–26a.

Wei Yuan: *Yuanshi xinbian* (Shanghai, 1936).

Wen Weijian: '*Luting shishi*', *Shuofu,* 8.

Wittfogel, Karl A. and Feng, Chia-sheng: *History of Chinese Society: Liao (907–1125).*

Wu Guangcheng: *Xi-Xia shushi* (Peking, 1930).

Wyngaert, A. van den: *Itinera et relationes Fratrum Minorum saeculi XIII et XIV, Sinica Franciscana,* vol. I (Florence, 1929).

Xin Tangshu, ed. Baina ben.

Xu Mengshen: *Sanchao beimeng huiban.*

Xu Ting: *See also* Peng Daya and Xu Ting.

Yagchid, S.: 'On the *daruɣači* of the *Yüan-shi*', *Bulletin of the College of Arts* (1964), pp. 237–441.

Yanai Watari: 'Gendai sekai no sanka', Mōkōshi no kenkyū (Tokyo, 1930).

Yao Sui: *Muanji,* ed. Sibu congkan.

Ye Longli: *Qidan guozhi,* ed. Saoye shanfang.

Yuan dianzhang ed. Shen Jiaben.

Yuanshi, ed. Sung Lien *et al.* (Beijing 1976).

Yule, Sir Henry: *The Book of Ser Marco Polo,* rev. Henri Cordier (London, 3rd edn, 1903).

——: Cathay and the Way Thither, rev. Henri Cordier, Hakluyt Society vols. 33, 37, 38, 41 (London, 1913–16).

Yuwen Mouzhao: *Da-Jin guozhi,* 4 ben, ed. Saoye shanfang.

Zhamtsarano, C.Z.: *The Mongol Chronicles of the Seventeenth Century,* Trans. Rudolf Loewenthal, Göttinger Asiatische Forschungen, vol. 3 (Wiesbaden, 1955).

——: 'Kult Chingisa v Ordose', *CAJ* (1961), pp. 194–234.

Zhao Hong: *Meng-Da beilu,* ed. Wang Guowei.

Zhao Yi: *Nianershi zhaji* (Beijing, 1958).

Index

This index contains some major alternative spellings which were used in the original version and which feature in the current notes. Notes, except for a few of the most important, have not been indexed.